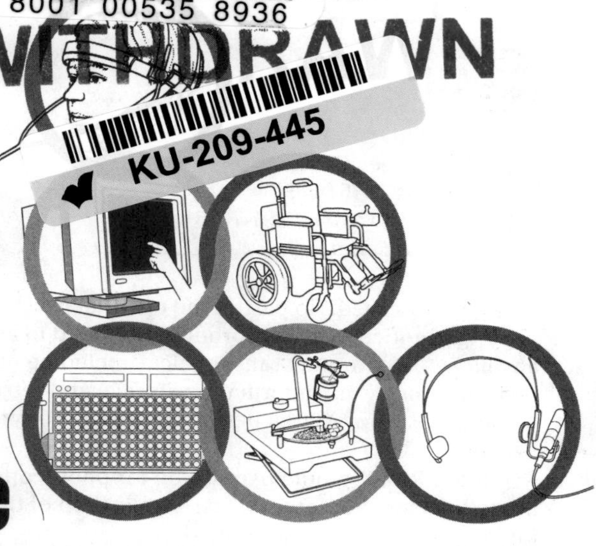

# Evaluating, Selecting, and Using Appropriate Assistive Technology

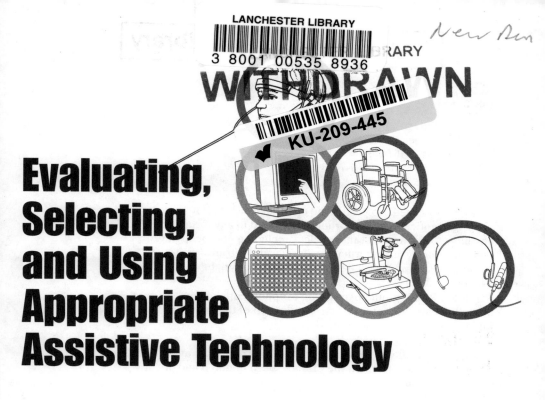

**Jan C. Galvin**
The Galvin Group, Ltd.
Tucson, Arizona

**Marcia J. Scherer**
Director
Institute for Matching
Person and Technology, Inc.
Webster, New York

8700 Shoal Creek Boulevard
Austin, Texas 78757-6897
800/897-3202 Fax 800/397-7633
www.proedinc.com

© 1996 by PRO-ED, Inc.
8700 Shoal Creek Boulevard
Austin, Texas 78757-6897
800/897-3202 Fax 800/397-7633
www.proedinc.com



The CD-ROM that was previously provided is no longer available. However, the resources on the CD have been updated and are now retrievable from the following web sites:
www.abledata.com
www.trace.wisc.edu

**Library of Congress Cataloging-in-Publication Data**

Evaluating, selecting, and using appropriate assistive technology / [edited by] Jan C. Galvin, Marcia J. Scherer.
p. ; cm.
Originally published: Gaithersburg, Md. : Aspen Publishers, 1996.
Includes bibliographical references and index.
ISBN 0-944480-35-7 (soft)
1. Rehabilitation technology. 2. Medical rehabilitation–Psychological aspects. 3. Self-help devices for people with disabilities. I. Galvin, Jan C. II. Scherer, Marcia J. (Marcia Joslyn) 1948–
[DNLM: 1. Disabled Persons—rehabilitation. 2. Self-Help Devices. WB 320 E914 1996a]
RM950.E836 2004
617'.03—dc21

2003046786

Previously published by Aspen Publisher under
ISBN 0-8342-0664-1.

Printed in the United States of America

3 4 5 6 7 8 9 10 08 07 06 05 04

# Table of Contents

# Contributors

**Peter Axelson, MSME**
Director
Research and Development
Beneficial Designs
Santa Cruz, California

**Sarah W. Blackstone, PhD**
Augmentative Communication, Inc.
Monterey, California

**Alexandra Enders, OTR/L**
Associate Director
Rural Institute on Disabilities
The University of Montana
Missoula, Montana

**Jan C. Galvin**
The Galvin Group, Ltd.
Tucson, Arizona

**Doreen Brenner Greenstein, PhD**
Senior Extension Associate
Agricultural and Biological Engineering
Cornell University
Ithaca, New York

**Judith E. Heumann**
The Assistant Secretary
Office of Special Education and Rehabilitative Services
United States Department of Education
Washington, DC

**Kathleen A. Kolar, MMSc/PT**
Clinical Specialist
Rehab Dynamics Incorporated
Minneapolis, Minnesota

**Peter Leech, MSW**
Project Director
MonTECH Program
Rural Institute on Disabilities
The University of Montana
Missoula, Montana

**Jay D. Leventhal, BA**
Senior Resource Specialist
Technology Center
American Foundation for the Blind
New York, New York

**Patricia E. Longmuir, MSc**
Consultant
Don Mills, Ontario

**Gary M. McFadyen, PhD, PE**
Lead Rehabilitation Engineer
Comprehensive Assistive Technology Center
Mississippi State, Mississippi

**Steven Mendelsohn, JD**
Attorney
San Francisco, California

**Joel N. Orr, PhD**
Orr Associates, Inc.
Chesapeake, Virginia

**Anita Perr, BS, MAOT**
Occupational Therapist
Convent Station, New Jersey

**William A. Peterson, MSME**
Director
Rehabilitation Engineering
National Rehabilitation Hospital
Washington, District of Columbia

**Lawrence A. Scadden, PhD**
Senior Program Director
Directorate for Education and Human Resources
National Science Foundation
Arlington, Virginia

**Marcia J. Scherer, PhD**
Director of Consumer Evaluations
RERC TET
Senior Research Associate
Center for Assistive Technology
University at Buffalo
Buffalo, New York

**Gregg C. Vanderheiden, PhD**
Director
Trace Research and Development Center
Waisman Center and Department of Industrial Engineering
University of Wisconsin-Madison
Madison, Wisconsin

**Anthony J. Vitale, PhD**
Senior Consultant Engineer
Assistive Technology Group
Digital Equipment Corp.
Maynard, Massachusetts

**Rachel A. Wobschall**
Minnesota Governor's Advisory Star Program
Minnesota Department of Administration
St. Paul, Minnesota

# Foreword

Those of us who are disabled and who personally use assistive technology on a daily basis to help us live our lives and work at our jobs more comfortably and efficiently know how wonderful and necessary this technology can be. Of course, low-technology, inexpensive solutions abound for many job-related and independent living challenges; however, the fact remains that many of the high-technology devices many of us use in our daily lives cost a great deal of money. For many people, these are dollars well spent, and no value can be placed on the independence, quality of life, and self-sufficiency that technology can provide under the right circumstances.

The problem is that this is not always the case. Any seasoned advocate, special education professional, or rehabilitation specialist can bombard you with stories of how the wrong technology was purchased for an individual—a braille display for an individual who prefers speech synthesis because of poor braille-reading skills, hearing aids that amplify inappropriate frequency ranges, wheelchairs that are too big or too small, and so on. Much of this technology ends up gathering dust; neither the individual who needed it initially nor the one to whom it could go instead gather any benefit from it at all.

These inappropriate purchases have other tragic consequences as well, as they reinforce the misperceptions that exist among the general public about the capacity of disabled people to function independently and to live normal and productive lives. Even worse, the disabled individual often ends up taking the brunt of the blame when the problem that was supposed to have been solved remains a problem. When the wrong device is bought, it can be easier to say, "He just doesn't want to work," than "We made a mistake in our evaluation of what he needed."

Enter the book, *Evaluating, Selecting, and Using Appropriate Assistive Technology* by Jan C. Galvin and Marcia J. Scherer, two long-time practitioners in the field of rehabilitation. This resource covers all aspects of assistive technology, including policy, legislation, funding, evaluation, selection, and maintenance. The book has as its goal the establishment of a process that will ensure that, to the extent possible, the right technological solution is adopted for the right individual. The book provides numerous examples and tips for properly evaluating not only the technology, but also the needs of the individual for whom the technology is being purchased.

This book is intended for both practitioners and consumers, because it stresses the partnership that must exist between the two groups if assistive technology is to be effective. It also seeks to provide an understanding of the various types of assistive technologies, since this understanding is crucial in establishing an efficient and outcome-oriented process to ensure an appropriate match between the technology and the person. Emphasizing the utilization of specific evaluation and selection criteria so that all team members will recognize and use the same fundamental elements, the book outlines a methodology that will lead to successful use and a satisfied user.

The editors of this book put their money where their mouthsticks are, as 10 of the 15 chapters are written by individuals with disabilities, covering all topics related to the use of technology in education, employment, and play.

This book, then, is for the busy consumer who needs assistance, and for the overworked and harried practitioner—the physical therapist, the occupational therapist, the teacher, the rehabilitation counselor, the independent living counselor, and others whose job it is to guide that consumer toward effective and long-lasting solutions to the problems that he or she faces. In short, this book stresses partnership. Therefore, it is invaluable in helping to create the environment that will yield the most positive outcome possible for the effort and dollars expended.

Technology for disabled people may start in a laboratory, a workshop, a university research facility, or in a garage, but its importance is not realized until it reaches the individual for whom it was designed. *Evaluating, Selecting, and Using Appropriate Assistive Technology*, then, will help this technology to fulfill its truest purpose: enabling individuals to be more productive and independent.

*Judith E. Heumann*
The Assistant Secretary
Office of Special Education
and Rehabilitative Services
United States Department
of Education

# Preface

Assistive technologies have enabled millions of individuals with disabilities to lead independent, secure, and productive lives. The impact of assistive technologies is evident in the growth of both the number of devices and the number of users of devices over the past several years.

As further evidence of the impact of assistive technologies, educational courses and training in assistive technology evaluation and selection are now offered in the fields of occupational therapy, physical therapy, rehabilitation counseling, special education, speech–language pathology, and social work. Rehabilitation engineering has become a discipline in its own right. Beyond professional educational efforts, parent and consumer groups are being trained to be more knowledgeable about assistive devices and ways to obtain them.

The range of choices available to consumers has expanded greatly. Many old, faithful, low-technology devices have been improved, and they have become more affordable and obtainable through local health care suppliers/pharmacies and consumer health catalogs. The miniaturization of computer components and the transfer of technology from the space program to the private sector have been boons to the development of smaller, transportable, and lightweight high-technology devices.

With more choices in technologies comes more decision points around their evaluation and selection. This book was created to help readers find their way through the system of assistive technology devices and services as it has come to exist today—a system that all too often can seem complex, confusing, even overwhelming. The book addresses a number of different issues that we believe are key elements in assistive technology service delivery. Rather than focusing on the bells and whistles of particular devices, each chapter concentrates on the criteria that are important in the selection of that type of device. If the selection process is done correctly, the match of person and technology will be appropriate, regardless of the particular device. Consumer satisfaction will result.

The book begins with a general overview of key issues related to assistive technology service delivery. Chapter 1 provides a model for service provision and outcomes assessment that emerged in part from the real life experiences of people with disabilities as described in Scherer's book, *Living in the State of Stuck: How Technology Impacts the Lives of People with Disabilities*. This model advocates a consumer-defined quality pathway to appropriate device evaluation and selection.

Chapters 2 through 10 focus on the evaluation, selection, and use of assistive technologies for various purposes and in a variety of contexts. The topics range from low-technology aids for grooming to high-technology devices for communication, from childhood to adulthood, from home to worksite, from basic activities of daily living to play and recreation. Each of these chapters presents information in the same format:

- the type of devices and services that fit within the particular category
- descriptions of what the devices do and how they enhance independence, employability, education, and so on through many case examples
- current technologies, future changes, and expected improvements (i.e., where they came from, where they are, where they are going)
- consumers who typically benefit from this type of technology
- quality pathways to selecting the most appropriate device in this category
- auxiliary considerations when selecting these devices

Many effective low-technology and do-it-yourself devices allow for inexpensive accommodations. Although it is important not to be carried away by the high-technology gloss of computers and computer access, more sophisticated technologies have enabled many people to lead independent lives who would not have been able to do so otherwise. The topics of computer access and interactive technologies are discussed in Chapters 11 and 12, followed by a projection of the next generation of technologies in Chapter 13.

The final section broadens the discussion once again. Chapter 14 addresses legislation and federal policy affecting the evaluation, selection, and procurement of all technologies; Chapter 15, the means to obtain funding for them. The Last Word drives home the point that consumers are pivotal in the evaluation, selection, and use of appropriate assistive technology devices and services.

It is impossible for a book like this to cover every aspect of assistive technology service delivery and each piece of assistive technology. Every week the number of new technologies on the market increases, while the resources available to pay for them decrease. Our goal in this book is to give the reader a firm understanding of the delivery process and to illustrate the appropriate use of assistive technology with examples. The reader needs to be aware of the basic policies that drive assistive technology service delivery, ways to approach funding sources, and the range of options available in assistive devices.

In summary, this book has been designed to lead the reader through the *process* of assistive technology selection while underscoring the need for a comprehensive evaluation before any assistive technology device or service is recommended or purchased. No matter what the technology is, the process begins with the same core task for achieving the most appropriate match of person and technology: the collection of as much information as possible about the person who will use the technology, the environments in which the technology will be used, and available technologies.

Assistive technology can be a powerful tool, but only if it has been designed with consumer input and selected with full knowledge of what is available, how it works, and how it interacts with the environment. Above all, this book puts the focus on the consumer of assistive technology. The consumer's needs and preferences must drive the evaluation and selection of assistive technology; to do otherwise will result in poorer person and technology matches that may lead to technology abandonment and, ultimately, to loss of functioning.

*Jan C. Galvin*
*Marcia J. Scherer*

# Acknowledgments

We acknowledge with gratitude the support and assistance of many people who made this book possible: Each of the contributing authors, the staff at Aspen Publishers, and especially our personal support systems Don Galvin and John Scherer.

We particularly wish to acknowledge those consumers and practitioners who provided us with the inspiration to create this book—namely those who have caused us to examine the ways in which assistive technology devices reach those who need them.

*Chapter 1*

# An Outcomes Perspective of Quality Pathways to the Most Appropriate Technology

*Marcia J. Scherer and Jan C. Galvin*

Matching people with the most appropriate assistive technology is a complex process, but the process need not be problematic and difficult. Appropriate technology interventions occur at all levels of technological sophistication and can be achieved through the implementation of a logical, systematic decision-making approach guided by certain fundamental principles.

## THE CHALLENGE OF ACHIEVING A GOOD PERSON–TECHNOLOGY MATCH

Assistive technologies help individuals with disabilities live more independent lives in their communities by minimizing "disability" and the need for assistance from other people. Although there are federal mandates for comprehensive, consumer-responsive assistive technology and technology-related services, obtaining such devices and services often remains an arduous task for both the individual and the professional. Part of the problem is that many myths surround assistive technologies. Ten of the most commonly held misconceptions regarding assistive technology devices and services have been highlighted by the SMART Exchange (1990) and are described in the following paragraphs. People with disabilities and those providing services should examine their own thinking to determine if they may unconsciously subscribe to any of these myths and whether those beliefs may affect their use or provision of assistive technology devices and services.

**Myth number 1: Assistive technology is the "be all and end all."** Assistive technology is a powerful tool useful to persons with disabilities in many ways and in a variety of situations. Some persons with disabilities believe that devices will take care of all the problems they encounter. Assistive technology devices can indeed make accomplishing a task easier. Technology alone does not end all the difficulties that accompany a disability, however. It is important for professionals to explore this issue with consumers and to help them understand that devices are not the "be all and end all."

**Myth number 2: Assistive technology is complicated and expensive.** Some of the assistive technologies used today are complicated and expensive, but some of the best solutions to the needs and preferences of people with disabilities are simple, inexpensive low-technology devices. Expensive and sophisticated devices are not necessarily a part of every solution.

**Myth number 3: Persons with the same disability benefit from the same devices.** The fact that two people have similar disabilities does not mean that they have the same assistive technology needs. Thus, it is important for professionals to assess assistive technology needs on an individual basis.

**Myth number 4: Professionals are the best source of information on assistive technology.** Since technology is always advancing, it is impossible for one person or group of people to be familiar with all the technology options currently available. Consumers, family members, and professionals should learn as much as possible about assistive technology and should share their knowledge and expertise with each other in order to reach the best possible solutions. Some assistive technology solutions rely more on the common sense use of everyday items from the hardware store than on highly technical information and expertise. While service providers are often connected to technology networks and resources, consumers and their families may join support groups and find the most creative and practical solutions. Necessity is the mother of invention, and persons with disabilities and their families are the ones who live the "disability experience" (Scherer, 1993). Personal experiences have spawned some of the best assistive technologies on the market today.

**Myth number 5: Assistive technology product descriptions are always accurate and helpful.** Too often, product descriptions are designed primarily to sell products to general audiences. It can be difficult to determine which information is useful and relevant to the specific needs of someone with a disability. This person may need other, more objective information to supplement the product descriptions.

**Myth number 6: A user's assistive technology requirements need to be assessed just once.** A particular assistive technology device may be useful to a person with a disability for his or her entire life span or for only a few months or years. As individuals expand their activities to encompass home, school, work, and community settings, they may have new or different needs. Ongoing self-assessment, as well as reassessment by professionals, ensures that changing needs are addressed.

**Myth number 7: Assistive technology devices will always be used.** Although assistive technologies are often crucial to the independent functioning of people with disabilities, many devices are eventually abandoned. The reasons for this abandonment vary. For example, the device may not have performed as expected, may be unreliable, or may be difficult to use. Research indicates that consumer involvement in technology decision making enhances the likelihood that the device will be used (Phillips & Zhao, 1993; Scherer, 1993).

**Myth number 8: Individuals with disabilities want the latest, most expensive devices.** Persons with disabilities are just like any other customers or consumers. Most of them want technology that is easy and comfortable to use, is reliable and affordable, and does the job as quickly and conveniently as possible.

**Myth number 9: Assistive technology is a luxury.** Once regarded as luxury items not meant for mass consumption, automobiles, telephones, and more recently computers are now essential technologies for functioning in today's world. For someone with a disability who relies upon assistive technology to perform a critical function or achieve a desired goal in life, assistive technology is very much a necessity. The fact that a device makes a task easier or more convenient does not make it a luxury—no matter what the cost.

**Myth number 10: Only people with certain types of disabilities find assistive technology useful.** The need for specific types of assistive technologies varies widely from person to person, but individuals of all ages, with varying abilities, and with diverse needs and preferences may be able to benefit from the use of assistive technology. The value of the technology depends on the goals and desires of the individual with a disability.

Once the myths that interfere with the process of matching person and technology are recognized and resolved, improved assessment (functional and outcome) and better interactions between the individuals who deliver services and those who receive the services will result.

## USE, AVOIDANCE, AND ABANDONMENT OF ASSISTIVE TECHNOLOGY

Data from the 1990 U.S. Census Bureau's National Health Interview Survey on Assistive Devices show that more than 13.1 million people in the United States (more than 5 percent of the total U.S. population) used assistive technologies in 1990. In 1969, 6.2 million people had used assistive devices. Thus, in 21 years, the number of persons using assistive technologies more than doubled. There are three key factors for this increase: (1) greater rates of survival following trauma and disease, resulting in longer lives for people with disabilities; (2) advances in microelectronics and the availability of microcomputers; and (3) the passage of legislation that has mandated the consideration of assistive technology for persons with disabilities.

There are no indicators of this population's predisposition to technology use in general, although it is known that people with disabilities differ in the degrees to which they use assistive technologies and to which they believe assistive technologies improve the quality of their lives. Many individuals with disabilities avoid technologies outright. Others try them, only to abandon them to the basement, closet, or bedside table. Depending on the type of assistive technology, nonuse or abandonment can be as low as 8 percent or as high as 75 percent; on the average, one-third of more optional assistive technologies are abandoned, most within the first 3 months (Phillips & Zhao, 1993; Scherer & Galvin, 1994). There is no information about the number of people who must continue to use devices that they are unhappy with because they cannot abandon the devices without severe consequences.

Technology abandonment can have a series of repercussions. Just as unused and abandoned technologies represent wasted resources, so does the inability of people to perform at their functional best. Nonuse of a device may decrease functional abilities, freedom, and independence, while it increases monetary expenses for caretakers. On a service delivery level, device abandonment represents an ineffective use of limited funds by federal, state, and local government agencies, insurers, and other providers.

A growing body of research on the abandonment of assistive technology devices illustrates the complexity of the interface between a person and a device. A review of that literature indicates that the overarching factor associated with technology abandonment is the failure to consider user opinions and preferences in device selection (Phillips & Zhao, 1993; Scherer, 1993). Other major reasons that consumers do not use devices are (in no particular order)

- changes in consumer functional abilities or activities
- lack of consumer motivation to use the device or do the task
- lack of meaningful training on how to use the device (especially for individuals who are elderly or who have cognitive impairments)
- ineffective device performance
- environmental obstacles to use, such as narrow doorways
- lack of access to and information about repair and maintenance
- no need for the device or minimal need for it
- device aesthetics, weight, size, and appearance

Most of these issues can be addressed appropriately in a comprehensive selection process that considers the person's ongoing needs and takes both a short- and long-term view of the individual's assistive device use and which is, first and foremost, consumer-directed. A better understanding of how and why technology users decide to accept or reject a device is critical to improving the effectiveness of assistive technology interventions and enhancing consumer satisfaction.

## MATCHING PERSON AND TECHNOLOGY MODEL

It is important to train the person, family, co-workers, and others for the realities and situations of assistive technology use. But successful assistive technology use requires adapting the assistive technology to the person's capabilities and temperament, not vice versa. One technique that has been found helpful in organizing the many influences on a person's predisposition to the use of an optional assistive technology is the Matching Person and Technology (MPT) Model (Scherer & McKee, 1989; Scherer, 1991), which advocates separately addressing

1. characteristics of the *M*ilieu (environment and psychosocial setting) in which the assistive technology is to be used
2. pertinent features of the individual's *P*ersonality, preference, and temperament
3. salient characteristics of the assistive *T*echnology itself

Some of the influences on assistive technology use as indicated in the MPT Model are shown in Table 1–1. The information in the chart demonstrates an attempt to profile a person's predisposition to the use of a particular assistive technology. For example, one person may have characteristics associated with assistive technology nonuse as far as milieu/environment variables, but appear to be an optimal user according to the characteristics listed for personality and technology. The milieu/environment influences on use may need some intervention or modification before the person can gain maximum satisfaction and function from use of the assistive technology. The following example of a hearing aid illustrates the need to consider various influences on assistive technology (AT) use.

One device with a high rate of abandonment is the hearing aid. According to a study conducted by Scherer and Frisina (1994), factors associated with the nonuse of hearing aids include such characteristics of the technology as discomfort with ear molds, cost, and visibility of the aids. A key characteristic of the person that influences the abandonment of hearing aids is the person's expectation that the aid will restore "perfect hearing." Milieu/environment characteristics that affect hearing aid use include the cooperation of significant others in avoiding noisy environments where it is difficult for the hearing aid user to discriminate a speaker's voice from background noise. Table 1–2 lists examples of questions for consumers to answer when considering assistive technologies in three broad domains: mobility, speech, and hearing.

The MPT Model consists of checklist-type assessment instruments to record consumers' goals and preferences, their views of the benefits to be gained from a technology, and changes in their self-perceived outcome achievement over

**Table 1–1** Influences on the Use of Assistive Technology

| | *Milieu* | *Personality* | *Technology* |
|---|---|---|---|
| **Use** | Support from family, peers, or employer | Proud to use device | Goal achieved with little or no pain, fatigue, discomfort, or stress |
| | Realistic expectations of family or employer | Motivated | Compatible with or enhances the use of other technologies |
| | Setting/environment fully supports and rewards use | Cooperative | Is safe, reliable, easy to use and maintain |
| | Pressure for use from family, peers, or employer | Optimistic | Has the desired transportability |
| | | Good coping skills | Best option currently available |
| | | Patient | |
| | | Self-disciplined | |
| | | Generally positive life experiences | |
| | | Has the skills to use the device | |
| | | Perceives discrepancy between desired and current situation | |
| | | Willing to challenge self | |
| **Nonuse** | Lack of support from family, peers, or employer | Fear of losing own abilities or becoming dependent on AT | Strain or discomfort in use |
| | Unrealistic expectations of others | Embarrassed to use device | Requires a lot of setup |
| | Setting/environment disallows, prevents, discourages, or makes use awkward | Depressed | Perceived or determined to be incompatible with the use of other technologies |
| | Requires assistance that is not available | Unmotivated | Too expensive |
| | Training not available | Uncooperative, resistant, hostile, or angry | Long delay for delivery |
| | | Intimidated by technology | Other options to device use are available |
| | | Overwhelmed by changes required with device use | Has been outgrown |
| | | Does not have skills for use | Is inefficient |
| | | Poor socialization and coping skills | Repairs or service not timely or affordable |

*Source: Guidelines for the Use of Assistive Technology: Evaluation Referral Prescription.* American Medical Association, Copyright © 1994.

time. One pair of instruments, the Assistive Technology Device Predisposition Assessment, was developed from a study (Scherer, 1986) of differences between assistive technology users and nonusers. The consumer version addresses individuals' subjective satisfaction with current functioning in many areas and identifies those areas in which improvement is most desired. The consumer version has two forms: (1) questions about temperament, psychoso-

**Table 1–2** Some Guiding Questions When Assessing the Match of Person and Technology

| | ***M**ilieu* | ***P**erson* | ***T**echnology* |
|---|---|---|---|
| **Mobility** | Where does the person want to go?<br>What barriers exist to getting there?<br>What forms of assistance are available?<br>What in the environment *needs* to be changed?<br>What in the environment *can* be changed? | With what does the person need/want assistance?<br>Does this person want the proposed device?<br>Does the person have realistic expectations for the device?<br>Will the use of the device require changes in the person's basic way of doing things?<br>Will the device fill an unmet need? | Is the device affordable for this person?<br>Is the device safe, reliable, and comfortable?<br>Will the device eclipse the person using it?<br>Is the device aesthetically pleasing?<br>Is the device easy to use, repair, and maintain? |
| **Speech** | Is the person being asked to use a device? By whom?<br>With whom does the person most communicate now?<br>Who does the person want to communicate with more?<br>Will all the person's primary environments support the use of the device?<br>Will the device put demands on others? | Does the person want a technical alternative to speech?<br>Does the person have the aptitude for success with this device?<br>Is the person easily frustrated or discouraged?<br>Does the person know and possess good conversational skills?<br>Does the person have the patience for a communication system? | What nontechnical options are available?<br>Is the device portable for this person?<br>Can the device be set up and used independently?<br>Does the device have the desirable speed?<br>Is the device easy to learn to operate?<br>Does it require other devices? |
| **Hearing** | In what settings does the person spend a lot of time?<br>What communication situations are challenging?<br>Have frequently used public places been properly equipped?<br>Is the workplace accommodating?<br>Are family members accommodating? | Does the person have a realistic view of hearing aid use?<br>Is the person social and outgoing or private and introspective?<br>How much is the person inconvenienced by a hearing loss?<br>How motivated is the person for device use?<br>Are there secondary gains for *not* hearing? | Does the device do what the person expected?<br>Can the person easily use the device?<br>Is the device comfortable?<br>Does the person feel embarrassed to use this device?<br>Is maintenance complicated? |

*Source*: Reprinted with permission from *Guidelines for the Use of Assistive Technology: Evaluation, Referral, Prescriptions*, p. 23, Copyright © 1994, American Medical Association.

cial resources, and views of "disability" and (2) questions about the consumer's views of and expectations for that particular technology. Companion professional forms are similarly constructed to permit criss-cross comparisons of professional and consumer views. Because the items emerged from the actual experiences of technology users and nonusers, they have "content validity." Additional psychometric evidence indicates that they are quality assessments (Crewe & Dijkers, 1995).

Regardless of the means employed to assess the potential quality of the match of person and assistive technology, it is crucial for professionals to ensure the following:

- Professionals have the support they need to become knowledgeable about a variety of technologies and relevant resources.
- Consumer needs, not particular features of an assistive technology or its availability, drive the matching process.
- Different perspectives of professional and consumer are openly addressed.
- A variety of interventions are considered, not all of which involve technology.
- Trial periods with the interventions in situations of actual use are arranged.
- Desirable interventions are selected with the necessary support systems established to ensure their success.
- Specific objective criteria by which to judge the intervention's usefulness to the consumer are identified, along with a timeline.

Individuals with disabilities who are involved in assistive technology selection in a meaningful way are generally more cooperative, more active and independent in using the assistive technology, and more satisfied with services overall.

## ESTABLISHMENT OF QUALITY PATHWAYS TO MATCHING PEOPLE WITH APPROPRIATE ASSISTIVE TECHNOLOGIES

To become more consumer-responsive, the professional must remember three words: ask, listen, and respond. The actual steps used for matching person and technology are similar to the steps used in any selection or decision-making process:

1. Establish goals/expectations.
2. Assess need for no-technology, low-technology, or high-technology device.
3. Match person and technology.
4. Select and fit assistive technology to the person.

5. Train person for assistive technology use.
6. Assess/evaluate outcomes of assistive technology use according to goals/expectations.
7. Return to Number 1.

### Identification of Goals and Tasks

One of the keys to achieving successful technology outcomes is the use of a collaborative approach throughout the matching process. Both the professional and the consumer are trying to achieve the same thing, and each has particular strengths to bring to the relationship. Consumers know their goals, interests, dislikes, priorities, and the practical aspects of their living situation. Professionals know about devices and systems, have experience matching technologies and people, and have access to a variety of resources. By forming a partnership in which each completes certain tasks, provides information, and makes certain decisions, they share the responsibility for achieving a good match of person and technology.

After the general goals and activities have been selected, it is necessary to conduct a task analysis of the activities to determine the actions required to accomplish them. In most cases, the evaluation of functional capabilities rests with clinical professionals, such as occupational and physical therapists. All practitioners can stimulate the discussion of the consumer's preferences, motivation, life style, adjustment to disability, goals, values, and view of and attitude toward various technologies, however. Together, consumers and practitioners can explore the relationship of these issues to the use of a particular assistive technology.

### Assessment of the Need and Desire for Technology

Information about the milieu/environment(s), the person, and the technology(ies) is essential. The assessment forms in the MPT Model facilitate assessment of the consumer's functional abilities and personal preferences, psychosocial resources, and view of the proposed technology. The consumer's goals, capabilities, and preferences determine the specific and objective criteria by which to judge potential solutions.

### Person and Technology Match

Write down the basic necessities and desired features for a device and develop a concrete criteria checklist that can be revised as necessary. Such an assessment should continue until the final decision is actually made—and then through follow-up.

There are a number of resources for information about devices, including people who use the type of product under consideration, occupational therapists, physical therapists, rehabilitation engineers, technology information specialists, product manufacturers and vendors, product catalogs, and local demonstration centers. Exhibit 1–1 lists a variety of agencies and individuals knowledgeable about assistive technologies. The professional, the consumer,

**Exhibit 1–1** Assistive Technology Providers

| ***Agencies*** | ***People*** |
|---|---|
| Medical Rehabilitation Facilities | Driving Educators |
| Acute Care Hospitals | Vehicle Modifiers |
| Extended Care Hospitals | Researchers |
| Home Health Care Agencies | Engineers |
| Veterans Facilities | Orthotists/Prosthetists |
| DME Facilities | DME Suppliers |
| P&O Facilities | Technicians |
| Rehab Engineering Centers | Physicians |
| Volunteer "Technologist" Groups | Occupational Therapists |
| State VR Agencies | Physical Therapists |
| Private VR Agencies | Speech/Language Therapists |
| Disability Management Agencies | Recreation Therapists |
| Private Nonprofit Agencies | Rehabilitation Counselors |
| Agencies Providing Sensory Aids | Special Educators |
| Special Education Technology Programs | Gerontologists |
| Students with Disabilities Support Systems | Industrial Designers |
| Developmental Disabilities Agencies | Architects |
| Independent Living Centers | Landscape Architects |
| Consumer Groups | Information Specialists |
| Agencies Serving the Aging | Computer Scientists |
| Agencies Serving Children | Building Contractors |
| Information Services | |
| Equipment Manufacturers | |

DME, Durable Medical Equipment
P&O, Prosthetics and Orthotics
VR, Vocational Rehabilitation

Courtesy of REquest Rehabilitation Engineering Center, National Rehabilitation Hospital, 1993.

and the consumer's family members and employer can each take responsibility for investigating certain resources. This approach encourages each person's active involvement and learning about technology.

The next action is to share the collected information and to brainstorm as many options for solving the problem as possible. It can be difficult to sort out all of this new information in a limited amount of time, so care is essential to avoid getting too little information, providing information too quickly, or overloading people with information. When brainstorming, those involved should accept all ideas and then measure each against the preestablished criteria.

Before the final decision, it may be necessary to make adjustments or compromises. In some cases, it may be necessary to redefine the problem. By the last step in the process, however, the one or two options that best meet the criteria are usually obvious. Because everyone involved developed the options together, it is not too difficult to agree on one or two possibilities and leave the final decision to the consumer.

There is a difference between judging the device itself and judging the fit of the device and the user. Table 1–3 notes some key considerations for narrowing the field of possible appropriate devices. The relative importance and meaning of each component varies, depending on the device and the values of the user. For example, securability is a more important consideration for a portable computerized device that will be used in many locations than for a device that will be used only in the bathroom (Lane, Usiak, Moffat, & Scherer, 1996).

Once the type of device has been selected, then a qualified supplier (dealer, vendor) must be located. Suppliers of assistive technologies range from the local pharmacy to large national distributors. There may be more than one supplier who can provide the device wanted, and it is important to check each of them. It may be wise to talk to more than one company representative, and it is certainly wise to look at as many devices of the type wanted as possible before making a final decision. A comprehensive evaluation of potential suppliers can save time, energy, expense, and frustration. Exhibit 1–2 is an interview guide that contains questions to ask suppliers.

### Selection of the Appropriate Assistive Technology

With the information now gathered, it is possible to weed out and narrow down the options. Finally, it can be determined which device best matches the person's needs and preferences.

### Training for Assistive Technology Use

Once the device is selected, the person who is to use it must learn about its operation and maintenance. It is important to explore the ergonomic aspects of

**Table 1–3** Key Components in the Evaluation of Devices

| *Questions* | *Importance* |
|---|---|
| **What does the device do?**<br>What proof exists to support performance claims?<br>Are performance expectations realistic?<br>How does it work?<br>Does it operate similarly to familiar devices?<br>Does it do more than necessary? | Sometimes manufacturers can make a device sound like magic and sometimes users imagine it's true. Getting objective information about what the device does and how it works ensures that performance expectations are appropriate and the skills required to use it match the intended user's abilities. If you understand how the device operates you can use it more efficiently and identify problems quickly. Demonstrations or trials with the device will help determine whether the device will be effective. |
| **Does device meet regulatory assurances?**<br>Is it new on the market?<br>Is it registered with FDA—Class I, II, or III?<br>Has the VA accepted it?<br>Does it meet applicable standards? | Most assistive devices must be registered with the FDA and many devices are evaluated by the VA for use in that system. Voluntary standards exist for a few products. These are the only established systems for quality assurance. If a device is new on the market these assurances are especially important. |
| **How was the device tested?**<br>Independent evaluations?<br>Tested in adverse conditions?<br>Performance results?<br>Reliability results?<br>Safety results?<br>Durability results? | Manufacturers usually test their products, but independent evaluations are rare. Make sure you know how the tests were conducted. Find out if the tests reflect worst-case conditions and check relevant performance issues. Do not be fooled by performance claims that are not important. |
| **Were user trials carried out?**<br>Who tested the device?<br>Under what circumstances?<br>How long did the tests last?<br>How do current users rate the device?<br>Is it easy to use? | User studies on a new device can help determine how well the device may work for you if the subjects were similar to you. Talking to other users of an established device can provide valuable information about device performance over time and ease of use. |
| **What maintenance and repair are required for the device?**<br>Who can do regular maintenance?<br>How often is it returned for repair?<br>Is there a warranty?<br>Who does repairs? Costs? | Assistive devices need regular care and can break down like any other device. These contingencies need to be planned for. |
| **What are the estimated lifetime costs?**<br>Initial cost?<br>Cost of regular maintenance?<br>Cost of replacement parts?<br>What are labor costs? | The lifetime cost of a device can be much different from the initial purchase cost. Make sure the lifetime estimates provided by the manufacturer are based on realistic "use estimates." Consider how a device is affected if it is used more or less than average. |

*continues*

**Table 1–3** continued

| *Questions* | *Importance* |
|---|---|
| **Are the aesthetics of the device acceptable?**<br>Is it attractive, quiet, etc?<br>Does it overwhelm the user?<br>How will it look after years of use? | It is important for the user to feel comfortable with the device. It should be as simple and unobtrusive as possible. |
| **Can the device interface with other equipment?**<br>Is it compatible with other devices?<br>Is it flexible?<br>Can it be expanded to accommodate new features? | When consumers use more than one device, compatibility is a must for effective performance. Devices that have options or can be expanded may serve a user more efficiently in the long run. |
| **Will the device be convenient to use?**<br>Is it easy to store?<br>Is it easy to transport?<br>Is it portable?<br>Is it easy to keep secure? | For devices that go everywhere with the user, these issues are particularly relevant. If an item is too heavy or bulky, it may not meet the user's needs. |
| **How easy is the device to learn to use?**<br>How complex is it?<br>How much training is needed to learn to use it?<br>What are the assembly and installation requirements?<br>Who will install it and provide training for use?<br>Is free technical assistance available?<br>Can the user explain how to use it? | The more complex the device, the more important it is to carefully assess these issues. If it is too difficult to use effectively, it will be abandoned by the user. The relative difficulty also depends on the abilities of the intended user. |

FDA, Food and Drug Administration
VA, Veterans Administration

***Note:*** For the most current information on key components in consumers' evaluation of devices, contact: Rehabilitation Engineering Research Center on Technology Evaluation and Transfer, University at Buffalo, Buffalo, NY 14214.

Courtesy of REquest Rehabilitation Engineering Center, National Rehabilitation Hospital, 1993.

device use and make any necessary environmental accommodations. The person who is training the individual to use the device should

- Plan and prepare for the session well ahead of time so that all the resources needed are immediately available.
- Prioritize what is to be achieved and pace the training session accordingly.
- Consider a "spiral curriculum" in which training begins with a familiar piece of equipment or means of access/input; gradually moves to the new, novel aspects; and ends with success and the enthusiasm that will accom-

**Exhibit 1–2** Evaluating Suppliers

| | | Suppliers Being Compared | | | | | |
|---|---|---|---|---|---|---|---|
| | | 1 | | 2 | | 3 | |
| Area | Question | Y | N | Y | N | Y | N |
| Sales | Demo/trial available? | | | | | | |
| | Delivery fee? | | | | | | |
| | Geographic limits? | | | | | | |
| | Quick delivery time? | | | | | | |
| | Ship products? | | | | | | |
| | Provide training? Fee? | | | | | | |
| | Installation? Fee? | | | | | | |
| | Accept funding source? | | | | | | |
| | Do funding paperwork? | | | | | | |
| Service and Support | Make modifications? | | | | | | |
| | Provide technical help? | | | | | | |
| | Provide service/repair? Service contract? | | | | | | |
| | Emergency service? | | | | | | |
| | While-u-wait service? | | | | | | |
| | Standard repair rates? | | | | | | |
| | Stock standard parts? | | | | | | |
| | Provide loaners? | | | | | | |
| | Pick-up & deliver? Fee? | | | | | | |
| | Geographic limits? | | | | | | |
| Company | Several years in business? | | | | | | |
| | Many devices sold? | | | | | | |
| | Good reputation? | | | | | | |
| | Knowledgeable staff? | | | | | | |

Courtesy of REquest Rehabilitation Engineering Center, National Rehabilitation Hospital, 1993.

pany it. Training can begin at that point the next time and "spiral up" to the next aspect to be mastered.

- Make sure that the person is attentive and is being challenged, but not frustrated. From the beginning, the person with the disability should feel ownership of the assistive technology and control of its use.

- Balance criticism and correction with reinforcement and encouragement.
- Evaluate short-term goals and relate them to long-term ones (e.g., independence, communication).
- Use this training as an opportunity to foster choice and teach decision making.

### Assessment of Outcomes of Assistive Technology Use

Although implementation has been described as a linear process, it is really an iterative (cyclical) operation. Information gathered at each step may require adjustments in decisions made earlier. For example, one criterion for a scooter may be that it cost less than $2,000. It is found, however, in gathering information that only scooters costing between $2,300 and $2,600 meet the performance criteria. Then, the issues related to price, performance, and supplier must be re-examined and a compromise reached.

It is important to consider the effects that a device selected for one activity may have on another activity. In a work setting, for example, hand-held typing sticks may be the best method for typing, but are they the best means of accessing other job-related equipment? Again, it is essential to weigh the benefits and drawbacks within the larger context.

The tasks to be accomplished, the consumer's functional abilities and personal preferences, the environment, and the device itself must all be considered in evaluating the use of the device. Exhibit 1–3 organizes these issues in the form of questions that the consumer should answer as part of the process of being matched with a technology.

## OUTCOMES MEASURES AND ASSISTIVE TECHNOLOGY SERVICE DELIVERY

Generally, it is no longer enough simply to provide a person with a technology. Now it is necessary to show how the technology helped a person get a job, improved the individual's quality of life, and enabled the individual to do what he or she wanted to do. It is also important to demonstrate the person's satisfaction with the result and provide evidence that the service was a cost-effective effort and an efficient use of staff time. Success in demonstrating outcomes is sometimes hampered by the lack of clear definitions for terms related to outcomes in assistive technology or even rehabilitation as a whole. Following are some definitions cited by Galvin and Wilkerson (1995) from the relevant literature:

> *Outcomes*—function and well-being, employability, performance of ADL [activities of daily living], client satisfaction. Insurers want

**Exhibit 1–3** Which Is the Most Appropriate Assistive Technology for Me?

**Functional Capabilities, Goals, and Tasks**

What is my disability? Is it stable or changing?
Do I have the physical and mental abilities to use the device?
Have I identified my needs clearly?
Can I change my activities so that I can do them without a device?
Is there a device that can help me meet my needs?
Will I need assistance to use the device?
Will an assistant need to use the device?

**Personal Characteristics, Capabilities, and Preferences**

What technology do I currently use?
How do I currently manage my daily activities?
Is it important to me to do things as independently as possible?
Does technology help me be more independent or dependent?
Am I comfortable using technology?
Will this device contribute significantly to my quality of life?

**Environment**

Where will I use the equipment? At home, work, community, all of those?
Is the environment architecturally accessible?
Is transportation available?
Does my environment(s) support the technology?
Are people available to assist, if needed?
Could the environment disrupt device performance (e.g., electronic interference)?
How would the device affect other people in my environment?
Will I have the training and support I need to use the device?

**Device**

What kind of device do I prefer?
Does the device reflect my life style, age, personality, values?
Have I considered all the devices available?
How well does the device work?
How much will it cost to buy and maintain the device?
Will it be easy to use and maintain the device?
How long is it likely to last?
Will I be able to try it before I buy it?

more than the latter. Currently Medicare bases the need for assistive technology on medical need, not functional need and independence. (p. 123)

*Outcomes Measurement and Management*—what happens to a person as a result of some intervention or treatment as opposed to a focus on the *process* of administering a particular intervention or treatment. An analysis of what assistive technology services ought to achieve for persons receiving them and how achievement can be identified and measured. (p. 123)

*Consumer-Responsive Outcomes Management Systems*—The Matching Person and Technology (MPT) Model and assessment instruments (Scherer, 1991) have consumers prioritize their own outcomes in terms of measurable changes in perceived quality of life rather than the absence of sickness or the ability to perform a number of functions. While measuring the outcome of walking, we need to know if the person can get to where he/she wants to go, whether by walking or some other means. The functional capability is only a means to the achievement of a goal and quality of life. It is crucial to find out what each person values and wants to accomplish on a personal level. Then interventions can be tailored to meet the person's goals. The consumer is compared to him- or herself over time and not to other persons since so many things vary from individual to individual. (pp. 123–124)

*Program Evaluation*—in the broadest sense, program evaluation is concerned with whether or not the programs or policies are achieving their goals and purposes. A program evaluation process uses measurable objectives to determine the patient's/client's progress and allows the measurement of individual elements within the program. One of the means of ensuring objective assessment of the effectiveness and efficiency of an assistive technology program is program evaluation. An example of an assistive technology program evaluation system would include *Outcome*—reflecting the benefits that people receive from program services; *Progress*—indicating the degree of patient/client progress toward objectives (i.e., discharge, independence); and *Efficiency*—determining the amount of patient/client resources that are expended in the pursuit of outcome and progress objectives (time and cost measures). (p. 124)

Outcomes measurement and management make up a central approach to improving quality health care (Ellwood, 1988; Morrison, 1992; Strickland, 1993; Zabuldoff, 1993). The Omnibus Budget Reconciliation Act of 1986 mandated that the Health Care Financing Administration begin to address outcomes of care. More recently, the need to increase accountability through quality management and improvement has been widely recognized and accepted during discussions of health care reform. In fact, uniform performance standards, outcomes research, practice guidelines, and consumer surveys have been common features among several plans under consideration.

The Consortium for Citizens with Disabilities (CCD) Health Task Force on Health Care Reform makes specific recommendations for a comprehensive system that includes access to durable medical equipment and other assistive devices, equipment, and related services. The consortium also points out that an appropriate system must provide services on the basis of individual need, preference, and choice. An appropriate health care system is one that encourages consumer participation; ensures consumer choice in relation to services and providers; and offers the appropriate amount, scope, and duration of services, as well as trained personnel.

The health care environment in the next century will undoubtedly demand objective proof of cost-effectiveness and cost benefits. Outcomes management programs must respond to the needs of multiple constituents that may have competing interests in quality improvement (Wilkerson, 1991). These constituents include consumers, providers, and payers of rehabilitation services. At the core are persons with disabilities; all other constituents' interests must be secondary (Smith, King, Frieden, & Richards, 1993). To the extent that data from outcomes measures support other interests, they should primarily support the interest of the person served. Consumer interests in high access, low-cost, wide-ranging services may often be at odds with the needs of provider organizations and payers, however. The appropriate application of an outcome measurement and management approach in assistive technology service delivery will benefit all three target populations.

**Consumers**

People with disabilities value the same things in any kind of service that people without disabilities value. Speed, efficiency, acceptable costs, convenience, choice, quick problem resolution, and flexibility in dealing with customer needs are often cited as key areas for customer satisfaction. Various studies conducted over the past 10 years reflect consumer perceptions of assistive devices (e.g., Phillips & Zhao, 1993; Scherer, 1986; Lane, Usiak, Moffat, & Scherer, 1996) and provide helpful insight into the needs, wants, and preferences of persons who use assistive technology. The data from these studies can and does contribute to the development of criteria for consumer satisfaction outcome measures (e.g., Scherer, 1991). With a few exceptions (e.g., Cushman & Scherer, 1994; Scherer & Cushman, 1995), there is a lack of data, however, to indicate the extent to which interventions have affected the lives and needs of consumers. In the past, anecdotal stories have sufficed; the future will demand the systematic collection of quantifiable data.

For consumers, the availability of more detailed information regarding outcome performance will enhance their judgment in choosing among providers and services. Additionally, a knowledge of consumers' opinions regarding their own individual outcomes and provider performance will promote the development of more consumer-responsive outcomes management systems.

### Providers

Although consumer satisfaction is a key component of quality service delivery, it is also necessary to measure objectively whether the assistive technology service was cost-effective and efficient. These issues are important in assessing quality of care. As services are streamlined, program evaluation criteria must be developed as part of an ongoing quality assurance assessment that covers all aspects of programs.

For providers, a practical outcomes management system will help them identify the areas in which they are doing well, improve their performance where there are deficiencies, increase the overall quality of their services, and achieve reductions in cost while maintaining quality and being competitive in the modern health care marketplace.

### Payers

Insurers and payers have two basic interests in outcomes data. First, they want to be certain that they purchase effective services. Second, they want reliable performance data and a steady track record to help them project future costs and outcomes. Employers and case managers will not be interested in discipline-specific outcomes only. Instead, they will be looking at consumer outcomes in terms of the entire spectrum of services received. Providers of assistive technology services must demonstrate that an outcomes-driven philosophy is ultimately more beneficial for both consumers and payers. Organizations can then use successful outcomes, rather than price, as a standard for reimbursement.

For payers, more valid and reliable information about outcomes, used in an appropriate and technically correct manner, will clarify choice among quality providers. Reductions in cost without a reduction in quality will improve options for purchasers.

## DEVELOPMENT OF A QUALITY MEASUREMENT SYSTEM

Assistive technology providers have different needs for quality measures based on size, operating environment, region, reimbursement policies, and resources for outcomes management. Other substantive issues, as noted by Galvin and Wilkerson (1995), include

- *defining assistive technology outcomes and determining what methods and measures to use.* Many sophisticated organizations have resources to address this issue, but the vast majority of assistive technology providers need more information and guidance. Uniformity of measures and language will be important also. Flexibility in approach is necessary, but contradicts the need for uniformity, common methods, and language. Can useful guidance be given under such circumstances?
- *deciding how many and what type of resources should be invested in outcomes measurement and management activities.* Can an organization conduct a meaningful program evaluation/outcomes management without computers, without standard tools, with minimal resources? What is the right or best practice in terms of resource allocation?
- *integrating systems to respond efficiently to multiple demands for outcome information.* Purchasers are beginning to request outcomes information. The development of quality pathways and the capabilities of electronic information systems are making it easier to integrate outcome data. How can an assistive technology program best organize, operate, and respond effectively and efficiently to the demands for various outcome data?
- *building a useful outcomes management information system that also functions as a relevant clinical tool.* What practices or tools need to be developed or already exist that can accomplish that balance? How is the clinical team involved or not involved?
- *communicating outcomes information fairly, completely, and accurately.* Should there be guidelines for reporting outcomes data? What should those guidelines look like?
- *making adjustments according to type of service provided, such as different populations reflecting primary disability groups, rural versus urban, different social/economic groups with different sources and levels of financial support.* An equitable outcomes measurement and management system must take such differences into account in the measurement of outcomes.

## Tools To Consider

The quality pathways presently being developed and used describe the appropriate clinical work of each professional and department as it relates to consumers' and families' measurable outcomes of that care. They are the quality standard toward which all other processes and interventions should be directed (e.g., clinical practices, formal structure for communication). Pathways to quality assistive technology service delivery fit a range of 30 to 70 percent of the consumer population and are minimum standards for all consumers of that same population. Quality pathways delineate essential components of care for every consumer with a given diagnosis. They identify key tasks or events that relate to consumer problems or areas of concern.

Functional status measures, such as the Functional Independence Measure (FIM), could form the basic framework for evaluating outcomes in assistive technology, but their use for this purpose has drawbacks. For example, the underlying assumption of the FIM is that the level of an individual's disability implies a cost or burden of care to the individual. The basic cost or burden of disability is the amount of assistance from another person or device that the person with a disability needs to perform the activities of daily living (ADLs). Current independent living policy does not consider a person less independent if he or she needs personal assistance or assistive technology to accomplish the goals, however. For example, if a young woman with a disability decides to have a personal care assistant to help with ADLs so that she is free to conserve her energy for work, she does not consider her independence diminished. These issues of personal and program values must be taken into consideration when developing outcomes measurements.

An additional tool is under development by the Rehabilitation Engineering and Assistive Technology Society of North America (RESNA). This organization has been awarded a grant by the National Institute on Disability and Rehabilitation Research to develop systems and tools to ensure quality in assistive technology through the

- development of methods of measurement and standards to determine the most appropriate technology for an individual user
- evaluation of the effectiveness of specific applications of technology as used by an individual for specific purposes
- development of tools to provide evaluators with the capacity to make objective appraisals of assistive technology and its delivery systems

**Further Needs**

It is essential to provide products and services that are efficient, effective, and consumer responsive, and to document this through program evaluation and follow-up activities. With the move to a managed health care environment and specific dollar amounts paid for procedures, it is important to document time and materials when providing devices and services so that there are meaningful data on the true costs of providing assistive technology services. Furthermore, it is time to move beyond the anecdotal stories and document improved function, employability, and independence. Devices and services must be both safe and appropriate, and the personnel providing assistive technology services should meet the minimum requirements for standards of qualifications as developed by recognized professional groups (or as are being currently developed by RESNA).

Outcome measures that include both functional and consumer satisfaction criteria, as well as service delivery quality assurance criteria, must be developed. One partial means of approaching this is shown in Figure 1–1 and Table 1–4. As depicted in Figure 1–1, the evaluation of the need for an assistive technology proceeds from the outer circle to the inner one. First, the person's general physiological, psychological, and psychosocial characteristics are considered. At any given point in time, these characteristics determine the person's view of quality of life, rehabilitation success, and experience as a person with a disability (Scherer, 1993). These, in turn, determine the milieu, person, and technology influences on the match of this person with a particular assistive

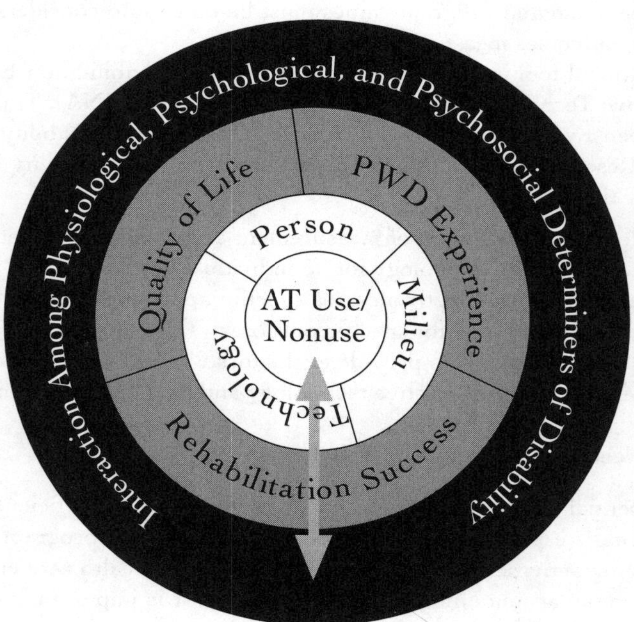


**Figure 1–1** Matching the Person with the Most Appropriate Assistive Technology. AT, assistive technology; PWD, person with a disability.

**Table 1–4** Outcomes of Persons Matched with Manual Wheelchairs in Fiscal Year 1996

| Diagnosis (Need) | Age | FIM D/C, F | MPT D/C, F | Where Living? | Indep/ PCA/ or Family Caretaker? | WC Model | Seating System | Currently Using? Time/ Consistency | Abandoned? | Reason | Other AT | Comments |
|---|---|---|---|---|---|---|---|---|---|---|---|---|
| CVA: Left | | | | | | | | | | | | |
| Right | | | | | | | | | | | | |
| Other | | | | | | | | | | | | |
| SCI: C __ | | | | | | | | | | | | |
| T __ | | | | | | | | | | | | |
| L __ | | | | | | | | | | | | |
| Amputation: BK Left | | | | | | | | | | | | |
| Right | | | | | | | | | | | | |
| Bilateral | | | | | | | | | | | | |
| AK Left | | | | | | | | | | | | |
| Right | | | | | | | | | | | | |
| Bilateral | | | | | | | | | | | | |
| MS Involvement | | | | | | | | | | | | |
| [Etc.] | | | | | | | | | | | | |

AK = Above the knee
BK = Below the knee
C = Cervical level
CVA = Cerebral vascular accident
D/C = Discharge
F = Follow-up
FIM = Functional Independence Measure
L = Lumbar level
MS = Multiple sclerosis
PCA = Personal care assistant
SCI = Spinal cord injury
T = Thoracic level
WC = Wheelchair

technology. The center circle, or core, is having and using the assistive technology. To understand the outcome of assistive technology use or nonuse at a future point in time (after the individual has tried and used the assistive technology), it is necessary only to examine the process as it moves outward from the core to the milieu, person, and technology characteristics that are affecting actual assistive technology use at that time to the person's resulting views of quality of life, experience as a person with a disability, and rehabilitation success. These will have an effect on the individual's physiological, psychological, and psychosocial resources. Thus the whole process begins again; the cycle is continuous.

It is difficult to isolate a particular influence on assistive technology use or nonuse because there are so many variables that are hard to quantify (e.g., assistance given by family members, the amount of training that the person had in using the assistive technology). In trying to develop quality pathways to assistive technology service delivery, a data collection form such as that shown in Table 1–4 may be helpful. This is similar to the form used in the research by Scherer and Cushman (1995) and it organizes information about persons with different diagnoses routinely provided with a particular assistive technology (in this case, a manual wheelchair). Data are collected on the use of the various models of wheelchairs, reasons for nonuse, and any alternative or replacement devices; for example, a man may have purchased a manual wheelchair and later found that he could get along with a walker. Scores from the Functional Independence Measure (FIM) at discharge and follow-up can be compared to the FIM goal and Matching Person and Technology (MPT) data collected at discharge and follow-up to capture functional and personal influences on use.

For service delivery quality assurance, information on length of stay, professional costs and services, living situation at discharge (e.g., home, skilled nursing facility), and primary caregiver is also important. Data on assistive technologies should indicate whether devices are purchased or rented, and the costs of the device, supplier, and payer. All this information can be used to compare services provided to individuals within a single facility or as a means to integrate information across facilities and rehabilitation providers.

The central motivation for developing outcome measures for assistive technology is to improve our understanding and documentation of the effectiveness of assistive technology devices and services. This information will make it possible to enhance the independence of people with disabilities and the options and opportunities available to them. It is also important to expand access and avoid undue hardship for everyone involved in matching the most appropriate technologies to all persons who want them.

## REFERENCES


Crewe, N., & Dijkers, M. (1995). Functional assessment. In L.A. Cushman & M.J. Scherer (Eds.), *Psychological assessment in medical rehabilitation* (pp. 101–144). Washington, DC: APA Books.

Cushman, L.A., & Scherer, M.J. (1994). Measuring outcomes of assistive technology use through mixed methods. *Archives of Physical Medicine & Rehabilitation* [Abstract], *75*(6), 726.

Ellwood, P. (1988). Outcomes management: A technology of patient experience. *New England Journal of Medicine, 318*, 1549–1556.

Galvin, J.C., & Wilkerson, D.L. (1995). A quality assurance process in an assistive technology program. *Proceedings of the Eleventh International Seating Symposium, University of Pittsburgh*, Pittsburgh, PA (pp. 122–130).

Lane, J.P., Usiak, D.J., Moffat, J.A., & Scherer, M.J. (1996). *Consumer evaluation criteria for assistive devices: Guidelines for design, development and marketing.* Manuscript submitted for publication.

Morrison, M. (1992, October/November). On the threshold of outcomes management. *Rehab Management*, 105–107.

Phillips, B., & Zhao, H. (1993). Predictors of assistive technology abandonment. *Assistive Technology, 5*, 36–45.

Scherer, M. (1986). Values in the creation, prescription, and use of technological aids and assistive devices for people with physical disabilities. Doctoral dissertation, University of Rochester, and final report to the National Science Foundation, *Dissertation Abstracts International, 48(01)*, 49. (University Microfilms No. ADG87-08247).

Scherer, M.J. (1991). *Matching person and technology (MPT)*. Rochester, NY: Author.

Scherer, M.J. (1993). *Living in the state of stuck: How technology impacts the lives of people with disabilities.* Cambridge, MA: Brookline Books.

Scherer, M.J., & Cushman, L.A. (1995). Differing therapist-patient views of assistive technology use and implications for patient education and training [Abstract]. *Archives of Physical Medicine & Rehabilitation, 76*(6), 595.

Scherer, M.J., & Frisina, D.R. (1994). Applying the Matching Person and Technology Model to individuals with hearing loss: What people say they want—and need—from assistive technologies. *Technology and Disability, 3*(1), 62–68.

Scherer, M.J., & Galvin, J.C. (1994, February/March). Matching people with technology. *Rehab Management, 7*(2), 128–130.

Scherer, M., & McKee, B. (1989). But will the assistive technology device be used? In J. Presperin (Ed.), *Proceedings of the 12th Annual Conference: Technology for the Next Decade* (pp. 356–357). Washington, DC: RESNA Press.

SMART Exchange, (March, 1990). *Technology: removing the shroud of mystery: A collaborative paper.* PO Box 724704, Atlanta, Georgia, 30339.

Smith, L., King, K., Frieden, L., & Richards, L. (1993). *Health care reform, independent living, and people with disabilities.* A report of the National Study Group on the Implications of Health Care Reform for Americans with Disabilities and Chronic Conditions. Houston, TX: ILRU.

Strickland, D. (1993). Quality of care under reform: Practice guidelines and report cards. *Occupational Therapy Practice, 2*(2), 1–5.

U.S. Census Bureau. (1990). *National Health Interview Survey on Assistive Devices (NHIS-AD)*, Washington, D.C.

Wilkerson, D. (1991). Program and outcome evaluation: Opportunity for the 1990s. *Occupational Therapy Practice, 2*(2), 10–15.

Zabuldoff, J. (1993, August/September). A conversation with Paul Ellwood, MD. *Rehab Management*, 27–32.

*Chapter 2*

# Low-Technology Aids for Daily Living and Do-It-Yourself Devices

*Alexandra Enders and Peter Leech*

There is no greater increase in function than from nothing to something.

*Peter Leech*

Everyday technology is often taken for granted, even by advocates with disabilities, but tools for daily living are frequently needed *before* the rest of the technology can be beneficial. Usually more mundane than glamorous, everyday technology rarely involves high-technology or computer applications. If it is working right, and working as a system, it can and should fade into the background.

Technological support for everyday living is all pervasive. It is also intrinsically related to adaptive strategies and personal assistance services. Without some combination of these three supportive services, a person with a disability may not be able to get out of the house, into bed, eat dinner, take a bath, or put on clothes. The combination of supportive services used is very individualized and changes over time and circumstance.

In many ways, everyday technology is the most challenging of all technological interventions. It can be highly personal and can involve body functions in very private ways. It has the least amount of funding available, however, because it does not easily fit into most medical, vocational, or educational categories. Furthermore, because it is by definition home- and community-based, it does not fit well into the traditional service delivery categories. The basic principles that guide wise choice and use of everyday technology need to be tightly woven into all the aspects of technological support systems, high-technology and specialized products included. Unfortunately, these principles are sometimes in direct conflict with reimbursement requirements; for example, Medicare's regulatory demand that the device not be useful to a healthy or uninjured person makes it difficult to buy an off-the-shelf product at a discount store and adapt it for a person with a disability. People with disabilities must learn to differentiate between the medical model problem-solving rationale that drives third-party reimbursement and a more practical approach that will work for them—whether or not third-party payment is available. Professionals should help people with disabilities learn pragmatic principles for choosing and using tools for living, especially since they must pay for most everyday technology.

## BENEFICIARIES: EVERYONE

The usefulness of everyday technology is not limited to any particular group of people. Everyone uses it, and poor design appears to be a universal problem (Norman, 1988; Papanek, 1983; Papanek & Hennessey, 1977). Improvement in design to make a product intrinsically more accessible to people with disabilities promises to improve the product for everyone.

Everyone whose life is touched by a person with a disability sooner or later comes into contact with that person's tools for living. Equipment selection should take into account the everyday contacts, such as caregivers, assistants, classmates, and co-workers. If the device works for the individual with a disability, but detracts from the life of co-workers, or is potentially dangerous to a caregiver or personal assistant, something went amiss in the original selection process. The same is true if the device is effective, but has an aura of stigma and creates interpersonal barriers for the people who use it. This is the assistive technology equivalent of "the operation was a success, but the patient died."

Everyday technology that works, generally works for everyone. Those with disabilities who find or invent practical technology to help them in the activities of daily living (ADL) are not usually surrounded by appliance-like equipment; they have aesthetically pleasing, helpful gadgets that do not look out of place, even when they are performing a task for which they were not designed. When they work, they are clever—so clever that a person without a disability may find them useful.

## DEVELOPMENT OF TOOLS FOR DAILY LIVING

### Left to Your Own Devices

Many gadgets in the professional catalogs and literature are focused on the daily living needs of people with disabilities. The most successful items, as well as the best methods for evaluating, selecting, and using appropriate devices, are developed primarily through self-help, however, based on trial and error rather than professional intervention. Thus, leaving people with disabilities "to their own devices" is not necessarily a bad thing. The more control these people have over their technology, the better. It is detrimental for professionals to try to assume control of an individual's tools for living, because their control creates an undesirable dependency and reduces the individual's motivation to become a designer, an inventor, and a problem solver.

Even so, people with disabilities should not just be abandoned to their own wiles in the jungle of daily living. There is a significant role for professionals in daily living technology. The transitions from the role of patient, the role of consumer, and then to the role of inventor are important in the career of a person with a disability. The professional may begin as a teacher, evolve as a coach, and ideally become a partner, even a student, as the person with a disability develops strategies that can be shared with peers and professionals.

From the perspective of the person with a disability, the locus of control moves from the external to the internal. The capacity for change and growth becomes self-directed. Therefore, the process of acquiring the device can be very important. The person's development of a self-help orientation for everyday technology can have a profound impact, providing a tangible mechanism through which that person can regain control of his or her life in everyday activities and decision making. Professionals need to foster problem-solving skills. If the individual does not understand how the professional developed the solution, the individual will not be able to develop strategies in the future. Reinvention is a successful strategy and outcome if performed by a person with a disability. The difference between giving someone a fish and teaching someone to fish is particularly applicable in the realm of tools for daily living.

An individual's need for experience and practice with the devices that may become a part of his or her ongoing support system is frequently overlooked. A survey of occupational therapists indicated that less time was spent on training in independent living skills than may be necessary or desirable (Pendelton, 1990). Occupational therapy consumers have described training in home- and community-based skills as the most deficient, least addressed form of intervention during their rehabilitation stay (Rogers, 1979). Professional rehabilitation intervention is often not available after hospital-based rehabilitation is finished, usually because of the lack of funding. In rural areas, the distance from a source of professional services may be an additional complication.

Consumers and their families should learn about the benefits and availability of professional services, as well as the best way to seek these services when needed. They also need to understand the value of being self-reliant and taking charge of their own ongoing "rehabilitation." For example, in order to optimize function, they need to know how to select mass market products for desirable characteristics and where to get updated, reliable information in the future. Ideally, the teaching of these consumer skills would be part of the initial hospital-based rehabilitation process; but instruction in community-based independent living skills is not usually a component of the inpatient rehabilitation experience. There are notable exceptions, such as the independent living skills training programs designed for older people who are losing their vision that focus almost exclusively on skills needed for integration into the community. These programs rarely use a medical model, focus on person–environment interactions, and highlight consumer-identified ongoing community-based needs.

### Disability As a Difference in Degree

The do-it-yourself (DIY) approach to tools for daily living is as old as humankind. In fact, one of the characteristics that distinguishes the human animal from the other apes is the human's ability to develop and elaborate on tools. It is most likely that we survived as a species because we were clever enough to develop tools that make up for our frailties; protect us from predators; and help us to find food, create shelter, and use fire. Tools and devices have become so commonplace that they are taken for granted in daily life and are "invisible" as special devices. Most people rarely consider their dependence on some adaptation of the wheel to get around until the car, elevator, or bicycle breaks down. Nor does anyone think about dependence on electricity until the power fails.

People with disabilities are different from other people only in degree. Having a disability means only that one's functional envelope may have less range or flexibility and that one's tools must be designed or adapted to build on existing functional abilities. The daily living needs are the same. The question of "dependence," or the degree thereof, is a matter of perspective.

Building on functional abilities rather than compensating for functional deficits is a paradigm shift. Extending one's mindset about disability beyond "let's fix it" can and often does make the difference between living and just existing. People with disabilities are increasingly vocal about the fact that they do not need to do things as if the disability does not exist; they just need to get the job done. The best approach is the "whatever it takes" model. The message—help me build on my strengths, and not just fill in for perceived deficits—is indeed a different approach to disability services.

## TECHNOLOGY: NOT A STAND ALONE SOLUTION

Independence is defined in terms of how much control a person has over his or her environment, not in the number of tasks that the person can do without assistance. Tools have always improved the odds, as has cooperative effort. We are not only tool-making animals, but also strategy-using, social animals; as often as we have developed a tool, we have developed a strategy to use it and have reached out for assistance from our associates when necessary. In fact, this combination of tools, strategy, and cooperation may be characteristic of humanoid evolution from one level of accomplishment to another. This triad of support can be illustrated graphically by a triangle, each side of which represents one of the aspects of common functional supports (Figure 2–1).

Although the proportions may vary with the particular endeavor, some level of input from each of these three elements is always evident. A particular activity may appear to involve primarily strategy and tools, but cooperation undoubtedly plays a role somewhere. For example, a person who decides to drive across the country alone may consider this a triumph of independent effort: human and machine against the odds. The importance of cooperative effort may recede into the background until the machine needs fuel or the driver considers all the effort that went into building the machine and the road upon which it runs. Clearly, we are all very fragile animals, extremely dependent upon one another, our tools or machines, and our wits for survival.

Despite the fact that everyone relies heavily on this support system, conceptualizing the needs of a person with a disability seems to lead to new "special needs" categories (Figure 2–2). Tools and machinery become "applied technology," "assistive devices," "ADL equipment," "technical aids for the handicapped," or "technological support." Strategies become "adaptive strategies"; cooperative effort becomes "personal assistance services." For people with disabilities, the need for a support system is no less pervasive or necessary than for others, but such a system always includes technological support, adaptive strategies, and personal assistance (people support). Achieving independence means

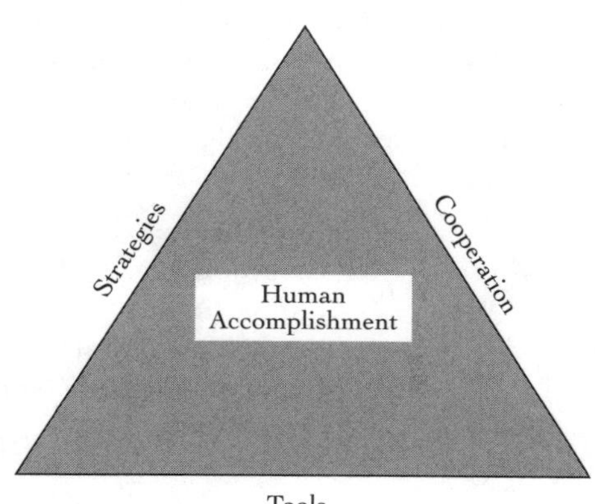


**Figure 2–1** Three elements of a human accomplishment support system

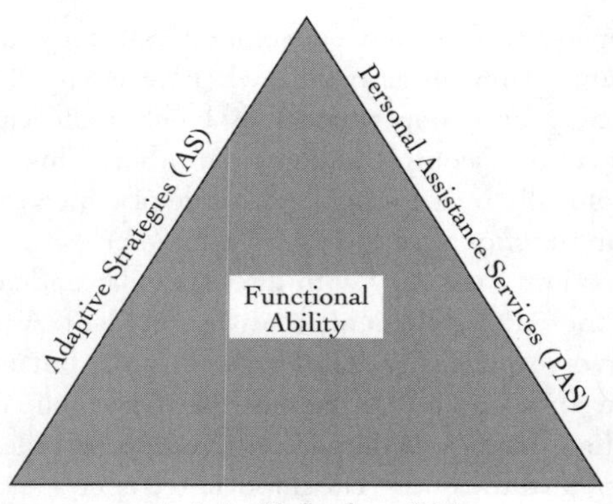


**Figure 2–2** Three elements of a functional ability support system

being in control of one's life—defining one's own support system, including the tools, the strategies, and the people support necessary to accomplish any given task or objective, in all the environments in which it is needed.

## FEATURES OF A TRUE SUPPORT SYSTEM

A comprehensive list of everyday technology would fill an encyclopedia. In some functional areas, however, tools for daily living may be critical for a person with a disability (Figure 2–3). A few functional tasks, such as lifting, are needed across environments (e.g., work, school, community). It is important to consider these tasks in everyday technology so that the functional solution is unified; for example, the individual should be able to reach out to pick something up in all environments.

Daily living technology includes technological support systems in the following areas:

**Shelter:**
- Access
- Safety/security
- Environmental control
- Sleeping

**Interpersonal relationships:**
- Communicating (speaking and writing)
- Sex/intimacy
- Child care

**Personal care:**
- Breathing
- Eating (input)
- Excreting (output)
- Grooming/hygiene (surface)
- Dressing
- Health management

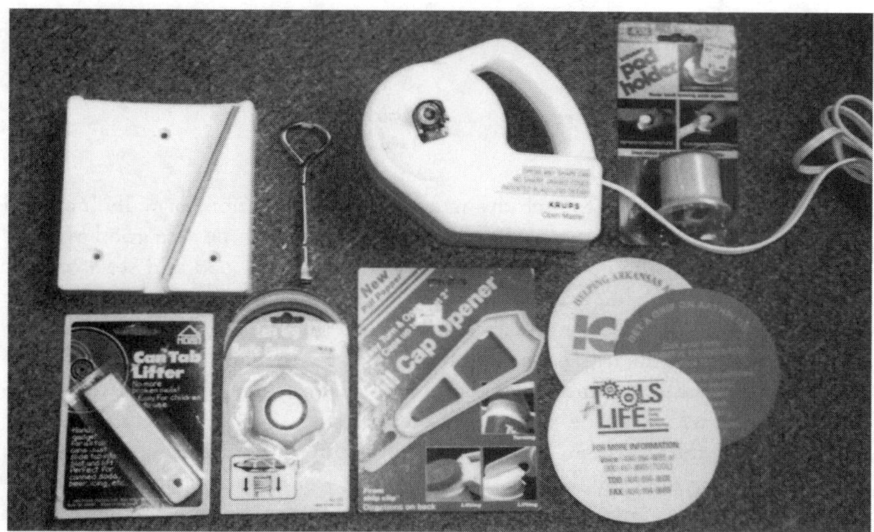


**Figure 2–3** Assistive opening devices that come from the grocery store and the hardware store. Round grippers with advertising are freebies from disability programs.

---

**Figure 2–4** Glue traps for tiny game hunting

**Home management:**
Storage
Food preparation
Cleaning/household chores

**Functional tasks:**
Lifting
Reaching
Holding
Transferring

Each of these categories includes many tasks that are not normally included in activity lists and assessments. For example, Figure 2–4 shows a good product ridding the home of mice and bugs. Some people cannot load and set a regular mouse trap. With a glue trap, all they have to do is place the trap where there has been mouse activity—no peanut butter, no fingers caught in the bale, no spring to release if the trap is not set on the floor gently enough. The mouse gets stuck and dies, and the entire trap is discarded. For bugs that are attracted to windows, the traps can be set on the window sill; for cockroaches and other kitchen pests, the traps can be safely set on counters because they contain no poison. It seems unlikely that "mouse trapping" would appear on any ADL assessment form, but anyone who has lain in bed listening to mice chew through the kitchen knows it can be an important activity.

A support system is never static. A functional bathroom that incorporates tools, strategies, and cooperative effort is a jail, not a support system, if the person can use the shower or go to the toilet only at home. The person may need to wash up when traveling or go to the toilet at work. The goal is to maintain the same degree of functional ability, no matter what the environment. Different situations may call for different balances among the elements of a personal support system (Figure 2–5). For example, there may be a fair balance between assistive technology, adaptive strategies, and personal assistance at home. When people travel, however, they are likely to rely more on adaptive strategies and personal assistance. In some places, visitors with disabilities can rent or borrow equipment, formally or informally, that is not readily transported from home.

Recognition that people with disabilities travel is evident in the increased availability of accessible recreation vehicles (RVs). The variation of personal preference is also evident in the range of vehicles seen, from top of the line accessible RVs to the DIY accessible camper/van shown in Figure 2–6. The latter is a van adaptation that includes an accessible cooking set-up. Six-inch deep cabinets were designed to fit onto each rear door. One side houses a fold-down shelf that contains a camp stove with shelves above; the other features a "pantry" covered by a fold-down preparation table with shelves above designed to hold dishes and utensils. Storage bins with rope handles slide underneath the platform, which converts from seat to bed.

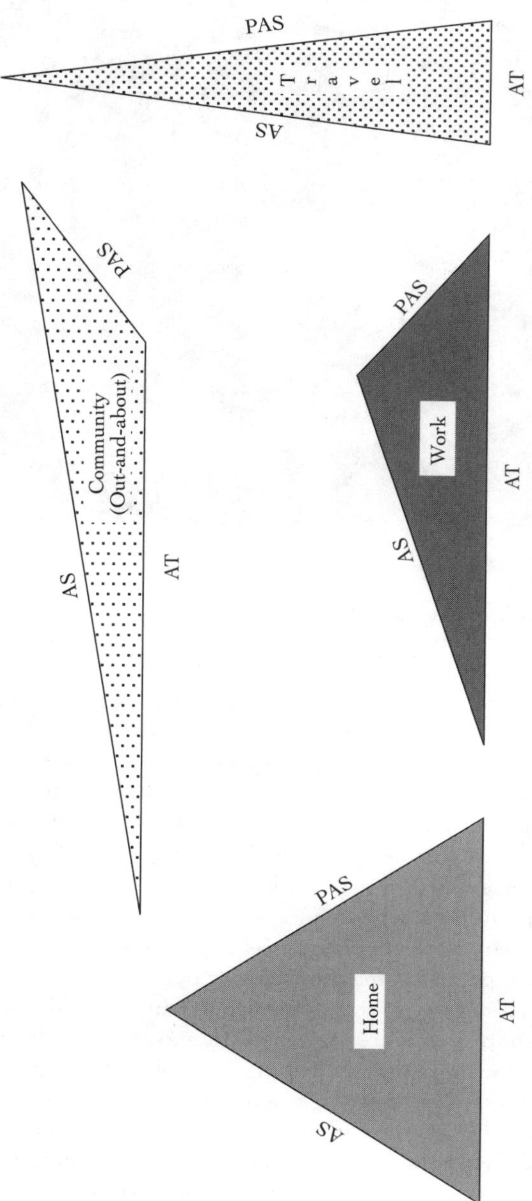


**Figure 2–5** Different balances among the elements of a personal support system. AT, assistive technology; AS, adaptive strategies; PAS, personal assistance services.

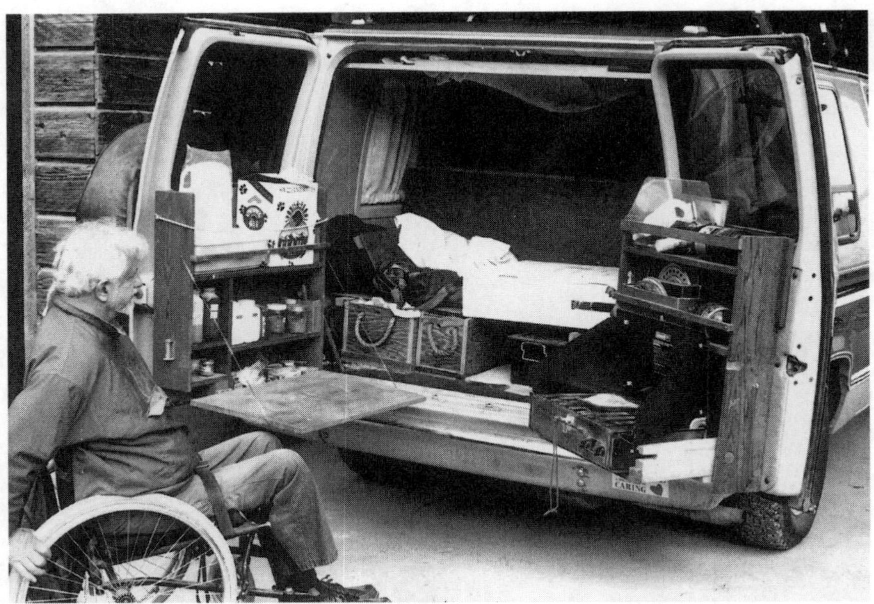

**Figure 2–6** Peter Leech's van with accessible cooking set-up

---

Support systems must take into account changes in functional performance, as well as changes of environment. Changes in medication, fluctuations in hormonal levels (e.g., increased muscle tone and spasticity in some women during their menstrual periods), fatigue level, time of day, changes in strength and stamina that accompany aging, decline in ability related to specific disabilities (e.g., multiple sclerosis or amyotrophic lateral sclerosis [ALS])—all influence the proportions of supports needed. Thus, there is a danger of developing baseline support systems that require a performance level not always available. Although this is true for all assistive technology, it is critical for daily living tools; no one should have to operate at maximum peak performance on an everyday basis. If an individual's ability to transfer independently or assist in a transfer always draws on resources that are very close to maximum performance, provision must be made for those times when this level of performance is not possible. Even people who do not normally use adaptive equipment may need to have it available for days when they are not functioning at their best.

If the technology works only when the "functional envelope" is at its broadest range, there is likely to be a high degree of dissatisfaction among those who use that technology. Furthermore, those who use it are likely to blame themselves for the failure of the technology. This can discourage an individual with a disability from considering technological solutions again or even from trying to accomplish the task in the belief that the task is beyond his or her skill and capabilities. Norman (1988) described the cycle of technology as learned helplessness. He suggested that the design of everyday things seems almost guaranteed to produce technology phobia. Norman was describing everybody's everyday technology, not assistive technology. People think that the failure is their fault and generalize this to other technology, coming to believe that they just have no aptitude for technology. This phenomenon is probably even more rampant in the disability field, where the marketplace has even less control over good design characteristics.

## DEVELOPMENTAL MODEL

A newly disabled person may not at first recognize the challenges in moving beyond a home environment or may not be ready to look for solutions during the early stages of rehabilitation. Because professionals seldom participate in such planning, technologists often see an individual later in his or her career as a person with a disability. At this point, the person may be so used to problem solving alone that the subject of daily living issues does not arise. That does not mean that everyday technology should be overlooked, however.

### Function Away from the Primary Environment

The support system required to achieve independence will vary with the distance and length of time a person can stay away from his or her primary residence. If a person's reentry into life and community is to be accomplished with any efficiency, the support system must include the useful tools, strategies, and cooperative effort associated with the common ADLs, especially when it is necessary to accomplish them away from the immediate residence. The most efficient support system involves people with a similar disability who have managed to reach a higher level of independence so that the newly disabled person loses less time in "reinventing the wheel." This element of peer counseling is often overlooked.

After learning to function in their primary environment, people begin to want to venture away from it. Whether a woman who has a mobility impairment, for example, can go out depends on her mobility and access. Given a functional manual wheelchair or a reliable power wheelchair, adequate ramping, and wide enough doorways, she may begin to test her ability to function in the yard or on the street. How long she may venture away depends on her ability to manage eating, drinking, and bladder and bowel functions away from her primary environment. This often requires either that different strategies be employed in order to function in the absence of a support person or that a support person go along for the ride.

It is essential to test a person's ability to function in each one of the daily living areas away from the primary environment before that person can begin to consider the demands of education, vocational training, or employment. Being away from the primary environment from early morning to evening on a daily basis also necessitates modification of the self-care regimen at home (e.g., bathing, grooming, bowel care, dressing) so as to be accomplished before or after the day away. If in need of personal assistance for these activities, then the person must have control over scheduling.

## Personal Technology

Touching every aspect of daily life, tools for living can be highly personal—especially when they involve basic body functions. It can be difficult and embarrassing for everyone to discuss the intimate details of bladder and bowel function, menstruation, sexuality, and personal hygiene, for example. There are privacy and confidentiality issues. Even more important are the vulnerability and emotions associated with changes in function or in ways of handling such personal activities.

There is not even commonly accepted language to ease the awkwardness of such discussions. People may write down bladder function and talk about urination, but most still say "pee." In 1994, Enders planned an informal discussion group at a national technology meeting, "Going with the Flow: Peeing and Bleeding for Women and Very Enlightened Men." The announcement of the session and the language used caused quite a stir. It is critical to find appropriate ways to talk about these issues.

Apparently, it is difficult even to write about some areas. For example, there is almost nothing in the literature on menstruation except in the English book *Disabled Eve* (available from the National Rehabilitation Information Center, 8455 Colesville Rd., Suite 935, Silver Spring, MD 20910). The few references that do exist provide little detail on the physical manipulation of female sanitary products. A tampon inserter is commercially available in England, but none is readily available in the United States. This is not an obscure issue—half the population deals with the issue of menstrual bleeding and hormonal flux for at least 30 years. A DIY solution is shown in Figure 2–7. When tampons on a stick

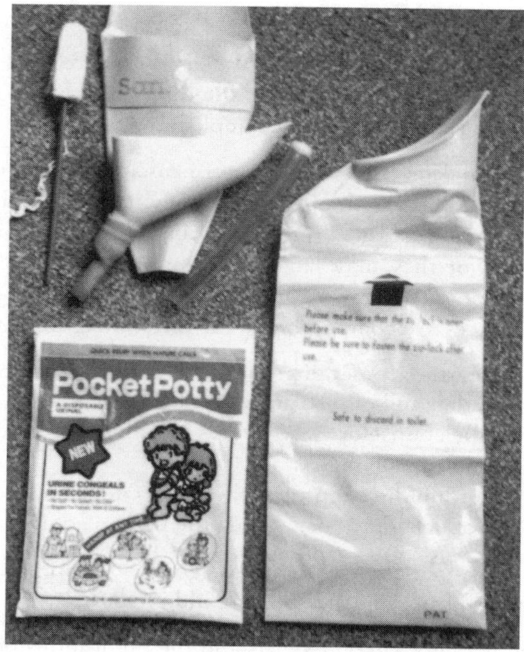


**Figure 2–7** Funnels for urination. Do-it-yourself tampon inserter, top left

were no longer commercially available, a consumer started making her own by inserting a thin plastic paint brush handle into an OB brand tampon. She stresses the importance of placing a washer or something similar on the handle to prevent it from moving all the way through the tampon and coming out the far end during insertion. The handle can be washed and reused. This woman also uses a carefully planned adaptive strategy for inserting and removing the tampon.

Differences in comfort levels and in values (e.g., attitudes about birth control, sexual orientation) come into play when intervention is needed. Although a nurse may be very comfortable discussing body functions, some technologists may be uneasy in such discussions. If the professional is uncomfortable, it will be very difficult for the person with a disability or a family member to bring up these issues. It is critical to recognize one's personal comfort level. If discussions of such issues as toileting, sexuality, and tampon insertion create embarrassment for either the individual or the professional, another team member, a peer counselor, or an outside referral may resolve the problem.

## SELECTION OF APPROPRIATE DEVICES

- What does the person want to do? When and where?
- What functional abilities, skills, and interests does the person have?
- What tools can best be used to accomplish the task?

Assessment, formal or informal, is one means of determining consumer needs. Depending on the length of time that they have had a disability, people may need a traditional assessment, they may be full partners in identifying issues and solutions, or they may have the solution worked out and just need assistance in obtaining, customizing, and installing equipment. The differences in these circumstances are comparable to the differences in working with

1. a dentist, who does something to a person and asks questions while the person's mouth is full of instruments
2. an educator or counselor, who shares learning and discovers a process for future problem solving
3. an architect or building contractor, who has demonstrated expertise and is hired to produce a product, which the person controls and pays for

Whether part of an assessment, a shared goal-setting process, or a contractual relationship, information gathering should include:

- data on the person's current status and the point in his or her career as a person with a disability (see Developmental Model)
- any expectations of change in the person, resources, or environment;
- identification of the person who wants change to occur
- the basis on which success will be evaluated

This information is necessary for all technology interventions. The approach used depends on where and when the professional is called into the process. The issues may reflect a global need, such as opening and closing doors in all environments. Sometimes, the person needs recommendations for a specific environment, such as the home bathroom or kitchen. Sometimes, the professional is asked to look only at possible applications of assistive technology, while others consider alternative options and pull the process together. Sometimes, the technologist is called in after everyone else has given up, in the hope that technology can solve the problem.

When looking at everyday technology, it is important to understand why the individual seeks intervention at this time. These activities usually have been occurring everyday for some time. What is different now? Have expectations been raised (or lowered)? Have functional skills changed, and are they now stabilized or is more change expected? Has an essential element of the person's overall support system changed (e.g., a personal assistant is leaving)? Will the environment change (e.g., the person is leaving for college)? Has other technology caused a change (e.g., a new wheelchair causes a problem with bed and toilet transfers)? One of the founders of the Independent Living movement told the story of being motivated to find a way to control a power wheelchair when he fell in love; he decided that having an assistant along pushing his wheelchair was not conducive to a romantic relationship with his girlfriend. The reasons for a desired change in everyday technology are not always as straightforward. A mother who is looking for a better way to help her 14-year-old daughter with cerebral palsy in the shower may really be looking for ways to handle her daughter's menstrual periods in a manner that is acceptable to both of them. The teenager may be bigger and heavier, and may have outgrown her current bathtub equipment, but only probing questions such as "why does she need more showers now than she did 2 years ago?" are likely to lead to an acceptable solution.

Problem identification should incorporate all the aspects of the functional activity, not just a specific and isolated task that has been focused on as the problem. Keeping the questions "what's different?" and "why now?" in mind can help. Sometimes, when the individual recognizes what the real issue is, he or she or a family member can readily solve it. Sometimes, understanding "why now?" suggests a more appropriate professional relationship. For example, a woman who wants to change because she saw someone else doing an activity and thinks she could find a way to do it, too, may be ready for a partnership/problem-solving model or an introduction to peer mentors.

## CRITERIA FOR EVALUATING EVERYDAY TECHNOLOGY

Even though applied to the same range of human activities as are other tools, assistive technology devices are often evaluated by different criteria. The only real difference, however, is that they may need to address a larger or more varied degree of limitation. This does not seem a valid reason to treat them as a special category of tool or to judge their performance, economics, or aesthetics by less rigorous criteria than those applied to other tools.

If it is to be effective, any tool must succeed on two counts:

1. **Technical features**
   Does it work?
   Is it strong and safe?
   Is it compatible with other equipment?
   Is it reliable?
   Is it durable?
2. **Ergonomic (human factors) features**
   Is there a feeling of security when using it?
   Is it simple to use?

Is it the correct size?
Is it comfortable?
Is it aesthetically appealing?

The technical features can be objectively measured; the ergonomic features are more subjective and should be evaluated in relationship to the device user and/or caregiver. If an elderly woman does not feel secure on her elevated toilet seat, for example, she probably will not use it. Surveys in the United States (Grall, 1979) and England (Page, 1981) have shown that adaptive equipment often does not measure up very well to these standard criteria for useful tools.

To ensure that they are not using a double standard, professionals who use, build, prescribe, or recommend equipment for an individual with a disability should apply one question to every piece of equipment: "Would I want this piece of equipment in my house, my office, my car?" If the honest answer is not "yes," then it is time to go back to the drawing board or the file cabinet and look for another solution. An additional set of functional criteria can be called the "closet test" in answer to the question, How do you keep equipment out of the closet? These questions are implicit (or should be) in the purchase of any product. Because equipment decisions are not always in the control of a person with a disability, outside "helpers" or developers may need to be reminded to address questions such as the following:

- Would I want this thing in my house?
- What impact is it really going to have on this person and his or her family?
- Is it worth the effort to use the device?
- How labor-intensive is it to set up, fit, clean, maintain, and store?
- What options does the person have if he or she does not use this thing?
- What incentive is there to use it?
- What disincentives are there?
- Is it possible to get by with less, to reduce the overall number of devices?
- Does the person need more? Is this just one piece of a system?
- Who will do routine maintenance? Do repairs?
- Where will it be stored when not in use?

A whole field of questions relate to the theme, "Would I want to use this thing?" Questions will be specifically different for each type of device, but the general tone is

- for an eating device: Would I use it in a restaurant?
- for adaptive clothing: Would I wear this in public? On a date?
- for a transfer device: Would I use it in public?

## FINDING INFORMATION, SERVICES, RESOURCES, AND PEOPLE

There is no great mystery about assistive devices; they are just tools! People who are unfamiliar with the way tools work, however, may need to learn that all tools or machines are simply combinations of mechanical, electrical, or electronic devices arranged in a way to accomplish a certain task. Once they can relate their assistive technology to the technology that already exists in the community, people with disabilities can develop their own "circles of support" to attend to their assistive technology needs. Rather than formal dealers and repair services that are inconveniently located or unavailable altogether, local service people can repair the mechanical, electrical, or electronic components of most assistive devices; others can invent and fabricate special devices when asked to do so. These are the same people who keep the other tools and machinery of modern life up and running. They can keep people with disabilities up and running as well.

When approaching nontraditional service people for repairs or maintenance on assistive devices, it is important to ask questions that fit within their frame of reference. For example, it is appropriate to call a welder when the frame of a wheelchair needs repair, but rather than ask whether the welder "repairs wheelchairs," it is more useful to ask whether he or she can weld the metal of which the wheelchair is made (e.g., stainless steel, chrome-moly, aluminum). This, of course, requires that the person with the disability be familiar with the equipment and its component parts. Other possible questions might include, Can you check the charging capacity of a deep cycle battery? or, Can you check my machine for a short circuit or a defective switch?

Asking a helpful hardware dealer for assistance with a DIY project can have unexpected benefits. For example, when Leech wanted to set up a sprinkling system that he could turn on from his porch (Figures 2–8 and 2–9), he asked a hardware dealer about outdoor water faucets with lever handles. The discussion that followed not only yielded the faucets, but a great deal of other useful information about what size plastic pipe to use, how to fit it together, and what sprinkler heads are best and how to install them. Often, hardware dealers know other people who can be helpful with a project.

It can also be useful to investigate what else has this component or something like it? Leech spotted a wheelchair ramp in another city that had an open-wire mesh covering so that snow could pass through it. This seemed like a good idea, so he called a building supply store and talked with someone there about what the material looked like, the usage that it would get, and the weight that it had to support. He learned that an extruded steel mesh would do the job and built that into his ramp plans (see Figure 2–9).

**Figure 2–8** Peter Leech turning on the top faucet lever on his complex watering system

In the mainstream consumer marketplace, in a specialized part of it, or in a specialized industry, there may be someone who needs to do exactly the same thing. For example, pilots and passengers in small planes that do not have toilets may have some creative suggestions about what to do when they need to urinate. Function-oriented features may appear in product literature, and knowledgeable salespeople can help. Usually, there are no features labeled "access" or "handicapped," as manufacturers do not yet understand this market. Even when there are such labels, the features need careful examination for utility, because manufacturers sometimes use a very narrow interpretation of access.

researchers feel that URINE is an appropriate name for product development and research into everyday technology. It is not quite accurate to say that the research is not exciting, because a breakthrough is very exciting. Breakthroughs tend to be the result of real creativity, frequently outside the realm of the originally planned research. The best "labs" are usually in the homes of tinkering people with disabilities.

The best way to develop accessible aids to daily living products may actually be by increasing the awareness of product design professionals. Realistically, most of the significant advances in daily living aids for people with disabilities have been mass market products and services: modular environmental control units available at the hardware store, automatic garage door openers, microwave ovens, bidet type toilet seats, waterbeds, edible TV dinners and other convenience foods, food processors, oven rack pullers, automatic dishwashers, home security systems, Niagara beds, Velcro shoe closures, jogging clothes as acceptable streetwear, vibrators, hot tubs, hand-held shower massage units, electric toothbrushes, electric can openers, remote controls for almost everything, and on and on. Until the architects and product designers incorporate universal product design into the total environment, however, people with disabilities will have to look for more immediately available forms of technical aids to retrofit personal environments and everyday technology.

## CONCLUSION

For everyday technology, the changes in equipment for people with disabilities are probably less important than the changes in the process. The best way to retrofit everyday technology is with a self-help approach to problem solving. Do-it-yourself is more a process than a product or technique. Once people learn to explore a wide range of potential resources and develop a broad view of how and where technology can assist in everyday life, self-help and the process of everyday DIY technology become routine parts of independent living. This ability to take control of the technology is a powerful starting point in breaking the dependency cycle that is inherent in so many disability-oriented services.

Do-it-yourself is not really a matter of how many things one can saw or solder, but how one manages the everyday tools of living. The biggest challenge is to incorporate both professional and self-help approaches into a support system that is flexible and adaptable in multiple environments over time.

---

### REFERENCES

Darjes, R. (Ed.). (1990). Families caring for people with dementia; Are they using the technology? Which technologies are they using? *Windows on Technology, 7* (1), 4.

Grall, T.B. (1979). *A feasibility study of product testing and reporting for handicapped consumers*. Sheboygan Falls, WI: Interdisciplinary Design Consultants.

LaPlante, M., Hendershot, G., & Moss, A. (1992). Assistive technology devices and home accessibility features: Prevalence, payment, need, and trends. *Advance Data: Vital Health Statistics*, September 16, 1992, Vol. 217.

Longino, C., Jr. (1994, August). Myths on an aging America. *American Demographics*, 36–43.

Manton, K., Corder, L., & Stallard, E. (1993). Changes in the use of personal assistance and special equipment from 1982 to 1989: Results from the 1982 and 1989 National Long-Term Care Study (Hyattsville, Md). *Gerontologist, 33* (22), 168–176.

McCuaig, M., & Frank, G. (1991). The able self: Adaptive patterns and choices in independent living for a person with cerebral palsy. *American Journal of Occupational Therapy, 45*, 224–234.

Norman, D. (1988). *The psychology of everyday things*. New York: Basic Books.

Page, M. (1981). Why technical aids do not always work. *New Scientist*,

Papanek, V. (1983). *Design for human scale*. New York: Van Nostrand Reinhold.

Papanek, V., & Hennessey, J. (1977). *How things don't work*. New York: Pantheon.

Pendelton, H. (1990). Occupational therapists' current use of independent living skills training for adult inpatients who are physically disabled. *Occupational Therapy in Health Care, 6*, 93–108.

Rogers, J. (1979). Psychosocial parameters in treating the person with quadriplegia. *American Journal of Occupational Therapy, 33*, 432–439.

Wolff, H.S. (1972). Bioengineering: A many splendoured thing—But for whom? In R. M. Kenedi (Ed.), *Perspectives in biomedical engineering* (pp. 305–311). Baltimore: University Park Press.

# Appendix 2–A

## A DIY Process: Food Preparation and Nutrition

Good food preparation is the cornerstone of the good nutrition that is necessary to maintain good health and avoid the secondary illnesses that interfere with an active, independent life style. Food preparation actually involves a number of separate, even though interrelated, tasks, all of which must be subjected to the same scrutiny as any ADL. A person with a disability should ask:

- Can I do it myself?
- Can I learn some new adaptive strategy to make it possible?
- Will some tools/assistive devices help me to do it?
- Do I need people-help? If so, how much?

The tasks include planning the meal (e.g., reading cookbooks, checking resources), shopping, transporting foods home, storing foods prior to preparation, cooking, serving, storing leftovers, and cleaning up.

### PLANNING THE MEAL

What do you like, what's good for your body, how much of it, and how often? What do you have to prepare, cook, and serve with? Stove, refrigerator, pots and pans, utensils, serving dishes, plates, cups, utensils, etc.?

What does it require to prepare this food? Knives: size, shape, sharpness? Cutting board? Bowls: how many, what size, ceramic or metal? Trays, plates, platters? Spoons: size, shape? Food processor or mixer?

What does it require to cook this food? Burner or oven? Sauce pans, sauté pans or skillets, lids, larger pots, baking pans? How many, what sizes?

What does it require to serve this food? Bowls, platters: how many, what sizes? Plates: how many, what sizes? Tableware? Glasses?

What will be necessary to store and use the leftovers?

All these questions make cooking seem like an overwhelming task; therefore, it is essential to start out simply. When I started cooking again after becoming disabled, I learned very quickly that I could continue to use only a few of the things that I had used before: a griddle with a bail handle (a heavy wire handle), a certain knife that fit the way my chopping/cutting hand works, and large bowls made of plastic rather than heavy ceramic or glass (I dropped and broke most of those before too long!). Over the years, I have learned from these experiences and now can fairly easily select those utensils that will work for me.

## SHOPPING

Where should you go to get the things that you want? Are those places accessible? Do you need help? What form should you purchase (e.g., fresh, dried, boxed, bottled), and how do you carry these things home with you? Generally, fresh fruits and vegetables weigh less than bottled, canned, or jarred items, but there are some things that you can find only in the bottled, canned, or jarred form. You should be prepared to deal with these as necessary in order to follow the dictates in your meal planning. If you limit your shopping because you cannot open cans or jars or because you cannot lift their weight, you may be limiting your nutrition or palate unnecessarily.

## TRANSPORTING FOODS HOME

Getting your purchases home requires lifting and carrying, unless someone else is doing the shopping. The store clerks can pack your groceries in manageable units, several bags if necessary, balanced so that *you* can lift their weight when you get them home. Checkers generally ask whether customers want paper bags or plastic. Environmental concerns aside, I have learned to say, "Both." A large paper bag *inside* a plastic bag gives the plastic bag shape and stacking ability, and the plastic bag has the handles and strength to be lifted, one-handed, as long as it is not loaded too heavily. It can take some trial and error to figure out just what works, but that leads to adaptive strategies. This approach is a great learning experience for managing independently, either doing it yourself or deciding where and when you want to get help because the time : energy equation does not work for you.

## STORING FOODS

Foods need storage in two forms: as ingredients or stock items before the cooking and as leftovers after the cooking. Almost invariably, some form of refrigeration or freezing is necessary to preserve the leftovers safely. Many types of storage bags and containers are available for these purposes. The reusable types are most desirable as long as they are workable for you. I prefer 1-quart and 1-gallon zip-lock bags for those things that I can enclose and lay down on the table so that I can "zip" by running my thumb along the "zipper." I recycle these bags as often as possible. For plastic containers, I look for those with a stiffening ridge around the bowl and lids that have a ridge around the top so that I can use my teeth and bite to accomplish the final closure. This configuration also facilitates the opening after they have been refrigerated and the cooling of the air has created a vacuum inside.

Jars are notoriously difficult to open for persons with diminished hand strength. There are two possible reasons for this difficulty. The jar may be fresh from the packer, and the *vacuum* resulting from the packing/preserving process is very strong; or the jar may have been opened, and the residue of sticky contents between the jar's edge and the lid, and the vacuum resulting from refrigeration and the cooling of the air inside, have combined to create both a mechanical and a vacuum seal. Many "jar openers" have been devised to make up for diminished hand strength, but most of them require hand strength to operate. The only one that I have been able to get to work for me consistently is a little known, but very effective "trick" that releases the vacuum so that the lid can be turned with relatively little hand grip and twist effort.

A tool that can pry out the lid just enough to release the vacuum is available from many paint supply dealers. Known as a paint can opener, it is actually a beer bottle opener (for the painting parties) with a flat hook on one end (to open the paint cans). The hook end of this tool can be slipped under the edge of the jar lid and the lower threads on the jar and used to "pry" the lid away from the jar (Figure 2–A–1). You will know that it is working when there is a hiss of air being sucked into the vacuum of the jar and a pop as the safety button on the lid pops up. The lid may then be turned with minimal hand strength. It sometimes takes several tries to find the exact spot between the lid and the threads that will afford the proper leverage to release the vacuum; it is best to start with the lowest threads and work upward until you find the right place to pry. With a little practice this procedure works every time. When a residue has been allowed to dry on the lid, creating a mechanical friction, you may also have to rinse with hot water under the rim to loosen the lid. The warming caused by standing the jar upside-down in the sink and running hot water down onto the lid edge may also release the vacuum. A few of these experiences will help you to remember to clean the rim of the jar before resealing. I have also used the rounded end of a table knife and the handle of a spoon to accomplish the prying when I have not had a paint can opener available. Anything that can fit into the threads will do.

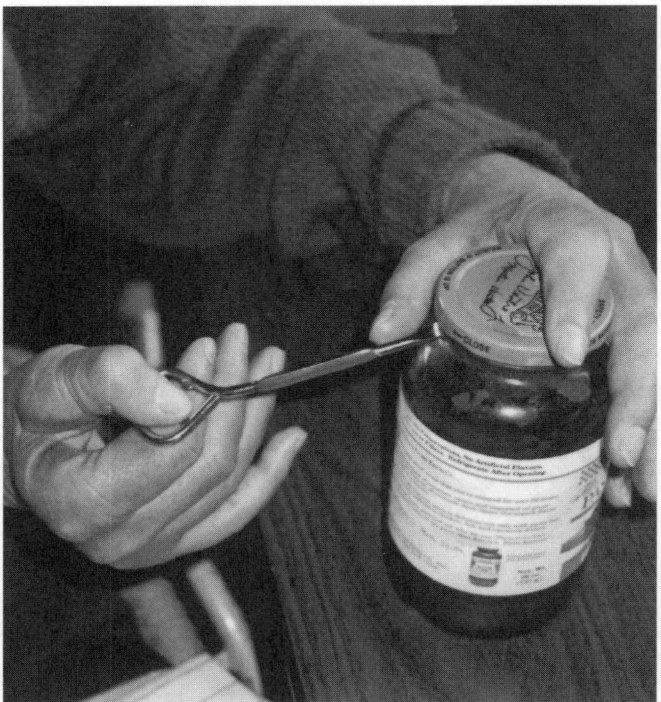

**Figure 2–A–1** Paint can opener used as a jar opener

## COOKING

As mentioned earlier, the tools available for cooking are so numerous and varied as to be overwhelming. It is essential to start simply and add to your cooking arsenal and repertoire slowly. Utensils must fit your strength, stature, and hand strength. Deciding the kinds of things you want to cook and examining the operations necessary to accomplish this determine the utensils required.

I select knives that are relatively lightweight and balanced so that the handle is about as heavy as the blade and has a shape that hooks down into the soft part of my hand between my thumb and forefinger. I cannot really grip the knife, so I balance it in the crook in my hand and guide it while the weight and sharpness do the cutting.

I choose pans that have flat handles. I do not have to grip this kind of handle in order for the pan to stay upright. For larger pans, I choose the flat handle plus a loop handle opposite the "sticky-out" handle so that I can lift it with both

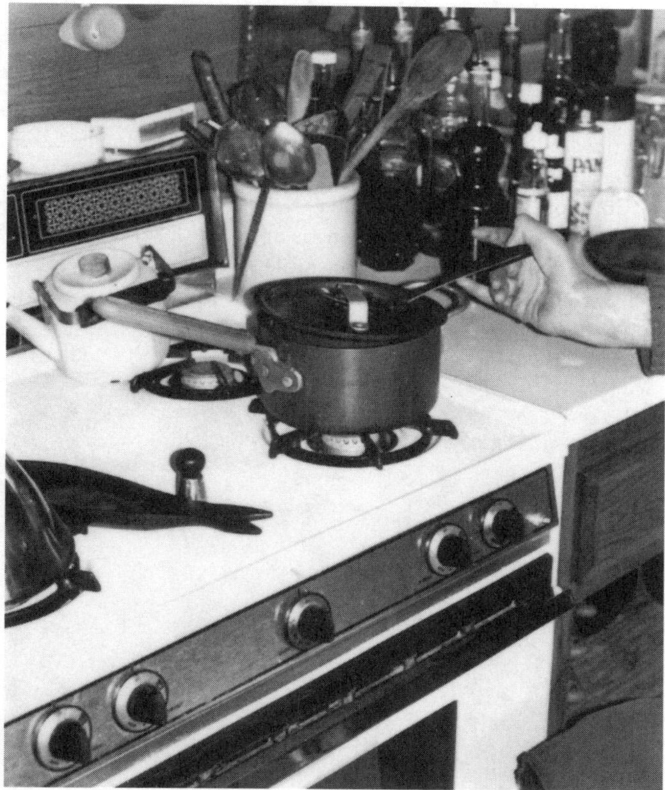

**Figure 2–A–2** Flat-handled pot with loop handle on opposite side. Spoon used to lift pot lid

hands without having to "grip" it. For larger "stock pots," I choose those with two loop handles for the same reason.

I can lift lids that have a flat loop handle with either a hot pad or a towel around my fingers, or I can use a spoon as a lever handle and lift the lid to set aside (Figure 2–A–2). Of course, the spoon that I use to lift the lid also has a flat handle, so I do not really have to grip it to balance the lid. In fact, most of the cooking utensils that I use (e.g., spatulas, spoons, serving spoons) have flat handles for the same reason.

I have learned that stainless steel bowls are lighter and do not break as easily as glass or ceramic. They are economical in that it is not necessary to replace them often. (Mine have lots of dents.) Over the years, I have collected an assortment of sizes and shapes.

I have a very "open" kitchen, carved out of a very compact space. I have had the doors and shelves under the sink taken out for "turn-around" space between the sink and the stove, and the hinged doors taken off the lower cabinets so that I can reach sauté pans and pots without acrobatics (Figure 2–A–3). Ingredients, herbs, and condiments are on open shelves or counters where I can reach them easily. Some lighter pans and utensils are on a (low) overhead rack where I can reach them from the preparation table that I use (Figure 2–A–4). Currently, this is a simple folding table that I can get my knees under and get close

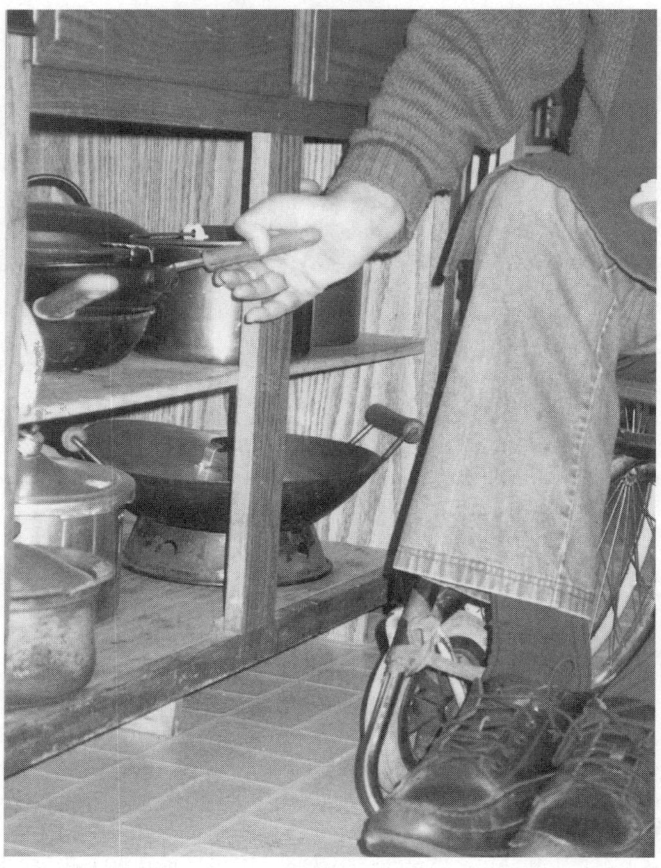

**Figure 2–A–3** Shelves without doors to allow access to pots and pans

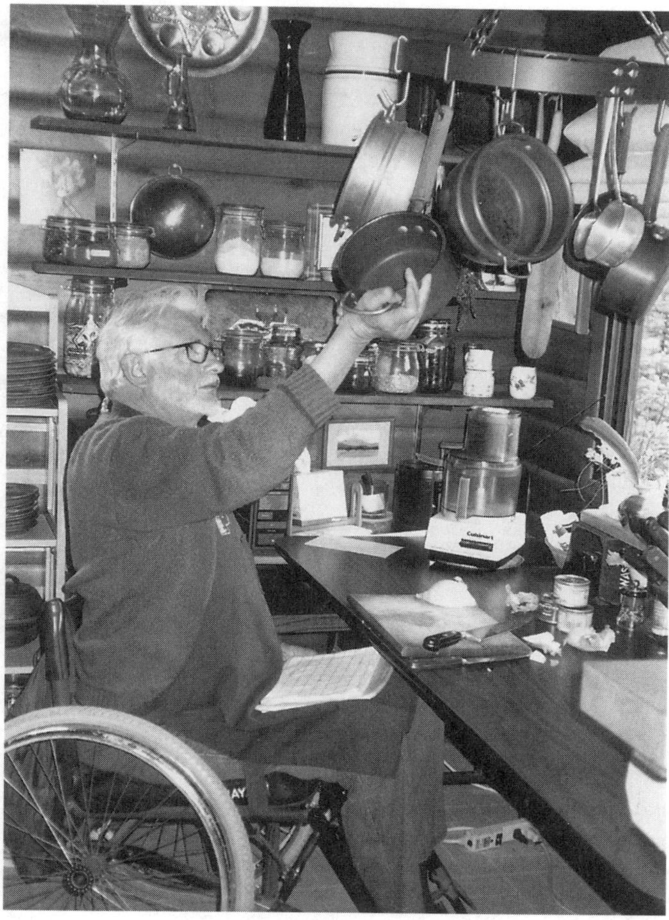


**Figure 2–A–4** Low overhead rack for lighter pans and utensils. Loop handle on pot allows easy gripping

---

enough to use for chopping vegetables and preparing other parts of a meal. I can reach things at the back of this table. My food processor, knife sharpener, and mixer are on a fiber pad or towel so that they slide easily to the front of the table when I need them, yet are stable during use (Figure 2–A–5).

I use a simple flat board on my lap, covered with a folded tea towel to carry things. After I chop things, I slide them off the cutting board into a light wooden

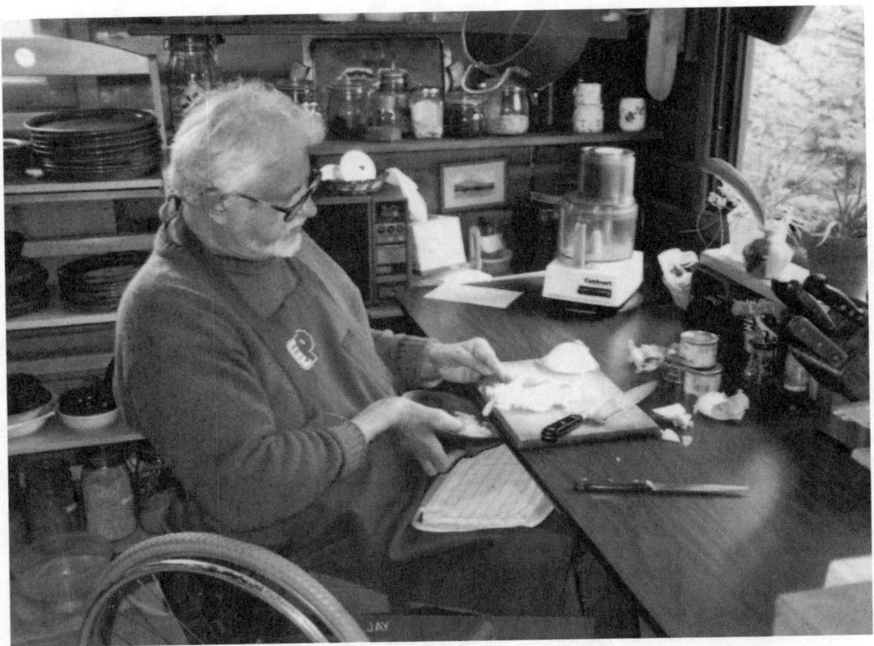

**Figure 2–A–5** Meal preparation area

bowl or plate to transfer them to the cooking pan on the stove (Figure 2–A–6). These wooden bowls and plates are available at Cost Plus and other Asian import stores.

I sometimes cook for larger groups and have learned to store the larger cooking and serving items on the higher shelves. After all, the only time I use them is when there are other folks around who can get them down (and clean) and put

**Figure 2–A–6** Using wooden bowl to transfer chopped food to cooking pan

---

them back up for me. So the upper shelves of my kitchen are decorated with these items. Usually, people are willing to trade their energy in preparation and clean-up for my experience and creativity in the cooking, and the end result is a sense of equal sharing.

**Bon Appetit!**

**Fig–2–A–7** Bon appetit!

---

*There are many other DIY projects that I could describe here that would contradict the commonly held view of what a person with a disability is capable of or interested in. In workshops, I have described myself as a father, a lover, a photographer, an artist, a winemaker, a flyer (of light airplanes), an organic gardener, a vegetarian gourmet cook, and what have you! I identify as a "person with a disability" only in a political sense and reject the idea that my physical limitations render me "dependent" in the popular or common view of people with disabilities.*

*Peter Leech*

## *Chapter 3*

# Seating and Wheeled Mobility Aids

*Kathleen A. Kolar*

Together, seating and wheeled mobility make up a complete functional mobility system. Seating is the interface between the person and the mobility device. It allows the person access to the mobility device at her or his highest functional level, thereby giving the person the greatest level of personal independence. Devices for seating range from a piece of plywood and foam inserted onto the sling of a wheelchair, to a custom mold that conforms to the exact body contours of the client. Wheeled mobility can be (1) manual or (2) powered by an external power source (e.g., a person) or by an intrinsic power source (e.g., a battery).

## SEATING

### Seating Components

When a person is in the seated position, the hips and knees are flexed (bent) to approximately 90 degrees; the pelvis, trunk, and head are upright and symmetrical; and the arms are at the side with the elbows flexed to 90 degrees (Trefler, Hobson, Johnson Taylor, Monahan, & Shaw, 1993). The components of seating or positioning systems are typically defined by the function they serve (Figure 3–1).

A *seat* supports the pelvis and posterior thighs when a person is in the seated position. The surface should extend from the posterior aspect of the buttocks with the pelvis in the most available upright position to an approximately two-finger width posterior to the popliteal fossa (behind the knees).

A *back* supports the posterior pelvis and spine. The surface should extend from the seat surface to the level of the top of the shoulder or lower, depending on the support needed by the individual.

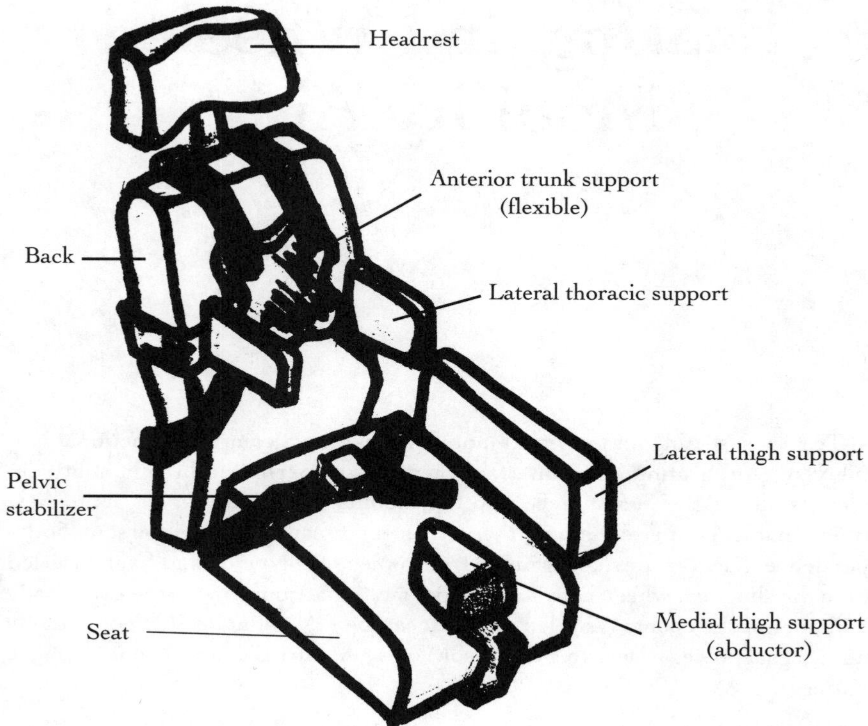


**Figure 3–1** Seated positioning components

A *lateral thoracic support* supports the lateral, or outside, aspect of the trunk. Usually used in pairs, lateral trunk supports are placed either symmetrically, no higher on the trunk than three fingers below the axilla or arm pit, or asymmetrically to assist in arresting or correcting a scoliosis (lateral curve) of the spine.

A *medial and lateral thigh support* supports the thigh. Like the lateral trunk supports, these are usually used in pairs: both placed medially or laterally to limit excessive hip abduction (upper legs flared out) or adduction (upper legs in knee together position), or one placed medially and the other laterally to assist in arresting or correcting a windswept deformity (one hip in relative abduction, one hip in relative adduction).

A *pelvic stabilizer* supports the anterior or front aspect of the pelvis of a seated person. The support is usually positioned anterior and inferior to the anterior superior iliac spines of the pelvis to limit or correct posterior pelvic tilt, pelvic rotation (one side of the pelvis more anterior than the other), or pelvic obliquity (one side of the pelvis more superior than the other). The support can be flexible (e.g., a seatbelt) or rigid (e.g., a subASIS bar, which is a padded, solid bar curved for bladder relief) (Kolar, 1989; Margolis, Jones, & Brown, 1985).

An *anterior trunk support* supports the anterior aspect of the trunk. The support, which can be rigid or flexible, is usually placed symmetrically on the trunk at a level below the sternal notch, or top of the breast bone, and above the sternal xyphoid junction, or bottom of the breast bone.

A *head support or headrest* supports the posterior or back of the head. Usually contoured to follow the shape of the head, it is placed at the level of the occiput or just above the junction of the head and neck. The head support may also have additional components to provide lateral or anterior support for the head. The anterior support, which can be rigid or flexible, is usually placed across the forehead.

Additional positioning devices are often individually fabricated to provide specific support for upper and lower extremities.

The system components can be fabricated from a variety of materials. The most common base materials are plywood, steel, plastic, and aluminum; a variety of foam types, gels, water, and air chambers provide the padding and support for the body segment.

### Functions of the Components

Seating components are used in a variety of combinations, based on the needs of the individual. Many forces act on the body structure. The skeleton is the framework, and the muscles are internal forces that act together in balance to support the structure in optimal alignment or "good" posture. If the internal forces (i.e., the muscles) do not act in balance because of a lack of strength or a lack of coordination, the external forces (i.e., seating and positioning components) must compensate for the malfunction.

The missing forces needed to balance the body are most often replaced when the primary goal of seating intervention is postural control to prevent or arrest deformities. Improving posture and body alignment also enhances functional movement by stabilizing the body and trunk. The proximal stability of the trunk provides a stable base for distal mobility or movement of the head or extremities. The functional movement of the head or extremities makes it possible to reach a communication device, run a computer, propel a manual wheelchair, drive a power wheelchair, or perform a myriad of other jobs. Secondary benefits of upright posturing and proper positioning include improved respiratory and internal organ function, as well as improved self-image (Ward, 1984).

Without proper positioning or support, an individual who has lost the ability to remain upright against gravity may appear to have greater deformities and functional limitations than truly exist. For example, an individual may be relying on the arms for support while seated because of lack of trunk strength or control. The individual cannot then use the arms for any other purpose because they are providing additional support for the body.

Proper seating also ensures pressure relief and comfort. Pressure problems are most common among individuals who have decreased or absent sensation, severe fixed postural deformities, or such severe motor control difficulties that they are unable to shift their weight (Cook & Hussey, 1995). Correct body alignment against gravity and for function is the first step in decreasing the risk of significant pressure problems and subsequent skin breakdown. Second, the choice of positioning components of the appropriate size, shape, placement, and composition can reduce pressures. Third and last, changing the body orientation in space alters the effect of gravity and, ultimately, pressure on different parts of the body. It may be necessary to proceed through all three steps to solve the pressure problems of some individuals.

Comfort becomes the primary factor in positioning for those individuals who are very ill or who have such a significant deformity that it compromises their internal body systems. In those cases, the goal is not to alter their body posture greatly, but rather to support them in a position that provides the maximum comfort possible.

### History and Trends in Seating

Considerations of seating and positioning really became more formalized during the late 1970s and early 1980s. There was no real attempt to follow general body contours at first, however. The components were often large, flat support surfaces fabricated from plywood and polyfoam, and upholstered in vinyl. Straps and seatbelts were often cumbersome and fabricated from leather.

As a variety of materials became available, components began to take on the shape of general body contours. Plastics and aluminum were added to plywood as choice options for fabrication. The development of foams that can be mixed and poured has allowed custom contour or molded components. Bags of small styrofoam beads and epoxy mixtures and flexible matrices add a variety of options to customize components for individuals. Waterproof coverings, two-way stretch materials, and vacuform vinyl are now options for covering the custom-molded components.

Because of the increasing costs of fabricating customized components, a modular approach to fabricating and combining seating components appears to be emerging. Present technology and materials make the modular approach a cost-effective solution for a majority of consumers, although fabrication of custom components is still necessary and available for the consumers who require it.

Typically, therapists have determined the success of seating and positioning on the basis of their professional observations and knowledge of the consumer needs. Recently, the use of pressure measurement devices has established reproducible criteria on which to judge the effectiveness of chosen components. Research into pressure, tissue density, and custom contouring of components, primarily seat cushions, is continuing. In addition, research is being initiated into the development of noninvasive, safe ways of monitoring posture while seating components are in place.

### Those Who Can Benefit

In general, anyone who needs additional support to maintain an upright position can benefit from custom seating and positioning. The most common conditions that require consideration of seating are shown in Table 3–1.

### Seating Selection

Areas evaluated in the selection of appropriate seating components are physical function, including strength and range of motion; muscle tone; primitive reflexes; fatigue; and endurance levels. Questions about medications and other issues related to body system function that may affect seating should be part of the initial request for background information. The client's existing equipment should also be checked.

After the initial information is gathered and the physical evaluation completed, the individual is observed in a seated position. The examiner typically begins at the pelvis; moves to the upper legs, the trunk, head and neck, upper extremities, and shoulders; and ends with the ankles and feet. Looking for normal body alignment in the forward facing or frontal plane and the side facing or sagittal plane, the examiner notes any deviations from the typical for each body segment, along with probable causes (i.e., neuromuscular, developmental, gravitational, biomechanical, or environmental) (Kolar, 1995). Once the deviations and probable causes have been identified, specific positioning components can be selected to address each need. The components may be commercially available, may need to be custom designed, or may be a combination of the two.

For example, there are many possible causes for an oblique pelvis. The obliquity may be fixed or flexible. It may be secondary to a scoliosis, which is structural, or secondary to a strong primitive reflex, which is neuromuscular. Knowing the cause can assist in determining the appropriate equipment component choice. If the obliquity is fixed, the seating should support the pelvis to provide a stable base for the trunk. If the obliquity is flexible, the seating should support the pelvis in a corrected position. If the pelvic obliquity is affected by a strong

**Table 3–1** Conditions That Require Consideration of Seating and Positioning

| *Condition* | *Description and Characteristics* | *Seating Considerations* |
|---|---|---|
| Cerebral palsy | Nonprogressive neuromuscular | |
| Increased tone (high tone) | Fixed deformity, decreased movements, abnormal patterns | Correct deformities, improve alignment, decrease tone |
| Decreased tone (low tone) | Subluxations, decreased active movement, hypermobility | Provide support for upright positioning, promote development of muscular control |
| Athetoid (mixed tone) | Excessive active movement, decreased stability | Provide stability, but allow controlled mobility for function |
| Muscular dystrophies | Degenerative neuromuscular | |
| Duchenne | Loss of muscular control proximal to distal | Provide stable seating base, allow person to find balance point |
| Multiple sclerosis | Series of exacerbations and remissions | Prepare for flexibility of system to follow needs |
| Spina bifida | Congenital anomaly consisting of a deficit in one or more of the vertebral arches, decreased or absent sensation | Reduce high risk for pressure concerns, allow for typically good upper extremity and head control |
| Spinal cord injury | Insult to spinal cord, partial or complete loss of function below level of injury, nonprogressive once stabilized, decreased or absent sensation, possible scoliosis/kyphosis | Reduce high risk for pressure concerns, allow for trunk movements used for function |
| Osteogenesis imperfecta | Connective tissue disorder, brittle bone disease, limited functional range, multiple fractures | Provide protection |
| Orthopedic impairments | Fixed or flexible | If fixed, support<br>If flexible, correct |
| Traumatic brain injury | Severity dependent on extent of central nervous system damage, may have cognitive component, nonprogressive once stabilized | Allow for functional improvement as rehabilitation progresses, establish a system that is flexible to changing needs |
| Elderly | | |
| Typical aged | Often, fixed kyphosis, decreased bone mass, and decreased strength, incontinence | Provide comfort and visual orientation, moisture-proof, accommodate kyphosis |
| Aged secondary to primary disability | Example—older patients with cerebral palsy may have fixed deformities | Provide comfort, support deformities |

primitive reflex, perhaps a rigid pelvic stabilizer would meet the individual's needs better than a flexible one. Once the decision is made as to the type of components, a choice between the currently, commercially available options can be finalized. The same approach can be followed for every deviation observed and the probable causes identified.

## WHEELED MOBILITY

### Wheelchair Components

As with seating and positioning, there are general categories of components that are common to all wheelchairs (Figure 3–2).

The *cross frame* determines the width of the chair. The frame in an X or cross design allows the chair to fold. The frame in an H or rigid design gives the chair additional stability, but does not allow folding. The upper part of the frame becomes the support for the attachment of the seat upholstery.

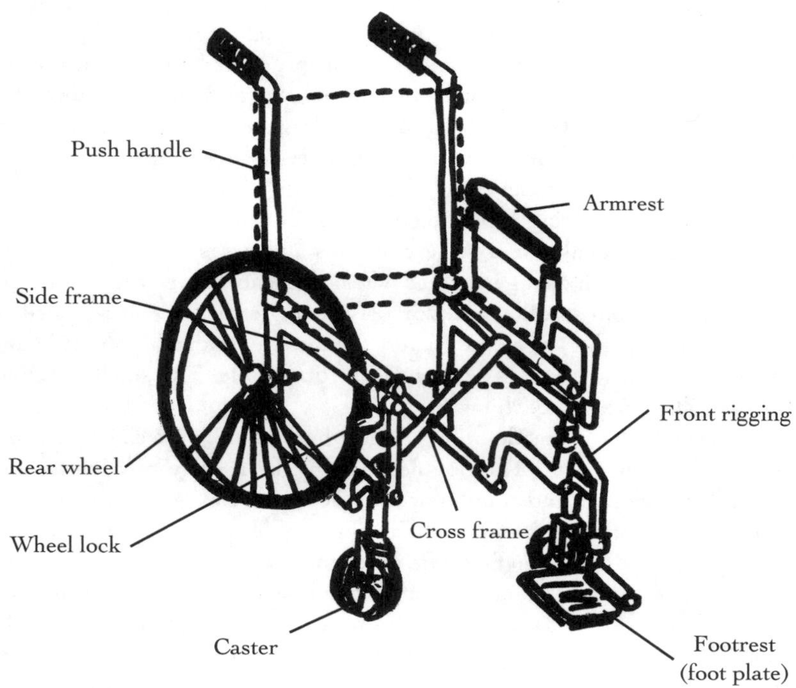


**Figure 3–2** Standard wheelchair components

The *side frame* is the part of the wheelchair to which the center frame attaches. The side frame is also the part of the chair on which the armrests, footrests, front riggings, wheels, casters, wheel locks, and rear anti-tip devices are mounted.

The *push handles*, or canes, are extensions of the side frame. They may be fixed or adjustable in height. The canes are used to push the wheelchair or as the lever to tilt the wheelchair to clear a curb or other obstacle.

The *rear wheels* attach to the side frame with a fixed axle mount or adjustable axle plate. The adjustable axle plate makes it possible to place the wheels for maximum stability or maximum propulsion through wheelchair-consumer interface. A quick release option is also available for easy removal of the wheels for storage without the use of tools. The rear wheels typically come in 24-inch diameter as standard. However, 20- and 22-inch sizes are now commonly available. Other wheel options include wire or molded rims, push rims with or without pegs for pushing, and various types of tires. Tires can be pneumatic, hard rubber, or equipped with flat-free inserts. Tire and wheel choice depend on the kind of wheelchair and frame on which they will be mounted.

The *wheel locks*, or brakes, are mounted on the side frame and, when engaged, prevent the motion of the rear wheels. The wheel locks can be on a high mount or a low mount, depending on the needs of the wheelchair user. A high mount typically allows ease of access, but a low mount prevents hand injuries to the fast or strong pusher during propulsion. Hill holders or grade aids allow the wheelchair to be propelled forward, but do not allow the chair to roll backward. Such a feature can be helpful if the pusher has decreased strength.

The *casters* are the two smaller front wheels of the wheelchair. They can move in all directions, thus making it possible to steer the wheelchair. Like the rear wheels, casters are available in a variety of sizes and types. Changes in caster size, in combination with changes in rear wheel size, can change the seat height of the wheelchair from the floor and/or tilt the angle of the seat forward or rearward. Generally, the larger the caster, the more comfortable the ride and the less likely the caster is to get caught in a rut or hole. The smaller casters provide less rolling resistance, however.

The *armrests* attach to the side frame of the wheelchair. There can be a single or double attachment point. The double attachments usually provide a more stable mount for laptrays and communication devices. Armrests can be removable or fixed to the frame of the wheelchair. Removable armrests, which can flip up, swing away, or lift out, can facilitate independent transfers.

*Front rigging*, or footrest hangers, can be fixed, swing away, elevating, or a combination. The riggings hang from the frame at different angles relative to the seat rails. The angles allow for foot placement with a knee bending angle of greater than, less than, or equal to 90 degrees, depending on the needs of the wheelchair user. The hangers also come in different lengths to adjust to differing lower leg lengths.

*Footrests*, or foot plates, come in different sizes and different materials. If foot abnormalities do not allow the foot to lay flat on the footplate, angle-adjustable plates are available.

## Sizes

Wheelchair sizes are given in terms of the seat depth and width measurements. The seat depth is the length of the seat rail measured from the front edge of the chair seat to the back uprights. The seat width is the measurement from the outside edge of the seat rail to the outside edge of the opposite seat rail. In other words, the seat depth and width dimensions are typically the dimensions of the seat upholstery. Two other wheelchair measurements, back height and seat height from the floor are important for proper fit and function of the wheelchair for the user. To determine the appropriate size wheelchair, the user's body dimensions or seating system dimensions are matched to the wheelchair dimensions (Axelson, Minkel, & Chesney, 1994).

A wheelchair of the proper size ensures that the user can reach the wheels easily for propulsion. A seat that is too wide or a back height that is too high can make it difficult for the user to get a full stroke when pushing the chair or even to reach the wheels at all. A wheelchair with a seat that is too narrow, too short, and too high off the ground can change the user's center of gravity in the wheelchair and make the wheelchair more susceptible to tipping.

In the past, wheelchairs were available in only a few width sizes that were considered standard. Currently, however, wheelchairs come in many width and depth sizes. Additionally, frames for extra wide or extra tall individuals can be obtained.

## Manual Mobility

The standard style of manual wheelchair has small casters in the front, large wheels in the rear, and a cross frame that allows the chair to pull together to fold. Manual wheelchairs can be categorized as dependent propelled or self-propelled. Users cannot maneuver dependent propelled wheelchairs by themselves. Wheelchairs with stroller-type bases, whether sized for a child or an adult, make up most of the wheelchairs in this category. The transport, and some indoor styles of manual wheelchairs, have front casters the same size as those on the standard wheelchair, but have small rear wheels. The four small wheels make the chair easy to maneuver in tight places, but impossible for the user to propel independently.

Self-propelled manual wheelchairs may be standard, or they may have special characteristics for special concerns of the user. For example, lightweight and ultra light wheelchairs are made of lighter materials and more streamlined to reduce weight. Sports style wheelchairs are often ultra light. In addition, sports wheelchairs may have a rigid H configuration, only a single front wheel, or altered seat and front rigging configuration.

A hemi or low seat style of wheelchair differs from the standard because its seat is lower to the floor. The lower seat height can help a user to propel the wheelchair using both feet or one foot and one arm. Some wheelchairs have a unique axle mechanism that translates a wheel stroke to both wheels. The one-arm drive mechanism can be designed to be accessed by an extra push rim on one side of the large rear wheel or by an additional pumping style handle. The extra axle mechanisms add weight to the chair and are often difficult to manipulate.

A manual wheelchair may have an amputee option, either a permanent change in the design of the frame or an add-on axle plate. In either case, the modification moves the rear axle rearward to move the user's center of gravity in the chair more rearward. This adaptation compensates for the loss of weight of the missing limb or limbs. Without the adaptation, the user has a greater risk of tipping the wheelchair backward.

Some manual wheelchairs are equipped with a device that, when activated, allows the user to come to a standing position in the chair. The ability to reach objects at table height and above, as well as the possible health benefits of weight bearing, are typical justifications for standing wheelchairs.

For those who use a manual wheelchair and occasionally need additional power to climb grades or curbs, power assist mechanisms are available. The wheelchair user engages the power assist mechanism while sitting in the wheelchair, usually by dropping a fifth, powered wheel to provide the extra "push" needed. The user continues to maneuver the wheelchair as a manual wheelchair.

Different from power assist mechanisms are the power add-on units. Also mounted on a manual wheelchair frame, these units use friction to drive the rear wheels of the manual wheelchair. The units can be engaged or disengaged. Unlike the power assist mechanisms, the add-on units convert a manual wheelchair to a power wheelchair. The added weight makes it difficult to propel the wheelchair manually. Also, because friction is used to drive the rear wheels, slipping can occur. Most people who need to use power choose a power wheelchair rather than trying to convert a manual wheelchair to a power wheelchair.

### Powered Mobility

The standard configuration of a power wheelchair has components similar to those of the standard manual wheelchair. In addition, however, the power wheelchair has two motors, batteries, a control box, and a joystick mechanism mounted on its frame. The wheelchair's frame is reinforced to support the extra weight of the batteries and motors. The wheels and casters are also wider and configured to bear the extra weight.

Power wheelchairs can be belt-driven or direct drive. In the belt-driven system, belts run from the motor to the rear wheel axle. The belts can slip and need to be replaced when worn or stretched. Direct drive systems are configured to allow the motors to turn or drive the rear axles.

### *Types of Powered Devices*

Traditionally, standard style power wheelchairs were made with a cross or X frame. Direct drive rigid frame styles with larger front casters and smaller diameter rear wheels, to match the caster size, have recently provided a reliable, less "medical" looking, wheelchair choice.

Power bases also have direct drive, larger front casters, and smaller diameter rear wheels similar to the standard style rigid frame. The frame that holds the seat has a single, central, pedestal type attachment to the base. The power base looks like an all terrain vehicle rather than a wheelchair.

Indoor power wheelchairs have smaller rear wheels, batteries, and motors to lessen their weight. These wheelchairs are easily taken apart for transport in a car trunk or other small space. Even when separate from the weight of the chair, however, the battery weight can be prohibitive. Improvements in the power and reliability of indoor or portable power wheelchairs make them a lower cost, practical alternative to the traditional power wheelchair for users who negotiate primarily level, fairly smooth surfaces.

Scooters or carts can have three or four wheels and be front or rear wheel drive. They have a pedestal seat, and most use a tiller-type drive with a rocker style mechanism on the handle. Scooters typically require the user to have fair to good sitting balance and upper extremity or arm control. Grocery stores sometimes provide scooters for their customers who have difficulty walking.

### *Control Mechanisms for Powered Mobility*

The joystick is the most common and the most desirable way to control a power wheelchair. It is usually attached to the wheelchair by means of a bracket affixed to the armrest, either right or left, depending on the user. Joysticks can also be mounted in positions where they can be operated by other parts of the body, such as the chin, head, foot, elbow, or shoulder. Today, special configurations of the joystick are commercially available for head and chin control for almost all types of powered mobility.

Joysticks often look like a ball on a stick, but the shape can be changed to match the need of the individual user. They can work in two ways. Proportional control joysticks have internal mechanisms that "read" the relative position of the joystick at any point along a continuum. Functionally, this makes the joystick behave much like the gas pedal of a car; the harder the driver pushes the pedal, the faster the car goes. For the proportional joystick, this "gas pedal" function occurs in any direction and allows accurate, smooth responses. Today, most joysticks use proportional control.

Some joysticks look the same as the proportional control joysticks, but are really activating four switches placed at 90 degrees to each other around a circular path. Pushing the microswitch control joystick forward activates the forward switch in an all or nothing fashion, for example. The same happens when the joystick is pushed rearward, left, and right. When the joystick is pushed on a diagonal, two switches are activated to initiate a turn. The chair responds with a preset speed, and driving is usually less smooth than with a proportional control joystick.

Switches configured to respond to various levels of pressure, breath or air, gravity, or change in electromagnetic field shape are now available in a variety of sizes, shapes, and colors. The ability to activate three switches permits independent driving in most situations, but typically does not allow for activation of on/off, reverse, or alternate modes used to access environmental controls or communication devices. The ability to activate four switches in any combination with any body part and any consistently reproducible movement provides an individual with the opportunity to experience fully independent mobility.

Switches can respond to activation in several ways. Not only can a switch be either on or off, but also some switches can latch, or stay on, once they are activated until they are activated again. This feature may allow the user who can activate a switch, but not maintain the activation, to drive, that is, she or he can activate a latching switch to go forward, then activate it again only when necessary to stop or to correct the course. Another switch response often used in powered mobility is a stepped response, which is commonly seen in a sip-and-puff or breath control on a power wheelchair. The user sips or puffs to start the wheelchair forward at an initial speed, gives a second sip or puff (whatever was used for the first activation) to increase the speed by a preset amount, and uses a third sip or puff to increase the speed a final preset amount. If the user sips or puffs again, the chair returns to the initial speed.

Knowing the options available for alternate control of a power wheelchair is important for the success or failure of an individual.

### Tilt and Recline Mechanisms

Both manual and power wheelchairs can be equipped with tilt and/or recline mechanisms. The mechanisms change the body orientation in space. They can be manually or power activated, depending on user need and wheeled mobility choice.

A tilt mechanism keeps the seat and back angle in the same relative position and tilts the body rearward in space, off vertical, like rocking back in a rocker, but being able to stop at any point. The whole seat moves back in space as a unit.

A recline mechanism moves the back rearward in space, off vertical, keeping the seat stationary, similar to an easy chair recliner. Elevating legrests are usually used in conjunction with a reclining back. With a standard recliner, the back goes down and back, and the user slides or shears across the surface of the back upholstery. Mechanically, this action can "push" the user out of position. For a wheelchair user, the shear force can contribute to skin breakdown. The zero shear or low shear back configuration of the recline mechanism is designed to eliminate as much of the "push" as possible when the user returns to upright by having the back move on tracks following the movement of the user's back.

**Selection of Wheeled Mobility**

The first decision in the selection of wheeled mobility is to choose between manual or powered mobility. For users who have no functional body movements to propel a manual wheelchair or to operate an alternate control mechanism consistently, a dependent manual wheelchair base is the logical choice. Independent manual wheelchair users generally have good upper extremity strength and control, and the endurance to propel themselves for moderate to long distances (Axelson, Minkel, & Chesney, 1994). For users who have some functional upper extremity movement, but insufficient strength to propel themselves, powered mobility is the logical choice. For those users who fall somewhere between these categories, additional factors must be explored to help make the appropriate mobility choice more apparent.

One significant factor in choosing between a manual self-propelled power base for a user is energy expenditure. Generally, if reaching a destination requires almost all of the wheelchair user's energy, powered mobility should be explored—even if the user is able to self-propel.

Often age, impaired vision, and decreased mental ability are considered contraindications to powered mobility. According to Trefler (1984), children as young as 18 months and adults in their 90s have successfully gained greater independent mobility through the use of a powered mobility device, however. Children typically begin to develop a sense of self and separation from their parents as soon as they can crawl or walk away; those with decreased physical skills should have the same opportunity at the same age. Just as any child who is mobile needs supervision, it is essential to set limits for the child who uses powered mobility. Individuals with low vision or who may be legally blind can still do well in operating power wheelchairs—even if they can only detect shadows. They learn to compensate just as an ambulatory, visually impaired person does. Below normal mental ability is no reason to deny the possibility of increased independence. Again, judgment and limit setting are needed. The goal is independence in mobility.

### History and Trends in Wheeled Mobility

Wheeled mobility has come a long way from the antique manual wheelchairs to the microcomputer-controlled power wheelchairs of today. The technological advances have made it possible for more individuals with more severe disabilities to have a chance at greater independence. A larger number of wheelchair users can now live on their own with attendant support rather than be institutionalized.

Wheelchair standards have been developed through safety, performance, and dimension criteria for both manual and power wheelchairs. The standards and the results of wheelchair tests give consumers greater buying power by giving them more information on which to base their choice of wheeled mobility.

Other research is continuing to improve the reliability and versatility of powered mobility through exploration of "smarter" controls. For example, controls may soon alert wheelchair users when they are too close to objects and may shut down power to prevent users from driving into objects. Who knows how far technology can go?

## TEAM APPROACH TO SEATING AND WHEELED MOBILITY

The ideal evaluation for seating or wheeled mobility originates in a team approach with the client as an equal or leading member of the team. The team involved in the evaluation process may include but is not limited to the following professionals: physical and occupational therapists, physicians, rehabilitation technology suppliers, rehabilitation engineers, instrument makers, speech and language pathologists, vocational rehabilitation counselors, teachers, employers, and orthotists. Each member of the team brings a unique area of expertise. The therapists bring knowledge of the body in the areas of movement, function, strength, growth, and development. The physician brings knowledge of diagnoses, disease progression, and seating and mobility contraindications. The rehabilitation technology supplier brings knowledge of the currently available equipment and funding-related issues. The engineers bring knowledge of electronics, mechanics, material properties, and design concepts. The instrument makers have the skill to fabricate the needed custom solution as determined by the team. The list can go on.

Different team members take a lead role at different times during the evaluation, depending on their area of expertise. Therapists and physicians would have the primary tasks of assessing physical status and identifying the type of equipment that the client needs. The rehabilitation technology supplier can provide currently available equipment options to match the type of equipment solutions requested. If custom options are needed, the engineers can design and interface components to existing commercially available equipment. The instrument maker can take primary responsibility for fabrication of the custom components. The client or consumer has a lead role in the final decision at each aspect of the evaluation process. Meeting the needs and expectations of the client about the technology and service requested is a primary outcome of the evaluation.

In addition to the considerations discussed throughout this chapter and the specifics for seating and mobility, the evaluator(s) must also assess the impact of family, communication, environmental, vocational, and transportation issues. Seating and mobility are only two aspects in the continuum of assisting an individual in achieving her or his highest functional potential.

---

## REFERENCES

Axelson, P., Minkel, J., & Chesney, D. (1994). *A guide to wheelchair selection: How to use the ANSI/RESNA wheelchair standards to buy a wheelchair*. Washington, DC: Paralyzed Veterans of America, 3–7, 11–16.

Cook, A.M., & Hussey, S.M. (1995). *Assistive technologies: Principles and practice*. St. Louis: Mosby–Year Book, 258–299, 525–558.

Kolar, K.A. (1989, May). Seated positioning: Seatbelt alternative. *NDTA Newsletter*, 1.

Kolar, K.A. (1995, February). *Creating a flow—Moving from evaluation results to technology selection.* Paper presented at the Eleventh International Seating Symposium, Pittsburgh, PA, 247–251.

Margolis, S.A., Jones, R.M., & Brown, B.E. (1985). The SubASIS seated positioning. Paper presented at proceedings of the RESNA 8th Annual Conference, Memphis, TN. Arlington, VA, RESNA, 45–47.

Trefler, E. (Ed.). (1984). *Seating for children with cerebral palsy*. Memphis: The University of Tennessee Center for the Health Sciences, 87–91.

Trefler, E., Hobson, D.A., Johnson Taylor, S., Monahan, L.C., & Shaw, C.G. (1993). *Seating and mobility for persons with physical disabilities*. Tucson: Therapy Skill Builders, 3–15.

Ward, D.E. (1984). *Positioning the handicapped child for function* (2nd ed. rev.). St. Louis: Phoenix Press, 1–16.

---

## SUGGESTED READING

Bergen, A.F., Presperin, J., & Tallman, T. (1990). *Positioning for function: The wheelchair and other adaptive equipment.* Valhalla, NY: Valhalla Rehabilitation Publications.

Scherzer, A.L., & Tscharnuter, I. (1982). *Early diagnosis and therapy in cerebral palsy: A primer on infant developmental problems* (Vol. 3). Dekker, NY: Pediatric Habilitation.

Trefler, E. (1992). *Technology in the classroom: Positioning, access, and mobility module*. Rockville, MD: American Speech-Language-Hearing Association.

Trefler, E., Kozole, K., & Snell, E. (Eds.). (1986). *Selected readings on powered mobility for children and adults with severe physical disabilities*. Washington, DC: RESNA.

Zollars, J.A. (1993). *Seating and moving through the decades. A literature review on seating and mobility through 1992*. Santa Cruz, CA: PAX Press.

*Chapter 4*

# Transportation

*William A. Peterson*

> The day I was discharged from the rehabilitation hospital I once called home, I was the proud owner of a sparkling new wheelchair and a pickup truck that could not be adapted. For six months I had to rely upon friends and relatives to drive me around. Every time I wanted to go somewhere, I had to ask for a ride. Though my friends and family were wonderful and tried the best they could, I still couldn't get over the fact that I was dependent upon them for my freedom. The day I picked up my newly adapted van, I felt like a bird being released from a small cage. I was free once again.
>
> (W.A.P., 1994)

People with disabilities want an education and the ability to compete for jobs that will enable them to make a reasonable living. They want to be able to relax at a restaurant or to be entertained at a movie theater. People with disabilities want the freedom to attend a church chosen on the basis of their beliefs, not its geographical location. Society today is extremely mobile, and in order to participate in it, people with disabilities need to be just as mobile as their able-bodied counterparts. Wheelchairs allow those with mobility impairments to get around locally, assuming sidewalks and buildings are accessible. Mass transit helps some, but is extremely limiting. The ability to get into an adapted vehicle and drive it anywhere at a moment's notice, however, is one of the greatest freedoms that a person with a disability can experience.

A person who is newly disabled must face many new challenges and make many decisions. Some of the challenges are personal, while others involve friends and family. Driving once again is a challenge that requires many well thought out decisions in order to prevent costly mistakes. Friends and family members can help with some of the decisions, but it is highly recommended that a driver evaluator/trainer and/or an adaptive equipment dealer be involved in this process.

Typically, a driver evaluator assesses the driving potential of a client by reviewing the client's medical history and current medical status, as well as the client's driving history and general driving knowledge. An evaluation includes an assessment of the client's sensory-motor and cognitive-perceptual functions, such as visual acuity, peripheral vision, night vision, reaction times, arm and leg strengths, transfer abilities, range of motion, attention span, decision-making abilities, depth perception, and spatial relationships (Kerr & Irwin, 1990). A driving evaluation is recommended for all persons with disabilities, whether physical or cognitive, who wish to drive. Local rehabilitation hospitals or the state vocational rehabilitation department should be able to provide referrals for the closest reputable driver evaluation program.

An adaptive equipment dealer is familiar with all the adaptive aids available to help persons with physical disabilities overcome barriers to their driving. Not only are dealers familiar with adaptive equipment currently on the market, but also they are keenly aware of which vehicles are the easiest to adapt since they are the ones who install the equipment. Therefore, it is helpful to involve an adaptive equipment dealer in the process from the beginning. It is important to match the person's disability with the appropriate vehicle and adaptive equipment. Reputable equipment dealers can be located through the state vocational rehabilitation department, the National Mobility Equipment Dealers Association (NMEDA), or the Department of Veterans Affairs.

## VEHICLE SELECTION

In choosing the correct vehicle for modification, there are a number of considerations. For example, the person's functional abilities, the vehicle's adaptability, and cost must all be taken into account:

- Is the person capable of independently transferring into the vehicle and pulling his or her wheelchair inside?
- Is the vehicle's doorway large enough to allow for such a transfer, and is there enough room to add the necessary adaptive equipment and to store the wheelchair?
- How much will the vehicle cost and how much will it cost to modify the vehicle?

Although standard concerns such as make, model, and color still apply, it is essential to keep an open mind when shopping for a vehicle that will be used by a person with a disability; the list of potentially adaptable vehicles becomes shorter as the severity of the person's disability increases. It is best to talk with a reputable adaptive equipment dealer prior to shopping for a vehicle to bring into focus the type(s) of vehicle(s) that will be most suitable and most satisfying for the individual. Generally speaking, two types of vehicles are appropriate: sedans and vans. Sedans require the ability to transfer, while vans are more versatile and, if adapted properly, allow an individual to remain in a wheelchair when driving.

If the person with a disability is capable of transferring independently, then a large two-door sedan is recommended. Two-door sedans typically have wider doorways than do four-door sedans, providing more room for transfers and easier access for loading and unloading a wheelchair. Bench seats are also recommended, because they allow the driver to slide over onto the passenger side of the seat to load his or her wheelchair or, alternatively, to enter the vehicle from the passenger side, slide over onto the driver's side of the seat, and pull the wheelchair in afterward. If at all possible, the person should practice transferring into and out of the vehicle before purchasing it to make sure that he or she can make unlevel transfers and that there is adequate space to load the wheelchair inside the vehicle. Once inside the vehicle, the driver will be able to determine if leg space is adequate. Before purchasing the vehicle, however, it is highly recommended that an adaptive equipment dealer be consulted to confirm that there is adequate space for the necessary adaptations.

Although a van is the vehicle of choice for quadriplegics because of their inability to transfer independently, the usefulness of vans is not limited to quadriplegics. In fact, many people prefer vans to sedans. Adapting a van for a person in a wheelchair is far more costly than adapting a sedan, however. In order to access a van independently, a person who uses a wheelchair needs to have: a lift installed along with a power door opener/closer; switching mechanisms, both inside and out; and hand controls. Depending on the person's functional abilities, it may also be necessary to install a four- or six-way power seat, as well as to raise the roof and/or lower the floor pan. A person's functional abilities will dictate how extensive the modifications are. An individual with high level quadriplegia may need more head room for entering and exiting the van as well as operating the van. Therefore, the roof may need to be raised and/or the floor pan lowered. The difference in cost between adapting a van and installing a set of hand controls into a sedan is clear, but van conversions are so special that they can be made to fit almost everyone's needs.

## ADAPTIVE DEVICES

Whether the person is planning to purchase a new sedan or van or simply wishes to adapt an existing vehicle, there are a number of options/factors to consider (Butler, 1991, pp. 9–11):

- automatic transmission. Relieving the driver of the need to shift gears is particularly important for quadriplegics and for paraplegics who have both hands busy operating the hand controls and steering the vehicle.
- power steering. If hand controls are used, power steering is essential.
- power brakes. Because of the small lever action of hand controls, power brakes require less strength to apply and respond quicker than do other brakes.
- tilt steering wheel. The advantage of this type of steering wheel is that it allows the driver to adjust the wheel to the most functional location and to move it out of the way while transferring.
- air conditioning. More than just for comfort, air conditioning is very important for quadriplegics living in warmer climates, because these individuals are unable to control body temperature.
- cruise control. Great for long distance traveling, cruise control frees up one hand.
- power windows. The driver can readily control all windows without having to stop.
- power door locks. The driver can readily control all door locks from the driver's position.
- power seat. A person with limited function can control seat position with ease.
- bench seat. Because it allows entry from either side of the vehicle, a bench seat is highly recommended for the front seat of a sedan.

**Hand Controls**

Designed in the form of a linkage system that enables the user to operate both the brake and the gas with one hand, most hand controls are easily installed. They clamp onto existing structures, thereby permitting normal operation of the vehicle. Hand controls can generally be installed for either right or left hand operation. At the time of installation, a dimmer switch and horn button should be mounted onto the handle portion of the control or in another position that is easily accessible to the user. Only a reputable dealer should install hand controls.

Three different control mechanisms are used with mechanical hand controls:

1. Push–pull hand control systems (Figure 4–1) operate just as the name suggests. The user pushes the control down toward the brake pedal to apply the brake and pulls the handle upward to accelerate.
2. Push–right-angle pull hand control systems (Figure 4–2) operate the brake in the same manner (i.e., by pushing down toward the brake pedal). To accelerate, however, the user pulls the control down toward the body at a right angle to the steering column.

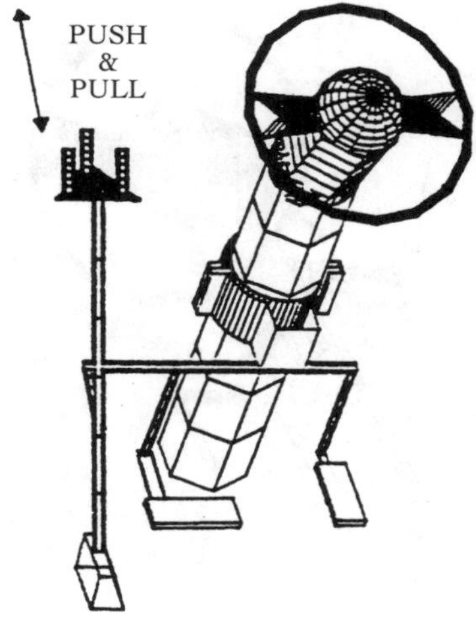


**Figure 4–1** Push–pull hand control

3. Push–twist (rotate) hand control systems (Figure 4–3) again operate the brake by pushing the handle down toward the brake pedal. The user accelerates by simply twisting the control handle, much like a motorcycle rider.

Although mechanical hand controls are not difficult to learn to operate, they do require some familiarity. Therefore, an individual should never drive in traffic using hand controls without proper evaluation and training.

Nonmechanical, servo-assist (electronically driven), control systems are available for quadriplegics who are unable to use conventional control mechanisms. With these systems, the driver simply exerts a slight pressure on the control handle in a push–pull motion. An auxiliary pump then augments that slight pressure to activate the appropriate gas or brake mechanisms. This type of control mechanism is extremely sophisticated and requires skilled installation and service.

### Steering Devices

When properly installed, steering devices allow the driver who is using hand controls to maintain a firm grip on the steering wheel at all times. One hand is busy operating the vehicle, while the other is busy steering. Steering devices also help the driver maneuver the vehicle in tight quarters.

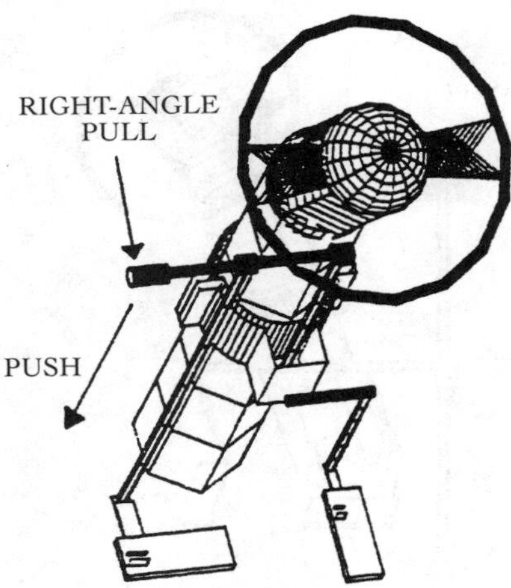


**Figure 4–2** Push–right-angle pull hand control

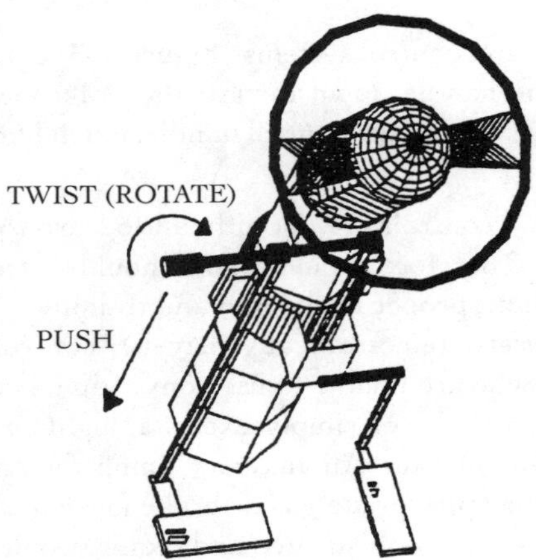


**Figure 4–3** Push–twist hand control

Steering devices either are clamped directly onto the steering wheel itself or are attached to a spreader bar that spans the inside diameter of the steering wheel and is fastened to the inside portion of the wheel on both sides. (If the vehicle is equipped with an air bag mounted inside the steering wheel, a spreader bar attachment should not be used because it would interfere with inflation of the air bag.) It is essential to check these steering devices from time to time to ensure a safe connection. Commercially available steering devices snap into steering wheel bearing casings and are easily removed by depressing a retainer clip, which allows able-bodied drivers to steer without interference from the device.

Each steering wheel device is designed to meet the specific needs of the user, and each design dictates how the user will interface with the steering wheel. There are four basic designs:

1. Spinner knob steering devices require good grasp and wrist strength (Figure 4–4). The user simply grabs the spinner knob with one hand, while the other operates the hand control. Care should be taken regarding the mounting position of a spinner knob, as a cumbersome position can cause early fatigue.
2. V-grip steering devices are typically used by quadriplegics who have adequate wrist strength, but a poor grasp (Figure 4–5). The driver slides one hand into the device, keeping the hand in an upright position, and holds onto the handle portion of the knob.

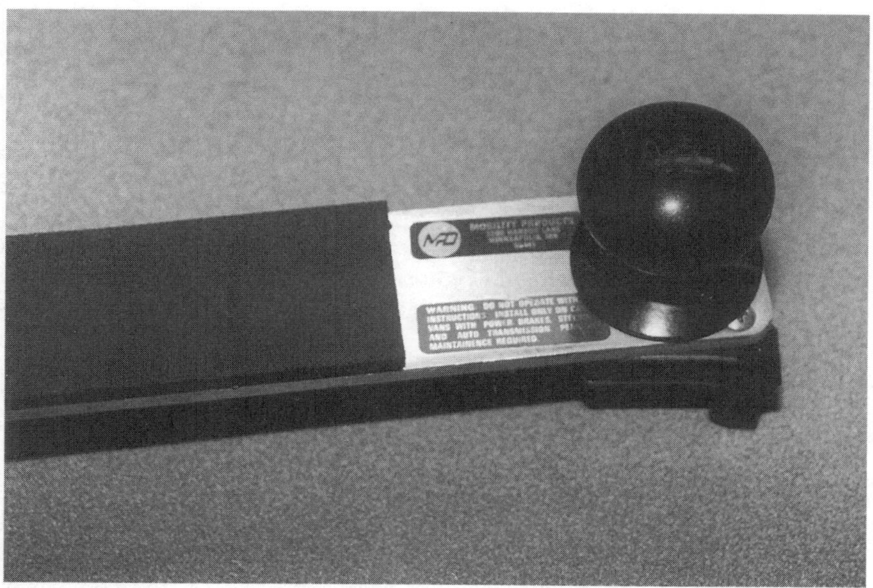

**Figure 4–4** Spinner knob steering device

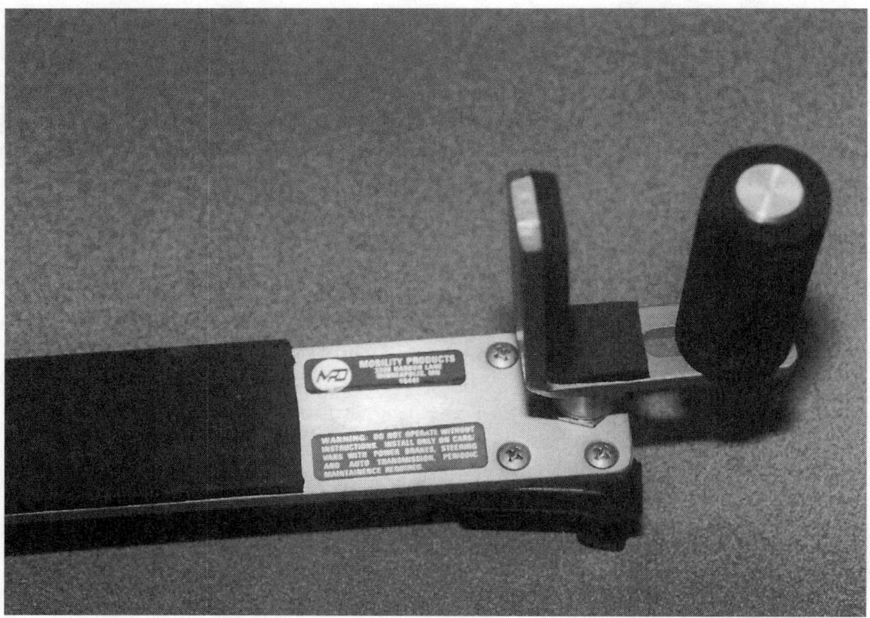

**Figure 4–5** V-grip steering device

3. Adjustable tri-pin steering devices are used by quadriplegics who have poor grasp and poor wrist strength (Figure 4–6). As with V-grip devices, the user slides one hand between the two supports and grabs onto the handle portion of the device.
4. Amputee steering devices are designed to work with an upper arm amputee's prosthetic hook (Figure 4–7). The user places the prosthetic hook into a hole provided in the steering device and steers with the prosthetic arm.

### Other Adaptations

A number of other modifications can be made to a vehicle to allow individuals with different types of disabilities to operate that vehicle both independently and safely. For example, because they are normally operated by some type of foot pressure, parking brakes must be modified for individuals who have limited leg strength or who are quadriplegics or paraplegics. There are two types of parking brake modifications available: (1) a parking brake extension that is

**Figure 4–6** Adjustable tri-pin steering device

**Figure 4–7** Amputee steering device

**Figure 4–8** Parking brake extension

mounted on the parking brake and extends upward to allow the driver to operate it by hand (Figure 4–8) and (2) an electric parking brake system that uses a motor to set and release the parking brake. The switching mechanism used to energize a powered system should be installed within easy reach of the driver.

Left foot gas pedals are used by individuals who are unable to use their right foot to operate standard gas and brake pedals safely, but who have good use of their left leg and foot. Left foot gas pedals are positioned on the left side of the brake pedal and are mounted on the original gas pedal so no major modifications are required.

Individuals with short legs can use pedal extensions to lift the operable surface of the pedals upward so that they can reach the pedals. The extensions must be extremely lightweight and should not be installed by anyone except a reputable dealer, since too much weight on either the gas or brake pedal can adversely affect control of the vehicle.

Cross-over gear shift levers are available so that individuals who have limited or no use of the right arm can shift gears with their left hand (Figure 4–9). Similarly, cross-over turn signal levers are available so that individuals who have limited or no use of their left arm can operate the turn signals with their right arm.

**Figure 4–9** Cross-over gear shift lever

## VAN CONVERSIONS

There are two types of vans: full-size vans and mini-vans. Both types require extensive modifications if people with disabilities are to drive them. Mini-vans are obviously smaller and more maneuverable than are full-size vans. They have much less head clearance than do full-size vans, however, requiring modifications (e.g., lowering the floor pan or raising the roof) that may not be required with a full-size van. Depending on the person's height, wheelchair size, and disability, these conversions may still be necessary in full-size vans, but not to the extent needed in mini-vans. Full-size vans typically seat a greater number of passengers than do adapted mini-vans, depending upon where the wheelchair lift is installed, an important consideration if space is an issue.

Several questions must be answered when working with a reputable adaptive equipment dealer and/or evaluator before purchasing a van:

- Will the driver drive from a wheelchair or transfer into the driver's seat?
- If the driver is to transfer into a driver's seat, does he or she have adequate strength to make the vertical transfers necessary, or should a four- or six-way power seat be installed to allow for horizontal transfers?

- Is there adequate space between the seat and the engine cowling to maneuver the legs and feet while swiveling the seat?
- If the person will be driving from a wheelchair, will he or she be seated too high to operate the vehicle safely? Will the driver need to be lowered while in the wheelchair? How will the wheelchair be locked down? A person either driving or riding as a passenger in a wheelchair should have the wheelchair tied down, as well as have a safety belt and shoulder harness in place, for adequate protection.
- Will the steering column need to be extended so that the driver's feet will not interfere with the gas and brake pedals?
- Is there adequate space for hand controls? What type of hand controls will best fit the driver's needs?
- Is there sufficient head clearance inside the van to allow the individual in a wheelchair to maneuver around safely? Will the van roof need to be raised or the floor pan lowered?
- Is there adequate space to maneuver a wheelchair when entering or exiting the van?
- Will the corrugated flooring found inside vans make it difficult to maneuver a wheelchair? If so, half-inch exterior plywood can be installed over the corrugated flooring to eliminate the rough texture.
- In which door will the lift be installed, the side door or the back door? A rear door access usually requires the removal of rear sofas or center bench seats, thus reducing the number of passenger seats.
- Is there sufficient head room for the individual in a wheelchair to enter safely through the lift-equipped doorway? Will it be necessary to raise the doorway to accommodate the person?
- What type of lift will be installed? Different lift designs require different amounts of space. Mini-vans typically use ramps that fold up into the doorway and are usually equipped with a device that lowers the mini-van to reduce the slope of the ramp and facilitate access.
- Will a power door be required? If the person in a wheelchair will be operating the van independently, a power door will be necessary since the lift or ramp will block access to the door and affect the ease of operation of closing or opening the door once inside the van.
- What type of switching mechanisms must be installed in order to operate the van's power door and lift/ramp, and where will these switches be installed?
- Does the vehicle have a dual battery system already installed? If not, such a system should be installed in such a way that the main battery cannot be drained when the powered equipment operates with the ignition off.

Answers to these questions will help determine the type of van that a person with a disability should purchase (mini-van vs. full-size van) as well as the extent of modifications and, therefore, the added costs for adapting the vehicle.

## Wheelchair Lifts

There are four general types of wheelchair lifts designed for van use: platform lifts, rotary lifts, under-the-vehicle lifts, and hoists. (REquest, 1992; ABLEDATA, 1994). All four operate differently when raising and lowering a wheelchair and its user into and out of a van.

Platform lifts, also called folding lifts (Figure 4–10), are mounted inside the side or rear doorways of a van. Some modifications inside the van are required when platform lifts are installed. They are usually supported by two vertical uprights, although some are supported by only one. The platform is stored in a folded, upright position just inside the van door and unfolds horizontally once the door is opened. The user rolls forward onto the platform and then lowers the platform and wheelchair to the ground before rolling forward off the platform. To enter the van, the user reverses the procedure. It takes approximately 8 feet

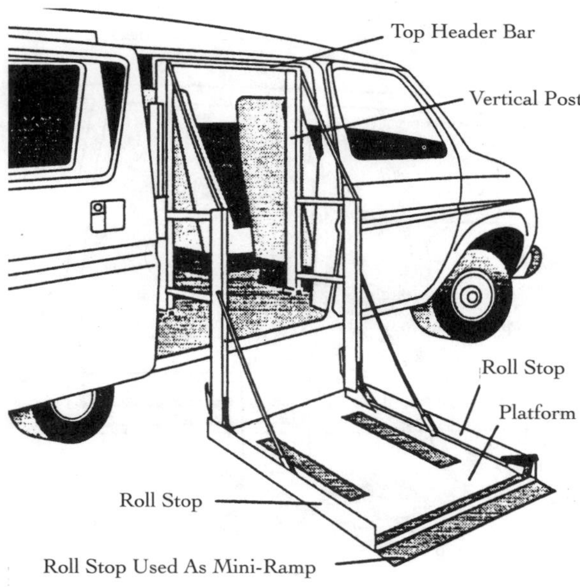


**Figure 4–10** Platform lift

of clearance to enter and exit a standard platform lift. Some platforms are designed to allow the user to roll off at an angle, thereby reducing the amount of clearance required. There are several styles of platforms: one-piece, folding, and split platforms. Folding platforms fold in half before storage; split platforms split in half and then each half is stored in the upright position. When stored, folding and split platforms provide an opening that allows able-bodied people to climb into the van.

Rotary lifts, also called swing lifts (Figure 4–11), have a platform that is supported by a single vertical upright. The platform rests on the floor in the middle of the van when stored. When ready to leave the van, the user rolls forward onto the platform, raises it slightly, rotates the platform about the vertical upright until it carries the user outside the van, then lowers the platform onto the ground before rolling backward off the platform. The process is reversed when the user wishes to get into the van. Rotary lifts require approximately 3 feet of clearance next to the van for the user to enter or exit the van. Rotary lifts can be installed only in the van's side door and require some modifications inside the van.

Under-the-vehicle lifts (Figure 4–12) are installed and stored in a metal enclosure under the van. When the user activates the lift to exit the van, the platform comes out from underneath the van and rises to the level of the van's floor. The user rolls out onto the platform, lowers the platform to the ground, and rolls

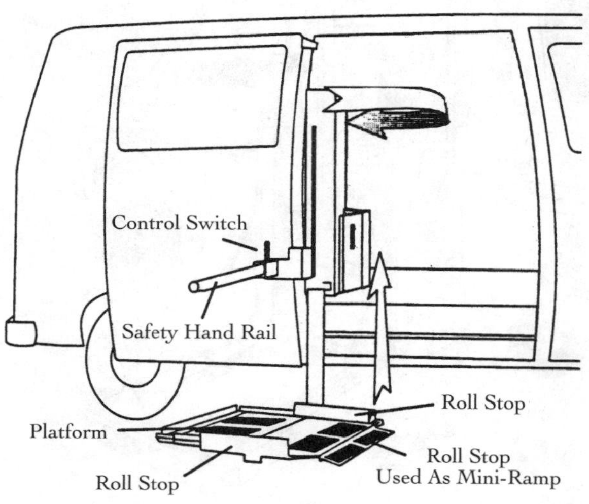


**Figure 4–11** Rotary lift

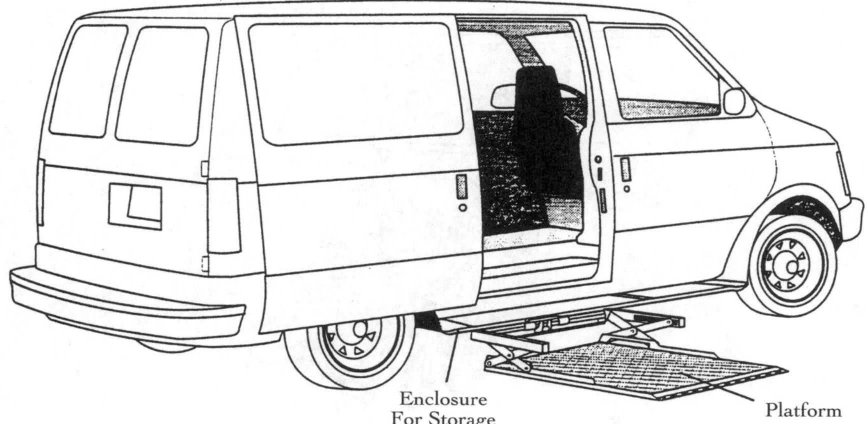


**Figure 4–12** Under-the-vehicle lift

forward off the platform. The steps are reversed to enter the van from the outside. Under-the-vehicle lifts can be installed only at the van's side door and may require modifications to the exhaust system and fuel tank.

Hoist lifts work differently, since there is no platform (Figure 4–13). Instead, the user attaches the lift's two straps to the wheelchair and these raise the wheelchair off the floor. A single arm supporting the wheelchair then swings outside the van and lowers the wheelchair to the ground. The process is done in reverse order when the user enters the van. Because there is no platform to deal with, the amount of space required outside the van in order to exit/enter the vehicle depends on the width of the user's wheelchair.

Most lifts have a mechanical backup system that allows the system to be operated manually, usually by another person. Such a system makes it possible for a person inside the van to exit the vehicle in cases of total power failure or in emergencies.

Vans equipped with lifts need control switches for access. The switches typically control both the lift and the power door. Usually, there are three two-way switches mounted near the rear of the van. One switch opens and closes the door, one folds and unfolds or rotates the platform outside the van, and the third raises and lowers the lift. Sometimes magnetic switches mounted inside the vehicle lights, e.g., tail lights, are activated with a magnet held over the location of the hidden magnets to operate the door and lift. Dash switches are also routinely added to the van to allow the driver to control the lift/door area from the driver's seat.

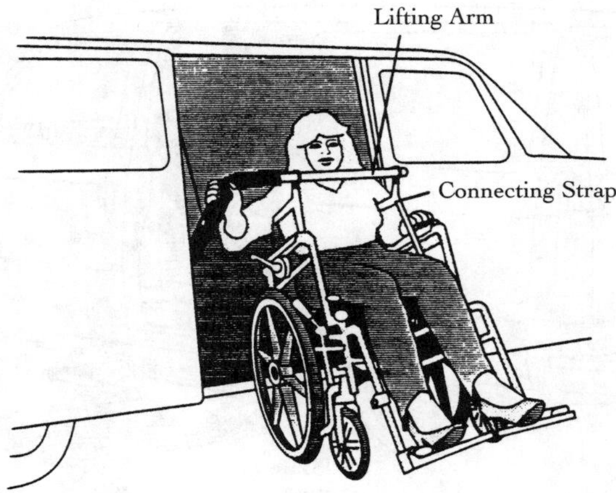


**Figure 4–13** Hoist lift

### Reduced-Effort Braking and Steering Systems

Some individuals do not have adequate strength in their upper body muscles to operate a vehicle using standard adaptations. Among the options available to them are reduced-effort braking and steering systems, which minimize the amount of effort required to operate the vehicle (Shipp, 1989, p. 25).

Depending on the system installed, reduced-effort steering systems reduce the amount of effort required to steer a vehicle by 40 to 70 percent. Systems that reduce the amount of effort by 40 percent are typically called low-effort steering systems, while those that reduce the amount by 70 percent are called zero-effort steering systems. These systems should not be installed without the installation of a backup power steering system that will allow the driver to maneuver the vehicle safely over to the side of the road in the event of engine failure. Reduced-effort braking systems work in a similar manner; they also include both low-effort and zero-effort systems. Backup brakes should also be installed to ensure that the driver can stop the vehicle in the event of engine failure. This equipment is extremely sophisticated and should be installed and serviced only by a reputable dealer.

### Other Van Modifications

One way to provide additional head space is to replace the van's original roof with a raised fiberglass roof. One problem with a raised roof is that the overall height prohibits the driver from parking in most parking garages.

If the person in the wheelchair requires additional head room once inside the van and does not want to raise the roof, it is possible to lower the floor. The original flooring is removed and replaced with smooth metal flooring, usually 4 to 6 inches lower. Typically, the floor is lowered from just behind the driver's seat back to the rear wheels. At times, the section just in front of the steering wheel is also lowered so that the driver can drive from his or her wheelchair.

The section of flooring in the driver's area may be removed and replaced with a power pan that can raise and lower the driver's wheelchair once it is in place behind the steering wheel. A motor raises and lowers this area.

Wheel wells are sometimes made in the driver's area so that the wheelchair user can roll his or her wheelchair into the grooves, thus lowering the driver's position at the steering wheel.

Four- and six-way power seats may be necessary if the wheelchair user has difficulty transferring into the original driver's seat. Four-way power seats have motors that control both up and down and forward and backward motions. Six-way power seats not only go up and down, forward and backward, but also rotate 90 degrees.

Restraining a wheelchair inside a van is extremely important, even if the user has transferred from the wheelchair into the driver's seat. An unrestrained wheelchair can quickly become a projectile if the driver is ever forced to stop quickly. A wheelchair can be restrained either manually or electrically. Four-point tie-downs are typically used when transporting individuals in wheelchairs as passengers, but they can also be used to restrain unoccupied wheelchairs. Electric tie-downs are used by individuals who sit in their wheelchairs while they drive; these tie-downs automatically lock the wheelchair into place once it is in position.

These and all adaptations should be made only by reputable dealers, and equipment should be routinely serviced to prevent costly breakdowns and to ensure safe operation. There are a number of dealers who specialize in vehicle modifications and in meeting the needs of disabled drivers.

## ACCESSIBLE PARKING

There are federal, state, and local laws that govern the number and design of accessible parking spaces required for each type of business. In general, businesses must designate approximately 2 percent of their spaces for accessible parking. Most of these spaces must have an access aisle that is at least 60 inches wide. Van-accessible parking spaces require an access aisle of 96 inches to accommodate lifts. One access aisle can be shared by two accessible parking spaces.

All states have laws regulating accessible parking permits. With proof of a person's disability (i.e., a copy of the diagnosis signed by a physician), the state's motor vehicle department will issue either a temporary or a permanent accessibility parking permit. People who have had some type of trauma or surgery that affects their ability to ambulate over a finite period of time typically receive a temporary permit to display on their vehicle's dashboard or suspend from their vehicle's rear view mirror. Permanent permits are granted to those individuals who have chronic disabling conditions (e.g., spinal cord injuries, multiple sclerosis, amputations). People with permanent permits can usually get specially marked license plates that remain on the vehicle. This works well for individuals who drive one vehicle only. Those who use a number of vehicles or depend on others to drive them around, however, may prefer a placard that they can move from vehicle to vehicle. Some states will grant both.

Drivers who use accessible parking spaces without the appropriate permit are subject to a fine, even if they have a disability.

## GAS STATIONS

With the current trend toward self-service gas stations, many drivers who are disabled find it difficult to have their vehicles serviced. Some states require gas stations with both full- and self-service pumps to pump gas for individuals with disabilities at self-service prices. Gas stations with only self-service pumps are not always required to pump gas for individuals with disabilities, but many owners of gas stations will provide these services when asked. Individuals who are unable to pump their own gas should check with local stations to see which ones will provide the necessary services.

---

### REFERENCES

ABLEDATA. (1994). *Van lifts*. ABLEDATA Fact Sheet. Silver Spring, MD: Macro International.

Butler, C.A. (Ed.). (1991). *The handicapped driver's mobility guide* Heathrow, FL: AAA Traffic Safety & Engineering Department, pp. 9–11.

Kerr, C.M. III, & Irwin, D. (1990). Driver assessment and training of the disabled client. In R.V. Smith & J.H. Leslie, Jr. (Ed.), *Rehabilitation Engineering* (pp. 317–327). Boca Raton, FL: CRC Press.

REquest Rehabilitation Engineering Center. (1992). *Lifts for vans*. Washington, DC: National Rehabilitation Hospital and ECRI, pp. 1–13.

Shipp, M. (1989). *Adaptive driving devices and vehicle modifications*. Ruston, LA: Louisiana Tech University: Center for Rehabilitation Science and Biomedical Engineering, p. 25.

# Appendix 4–A

## Resources

The following is a list of relevant resources which may be of assistance.

**American Automobile Association (AAA)**
1000 AAA Drive
Heathrow, FL 32746
(407) 444-7962
**American Association of Retired Persons (AARP)**
55 Alive/Mature Driving Program
601 E Street, N.W.
Washington, D.C. 20049
(202) 434-2277
**Department of Veterans Affairs**
Prosthetic and Sensory Aids Service
Mailing Code 117C
Washington, D.C. 20420
(202) 535-7293
**National Mobility Equipment Dealers Association (NMEDA)**
909 E. Skagway Avenue
Tampa, FL 33604
(813) 932-8566
**Association of Driver Educators for the Disabled**
P.O. Box 49
Edgerton, WI 53534
(608) 884-8833

The three major car manufacturers offer reimbursements for adaptive equipment conversion costs on eligible vehicles purchased or leased. For more information contact:

**Chrysler Corporation**
Automobility Program
P.O. Box 3124
Bloomfield Hills, MI 48302
1-800-255-9877
(810) 433-6682 fax

**Ford Motors Corporation**
Ford Mobility Monitoring
P.O. Box 529
Bloomfield Hills, MI 48303
1-800-952-2248
1-800-833-0312 TDD
(810) 540-7039 fax

**General Motors Corporation**
GM Mobility Assistance Center
P.O. Box 9011
Detroit, MI 48202
1-800-323-9935
1-800-833-9935 TDD
(313) 974-4383 fax

*Chapter 5*

# Selecting, Using, and Evaluating Communication Devices

*Sarah W. Blackstone*

## WHAT IS COMMUNICATION?

Communication means exchanging, transmitting, and receiving information, thoughts, feelings, and ideas. It allows people to establish, maintain, and deepen their relationships with each other. The human being is an elaborate communication system. Each sensory organ and motor act is a system component. People receive information by seeing, hearing, smelling, tasting, and feeling; they transmit information by looking, moving, touching, writing, and speaking. They are constantly exchanging information, even when they do not intend to do so. Communication happens both within and outside the periphery of conscious awareness.

Although the term *communication* generally implies the involvement of at least two people (interpersonal), some communication is intrapersonal. Communicating with one's self serves the functions of regulating behavior, planning, rehearsing, and perhaps worrying. It also is the source of creativity, poetry, insight, music, dreams, and fantasy.

Language is a powerful tool. It furnishes people with a shared code that connects them to each other across time and space. Language may be spoken, written, pictured, printed, even felt (Braille). Many, but by no means all, communication acts involve the use of language. In face-to-face communication, gestures, vocalizations, facial expressions, body language, eye movements, and gaze augment the linguistic forms of communication.

To a great extent, context determines the manner in which people transfer information and express thoughts and ideas. The characteristics and competencies of communicating partners, the situation, the activities, and the location of an interaction often dictate the modes of expression used. For example, deep sea divers gesture or write. People walking on a beach talk. Many authors use a computer with a word processing program to prepare their manuscripts. Family members who live apart talk on the telephone, send letters, or use e-mail.

Technology is having a profound impact on how and how often people transmit and receive information. Computer components and fiber optics have made it possible to communicate efficiently and quite effectively with almost anyone, anywhere, at any time, and in any form. Above all, technology is opening doors for people who are severely limited in their communication skills.

## WHAT IS A COMMUNICATION SYSTEM?

Each individual has a communication system. According to Vanderheiden and Lloyd (1986), an individual's communication system includes speech and standard augmentative communication techniques (e.g., gestures, facial expressions, telephones, computers, writing). For those with severe speech and/or writing impairments, special augmentative communication techniques are available. Examples are manual signs, communication devices, graphic symbol sets, communication wallets, rate enhancement strategies, and scanning techniques.

It is important for professionals who provide assistive technology services and for families of people with severe communication impairments to understand the concept of a "communication system." A communication device is never the only component of an individual's communication system. Assistive technology should never be the sole focus of augmentative communication intervention.

For example, Joey is a 3½-year-old with Down syndrome and delayed speech. He relied on gestures, facial expressions, and a stream of vocalizations to express his needs and participate in family activities until he learned to use the manual signs for "want" and "more" and also a communication display with pictures. Now he can select toys, favorite foods, and activities using language. Having access to language has allowed him to communicate about objects that are not present and to express a broader range of requests and comments.

If Joey's speech does not become intelligible, then his communication system will have to be expanded to incorporate other special augmentative communication techniques. He may require a communication board, a conversation book, a voice output communication device, or even a computer and special software to facilitate his language learning and interaction skills. As he grows older, Joey will continue not only to improve in his speech, but also to rely on body language, gestures, and other standard augmentative techniques—just like everyone else. In addition, he will have the special help and tools he needs to express language.

## WHAT ARE COMMUNICATION DEVICES?

Designed to help people accomplish specific tasks, communication devices can augment someone's ability to speak, hear, write, read, and even sign. These devices are commonly known as augmentative communication devices.

Low-technology augmentative communication devices are nonelectronic. They include, for example, communication boards and wallets, miniboards, schedule boards, and conversation books. Such devices are often homemade or clinician-made. They are useful for persons of all ages and can effectively meet a variety of communication needs. They are not just "backup systems" to be pulled out when a high-technology system fails; they are important components of an individual's communication system.

High-technology devices are electronic. They are either plugged into an electrical outlet or operated by a battery, generally a rechargeable battery. Because they are portable, they can be carried by the user or mounted on a wheelchair. High-technology devices provide individuals with a variety of options, including access to large vocabularies, speech output, print, and rate enhancement features. They often facilitate independence and participation. They are appropriate for very young children, very old adults, and many people in between.

Most high-technology augmentative communication devices are actually computers. They have certain hardware (component parts) and software (communication programs) features. Today's augmentative communication devices fall into two categories:

1. Dedicated communication devices are computers designed solely for the purposes of augmenting communication. Examples include the Liberator, Dynavox, and the Lightwriter.
2. Off-the-shelf computers (i.e., those used by the general population) can be adapted for use in the augmentative communication market. Since the advent of affordable laptop computers, manufacturers have been providing augmentative communication devices that "marry" communication software programs (e.g., Scanning WSKE, TalkAbout, Speaking Dynamically, and Gus), and various access and output features, to commercially available laptops.

For some individuals, off-the-shelf computers introduce a level of complexity that is unnecessary or undesirable. For others, adapted off-the-shelf devices are highly advantageous because they can be used for other purposes (e.g., word processing, computer-aided design, games, e-mail).

Both low- and high-technology devices place special cognitive, motor, perceptual, and learning requirements on the people using them to communicate and on their partners. Communication is itself very complex; the user must have appropriate training, and the devices require maintenance over time. In established augmentative communication clinical programs, data reveal that low-technology solutions are recommended *more often* than are high-technology devices. Reported ratios vary from 3:1 to 4:1 (Blackstone, 1991). Although professionals, family members, and users often experience difficulty learning to use augmentative communication equipment, it is well worth the investment of time and energy when used effectively.

Norm was a 42-year-old tenured college professor when his amyotrophic lateral sclerosis was diagnosed. As he was gradually losing his ability to speak and to write, he and his wife decided to find a way for him to stay "in touch"—no matter what. They did. Norm used a laptop computer with special communication software and a word processing program. With it, he completed his memoirs, wrote letters, prepared notes for his children, and carried on conversations with his family. In addition, Norm and his wife used an eye gaze board at night. She said the board was useful any time he was not in his wheelchair. "We were still having conversations until the day before he died," she said. "It made a profound difference to us both."

## WHAT CAN COMMUNICATION DEVICES DO?

The ultimate goal of the field of augmentative communication "is not to find a technological solution to communication problems, but to enable individuals to efficiently and effectively engage in a variety of interactions" (Beukelman & Mirenda, 1992, p. 7). Successful applications of augmentative communication devices encourage people to be more active participants during communicative interactions. Light (1988) described the purposes of communicative interaction as (1) expression of needs/wants, (2) information transfer, (3) social closeness, and (4) social etiquette (Table 5–1).

It is often possible to meet social closeness and social etiquette requirements without any augmentative communication device. Waving and smiling, for example, are perfectly acceptable ways to greet someone. Holding hands fulfills a desire to feel close, and vocalizations are sufficient to acknowledge an opinion and signal agreement (or disagreement).

Gestures can express basic wants and needs, but the expression of complex desires and needs, as well as any reference to the past or future, requires the use of language. The exchange of information is even more linguistically bound. Thus, augmentative communication devices are most often used for expressing wants and needs and exchanging information.

Both low- and high-technology devices fulfill interactive needs. Under some conditions, such as conversations with friends and family, or in certain environments, such as the beach or a restaurant, users may prefer to use low-technol-

**Table 5–1** Characteristics of Interactions Intended to Meet Various Social Purposes

| | Social Purposes of the Interactions | | | |
|---|---|---|---|---|
| *Characteristics* | *Expression of Needs/ Wants* | *Information Transfer* | *Social Closeness* | *Social Etiquette* |
| Goal of the interaction | To regulate the behavior of another as a means to fulfill needs/wants | To share information | To establish, maintain, and/or develop personal relationship(s) | To conform to social conventions of politeness |
| Focus of the interaction | Desired object or action | Information | Interpersonal relationship | Social convention |
| Duration of the interaction | Limited. Emphasis is on initiating interaction | May be lengthy. Emphasis is on developing interaction | May be lengthy. Emphasis is on maintaining interaction | Limited. Emphasis is on fulfilling designated turns |
| Content of communication | Important | Important | Not important | Not important |
| Predictability of communication | Highly predictable | Not predictable | May be somewhat predictable | Highly predictable |
| Scope of communication | Limited scope | Wide scope | Wide scope | Very limited scope |
| Rate of communication | Important | Important | May not be important | Important |
| Tolerance for communication breakdown | Little tolerance | Little tolerance | Some tolerance | Little tolerance |
| Number of participants | Usually dyadic | Dyadic, small or large group | Usually dyadic or small group | Dyadic, small or large group |
| Independence of the communicator | Important | Important | Not important | Important |
| Partner familiarity | Familiar or unfamiliar | Familiar or unfamiliar | Usually familiar | Familiar or unfamiliar |

*Source:* Reprinted with permission from________.

ogy augmentative communication devices. Familiar partners often communicate faster using low-technology devices, because partners can predict messages based on shared knowledge and experiences. Some interactions, such as telling jokes, giving speeches, putting unfamiliar listeners at ease, and getting attention, are accomplished more easily through speech output devices. Even more important for people with severe communication impairments, high-technology devices are literally opening the doors to education, employment, intimate personal relationships, community participation, and independent living opportunities.

## DEVELOPMENT OF COMMUNICATION DEVICES

In 1975, there were few augmentative communication devices on the market. In 1985, there were approximately 50. By 1995, more than 100 were being manufactured in the United States alone. This rapid growth in the communication device industry reflects a growing awareness of the needs of persons with disabilities, as well as an expansion in the electronics and computer industries. By bringing to market more computer memory, smaller components, intelligible speech, high-resolution displays, and color graphics, manufacturers of augmentative communication devices are facilitating communication for people with severe speaking and writing impairments.

Important features of augmentative communication devices are price, rental options, manufacturer, distributor, and the support provided to the consumer over time (Center for Applied Science and Engineering in Rehabilitation, 1996, in press).

As new technologies become available, device characteristics change. The primary feature categories of augmentative communication devices are likely to remain the same, however. These are input (methods of accessing the device), language options (linguistic characteristics), and output options (e.g., print or speech).

### Input/Access

How will the person select messages? What is the best interface between the device and the individual? Two primary techniques are available.

#### *Direct Selection*

"The user directly indicates the desired item from the selection set" (Beukelman & Mirenda, 1992, p. 58). Some techniques require the user to make direct contact with the device (e.g., typing, finger pointing, touching, headstick); others require no physical contact with the device (e.g., light pointer, eye gaze, voice recognition).

### *Scanning*

When individuals are unable to select messages directly, they can select them by scanning. Items in the selection set are displayed for visual scanning or spoken for auditory scanning, either by a trained communication partner (person) or a low-technology device, or by an electronic device, in a predetermined configuration. The augmentative communication device user waits until the partner or device scans through undesired items. When the desired item appears, the user indicates his or her choice (e.g., by hitting a switch).

Scanning arrays may be linear, circular, or group item. Because a group item scanning arrangement greatly increases efficiency, it is preferable whenever possible. One example of group item scanning is a row-column visual scan. Rows are electronically highlighted until the user selects the row that contains the target item. Then individual items in that row are highlighted one at a time. The user stops the scan at the specific item desired, and the device speaks the message.

## Language

How will vocabulary be represented (e.g., graphic symbols, pictures, alphanumeric characters, semantic icons)? How will symbols be arranged on the display? How will language be stored and retrieved? How can the rate of communication be increased?

The process of generating language by means of an augmentative communication device is much, much more difficult than talking, which people do automatically. By far, the most complex features of all augmentative communication devices relate to the presentation, storage, and retrieval of language. In fact, unless users can understand, find, and use the language symbols, they cannot use an augmentative communication device, no matter how easy the access may be, how attractive the device may look, or how intelligible the speech may sound.

### *Symbols*

Clearly, it is essential for the symbols to be meaningful to the individual who uses them. Symbol options currently being used in augmentative communication devices include real and miniature objects, textured and tangible symbols, photographs, line drawings, graphic symbol sets/systems (e.g., Mayer-Johnson, Picsyms, Blissymbols, ComPic, Pictogram Ideograph Communication [PIC], orthography, braille, and the Morse code). In the United States, the Mayer-Johnson symbol set, traditional orthography, Picsyms, and Minspeak icons are most commonly used on communication displays. No matter which symbols are used, they must be organized in ways that take into account the visual, motor, linguistic, and cognitive abilities of the augmentative communication device user.

### *Rate Enhancement Techniques*

At best, conversational rates with augmentative communication devices approach 15 words per minute (Foulds, 1987). This is a mere fraction of the 150 to 250 words per minute typical of natural speakers (Goldman-Eisler, 1986). In addition, the use of such devices alters the timing of communicative exchanges. "Communication inefficiencies and message-timing limitations interfere with the communication interactions of AC [augmentative communication] users" (Beukelman & Mirenda, 1992, p. 35). To enhance the rate of communication and still provide access to large vocabularies, several options are available. Many augmentative communication devices now offer more than one of these options.

***Message Encoding.*** Both low- and high-technology devices can use coding schemes. Users retrieve words, phrases, even paragraphs by means of codes. Current coding strategy options include iconic, numeric, alphanumeric, color, and letter codes. Because the use of codes requires memorization or constant access to a reference sheet, coding techniques increase cognitive demands. Once memorized, however, encoding strategies can be automatic.

***Prediction.*** Message prediction is a dynamic retrieval process in which the offered options change according to the portion of the message that has already been formulated. Familiar communication partners, for example, often predict entire messages after reading or hearing only a portion of them. Similarly, some augmentative communication devices now can predict additional portions of a message based on single letters, words, or phrases/sentences. These linguistic prediction techniques not only can accelerate communication rates, but also can improve the grammatical performance and literacy skills of some persons with language and learning disabilities (Beukelman, Garrett, Lange, & Tice, 1988). This strategy requires users to remain vigilant and to make decisions continuously about whether to accept (or reject) the predicted fragment, however, and some users dislike this feature.

***Levels.*** All low-technology aids have static displays. So do a number of high-technology devices. Accessing large vocabularies, however, requires the use of multiple displays or overlays. Each overlay corresponds to a "level." Changing levels often requires changing overlays, a demand that surpasses the motor skills of most augmentative communication users.

A dynamic (or transient) display is a computer screen that changes in response to user input. With dynamic displays, the user can change overlays simply by touching a switch. Along with the expanded memory capacity of laptop computers and improved display technology, this feature gives individuals with disabilities independent access to large vocabularies without recalling codes or using message prediction.

### Output Options

What communication modes can the device produce? Can the output be understood by communication partners?

Users of low-technology devices remain dependent on their communication partners to interpret symbols, words, or letters on the spot. High-technology augmentative communication devices allow individuals to prepare messages in advance, write, talk on the telephone, and have the benefit of feedback to refine messages before sending them.

Speech output (both synthesized and digitized), visual output on computer displays, and printed output modes are features common to most communication devices. Optional features may include an interface with a modem, environmental control unit, computer, telephone, and electric wheelchair. The more output options, the greater number of potential communication partners for an augmentative communication user.

## CURRENT FEATURES

Because no augmentative communication device contains all available features, no device is appropriate for everyone. Manufacturers design devices with a spectrum of features so people with different capabilities can use them. In choosing a device, it is necessary to match the features of the device to the characteristics of the individual. As more features become available in devices that reach the market and costs decrease, some people may use several devices. For example, a small, simple portable device may be best on community outings or in the car, while larger, more sophisticated devices are preferable to accomplish tasks at work, give speeches, and write poetry.

While all communication devices share certain qualities, each has a unique combination of features that distinguishes it from the other. It is not possible to describe specific devices or even all feature categories, given the long list of options currently available. The following four features are among the most exciting however: (1) auditory scanning, (2) dynamic displays, (3) digitized speech, and (4) portability.

### Auditory Scanning

Until recently, available technology was not meeting the communication needs of individuals with severe visual and motor impairments. Now, auditory scanning allows someone to listen to a menu of words and phrases, and then hit a switch when a desired message is heard.

*Waitress*: How are you today?
*Ann*: (*Hitting switch*) The device says, "Greetings, comments, waitress, music." Then, it repeats, more slowly, "Greetings." (*Ann hits the switch.*) The device says, "Hello, Fine." (*Ann hits the switch.*) The device says, "I'm fine, How are you doing?"
*Waitress*: I'm okay. What's new?"
*Ann*: (*hitting switch*) The device says (again), "Greetings, comments, waitress." (*Ann hits the switch.*) Then the device says, "Menu, order." (*Ann hits the switch.*) The device says, "I'm ready to order."

Individuals who use auditory scanning are limited to painfully slow communication rates. Because items must be presented in a linear fashion (i.e., one at a time), accessing vocabulary can be tedious. It is generally necessary to hit the switch multiple times before reaching the desired message. Thus, an important feature to consider in selecting a device that uses auditory scanning is how language is presented.

Branching is a presentation technique that allows someone to navigate through multiple levels until the desired message occurs. The purpose of branching is to get to the message in the minimal amount of time, with the smallest possible number of switch activations. Simple devices may have only two branches, but sophisticated devices can have an almost unlimited number. Conceptually, branching is comparable to group item scanning.

Some devices offer the option of using two different voices. One voice scans the categories, and another speaks the message. Ideally, only the user should hear the auditory scan, as this can be very disruptive to others, particularly in a classroom environment. Scanning can be accomplished either by using an earphone or by mounting a speaker close to the user's ear (e.g., on the headrest of a wheelchair). Volume control is very important, as sound that is too loud can damage hearing. Table 5–2 lists examples of devices that offer auditory scanning. Shaded areas indicate that the device has the listed feature.

### Dynamic Displays (Computer Screens)

While input (touch screen) and output (visual feedback) are important, the most critical function of the dynamic display on augmentative communication devices is the presentation of language. Some portable computers and high-resolution displays have sufficient memory to allow storage of libraries of pictures, symbols, animation, text, sounds, and speech. Users can configure the size, color, and arrangement of symbols, words, and phrases on the screen, and

**Table 5–2** Features of Portable Auditory Scanning Devices

| FEATURES<br>shaded areas = + feature<br>n/a = not applicable | Alphatalker | Digivox | Dynavox | Ke:nx | Liberator | Macaw | Message Mate | Speak Easy | Speaking Dynami-cally | Talking Screen | Whisper Wolf |
|---|---|---|---|---|---|---|---|---|---|---|---|
| LANGUAGE PRESENTATION and AUDITORY STRATEGIES (Way device presents language auditorily and strategy options) | | | | | | | | | | | |
| Number of branches allowable | 3 | 2 | +3 | +3 | +3 | 2 | 2 | 0 | +3 | +3 | 2 |
| Sequencing locations | | | | | | | | | | | |
| Auditory word prediction | icon | | w/ Dynawrite | w/ Cowriter | icon | | | | w/ Cowriter | | |
| VOICE OUTPUT (Whether speech output is digitized or synthesized. Whether device allows for two speakers—one for the user to listen to the scan and the other for the partner to hear the selected message. Whether voices heard by the user and partner are different.) | | | | | | | | | | | |
| Digitized/recorded | | | | | | | | | | | |
| Synthesized | | | | | | | | | | | |
| More than 1 voice option | | | | | | | | | | | |
| Personal speaker/earphone | | | | n/a | | | | | n/a | n/a | |
| Vol control for ext. speaker<br>Vol control for int. speaker | | | | n/a<br>n/a | | | | | n/a<br>n/a | n/a<br>n/a | |
| User volume control | | | | n/a | | | | | n/a | n/a | |
| SINGLE SWITCH SCANNING OPTIONS (Type of scanning strategies available to user) | | | | | | | | | | | |
| Step or manual | | | | | | | | | | | |
| Automatic | | | | | | | | | | | |
| Inverse | | | | | | | | | | | |
| LANGUAGE PRESENTATION—VISUAL (Way device displays language visually) | | | | | | | | | | | |
| Symbols—Text | S,T | S,T | S,T | S,T | S,T | S,T | S,T | S,T | S,T | S,T | S,T |
| Display—Static | | | | | | | | | | | |
| Dynamic—mono | | | | | | | | | | | |
| Dynamic—color | | | | optional | | | | | optional | optional | |

*Source:* 

they can change screens quickly. With the advent of laptop computers, these devices have become portable if they are mounted on a wheelchair, but they are not yet small or light enough to be carried by most ambulatory users.

A major advantage of dynamic display technology is that users can select (and construct) messages without remembering codes or physically switching overlays. Many professionals feel that transient displays not only enhance the rate of communication, but also substantially reduce cognitive and perceptual demands. The cognitive, motor, visual-perceptual, and learning loads inherent to dynamic displays challenge some users, however. For example, moving between and among screens to construct messages requires visual attention and decision making. Although memory demands decrease, users may need time and experience before they can generate messages (or parts of messages) automatically and routinely. See Table 5–3 for examples of both dedicated devices (e.g., Dynavox, Lingraphica, System 2000 Versa), and communication software designed to turn laptop (or desktop) computers into augmentative communication devices with dynamic displays.

### Synthetic and Digitalized Speech

Intelligible speech is available on augmentative communication devices. High-quality speech synthesis is now built into most dedicated devices and can be added to many laptop computers. Intelligible text-to-speech synthesis allows people who are literate to say "anything." It also provides access to text for people who have visual impairments (and those who are unable to read because of learning problems) and immediate feedback for those who are learning to write and those who have learning difficulties. The high-quality text-to-speech synthesizers DECtalk and Infovox both have male, female, and children's voices and are available in several languages. The Dynavox, Liberator, Lightwriter, and Voice 160 have DECtalk built in.

The affordability of digitized (recorded) speech has greatly increased the accessibility of speech output for those who need augmentative communication devices. Digitized devices are easy to program. Because messages are recorded using voice, they can be changed more easily than typing in the change. Also, this type of device can reflect the personal characteristics of the individual (e.g., age, gender, dialect, language, culture, personality). Individuals can select a friend to be their "voice." People with degenerative neurological conditions may even have an opportunity to record their own voice in anticipation of being unable to speak at some later time.

Digitized speech devices vary widely in the amount of recording time available, maximum number of messages allowable and assigned time per message, message space (dimensions of the space where messages are located and sym-

**Table 5–3** Dynamic Display Devices and Features

| *Features* | *Dynavox* | *Gus* | *Ke:nx* | *Lingraphica* | *Speaking Dynamically* | *System 2000 Versa* | *Talking Screen* | *Talk-About* |
|---|---|---|---|---|---|---|---|---|
| Hardware require-ments | Dedicated | Any Microsoft Windows compatible PC | Macintosh System 7 w/ 8 MB RAM and 80MB hard drive | Dedicated | Macintosh-Classic w/ hard disk, 4 mb Mac-LC 1,2,3, quadra performa | NEC Ultra-Lite, VERSA | IBMcompatible 386, 4 mb ram, 40 mb hard drive; w/color | Macintosh System 7 w/ 8 MB RAM and 80MB hard drive |
| Display | 12 × 9″ built-in touch panel mono-chrome | Microsoft Windows display mono/color | Mac display mono/color Supports ext. monitor | 10 inches diagonal mono | Mac display mono/color Supports ext. monitor | 9.5″ diagonal mono/color Supports ext. monitor | IBM compatible mono/color Supports ext. monitor | Mac display mono/color Supports ext. monitor |
| Language options | 8 languages 2000 Dynasyms; Dynawrite or both included | 4+ languages Any Windows bitmap or symbol set | English Mayer-Johnson, Dynasyms, COMPIC, etc. | English 2000 concept scenes, images, text | 9 languages Mayer-Johnson symbols/ Boardmaker Word processing | Runs IBM software Talking Screen (next column) EZ Keys (English) included | 5 languages Mayer-Johnson, Compic, Blissymbols PCX files | English Text based For use with Cowriter |
| Speech options | Built-in DECtalk; 15 secs recorded speech/ sound | Synthesizer included; recorded speech/ sound | MacinTalk II/ Pro; ext synthesizer recorded speech/ sound | Digitized built-in | MacinTalk Pro (or ext. synthesizer); recorded speech/ sound | VocaLite or Multivoice synthesizer; recorded speech/ sound | VocaLite or Multivoice synthesizer | MacinTalk II/ Pro; ext. synthesizer; recorded speech/ sound |

*continues*

**Table 5–3** continued

| *Features* | *Dynavox* | *Gus* | *Ke:nx* | *Lingraphica* | *Speaking Dynamically* | *System 2000 Versa* | *Talking Screen* | *Talk-About* |
|---|---|---|---|---|---|---|---|---|
| Other options | Printer, ECU | Printer, modem, CD | Printer | Printer | Printer, CD | Printer, ECU, CD, modem | Printer, ECU, CD | Printer |
| Physical access options | Includes touch screen, keyboard; supports all but optical pointer and eyegaze | Includes switch interface<br>Supports all except direct eyegaze | Supports all except direct eyegaze | Includes trackball, keyboard | Supports all except direct eyegaze | Includes touch-screen, switch interface, joystick, trackball<br>Supports all except eyegaze | Includes switch interface<br>Supports all except direct eyegaze | Supports all except direct eyegaze |

*Source:* Copyright © 1994, Augmentative Communication, Inc.

bols placed), access options (i.e., direct selection and scanning), language options (text and/or symbols), strategies available for accessing vocabulary (e.g., coding, levels, prediction), and portability (i.e., size and weight of the device). Features of voice output communication aids (VOCAs) that use recorded speech are summarized in Tables 5–4 and 5–5.

Although digitized speech is not likely to replace synthesized speech, particularly for those who need access to large vocabularies across multiple contexts, digitized speech devices offer an excellent way of accomplishing a variety of communication tasks: making emergency calls, making choices/requests, participating in choral activities, meeting/greeting, initiating interaction, telling jokes and stories, and relaying messages.

### Portability

An individual's age, weight, manual dexterity, ambulation skills, and ability to manage a device while walking determine a device's portability. Until recently, people who walked, but did not talk, had few options if they wanted to use a speech output device.

Table 5–6 gives examples of portable voice output devices that are now available. Some are text-based and have small keyboards. Users can select a limited number of stored messages for the device. Some devices allow people to use pictographic symbols. One such device is the Walker Talker, a computer and speaker worn around the waist; it delivers up to 60 recorded messages through a small 16-location touchpad.

## WHO CAN BENEFIT FROM COMMUNICATION DEVICES?

Anyone can benefit from communication devices. On a recent trip to Portugal, for example, my watch stopped. Being unable to speak or understand Portuguese and needing to buy a new battery for my watch, I prepared a communication display using an English-Portuguese dictionary. Writing words in Portuguese with English subtitles, I looked up words for "battery," "how much," "can you open it," "can you fix it," "thank you," and "please." In the shop, I pointed to the words on the display. It worked! The transaction was successful, efficient, and fun, even for the shopkeeper.

In contrast to this type of environmentally based communication impairment, there are various congenital and acquired causes of severe communication disorders. The most common congenital causes are mental retardation, cerebral palsy, autism, specific language disorders, and developmental apraxia of speech (Mirenda & Mathy-Laikko, 1989). Acquired impairments resulting in the need for augmentative communication assistance include amyotrophic lateral sclero-

**Table 5–4** Digitized Speech Devices Costing Less Than $500 US

| *Features* | *Cheap Talk 4 $69* | *Lynx $250* | *Say It Switch $40* | *Say It Rocking $50* | *Scan Mate 4 $385* | *Speak Easy $365* | *Switch Module 4 $45* | *Switch Mate 4 $360* | *Talk Back III $275* | *Voice Pal $424* | *Message Mate 20 $499+* |
|---|---|---|---|---|---|---|---|---|---|---|---|
| Output time | 20 sec | 16 sec | 20 sec | 20 sec | 16 sec | 2 min | 20 sec | 16 sec | 20 sec | 20 sec | 20 sec |
| Max # of messages | four | four | one | two | four | twelve | four | four | three | five | twenty |
| Time per message | 5 sec | 4 sec | 20 sec | 10 sec | 4 sec | 120 sec; recorded in sequence | 5 sec | 4 sec | 5, 10, 20 sec | 4 sec | variable |
| Message space | 2 × 2″ | knobs/ switches | 5 × 8″ | 4 × 12″ | ¾ × ⅞″ | ⅝″ | depends on switch | ¾ × ⅞″ | buttons/ switches | Any size taction pad | ¾ × ¾″ variable |
| Physical access options | Direct—touchpad | Direct–knob/ switch Scan—vis/aud | Direct—touchpad | Direct—rocking plate | Direct—touchpad Scan—visual | Direct—touchpad or 12 switches | Direct—four switches | Direct—touchpad 1 or 2 switches | Direct—buttons; 3 switches | Direct—taction pad | Direct—touchpad Scan—visual |

*Source:* Copyright © 1994, Augmentative Communication, Inc.

**Table 5–5** Digitized Speech Devices Costing More Than $500 US

| *Features* | *Alpha Talker* | *Dac* | *Digivox* | *Macaw* | *Parrot* | *Message Mate 20 or 40* | *Walker Talker* |
|---|---|---|---|---|---|---|---|
| Output time | 3–*25 minutes | 18–*72 minutes | 4.5–*35.5 minutes | 1–*8.5 minutes | 32–64 sec | 40 sec–*4 min | 1–*8 minutes |
| Max # of messages | variable | variable | variable | variable | 16 recorded in sequence | variable | variable |
| Time per message | variable | variable | variable | variable | variable | variable | variable |
| Message space | 32 locations 1″ + squares | 128 locations ¾″ or 1″ squares | 48 locations ¾″ + squares | 32 locations 1⅛″ + squares | 16 locations 7/16″ squares | 20 or 40 locations | 16 locations ¾″ squares |
| Physical access options | Direct—touchpad, *optical pointer, *remote switch box Scan—vis/aud | Direct—touchpad Scan—visual | Direct—touchpad Scan—visual | Direct—touchpad Scan—visual | Direct—touchpad & external switches | Direct—touchpad Scan-vis-20, vis/aud-40 | Direct—touchpad |
| LCD display | no | 16 characters | 16 characters | no | no | no | |
| Language access option | Minspeak, icon prediction | Levels 1–4 coding | Levels 1–4 coding/sequencing | Levels coding | no | no | no Minspeak |
| Language options | symbol, word, computer emulation | symbol, word, limited vocabulary spelling | symbol, word | symbol, word | symbol, word | symbol, word | symbol, word |
| Storage on disk | yes | yes | *yes | no | no | no | no |
| Carrying case | *yes | *yes | *yes | *yes, strap on unit | *yes, strap on unit | *yes | yes |
| Weight | 2.2 lbs. | 8.5 lbs. | 3.8 lbs. | 2.7 lbs. | 13 oz. | 1.5 and 1.8 lbs. | 1.8 lbs. |

** = Additional cost.*

*Source:* Copyright © 1994, Augmentative Communication, Inc.

**Table 5–6** Portable Devices (Less Than 3 lbs/1360 gms)

| Devices | Approximate Weight | Speech |
|---|---|---|
| **TEXT** | | |
| Canon | 18.5 oz. | |
| Crestalk | 9.0 oz. | |
| Finger Foniks | 12.2 oz. | |
| Franklin | 2.7 lbs. | All use synthesized speech |
| Lightwriter | 1.8 lbs. | |
| Say It All | 2.3 lbs. | |
| Secretary | 2.0 lbs. | |
| **SYMBOLS** | | |
| Alph Talker | 2.8 lbs. | |
| Digivox | 2.1 lbs. | All use digitalized/recorded speech |
| Macaw | 2.7 lbs. | |
| Message Mates | 1.8 lbs. | |
| Parrot | 13.0 oz. | |
| Walker Talker | 2.0 lbs. | |

*Source:* Copyright © 1994, Augmentative Communication, Inc.

sis, multiple sclerosis, traumatic brain injury, stroke, and spinal cord injury (Beukelman & Yorkston, 1989). Persons with congenital and acquired conditions that interfere with the production of intelligible speech face a lifelong struggle with the communication process. Typically, the muscles involved in speech production do not function well, if at all, because of brain damage. Some individuals have dysarthria (i.e., some degree of muscle paralysis). Others have dyspraxia (i.e., lack of muscle coordination). Language-based and cognitive difficulties often underlie severe speech impairments.

In the United States, approximately 0.8 percent of the population is unable to speak. An additional, unknown number of individuals have severe writing and/or gestural impairments. Although persons with severe communication disorders represent less than 1 percent of the general population, even this small percentage translates into millions of individuals worldwide (Beukelman & Mirenda, 1992).

People who can benefit from augmentative communication techniques and strategies come from all age groups, all socioeconomic groups, and all ethnic and racial backgrounds. The American Speech-Language-Hearing Association defines these individuals as follows:

> Individuals with severe communication disorders are those who may benefit from AAC—those for whom gestural, speech and/or written communication is temporarily or permanently inadequate to meet all of their communication needs. For these individuals, hearing impair-

ment is not the primary cause for the communication impairment. Although some of these individuals may be able to produce a limited amount of speech, it is inadequate to meet their varied communication needs. (1981, p. 578)

## WHAT IS THE BEST WAY TO SELECT APPROPRIATE DEVICES?

One common misconception is that the purpose of an augmentative and alternate communication (AAC) assessment is to answer the question, What device should I buy? It is not. While equipment recommendations are appropriately embedded in the AAC assessment process, they are rarely the sole focus of the assessment. There are many reasons. A community team may ask an augmentative communication team to address specific questions (e.g., best means to access a specific device), for example. An individual who is computer literate and cognitively intact may request a device recommendation only. People with amyotrophic lateral sclerosis sometimes approach AAC assessment in this manner.

It is sometimes argued that the only prerequisite skill for communication is consciousness (Mirenda & Mathy-Laikko, 1989), although there are certainly prerequisite skills for using specific communication devices, attaching meaning to graphic symbol sets, pointing to letters to spell words, hitting a switch to select scanned messages, and so on. The fact that people *can* use a device does not mean they *will* use it to communicate, however. Psychosocial and cultural variables heavily influence a person's use of assistive technology. Acceptance of the device by the person's family or peer group often underlies success.

The challenge is to create assistive technology teams that are consumer-responsive (Blackstone, 1992). Professionals can no longer be "evaluators" of people and "prescribers" of equipment. They must be collaborators, helping to guide the consumer in an important decision-making process. Selecting technology entails matching a person's needs, communication abilities, and temperament to features of available equipment and then orienting the person and his or her family to the realities and situations of device use (Scherer, 1991a). Assistive technology, in general, and augmentative communication devices, in particular, are rapidly expanding and changing. This challenges AAC consumers, professionals, and third-party payers.

Developed by Scherer (1991b), the Matching Person and Technology (MPT) Model aims to help consumers, families, and professionals make informed technology decisions. Table 5–7 illustrates three major factors that influence the use of technology.

Based on the MPT Model, Scherer and her colleagues developed three clinical/research instruments: Survey of Technology Use (SOTU), Assistive Technology Device Predisposition Assessment (ATD PA), and the Educational Technology Predisposition Assessment (ETD PA). These tools are designed to

**Table 5–7** Factors Influencing Consumer Use of Assistive Technology

| | | *Milieu* | *Person* | *Technology* |
|---|---|---|---|---|
| USE | Optimal | | | |
| | Partial/Reluctant | | | |
| NONUSE | Avoidance | | | |
| | Abandonment | | | |

*Note:* Milieu: characteristics of the environment and psychosocial setting in which the device is used. Person: pertinent features of the individual's personality and temperament. Technology: salient characteristics of the equipment.

(1) identify the people who are likely to use technology, (2) help determine the appropriate training strategies in certain situations, (3) provide a rationale for funding for device and training, and (4) demonstrate improvement in functioning over time. Each has a consumer and a professional version to help consumers, professionals, and educators consider all relevant influences.

Information is the key to consumer participation in any decision-making process. Grady, Kovach, Lange, and Shannon (1991) suggested the following guidelines to enhance consumer participation:

- Give information about all the devices that interest the family, including mobility, computers, communication, environmental controls, adapted toys.
- Provide information on resources, and help address other factors, such as training options, vendors, funding sources, books, publications.
- Prepare information in multiple forms to accommodate a variety of learning styles: hands-on experience, demonstrations, loans/trial use, training, pictures, written (binders with product brochures, handouts, lists), and computer printouts. Let consumers take home written information and pictures of devices.
- Organize information in logical ways. Build a foundation of general knowledge on which to base an understanding of individual devices.
- Present a separate "pyramid of information" on each device so consumers can understand the relationships between various devices and learn how devices can be used together (Exhibit 5–1).

**Exhibit 5–1** Information Pyramid

| |
|---|
| Provide General Technical Information "This is a computer" |
| Categorize Technical Information "This is an alternative keyboard" |
| Label Assistive Technology Device "This is the Unicorn Keyboard" |
| Explain how device is used "This is designed for larger movement" |
| Describe Applications "You can operate an educational program with this overlay" |
| Explore specific user applications "You can use this device for . . ." |

*Source:* Copyright © 1991, Augmentative Communication, Inc.

Figure 5–1 illustrates a clinical management process, adapted from an engineering design process model that is useful in selecting equipment (Blackstone, 1988). The process is somewhat analogous to shopping. For example, a young woman who is going to a party "needs" a new shirt. Her *goal* is to get just the right shirt. She need not go to every store in town, trying on every shirt, because she has already done a great deal of *research* (e.g., size, favorite color, stores with merchandise in her price range, places she will be likely to wear the shirt, weather conditions). In fact, she is unlikely to leave home or try on a single shirt without first considering a long list of *specifications*. Chances are she has even prioritized her specifications. She may consider it essential that the shirt go with her favorite pair of pants and have long sleeves, for example, but be willing to compromise on the fabric. At the store, the young woman looks around and *conceptualizes* which shirts might fit her specification list. With the help of a good salesperson (expert), she eventually selects a few shirts to try on. Then, she starts *analyzing the facts*. Does it fit? Look attractive? Feel good? Finally, she decides on one, her *solution*. She takes it to the clerk and *procures* (buys) it.

The decision-making process for assistive technology is similar. Unfortunately, many teams omit one absolutely critical step, listing and prioritizing *specifications*. Specifications begin with the word *must:**

- Must be acceptable to individual and family
- Must provide an efficient way to engage in conversational exchanges
- Must allow him or her to create, store and retrieve messages, produce written work and access computers
- Must permit him or her to access keyboard using index finger on left hand

* specifications list, copyright © 1994, Augmentative Communications, Inc.

- Must allow for elbow to be supported and movement excursion of 5 inches
- Must be elevated 2 inches on his tray and mounted at approximately a 30 degree angle
- Must permit use of a single switch/joy stick for leisure activities & computer assisted instruction
- Must cost less than . . .
- Must have symbol configuration that permits easy access to frequently used phrases
- Training must be available to learn mechanics of operation
- Training in class and community must be available for at least one year. (Blackstone, 1992a, pp. 4–5)

After generating a list of specifications, team members can begin to consider which devices can fulfill the requirements. From a shortened list, two or three devices may be selected for a trial period. The data obtained from these trials are the basis for a device recommendation.

## HOW GOOD ARE PROFESSIONAL RECOMMENDATIONS?

Studies on the abandonment of technology and the personal experiences of augmentative communication team members have made many professionals reluctant to recommend purchasing a communication device until after the person with a disability has had an opportunity to use the device in everyday life. Along

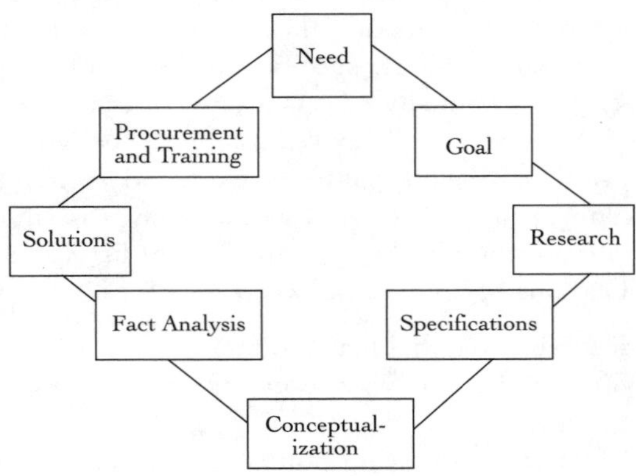


**Figure 5–1** Clinical management model. *Source:* Copyright © 1988, Augmentative Communication, Inc.

a continuum from optimal use to abandonment, a person may be an optimal user of the technology itself, but a reluctant user of the technology in some milieus. Or, a user who has more than one device may be an optimal user of one device, but avoid using a second device (Scherer, 1991a).

Many AAC manufacturers rent devices to potential buyers. Equipment loan programs are another option. From 1987 to 1992, the Los Angeles Unified School District, the second largest in the United States, purchased more than 250 AAC devices for students. Many devices were abandoned or were not used to the fullest extent possible. Among the reasons identified were the following:

- Technology selections were often based on what professionals believed was correct. The consumer and family were expected simply to agree.
- Equipment was selected according to the clinician's familiarity or preference.
- Little attention was paid to the psychological and social aspects of assistive device selection and use (Cottier, 1993).

In a retrospective study of 76 students for whom devices were recommended during the 1991 and 1992 school years, Cottier (1993) investigated the impact of a device loan program. An augmentative communication team had matched each student's capabilities and needs to the features of devices and made a recommendation. The devices considered most appropriate were then loaned to students for approximately 2 months, with the augmentative communication team providing consultative support. In addition to this consultative support, more than half (42) of the students had one-on-one instructional assistants. Seventy received speech therapy at school, and 25 had private speech therapy. Students ranged in age from 5 to 22 years and attended both regular education (N = 49) and special education (N = 27) campuses. Disabling conditions included cerebral palsy, autism, mental retardation, severe language impairment (aphasia), and multiple handicaps.

Cottier (1993) found that 20 different AAC devices were ultimately purchased from 10 different manufacturers. Fewer than one-third (24/76) of the devices originally recommended by the augmentative communication team were subsequently purchased for the students (Table 5–8). An additional 34 devices were purchased after students had tried 2 to 5 devices through the loan program. For 18 students, no device was bought. Closer examination of these data reveals that the team's original recommendations were more likely to be successful with younger students. For example, the originally recommended devices were purchased for 63 percent of elementary school children, but only for 15 percent of middle school and 0 percent of high school students. Devices not originally recommended by the augmentative communication team were purchased for 56 percent of the high school, 62 percent of the middle school,

**Table 5–8** Devices Purchased by Age/Grade Level

| *Devices Purchased for Students* | *Elem = 32 (5 yrs–13 yrs)* | *Middle Sch. = 26 (12 yrs–15 yrs)* | *High Sch. = 18 (15 yrs–22 yrs)* |
|---|---|---|---|
| Original device N = 24 | 20 (63%) | 4 (15%) | 0 (0%) |
| Different device N = 34 | 8 (25%) | 16 (62%) | 10 (56%) |
| No device N = 18 | 4 (12%) | 6 (23%) | 8 (44%) |

*Source:* Blackstone, S. (1994). Equipment loan programs: A rationale. *Augmentative Communication News, 7* (1):4.

and 25 percent of the elementary school students. Cottier concluded that, during the assessment and selection process, professionals may need to pay more attention to determining

- if the student is *willing* to use a device, not just *able* to use it.
- what the student and parental interest, motivation, and attitude are toward the device.
- what the student and family priorities are. For example, high school students were focused on academics, not communication. Many wanted writing systems only.
- how strong a student's support system is.

## EVALUATION OF AUGMENTATIVE COMMUNICATION DEVICES

Developments in computer technology have brought an explosion of assistive technology products, making it increasingly difficult to choose from among the many available. More than 1,000 new assistive technology products are introduced every year. The shelf life of assistive technology is approximately 3 years, and assistive technology centers may spend $10,000 per year on the purchase of new equipment and maintenance of old equipment (Blackstone, 1992b). Table 5–9 displays the expenditures of the government of Ontario, Canada, for some assistive devices. The average cost per person was higher for a communication device than for seating or hearing devices. During 1989 to 1990, however, the Canadian Ministry of Health through the Centralized Equipment Pool Project administered through the Hugh MacMillan Rehabilitation Center Augmentative Communication Service noted that augmentative communication devices represented only 1.7 percent of the total money spent ($77.7 million Canadian) (Blackstone, 1992c,d).

With so much money spent on assistive technology, payers might be expected to conduct formal performance evaluations of AAC devices. Sweden and England require the testing of devices before government programs can fund

**Table 5–9** Assistive Technology in Ontario (1989–1990)

| *Assistive Technology* | *AC Devices* | *Seating Devices* | *Hearing Devices* |
|---|---|---|---|
| Total cost in millions | $1.4 | $28.9 | $19.1 |
| # of people benefiting | 861 | 30,000 | 52,000 |
| Average cost per person | $1626 | $963 | $367 |

*Note:* AC, augmentative communication.



them. Likewise, in Ontario, Canada, the Ministry of Health requires the evaluation of augmentative communication devices before allowing them to be placed in the loan program or purchased for individual users. In the United States, the Assistive Device Center in Pennsylvania has collected data about the performance, maintenance, and use of equipment. They purchased approximately 1,000 devices in 1992 for the students' use. Of these, 822 were in the field with students. In addition, they had 2,000 pieces of equipment available for short-term loan. Unfortunately, because of legal considerations, available data on device performance are rarely shared beyond the fact that augmentative communication devices require very few repairs and, in general, receive good support from manufacturers.

It is very difficult to evaluate the available augmentative communication products or to compare the performance of similar products. A wheelchair's function is obvious, but communication is a more complicated process. By definition then, assistive technologies involved in enhancing communication options are complex and the effectiveness of a device often depends on variables that have little to do with the equipment. Nevertheless, basic principles apply to the evaluation of all assistive devices. For example, both an engineering analysis and a clinical analysis are needed. Engineering considerations address such issues as whether the device is safe, whether it does what its manufacturer says it does, and whether it meets the established standard, if available, for the device category. Clinical considerations take into account the device's ease of use, the user's experience with the device, the way in which it is used, and any published reports or interviews with users.

Equipment evaluations need to be rigorous, as objective as possible, and carried out by experts who adhere to a well-established protocol. Although consumers must be the ultimate evaluators of whether a device is, or is not, satisfactory (Williams, 1992), consumer-based evaluations remain infrequent. Information on the performance of AAC devices and a critical comparison of those with similar purposes should eventually be available to consumers, practitioners, the manufacturers, and third-party payers.

## SERVICE DELIVERY OUTCOMES

The outcomes of augmentative communication services and devices are of concern not only to consumers, but also to third-party payers, professionals, administrators of programs, and manufacturers. Many augmentative communication teams that deliver assistive technology services work in rehabilitation or university-based centers. These center-based programs offer a broad range of assistive technology services (e.g., seating, access, communication, environmental control, mobility), but they are costly to maintain. Moreover, follow-up has been difficult. Over the past decade, an increasing number of augmentative communication professionals have begun to work in the communities where people live, work, and have fun. Their hope is to improve the communication outcomes of people who use augmentative communication devices.

One outcome of a community-based approach to service delivery is an increased awareness of the need to be creative in obtaining access to equipment. Strategies to provide equipment at a reasonable cost are critical. One concept currently being considered is equipment pooling. The idea is to keep track of equipment already purchased in a community and to determine whether that equipment is available before buying duplicates. The extent to which equipment pools are likely to contain costs remains unclear, however.

## CONCLUSION

Toddlers and preschoolers, school-aged children, adolescents, young adults, middle-aged and older adults—all may experience severe difficulties communicating for a variety of reasons. At each stage of life, however, the isolation and lack of control that accompanies a severe communication disability is devastating to the individual and to those who share the person's life.

Janet is in her 30s. She was born with cerebral palsy and has very minimal control of her body, except that she can hit a switch with her head. Her possession of a communication device, a computer, and an electric wheelchair has allowed her to plan to move into her own apartment with an attendant and to go to a local community college. She actively uses her modem to access a local Bulletin Board and is exploring ways to get on the Internet. When Janet graduated from high school at the age of 21 years, she was unable to read or write independently, but she could spell simple words using a nonelectronic eyegaze system called an ETRAN. With word prediction communication software and tutoring at college, she developed literacy skills. She recently had a paper accepted for presentation at an international conference. Communication technology has helped her interact with her family and friends and has built a bridge for her to literacy and an adulthood in which she herself can define the direction of her life.

This chapter explores the options that are available for people like Janet, Norm, and Joey. Further, it seeks to reinforce the notion that it is people, as well as technology, that can expand the options for individuals with severe communication difficulties.

---

**REFERENCES**

American Speech-Language-Hearing Association. (1981). Position statement on nonspeech communication. *ASHA, 23*, 577–581.

Barker, P., & Henderson, J. (1994, March). *Auditory scanning device characteristics*. Paper presented at the CSUN Technology and Persons with Disabilities Conference, Los Angeles, CA.

Beukelman, D., Garrett, K., Lange, U., & Tice, R. (1988). *Cue-Write: Word processing with spelling assistance and practice manual*. Tucson: Communication Skill Builders.

Beukelman, D, & Mirenda, P. (1992). *Augmentative and alternative communication: Management of severe communication disorders in children and adults*. Baltimore: Paul H. Brookes.

Beukelman, D., & Yorkston, K. (1989). Augmentative and alternative communication applications for persons with severe acquired communication disorders: An introduction. *Augmentative and Alternative Communication, 5*(1), 42–48.

Blackstone, S. (1988). Augmentative communication: A clinical management process model. In L.E. Bernstein (Ed.), *The vocally impaired: Clinical practice and research* (pp. 136–166). Philadelphia: Grune & Stratton.

Blackstone, S. (1991). Equipment: Did you know that . . . ? *Augmentative Communication News, 4*(6), 6.

Blackstone, S. (1992a). The selection process: Ideas and strategies. *Augmentative Communication News, 5*(3), 4–5.

Blackstone, S. (1992b). Rethinking the basics. *Augmentative Communication News, 5*(3), 1–3.

Blackstone, S. (1992c). Decreasing the likelihood devices and people are abandoned. *Augmentative Communication News, 5*(3), 6.

Blackstone, S. (1992d). Product evaluations. *Augmentative Communication News, 5*(3), 5–6.

Blackstone, S. (1994). Equipment loan programs: A rationale. *Augmentative Communication News, 7*(1), 4.

Center for Applied Science and Engineering in Rehabilitation. (1996, in press). The *Chart of Augmentative and Alternative Communication Services* (revised). Applied Science and Engineering Labs, University of Delaware, A.I. duPont Institute, 1600 Rockland Rd., Wilmington, DE 19803.

Cottier, C.A. (1993, November). *How good is our first guess*? Miniseminar presented at the American Speech-Language-Hearing Association Convention, Anaheim, California.

Foulds, E. (1987). Guest editorial. *Augmentative and Alternative Communication, 3*, 169.

Goldman-Eisler, E. (1986). *Cycle linguistics: Experiments in spontaneous speech*. New York: Academic Press.

Grady, A., Kovach, T., Lange, M., & Shannon, I. (1991). Promoting choice in the selection of assistive technology devices. *Proceedings of the 6th Annual Technology and Persons with Disabilities*, Los Angeles, 315–324.

Light, J. (1988). Interaction involving individuals using AAC systems: State of the art and future directions. *Augmentative and Alternative Communication, 4*, 76.

Mirenda, P., & Mathy-Laikko, P. (1989). Augmentative and alternative communication applications for persons with severe congenital communication disorders: An introduction. *Augmentative and Alternative Communication, 5*(1), 3–13.

Scherer, M. (1991a). Assistive technology use, avoidance and abandonment: What we know so far. *Proceeding of the 6th Annual Technology and Persons with Disabilities*, Los Angeles, 815–826.

Scherer, M. (1991b). *The Scherer MPT Model: Matching people with technologies*. Webster, NY: Scherer Associates.

Vanderheiden, G., & Lloyd, L. (1986). Communication systems and their components. In S. Blackstone (Ed.), *Augmentative communication: An introduction*. Rockville, MD: American Speech-Language-Hearing Association.

Williams, M. (1992). Strategies that result in integrating AAC users into the community: Education, work and other aspects of community function. *Consensus Validation Conference, Resource Papers: Augmentative and Alternative Communication Intervention*. Washington, DC: The National Institute for Disability and Rehabilitation Research.

## *Chapter 6*

# Assistive Devices for People Who Are Blind or Have Visual Impairments

*Jay D. Leventhal*

In the book, *Visual Impairment: An Overview* (Bailey & Hall, 1990) published by the American Foundation for the Blind, the following characteristics of vision loss are provided:

> *Low vision refers to a vision loss that is severe enough to impede performance of everyday tasks but still allows some useful visual discrimination. Low vision cannot be corrected to normal by regular eyeglasses or contact lenses. It may be the result of eye disease, trauma, diseases affecting visual pathways in the brain, or changes associated with aging. Congenital low vision may result from abnormal development of the visual system or from disease or trauma in very early infancy. Low vision covers a range from mild to severe vision loss but excludes full loss of functional vision; the majority of persons who are legally blind are included within the low vision classification.*
>
> *Visual impairment technically encompasses all degrees of vision loss, including total blindness, that affect a person's ability to perform the usual tasks of daily life. Since the term "visual impairment" may not always connote total blindness to the general reader, the collective phrase "blindness and visual impairment" is often used to refer to the full range of vision loss. . . .*
>
> *Over 70% of visually impaired people in the United States are over age 65. Consequently, the most common causes of low vision are diseases or conditions that are strongly associated with aging, such as age-related maculopathy, cataract, diabetic retinopathy, glaucoma, and vascular retinopathy. Dry-eye syndromes also increase in frequency with age. Visual impairment early in life is most often associated with inherited congenital disorders, abnormal fetal development, and problems associated with premature birth. In addition, some diseases, such as rubella, can cause vision*

*loss and other damage to the fetus if contracted during pregnancy, particularly in the first trimester. . . .*

*Even though medical intervention cannot restore normal eyesight to people with low vision, other forms of assistance, such as optical devices and adaptive techniques, can help promote the effective performance of necessary tasks.*

*People and their life situations are different, and the way in which vision loss affects an individual depends on his or her unique circumstances.*

*People with visual impairments are found in a great variety of jobs and are capable of the most exacting work tasks and demands.* (pps. 2,15,18)

## INFORMATION ACCESS AND TRAVEL

Products for people who are blind or visually impaired are designed primarily to provide access to information or to ensure safe travel. Access to information may mean determining the time on a watch, identifying money, reading today's mail, reviewing text on a computer screen, differentiating between black and white chess pieces, or preparing dinner without being burned. The information may be transmitted in tactile form, as synthetic or digitized speech, or through the use of some sort of visual enhancement such as optical or electronic magnification. People who are visually impaired typically have sufficient residual vision to permit them to perform most of their daily activities with the assistance of optical aids. These include magnifying glasses for identification of print or other small items that can be viewed up close and either monoculars or binoculars for viewing distant signs or objects.

For people with low vision, increased illumination is frequently essential to their use of residual vision. Small tensor lamps placed near printed text, for example, can improve reading. Large, bright lights that illuminate large areas can be detrimental; not only do they commonly produce enough heat to be both uncomfortable and potentially dangerous, but also they tend to create a widespread glare. It is necessary to minimize the effects of glare from reflective surfaces, because people with low vision often need far more time to recover from the effects of glare than does someone with normal vision. It is also usually very helpful to provide a high visual contrast between materials to be read or manipulated and their background. Either environmental adaptation or optical filters can help to provide the desired visual contrast. Safe travel means being able to get from point A to point B independently without being injured. Almost all people who are blind accomplish this through the use of a long cane or a guide dog.

Twenty years ago, a person who was blind wrote braille on a manual braille writer—a machine with six keys representing the six dots in a braille cell and a spacebar—or one dot at a time on a metal slate with a stylus. Any document intended to be read by a sighted person had to be typed on an inkprint typewriter or dictated onto tape. Only those books and magazines produced in braille or recorded by the Library of Congress' National Library Service for the Blind and Physically Handicapped (NLS) or other agencies, or read by human readers were accessible to people with a visual impairment.

Computer technology has drastically changed the lives of people of all ages who are blind or visually impaired (Scadden, 1991). They can now use a standard computer word processing program to produce, edit, and print out a document for a sighted person to read. They can read books and magazines using optical character recognition systems (OCRs.) As a result, information is infinitely more accessible to them today, and it is much more available as a tool for education, employment, and recreation.

According to Iris Torres, coordinator of the Vision Resource Center of the New York City Board of Education, blind and visually impaired students use assistive technology in classrooms and in resource rooms. They take examinations on braille notetakers and print their answers out for their teachers. Handouts are provided in braille. Large print is produced by means of the enlargement feature of copying machines. High school students take courses in assistive technology at Baruch College in New York during their winter break and use what they learn to function in computer laboratories alongside sighted students.

## TYPES OF ASSISTIVE TECHNOLOGY

### Synthetic Speech

Synthetic speech systems have two parts: a speech synthesizer (i.e., a box attached to a computer port or a card installed in the computer) and a speech program loaded in the computer's memory. The synthesizer's programming includes all the phonemes and grammatical rules of a language so that it can pronounce words correctly. The speech program instructs the synthesizer to read a line, say a word, or spell a word. The user issues these commands by pressing different combinations of keys on the keyboard. Synthetic speech systems can cost from $150 to $1,500.

### Screen Magnification Software

Some computer programs enlarge print on the monitor's screen, enabling the user to review a document with the text magnified to a comfortable size and with the colors of the screen adjusted for best contrast. The user can view any part of the screen by scrolling up, down, or across. Screen magnification software ranges in cost from $80 to $600.

## Closed Circuit Television Systems

The magnification of printed material by a closed circuit television system allows the user with a visual impairment to read books, magazines, newspapers, handwriting, labels on bottles and cans, and so on. These systems are available in desktop models, for which the reading material is placed on a table that moves freely under the screen, or in portable models with hand-held cameras that let the user magnify everything from a telephone keypad or a card in an address file to books or magazines. Closed circuit television systems that can be connected to a regular television set cost less than $1,000. Full-featured systems are in the $2,400 to $3,400 range.

## Braille Technology

### *Braille Printers*

Generally slower and much noisier than print printers, braille printers use pins driven by solenoids to emboss braille dots on a page. Braille printers range in price from $1,700 for a 10 characters per second unit designed mainly for home or light office use, to $10,000 to $20,000 for heavy office or production units, to $80,000 for units used in publishing houses.

### *Refreshable Braille Displays*

A refreshable braille display is a separate device that displays 20, 40, or 80 characters of the text. The display attaches to one of the computer's ports. The braille letters are formed by sets of pins being raised and lowered electromechanically. These displays are refreshable, meaning that they allow the information displayed to change as the user moves the display window around the screen. Each refreshable braille cell (for the display of one character) currently costs approximately $70 to build. Because of this cost, in addition to the other costs (e.g., research and development, other materials, and marketing), a 40-character braille display costs $5,000 to $6,000, and an 80-character display costs $12,000 to $13,000. The extremely high price of braille displays for people with a visual impairment, the equivalent of a sighted person paying $5,000 for a 40-character monitor, forces many people who would prefer braille access to use synthetic speech instead (Figure 6–1).

### *Braille Notetakers*

Small, battery-operated devices, braille notetakers are designed mainly for storing information such as telephone numbers and addresses, and for writing short documents. They do not have the capacity necessary for full-blown data-

**Figure 6–1** Alva braille terminal, distributed by HumanWare. This device shows the user the text displayed on the computer screen in braille.

---

bases, spreadsheets, or other applications. The user enters information on a braille keyboard and reviews the information through the use of synthetic speech or a braille display. Because braille notetakers are about the size of a paperback book, they are extremely portable; they are ideal for use in meetings, classrooms, or while traveling. The information stored in memory can be saved to computer disk or printed when the user returns home or to the office. These devices range in price from approximately $1,000 to approximately $4,000 (Figure 6–2).

### *Optical Character Recognition Systems*

Today, many people who are blind or visually impaired have direct access to printed text through optical character recognition (OCR) systems that scan printed or typed documents automatically and display the text rapidly in either synthetic speech or braille. These individuals had direct access to print for several years before OCR systems were introduced into the marketplace, however. The Optacon (Optical to Tactile Conversion) centers around a small camera the size of a jackknife that the user moves manually across a line of print with one hand. The index finger of the other hand rests on a two-dimensional array of vibrating pins that displays an accurate facsimile of each image viewed by the camera. Although even dedicated Optacon users rarely achieve reading speeds

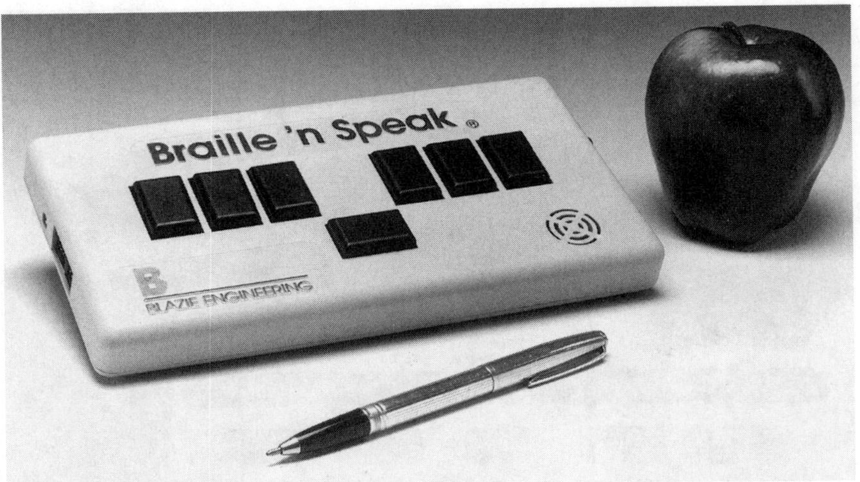


**Figure 6–2** Blazie Engineering's Braille 'n Speak, the most popular braille notetaker.

of more than 50 words per minute, the portability of the unit (the size of a print book) allows users access to printed material wherever they take the device.

An OCR system has three parts: (1) a scanner that uses a camera to take a picture of the printed page, (2) the recognition software that converts the picture into text, and (3) the speech synthesizer that speaks the text. Manufacturers package these three components and provide a spoken menu for the system.

Users have two options when purchasing an OCR system. Stand-alone systems are preferable for people who are not computer users, since their operation requires a minimum of computer knowledge. Computer-based systems require not only computer literacy, but also a synthesizer to read scanned text.

OCR systems are prime examples of ways that generally available components can be combined to produce a system that benefits people who are blind. Raymond Kurzweil developed the first OCR system in the mid-1970s. It was approximately 3 feet high, 2 feet wide, and 2 feet deep, and it cost $50,000. After undergoing significant refinements, a later generation of this OCR reading machine, the Kurzweil Personal Reader, appeared in 1987. This model was a table-top machine that did a far better job of text recognition, was much smaller, and cost $12,000. The current stand-alone model, the Reading Edge, is even smaller—6 inches high by 18 inches by 20 inches—and does a still better job of text recognition and costs approximately $5,000. Personal computer-based versions cost approximately $1,500 (Figure 6–3).

Computers also should be considered "reading machines," because when they are equipped with speech synthesizers or refreshable braille displays,

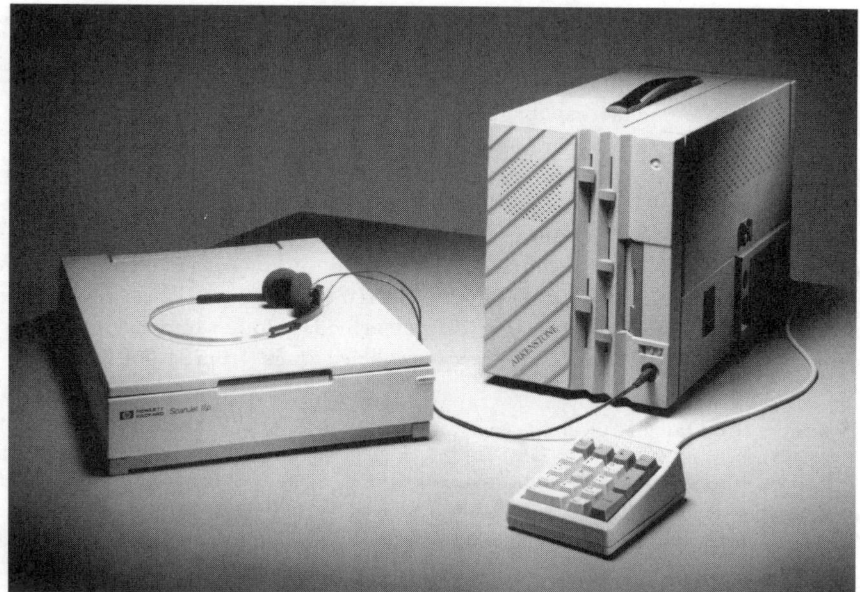

**Figure 6–3** An Open Book is a stand-alone optical character recognition system manufactured by Arkenstone, Inc. of Sunnyvale, CA.

---

people who are blind can read many documents available on computer disks or accessible through the Internet and the World Wide Web.

### Travel Aids

The two main travel aids used by people who are blind or visually impaired are long canes and guide dogs. Cane users swing their cane back and forth in an arc in front of them while walking. The cane alerts them to obstructions, steps, changes in the terrain, and so on.

Guide dogs are trained to lead their owners around objects and to respond to commands, including "forward," "left," "right," and "inside." They provide their owners with a trained pair of eyes, a tool that the owners can use to navigate safely through both urban and rural areas. Guide dogs can also provide some judgment, based on their training, and "disobey" commands that may expose their owner to danger.

There are about 15 schools in the United States that train guide dogs and their owners. Each potential guide dog user must apply to a school and show that he or she has a sound reason for getting a guide dog. Emily Biegel, director of Program Services for the Guide Dog Foundation in Smithtown, New York pointed out that owning a guide dog is a responsibility. The potential user "should have some acquaintance with dogs, as well as independent travel skills." There are also financial responsibilities, such as feeding and veterinary care.

Over the years, several electronic travel devices have been introduced to improve the quality of travel for people who are blind or visually impaired. The Laser Cane from Nurion, Inc. of Paoli, Pennsylvania, for example, emits sounds and vibrations to alert the user to obstructions and drop-offs in advance of cane contact. Other devices emit ultrasound waves, and the user listens through an earphone or a speaker to detect echoes reflected by obstacles. These devices are not used extensively, because they do not provide enough improvement over canes and guide dogs to justify their expensive price tags (from $1,000 to $3,000).

**Products for Daily Living**

People who are blind or visually impaired often need to adapt appliances and other items used in the activities of daily living. Many of these adaptations are "low-technology." For example, braille or large print labels can be placed on the control panels of appliances to assist in their operation. Some commercial appliances and products are available with such adaptations. Other specialized products are available from agencies for the blind and mail order houses.

Many products that are useful to all people, but especially to those who are blind or visually impaired, are available with computer chips that provide digitized human speech output. Clocks, calculators, and scales, for example, may have speech output. Over the past 10 years, general market manufacturers such as Sharp and Panasonic have introduced products that use digitized speech. Most of these products were produced as novelty items for the general public, but they quickly became necessities for people who are blind. Suddenly, a student who could not see well enough to read a digital display could use a calculator in math class. Moreover, these products were available in electronics stores at discount prices.

Unfortunately, the novelty of these products wore off quickly for the general public, and many of them disappeared from the market. There has been enough demand from people who are blind for talking clocks and calculators to keep them available through specialized mail order houses, but those who own talking videocassette recorders or talking clock radios take particularly good care of them because these appliances are no longer manufactured.

Several home medical aids with digitized speech output have been developed, although they are not yet widely available. With the growing number of older people who are blind and visually impaired, there is likely to be an increased demand for such products. Three of the most important are thermometers, blood pressure monitors, and blood sugar analyzers used by people who are diabetic.

## IMPACT OF ASSISTIVE TECHNOLOGY ON EMPLOYMENT

Assistive technology has changed the way people who are blind or visually impaired do their jobs and opened new fields of employment to them. Before the proliferation of assistive technology during the past 5 years, people who were blind typically needed someone to help them read mail, memos, and journals. They used a tape recorder or braille writer to dictate or write correspondence. People with some vision used magnifiers for reading and felt-tip pens for writing.

Now these job tasks are accomplished much more quickly and efficiently through the use of synthetic speech, electronic magnification, OCR systems, and braille technology. Mail can be scanned and sorted with the help of an OCR system, and only selected items are saved for a human reader. Large documents can be scanned and read when needed. Documents can be written on a computer, which has the additional advantages of endless opportunities for revision and access to a dictionary and thesaurus (Figure 6–4).

New job possibilities have opened up for people who are blind or visually

**Figure 6–4** The Language Master SE, a device that adds synthetic speech to a hand-held dictionary and thesaurus. From Franklin Electronic Publishers of Mount Holly, NJ

impaired because of assistive technology. Computer programming is a striking example. The American Foundation for the Blind maintains a database called the Careers and Technology Information Bank (CTIB). The CTIB contains information about the jobs held by and technology used by more than 1,700 people who are blind or visually impaired nationwide. Of the people in the CTIB, 75 percent are employed. (Unfortunately, the opposite is true of the entire population of working age people who are blind or visually impaired; 70 percent are not employed.) More than 100 of the employed people in the CTIB are computer programmers. Clearly, assistive technology has made a job that was uncommon among people who were blind or visually impaired 10 years ago much more common today. Computer programmer has joined rehabilitation counselor, attorney, and professor as one of the most common job titles for people in the CTIB.

A significant number of people who are blind or visually impaired and who have been unable to find full-time employment have used assistive technology to start their own businesses. Some of the 92 home-based businesses listed in the CTIB include braille transcription, computer consulting, real estate, recording studio, and travel agent.

## EVALUATION OF ASSISTIVE TECHNOLOGY

A number of questions must be asked and answered before the purchase of an assistive technology device. Some of these are general, while others are specific to the type of product being considered.

### General Questions

What will the product be used for? The consumer should be able to answer this question before investing in expensive technologies. A computer has many potential uses, for example, and the user can accomplish some intended tasks more efficiently on specific systems or without using a computer at all. If a visually impaired college graduate is going into a career in publishing or music composition, a Macintosh computer with inLARGE, a screen magnification program from Berkeley Systems of Berkeley, California, provides access to the most commonly used programs in those fields. An engineer needs a faster, more powerful computer, however.

Is the product's documentation easy to understand and use? Is it available in accessible formats? Many assistive technology products are shipped from companies that are thousands of miles away, and the users must then set up and learn to use the products. The best, most accurate OCR system or the most powerful closed circuit television system is of little use if the user cannot get it up and running.

A surprising number of manufacturers do not provide braille documentation for assistive technology products. They note that braille is expensive to produce and that many people who are blind do not read braille. Searching for information on a cassette tape can be very time-consuming and frustrating, however. Furthermore, documentation on disk can present an interesting paradox; a new user of a synthetic speech program must know how to install that program and learn its basic commands before being able to read a text file, but will be unable to read the instructions if they are only on disk. Braille documentation should be available for a small additional charge, if necessary.

What sort of technical support is available from the manufacturer? Problems often arise in the installation of assistive technology. It is important to be able to reach a representative of the manufacturer who knows the product being installed and who can suggest a quick solution or walk the user through any problem. Potential users should find out if the manufacturer maintains a toll-free technical support line for just such a purpose.

What warranty and service contract are available? This question is important for two reasons. First, much assistive technology is expensive to purchase and to repair. Second, when the product is being repaired, there may be no readily available substitute for the assistive technology. Therefore, it is important to inquire about replacement policies, such as the loan of a unit while the user's unit is being repaired.

### *Cost*

Unfortunately, the cost of assistive technology must almost always be a major consideration for consumers with disabilities and for the rehabilitation professionals who work with them. Because most products for people who are blind or visually impaired are manufactured by small companies for a relatively small market, the high costs of product research and development are passed on to the consumer. It is common for a blind or visually impaired person to spend as much or more than the original purchase price of a computer to make that computer accessible, for example.

Blind and visually impaired consumers are often caught in a difficult dilemma. They need a particular device to get a job or a promotion, but they cannot afford the device. As a result, they try to perform their job tasks with outdated equipment and may not receive a job or promotion because they do not have access to the equipment that they need.

The high cost of assistive technology often makes it necessary for people who are blind or visually impaired to seek support from third parties, such as state agencies for vocational rehabilitation. Students who are blind or visually impaired may become clients of the state department of vocational rehabilitation during high school, for example. State agencies give preference to equipment purchases that lead directly to jobs.

### *Job Placement*

According to Don Sims, a rehabilitation specialist for the Alabama Department of Rehabilitation Services, the client's employment experience is the most important consideration in Alabama. Technology vendors are very aggressive in promoting their products to rehabilitation counselors, but "the play is taken away by what equipment the employer is using and what will interface with it." Sims noted that counselors learn which vendors provide the best service, training, and technical support.

Sims pointed out that the Americans with Disabilities Act has opened up many low-technology jobs to people who are blind or visually impaired. He also stressed that state counselors must often negotiate with employers to secure jobs for their clients. One bank wanted to hire a person who is blind as a programmer, but the bank officials were very concerned about releasing bank codes to be brailled for the use of the new employee. The problem was solved by having three different organizations each do part of the braille transcription. The person now works at the bank as a programmer.

John De Witt, a consultant who has worked with the New Jersey Commission for the Blind to place clients in a variety of jobs, has noted that the client's experience and work environment are the key components of a successful placement. In some cases, a high-technology solution is not necessary. A person who is blind may need access to only a telephone system to do the job. A light probe, a device that makes a sound when it is pointed at a light source, such as a light flashing on a phone console, may be all that is necessary.

Rehabilitation counselors and technology consultants agree that there are no easy answers when it comes to matching a person with the right technology to perform a specific job. Consumer and counselor both must be involved in a process whose primary focus is to enable the consumer to perform the tasks required on the job in question.

## Specific Questions

The following is a checklist for consumers and rehabilitation professionals to use when evaluating assistive technology.

### *Speech Synthesizers*

- Does the user need high-quality speech, which is more expensive, or can the user function comfortably and efficiently with lower-quality speech?
- Can the synthesizer read text fast enough for the user to perform the job efficiently?

- Does the synthesizer mispronounce many words? Can the user listen to it comfortably for more than 15 minutes without getting a headache?
- Is the synthesizer to be used on one desktop machine or in more than one location? If the synthesizer is to be used in one location, an internal card may be preferable because it does not occupy a computer port.

### *Speech Programs*

- Does the program provide the power and versatility that the user needs?
- Can the program be configured to work effectively with the application programs already in use?
- What keystrokes are used for the program's basic and advanced functions? Are the keystrokes easy to remember? Is it possible to change the key combinations if they conflict with those used by application programs?
- Is the speech program compatible with the synthesizer being considered? Some speech programs are compatible only with synthesizers manufactured by the same company.

### *Closed Circuit Television Systems*

- Will the unit be used in one location or carried from home to the office, to meetings, or elsewhere?
- Is a low-cost model sufficient for the user's needs, or is a higher cost, full-featured unit required? The hand-held cameras of the low-cost units require hand-eye coordination, but they allow the user to bring the camera to the material to be magnified. High-cost units require a fixed workspace, but they leave the user's hands free for handwriting.
- Does the unit provide the magnification level and contrast that the user needs?
- What size monitor is required? The larger the monitor, the more information will fit on the screen.
- Is a black and white monitor sufficient, or is a color monitor required?

### *Screen Magnification Systems*

- Would a larger monitor suffice, or does the user actually need a screen magnification program?
- What equipment will be used? The monitor, graphics adapter, and display driver, as well as the amount of memory available, must be considered.
- What keystrokes are used for the program's basic and advanced commands? Are they easy to remember? Is it possible to change the key combinations used if they conflict with those used by application programs?
- Will the user benefit from using a speech program in addition to a screen magnification system? Fatigue is an important consideration.

### *Braille Printers*

- How much printing will be done? Is a slow-speed (10 characters per second) printer adequate, or is more speed required?
- Is a basic printer sufficient or is a powerful printer with advanced features required? Among the possible advanced features are the following.
  1. interpoint braille. Embossing braille on both sides of each page saves money and space.
  2. sideways printing. Each print page can be divided into blocks as wide as a braille page and printed across up to four pages. This is useful for reading charts, graphs, and maps.
  3. graphics. The ability to produce solid lines and geometric figures is essential for mathematics and science, and it is useful in other disciplines as well.
  4. foreign braille codes. Each language has its own braille code, including punctuation marks, accent marks, and contractions.
- Will the noise of a braille printer be disruptive? If so, a quietizer, a box designed to suppress the printer's noise, may be required.
- How are the parameters set? Is there a built-in speech synthesizer or another method of setting parameters that allows someone who cannot read braille to produce documents without relying on a braille reader's assistance? Being able to set parameters through synthetic speech also reduces braille paper costs. The printer "speaks" the settings to the user instead of printing them on paper. It greatly reduces the amount of time or paper needed to create the finished product.

### *Braille Displays*

- Is the user in a field where a braille display will have strong advantages over synthetic speech? Computer programmers, scientists, and mathematicians often prefer to check their work tactually.
- Is the user's work environment too noisy to use synthetic speech? Does the user do a significant amount of telephone work? Some people may find it distracting to listen to a speech synthesizer while trying to talk on the telephone.
- Does the user have a hearing impairment that could limit or preclude the use of synthetic speech?
- Is the user likely to be uncomfortable listening to synthetic speech several hours a day and, therefore, likely to prefer a braille display?

### *Braille Notetakers*

- Are the keys of the braille notetaker comfortable to the touch? Does brailling require much pressure? Are the keys noisy or quiet?

- Is the synthetic speech understandable? The emphasis is on portability in the design of a braille notetaker; the combination of a small speaker and a low-cost speech chip can produce low-quality speech.
- Does the user require a braille display because of a hearing impairment or because of the type of work being done?
- Are the commands easy to learn and use? Speech commands on braille notetakers are issued through "chord commands"—pressing the spacebar together with other keys. Are these commands pneumonic?
- Does the notetaker fit the purpose for which it is being purchased? Braille notetakers have a limited amount of memory. If the user intends to build a high-powered database or do desktop publishing, then other devices are more appropriate.
- What options are available for file transfer and storage? It quickly becomes necessary to transfer or erase files from the notetaker in order to have room for new ones. Therefore, the user should ask about transferring files to (1) another computer or a printer, (2) a disk drive, and (3) random access memory (RAM) cards.

### *Optical Character Recognition Systems*

- Does the user do enough reading to justify the purchase of an OCR device? If the user will use the machine rarely, it may be more cost-effective to pay someone to read the material.
- Should the user have an OCR system installed in a computer that is also used for other applications, or should the user have a dedicated system? Personal computer-based systems are much cheaper (beginning at $1,500 versus $4,500 for stand-alones) and allow the user to save documents directly to the hard disk. Stand-alone units require a minimum of computer knowledge, however. The user just presses a button and the OCR system scans and then reads the text (Figure 6–5).
- How well does the OCR device recognize the types of documents that the user wants to read? Will it read books, magazines, catalogs, bank statements, and take-out menus? It is important to test the OCR device's capacity to handle columns, different fonts, different colors, and different sizes of print.
- Does the OCR device maintain the original layout of each page scanned? Does it handle columns, headings, and sidebars correctly, or are parts of sentences scattered all over the page? If the text is not formatted properly, the user may find it difficult to follow what is being read.
- Can the OCR device use a sheetfeeder that will feed loose sheets to be scanned automatically? This feature allows the user to do something else while the document is being scanned.

**Figure 6–5** The Reading Edge, a portable, stand-alone optical character recognition system from Xerox Imaging Systems in Peabody, Massachusetts

---

### *Canes*

- Is it more important to have the sturdiness of a straight cane or the convenience of a folding or telescoping cane that can be put away when it is not in use? Folding canes separate into sections; telescoping canes collapse into one small piece.
- Is the cane length correct for the user? When the cane is standing up straight, the top should be level with the middle of the user's chest.
- Is the user comfortable carrying and getting information from the cane? Is the user comfortable with the cane's weight? The user should be able to detect the difference between various surfaces with the cane—concrete versus marble versus grass, and so on.

### *Guide Dogs*

- Does the person like dogs? Is he or she experienced in and comfortable with feeding, grooming, and caring for an animal?
- Will the user give the guide dog enough work to enable it to get enough exercise and retain what it has been taught? The user and the dog are a team and must work together regularly.
- Does the person have any health problems that will make it difficult to travel with a dog? Does the person have an allergy to dogs?

- Does the person have too much vision to work well with a dog? If the person responds to visual cues without waiting for the dog to react to obstacles, the dog's effectiveness will decline.

## CONSUMER INPUT

There is not enough consumer input into the process of evaluating and selecting assistive technology. In fact, it is surprising how few consumers know the manufacturer of the closed circuit television or the speech synthesizer that they use. When agencies for the blind or employers, rather than the consumer, purchase the equipment, the consumer either feels no obligation or has no opportunity to research thoroughly what products are available and then make an informed decision about what to buy. The consequences can be severe, because any major investment in technology has an impact on job performance and/or other aspects of life.

Some manufacturers seem to focus much of their marketing activities toward agencies instead of toward consumers. Their high-powered salespeople are more likely to do product demonstrations for agency personnel than for groups of consumers. Rehabilitation professionals and consumers alike sometimes end the search when they find a product that appears to perform the desired functions and do not continue searching for a product that performs better and costs less.

Before purchasing assistive technology, consumers should collect as much product information as possible from as many manufacturers as possible and read product reviews. The American Foundation for the Blind's Technology Center in New York publishes objective product reviews of assistive technology on a regular basis. Technology-related publications, such as Tactic published by the Clovernook Printing House for the Blind in Cincinnati, Ohio and Technology Update published by Sensory Access Foundation in Palo Alto, California, are sources of product reviews by consumers and new product announcements by manufacturers.

Consumers who contact the American Foundation for the Blind's Technology Center for advice about assistive technology are encouraged to arrange demonstrations of products before deciding what to buy. If possible, it is helpful to talk with other users of the product. No matter how good a product, it may not be right for a particular person or in a specific situation. A screen magnification program may not provide the required enlargement or contrast. A speech synthesizer may not be understandable for a particular person. The consumer's needs must be the first priority in selecting the correct assistive technology. If this is not the case, the device chosen can clearly cause more problems than it solves.

## TRAINING

There is not enough emphasis on training people to use assistive technology. In most cases, rehabilitation agencies (1) assess the needs of new clients to determine what devices will allow them to participate in the workforce, (2) purchase those devices, and (3) provide a minimum of training. Then, the clients are on their own. As a result, many people do not learn to use the technology to its fullest capacity. They learn only what they need to get by and remain unaware of some important functions of the products that they own.

Finding training is even more difficult for people who are not agency clients. In most cases, general market computer hardware and software manufacturers and local sales people are unfamiliar with assistive technology. Manufacturers do not have the staff or resources to provide training, and rehabilitation agencies usually do not provide training for people who are not registered clients. As a result, many consumers train themselves through hours of trial and error.

### Training Checklist

- Find accessible documentation for all products, including general market products.
- Read books and magazine articles about the products you purchase, searching for undocumented tips and tricks.
- Find accessible tutorials, especially ones that integrate assistive technology with general market products.
- Contact local consumer organizations to find user groups and/or experienced users who may be willing to answer questions or provide training.

## ACCESS TO GRAPHICAL USER INTERFACES

Access to Microsoft Windows and other graphical user interfaces (GUIs) is a major problem for blind and visually impaired people. GUIs are designed to allow fast, easy visual access with very little training necessary. Words are replaced by pictures on the computer screen, and the user navigates and makes selections using a mouse rather than by typing commands at a prompt.

Users who need to enlarge the size of the print on the computer screen in order to read it comfortably have a number of options in Windows. It is possible to change font sizes, adjust the screen colors, and change the size and appearance of the mouse pointer. A Windows-based synthetic speech program must translate this highly visual environment into one that is understandable to the blind computer user. It must convey through speech the meaning of visual symbols such as dialog boxes, buttons, and icons. The highlighted choice on a menu must be read accurately and quickly. Keystrokes must be substituted for mouse movement and mouse clicks.

Currently, Windows-based synthetic speech programs, and to a lesser extent Windows-based screen magnification programs, struggle to convey the necessary information to users. The criteria listed earlier in this chapter still apply to evaluating and selecting the correct software for access to Windows. Additionally, since improved versions of these programs are announced on a regular basis, it is critical that the user get a demonstration before purchasing one of these products.

## THE FUTURE OF ASSISTIVE TECHNOLOGY FOR PEOPLE WHO ARE BLIND OR VISUALLY IMPAIRED

The key to assistive technology changes in the future is integration. Currently, people who are blind or visually impaired must purchase additional hardware and software to make computers accessible. When a new operating system, such as Microsoft Windows, comes on the market, people who are blind or visually impaired find themselves totally unable to use it until new assistive technologies are developed.

In the future, access will be a consideration at the product development stage so that off-the-shelf products will be immediately accessible. Voice recognition will replace keyboards; the user will give commands to the computer verbally. Through artificial intelligence, computers will talk back to the user. This will enable the user to confirm the information that has been entered, as well as the actions that have been taken by the system. Books and magazines will be available and accessible on-line and on CD-ROM.

The trend toward smaller, more powerful portable devices will continue in assistive technology. Through the use of a variety of devices, access to information will become increasingly faster and easier for people who are blind or visually impaired. Innovative, affordable electronic travel aids will allow people who are blind to locate addresses or plot a route through an unfamiliar neighborhood as easily as a sighted person with a printed map. The ultimate benefit will be the full participation of many talented, enthusiastic persons in all parts of our society.

---

## REFERENCES

Bailey, I., & Hall, A. (1990). *Visual impairment: An overview*. New York: American Foundation for the Blind, pp. 2, 15, 18.

Scadden, L.A. (1991). An overview of technology and visual impairment. *Technology and Disability*, 1, 1–18.

*Chapter 7*

# Aids for Hearing Impairment and Deafness

*Gary M. McFadyen*

A hearing impairment is unique among the disabilities. All other disabilities prevent or make it more difficult for an individual to "do things." A hearing impairment does not prevent an individual from performing an activity of daily living nor limit his or her ability to function effectively at a vocation. Quite often, however, such an impairment restricts the social development or maturity of the individual, because it prevents or makes it more difficult for an individual to "communicate with others." This must be taken into account in evaluating, selecting, and using appropriate assistive technology for hearing impairments and deafness.

A discussion of aids for hearing impairment and deafness must begin with an overview of the hearing system. This knowledge is especially important in understanding the benefits and the limitations of any technology designed to aid human hearing.

## ANATOMY AND PHYSIOLOGY OF THE HUMAN AUDITORY SYSTEM

The human auditory system includes the outer ear, the middle ear, and the inner ear (Figure 7–1). The outer ear consists of the pinna and the external ear canal. The middle ear extends from the tympanic membrane (eardrum) to the oval window of the cochlea and contains three bones that are collectively known as the ossicles. The cochlea is the inner ear. It is a fluid-filled structure that contains approximately 20,000 hair cells (Guyton, 1976). These hair cells are connected to the fibers of the auditory nerve.

The vibration of an object in the air causes the air molecules to vibrate, which produces pressure disturbances in the air. When these pressure disturbances reach the ear, the outer ear funnels them to the eardrum, causing the eardrum to

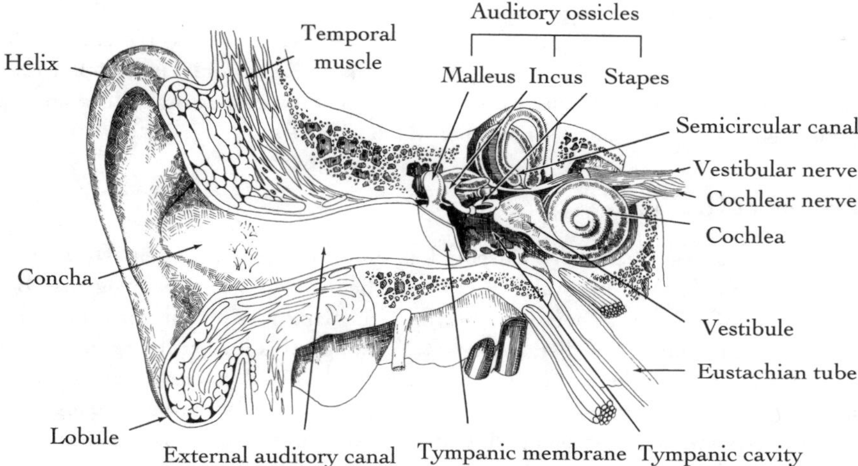


**Figure 7–1** Cross-section of the human auditory system. *Source:* Courtesy of Starkey Laboratories, Inc., Eden Prairie, Minnesota.

---

vibrate. The ossicles transfer the vibration of the eardrum to the oval window, and the movement of the oval window displaces fluid within the cochlea. This displacement causes vibration of the hair cells. When the hair cells vibrate, they generate impulses in the nerve fibers. As these impulses reach the auditory cortex of the brain, we perceive them as sound. The "normal" auditory system responds to vibrations (sound) in the frequency range of 30 to 20,000 Hertz (Guyton, 1976).

The intensity of sound is measured in decibels (dB). The threshold of "normal" hearing is denoted as an intensity of 0 dB. Each 3-dB increase represents a doubling of the sound intensity. Hearing loss is also measured in dB. A person with a 25-dB hearing loss would not hear a sound below 25 dB in intensity.

## Types of Hearing Loss

There are two types of hearing loss: conductive and sensorineural. A conductive hearing loss results when transfer of vibration from the eardrum to the oval window is impeded. This is usually caused by an obstruction in the outer ear canal or a degeneration or destruction of the ossicles in the middle ear. Conductive hearing losses generally respond well to medical intervention. Therefore, an individual with a conductive hearing loss should always undergo a medical evaluation before considering assistive auditory equipment.

A sensorineural hearing loss results from damage to the hair cells in the cochlea or damage to the auditory nerve. There are many possible causes, including prolonged excessive noise exposure, use of streptomycin or other ototoxic drugs, or tumors of the acoustic nerve. At the present time, little can be done medically to correct a sensorineural hearing loss.

### Degrees of Hearing Loss

Hearing losses are usually classified as mild, moderate, moderately severe, severe, or profound (Figure 7–2). A mild hearing loss is a hearing loss between 25 and 40 dB. A person with a mild hearing loss usually has difficulty hearing faint sounds and distant speech. Although this is a mild impairment of the hearing, the degree of handicap associated with such a loss depends on the individual. Some people are significantly handicapped by a mild hearing loss, while others are not affected at all. Children with mild hearing losses may have difficulty paying attention for an extended period, especially in a classroom situation.

A moderate hearing loss is a hearing loss between 41 and 55 dB. In general, people with a moderate hearing loss understand conversational speech at relatively close distances without great difficulty. The most common complaint heard from people with this degree of hearing loss is, "I hear fine, but everybody mumbles!" Most people with a moderate hearing loss benefit greatly from amplification. The speech of a person with this type of hearing loss will show articulation problems if the loss is acquired at an early age or if the person has had the loss for many years.

Individuals with a moderately severe hearing loss, which is a hearing loss between 56 and 70 dB, have considerable difficulty understanding speech in groups or in the presence of background noise. Without a hearing aid or other amplification device, they can understand conversational speech only if it is very loud. Persons with this degree of hearing loss often derive excellent benefit from amplification. Their speech usually shows more articulation problems than the speech of those with a moderate hearing loss.

A hearing loss between 71 and 90 dB is a severe hearing loss. Persons with such a hearing loss may identify environmental sounds, but usually have great difficulty understanding speech. In conversational speech, they may distinguish the vowels, but usually not the consonants. Their own speech may deteriorate without speech training. If this hearing loss occurs prelingually, speech may not develop.

A hearing loss that is greater than 90 dB is considered profound. In most instances, people with a profound hearing loss do not rely on hearing as their primary means of communication. Amplification may give these individuals an

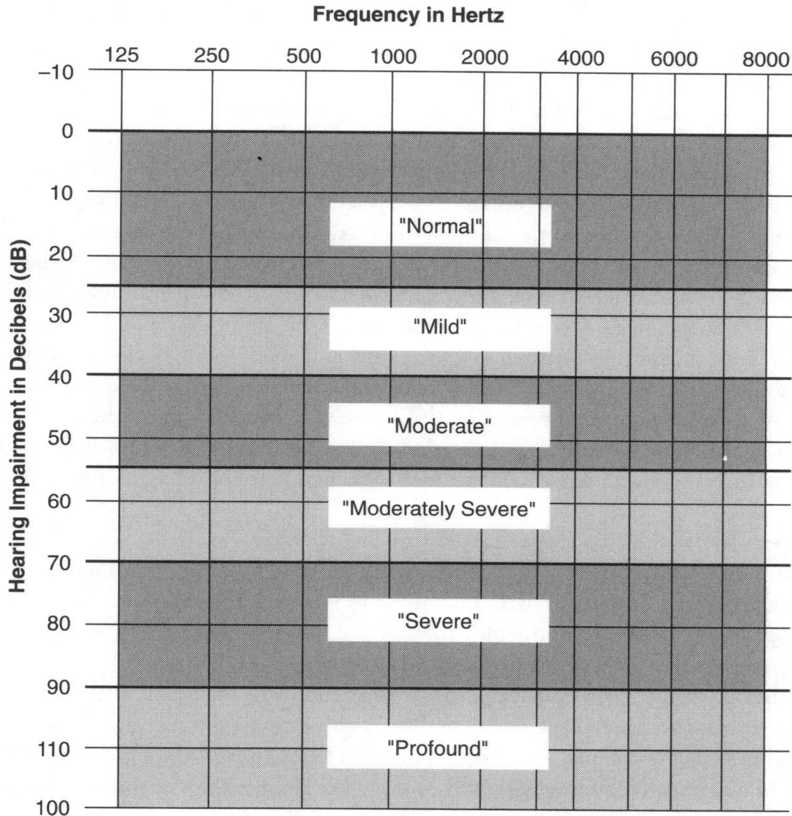


**Figure 7–2** Hearing loss classifications

awareness of environmental sounds, or it may provide auditory cues to complement other communication methods (e.g., lipreading). These individuals have poor speech, if they speak at all.

## SELECTION OF ASSISTIVE TECHNOLOGY

The main concerns in the selection of assistive technology for an individual with a hearing impairment are the degree of the impairment and the functional ability of the individual. If the impairment is profound or the individual is not fully functioning within society, the emphasis is on providing an awareness of environmental sounds, as well as any input necessary to help the individual maintain his or her speech. If the impairment is not as great or the individual functions well within society, the goal of any assistive technology is not only to improve hearing of speech and environmental sounds, but also to develop or maintain the individual's speech. As always, it is essential to examine each situation individually. Some people with a profound hearing impairment function better within society than others who have a mild to moderate impairment.

The most common assistive listening device is the hearing aid. Hearing aids are considered personal devices and are not usually covered by insurance, however. In addition, most states require those who provide hearing aids to have a hearing aid dispensing license. For example, the Mississippi State Department of Health Regulators Governing Licensure of Hearing Aid Dealers, section V. 5–1, states, "No person shall engage in the sale or practice of dispensing and fitting hearing aids or display a sign or in any other way advertise or hold himself out as a person who practices the dispensing and fitting of hearing aids unless he holds a current, unsuspended, unrevoked license issued by the Department, or is exempted pursuant to Section 9–1 of these regulations, or by statute."

A person considering a hearing aid for the first time should be advised, and is sometimes required by state and federal statutes, to have an examination by a physician to rule out any contraindications to wearing a hearing aid. The examining physician should not decide whether the hearing aid will help the patient. This is the proper role of the audiologist or hearing aid dispenser.

Although eyeglasses correct an abnormal focusing of the natural eye lens, hearing aids and other assistive listening devices do *not* correct impaired hearing. These devices primarily amplify sound. They can also filter the sound and amplify different frequencies at different gains. They can do nothing, however, to restore function to a nonfunctioning hair cell or auditory nerve.

## ASSISTIVE DEVICES AND TECHNOLOGIES

Assistive devices for people with hearing impairments and deafness can generally be classified as either alerting devices or communication devices. Obviously, these functions can overlap. An alerting device often communicates some information to the individual, and a communication device may well need to alert the individual that information is being communicated.

Alerting devices may use sound, light, vibration, or any combination of these three to provide the alert. The modality selected for a given situation depends on the abilities and preferences of the individual who will use the device, as well as on the environmental conditions ( Scherer & Frisina, 1994). If the person's hearing impairment is not great, an amplified sound-based alerting method or device may be adequate. If the use of amplified sound is impractical or ineffective, a light or vibration alerting device may be necessary. Because a vibration device needs to be in contact with the body, a light-based device is preferable for a stationary device in an environment where the hearing-impaired individual needs to move around. A vibration device has the advantage of being less obtrusive to others who may be nearby.

Many assistive communication devices consist of a receiver and a transmitter. The receiver is worn by the person with the hearing impairment. The transmitter either is worn by the speaker or is stationary within a given environment. Three primary methods of transmission are used for these devices: infrared (IR) radio frequency modulation (FM), and inductive coupling. Each of these has advantages and disadvantages (Table 7–1). Usually, IR transmitters and receivers are line of sight devices. The receiver must point directly at the transmitter, and there must be nothing to block the path of the transmission. Thus, these devices may not be suitable if the individual must be mobile. Large area IR transmitters, designed for use in theaters or auditoriums saturate the area with IR light. The reflection of the IR signal from objects in the room reduces or eliminates the line-of-sight requirement. Frequency modulation devices do not need a clear line of sight to be effective. Furthermore, they usually have more range than the other two methods. This allows the receiver to be further from the transmitter and still pick up the transmitted signal. Depending on the location, however, other transmitters or other electromechanical devices in the area can interfere with FM devices. Inductive coupling devices consist of a loop of wire connected to an amplifier. The loop is usually placed around the perimeter of a room. The individual with the receiver can receive the signal from anywhere within the loop. If the individual has a hearing aid with a telecoil, there is no need for an additional receiver. These devices can be the most discreet, but they are not usually portable.

Only the line-of-sight IR systems are considered confidential. Anyone with a receiver tuned to the transmission frequency can pick up an FM signal, and anyone with a telecoil-equipped hearing aid can pick up an inductive coupling signal. Furthermore, because the signal from inductive loops can extend beyond the loop, someone in an adjacent room can eavesdrop without being noticed. The value of the advantages and disadvantages of each of these types of systems will usually be the determining factor in the selection of these communication devices.

**Personal Devices**

Many assistive devices are available for the personal use of individuals who are hearing-impaired or deaf. These devices are helpful in using the telephone, listening to television, and performing other activities of daily living (ADLs).

**Table 7–1** Advantages and Disadvantages of Methods of Transmission for Auditory Assistive Devices

| *Method of Transmission* | *Advantages* | *Disadvantages* |
|---|---|---|
| Infrared (IR) | Confidential<br>Portable | Line of sight required between transmitter and receiver<br>Possible difficulty in bright sunlight<br>Not usually suitable for "walking around" use |
| Large area IR | Line of sight between transmitter and receiver not required<br>User allowed to move around within the room | Not confidential |
| Frequency modulation (FM) | Furthest range of all methods<br>Possible to operate multiple systems in same area with different frequencies<br>Portable<br>User allowed to move around within range of transmitter | Not confidential<br>Possible interference from other transmitters or electromechanical devices |
| Inductive loops | Direct interface to hearing aid telecoils<br>Most discrete<br>User allowed to move around within loop | Highly directional<br>Not confidential<br>User required to be within the loop for maximum sensitivity<br>Not portable while in use |

### *Devices for Using the Telephone*

*For Those Who Are Hearing Impaired.* Many hearing aids have a telephone switch on the aid that removes the microphone from the circuit and connects a coil of wire called a telecoil. This lets the hearing aid wearer use hearing aid–compatible telephones. Several years ago, it was difficult to find such a telephone. As a result of the Americans with Disabilities Act (ADA), these telephones are more common. Not all hearing aid–compatible telephones are compatible with all hearing aids, however. Before purchasing a particular telephone the individual who will use it should be sure it will work with his or her hearing aid.

Speaker telephones are not recommended for persons with hearing impairments. First, the speaker is further away from the ear than the handset would be. Second, if the volume of the speaker telephone is raised to a level high enough for the hearing-impaired individual to hear it (which is not always possible), the resulting echoes within the room make the person on the telephone harder to understand. Having the volume at this level is also a real nuisance for people in the room who are not hearing-impaired.

There is a wide variety of amplified telephones available. These telephones can be used with or without a hearing aid. The TeleTalker from Williams Sound and the Clarity from Walker, for example, are amplified telephones designed for persons with moderate to severe high-frequency hearing losses. Each telephone contains a control to boost the high-frequency sounds. The TeleTalker must be adjusted to fit the user's hearing impairment by an audiologist or hearing aid dispenser. The TeleTalker/CS is similar to the TeleTalker, but does not need to be fitted to the impairment.

Amplifiers can augment ordinary telephones for use by individuals with hearing impairments. The most economical type of amplifier is a battery-operated device that is placed over the receiver of the handset and is held in place with an elastic strap. There are three types of such amplifiers. The first type takes sound from the receiver, converts the sound to an electrical signal, amplifies the electrical signal, and outputs the signal as amplified sound. The second type takes sound from the receiver, converts the sound to an electrical signal, amplifies the electrical signal, and directs the amplified signal to a coil, which then outputs a magnetic field that can be detected by a hearing aid equipped with a telecoil. This type allows the individual to use a telephone that is not hearing aid–compatible. The third type of amplifier uses a coil to detect the magnetic field from the handset, converts the magnetic field into an electrical signal, amplifies the signal, and outputs amplified sound.

If more power is needed, an in-line amplifier that connects between the handset and the telephone can be used. These devices amplify the volume of the sound in the telephone handset. They use one 9-volt or four AA batteries. They contain a volume control for easy adjustment by multiple users, including those without impaired hearing. Because they are battery-operated, they are portable. They can be attached only to telephones with detachable handsets, however, so they will not work on public telephones. Some in-line amplifiers use an AC adapter instead of batteries, which makes them both less portable and more powerful than the battery-operated versions.

There are two special in-line devices that should be mentioned. The TeleLink is an adapter that is placed between the telephone base and the handset. It contains a connector that plugs into the Williams Sound PockeTalker and allows the telephone to be coupled to the telecoil of the hearing aid through a coil of wire around the neck. The second device is the AATIS/LAND from Phoenix Management. This device contains a plastic housing with a coil of wire inside. When placed over the ear behind the user's hearing aid, this device makes noncompatible telephones hearing aid–compatible and increases the strength of compatible telephones. The device can be configured to provide direct audio input (DAI) to a properly equipped hearing aid.

Another option is to replace the handset with an amplified handset. The older models contained a rotary volume control on the handset between the receiver and the mouthpiece. Newer models contain an electronic volume control that returns the volume to normal when the handset is hung up. This is a nice feature if the telephone is regularly used by both hearing-impaired and non–hearing-impaired users.

Cellular telephones are not hearing aid–compatible. The receivers for these telephones contain piezoelectric transducers, which require very little power to operate and, therefore, conserve battery power. They do not generate magnetic fields, however. Phoenix Management manufactures an adapter, called the AATIS/CELL, for cellular phones. This adapter is similar to the AATIS/LAND mentioned earlier. A special connector attaches a plastic housing containing a loop of wire to the telephone. This loop makes the telephone compatible with the telecoil in the hearing aid. These adapters must be ordered for each particular cellular telephone; they are not interchangeable between different brands or models of telephones.

*For Those Who Are Deaf.* Devices designed for hearing-impaired individuals will not help those who are deaf. Individuals who are deaf can communicate by telephone by use of a device called a telecommunication device for the deaf (TDD). The ADA refers to these devices as text telephones, or TTs.

A TDD contains a keyboard, a display, and some means of connecting to a telephone. Most TDDs are acoustically coupled to the telephone; that is, the telephone receiver is placed on a cradle on the TDD. The person on the other end of the line must also have a TDD. As each person types his or her message, the message appears on the displays of both TDDs. In the past, TDDs have been rather bulky (although not heavy), but newer versions fit into a coat pocket. A printer is available on some models. Several companies now manufacture telephones with built-in TDDs. Some of these telephones can function as computer keyboards, complete with built-in modems. Many telephone companies provide discounted rates for TDD calls because of the time involved in typing the messages.

Telecommunication devices for the deaf use a BAUDOT 5-bit communication protocol. Computer modems use an ASCII 8-bit communication protocol.

Some newer TDDs can convert BAUDOT to ASCII or vice versa, allowing the TDD to communicate with computer terminals. As more ASCII-compatible TDDs become available, the use of the BAUDOT code may eventually be phased out. The use of ASCII will allow TDDs to utilize a larger character set, including upper and lower case letters (BAUDOT uses only upper case letters). It will also allow non-printing keys to be used for command functions.

An individual who is deaf can communicate by telephone with a hearing individual who does not have a TDD by means of a relay service, which the ADA requires each state to make available. Either person can initiate the call. If, for example, a hearing individual wishes to call a person who is deaf, he or she calls the relay service operator, who then calls the other party on a TDD. The operator types whatever the hearing individual says and verbalizes whatever the deaf individual types. By law, the operator must maintain the confidentiality of the conversation.

*Telephone Alerting Devices.* Amplified telephones, hearing aid–compatible telephones, and TDDs are useless if the individual with a hearing impairment does not know when the telephone is ringing. A variety of telephone alerting devices are available. Amplified telephone ringers plug into a standard telephone jack and generate up to 95 dB of ringing sound. Some of these devices allow the user to adjust the volume, tone, and/or rate of the ring to best suit the user's hearing impairment. For all these devices, a two-plug telephone adapter is necessary if the ringer is to be connected to the same plug as the telephone.

Flashing telephone alert systems are recommended for individuals who cannot hear an amplified ringer, either because of the hearing impairment itself or because of background noise in the environment. These devices plug into a telephone jack and into a standard wall socket. Some models have a built-in strobe light that flashes when the telephone rings. Other models contain a plug for a user-supplied lamp or strobe. For night time use, a telephone alerting system such as a vibrator can be placed under the bed pillow.

### *Devices for Listening to Television*

Many hearing-impaired individuals, even those with mild impairments, have trouble understanding television. Few television speakers are high fidelity, and at a normal viewing distance of 6 to 10 feet, background noise and echoes within the room can make television listening difficult at best.

Assistive devices for listening to television may use any of the three transmission methods noted earlier. Frequency modulation and IR-based systems include a transmitter that connects to the audio output jack of the television set. Most manufacturers include a microphone for those televisions that do not have an audio output jack. The signal is transmitted to a headset that amplifies the sound. Some systems allow the user to adjust the receiver as necessary for his or her impairment. Because IR systems are line-of-sight systems, they require the receiver to be facing the transmitter. Frequency modulation systems do not have this restriction. In addition, some FM systems transmit a stereo signal. One such system is the Chaparral dB50. Most IR and FM systems have a jack on the receiver to connect a neckloop that makes the system compatible with a telecoil-equipped hearing aid. A neckloop is a loop of wire that is placed around the user's neck and connected to the receiver in place of the headset.

Inductive coupling systems are also available for listening to television. In these systems, the audio output jack of the television is connected to an amplifier. The output of the amplifier is a loop of wire placed around the perimeter of the room. A person wishing to use this system simply turns on the telecoil of his or her hearing aid. Receivers are commercially available for those who do not have telecoil-equipped hearing aids.

The Williams Sound PockeTalker is a portable, battery-operated amplifier that can be used in many different listening situations. When configured for television listening, the system includes a microphone with a 12-foot extension cord and either an earpiece, a headphone, or a neckloop. The microphone is placed in front of the television speaker, and the user wears the appropriate listening device. The neckloop makes the system compatible with hearing aid telecoils. Others in the room must take care to avoid tripping over the microphone extension cord. Other companies make similar devices.

The systems just described can be connected to a stereo sound system as well as the television. If the television is connected to the stereo, one system can be used for both. An economical solution for those households in which the television is already connected to the stereo system is to fabricate a homemade loop using wire from an electronics shop. It is important to match the impedance of the loop to the impedance of the stereo system. Loop systems transmit only a monaural signal, however, not a stereo signal.

For deaf individuals, there are closed captioning decoders that connect to the television and display text on the bottom of the screen. The program being watched must have been produced with closed captioning, and an increasing number of television shows and movies are indeed being produced with closed captioning. Decoders are necessary only for older televisions. By federal law, all television sets manufactured after July 1994 with 13-inch or larger screens must have a built-in closed captioning decoder.

### *Devices for Activities of Daily Living*

Many other devices are available to assist individuals who are hearing-impaired and deaf in their activities of daily living (ADLs). New devices are becoming available constantly.

A variety of sounds within a home indicate things that require attention; among these sounds are doorbells, smoke alarms, alarm clocks, babies crying, and telephones ringing. Alerting systems similar to those that inform individuals who are hearing-impaired or deaf of the ringing of a telephone are available for other sounds. These systems usually consist of one or more transmitters located at or near the source of the sounds and a receiver that may be either portable or stationary. Portable receivers vibrate when they receive a signal from a transmitter. A light-emitting diode (LED) on the receiver indicates which transmitter sent the signal. Stationary receivers plug into the wall. A standard table lamp or strobe is connected to the receiver, and the rate of the lamp's flashing indicates which transmitter has been activated. Complete systems can be purchased at one time, or components can be obtained individually as needed. Transmitters for these systems include doorbell monitors, door knock monitors, baby cry monitors, smoke alarm monitors, and general sound monitors that transmit a signal if any sound is heard.

Alerting devices are also available as standalone devices if a complete system is not needed. One standalone device is a smoke alarm that contains a flashing strobe light and a horn or siren. Xenon strobes usually emit the brightest light and are recommended for sleeping areas. Battery-operated devices are *not* recommended for sleeping areas. Most flashing smoke alarms are portable devices that plug into a standard wall socket.

Vibrating and flashing alarm clocks can be used to awaken an individual who cannot hear a standard alarm clock. Most of these alarm clocks contain a standard AC outlet into which the user plugs a lamp or a vibrator. Some have a bypass switch that makes it possible to turn the lamp on or off without activating the alarm. Portable, battery-operated, vibrating alarm clocks are useful for traveling.

Some individuals who are deaf prefer to use hearing ear dogs. These dogs are specially trained to alert their masters to the presence of different sounds. Like seeing eye dogs, these service dogs are allowed in all places of public accommodations.

### Devices for Business Use

Many devices and technologies are available to assist businesses in communicating with employees or customers who are hearing-impaired or deaf. In fact, many of the personal devices described can be used in a business setting. For example, a flashing doorbell set up on the counter of a retail business can alert hearing-impaired or deaf employees of the presence of a customer. Flashing telephone ringers can notify these employees that the telephone is ringing.

Several devices aid in one-on-one communication when one person is hearing-impaired. One such device is the PockeTalker from Williams Sound, which was mentioned earlier. This device is a small, personal amplifier with a microphone and a headset. (The headset can be replaced with a neckloop for those whose hearing aids have telecoils.) The microphone can be placed on the end of an extension cord so the speaker can hold it close to his or her mouth. This device works well if the speaker is close to the listener and remains nearby.

Personal communication systems can help hearing-impaired individuals either in a one-on-one meeting or in a group. These systems consist of a small portable transmitter with a microphone and a small portable receiver with an earpiece, headset, or neckloop. The speaker wears the transmitter and speaks into the microphone. The transmitter sends the signal by IR or FM (depending on the system) to the receiver, which amplifies the signal and outputs the amplified signal. With this device, the speaker can move around the room. Some of these systems have an additional microphone on the receiver that has its own volume control and allows the hearing-impaired person to pick up other sounds in the room.

The Chorus Universal Listening System is a personal communication system that has a receiver with removable input modules. One module receives FM signals, a second module receives IR signals, and a third module picks up the magnetic field from an inductive loop. This makes the system compatible with almost any large area assistive listening system.

In conferences, a transmitter can be connected to the conference microphone so that the hearing-impaired person can pick up all of the conversations. If individuals who are hearing-impaired are likely to use a conference room or other meeting room frequently, it may be wise to install an inductive loop around the baseboard of the room. The wire loop is connected to the output of an amplifier, and one or more microphones are connected to the input of the amplifier. The telecoil of a user's hearing aid or an induction receiver picks up the amplified signal. The Oval Window Microloop System is a portable inductive system that can be set up in almost any room; its 90-foot loop provides a listening area that is 20 by 25 feet in size. For larger areas, there are stronger systems designed to be permanently installed in a given area.

Deaf employees who need to use a computer may benefit from the KEYPlus keyboard from Ultratec, which is designed for use on IBM and compatible computers. In addition to all the features of a standard keyboard, the KEYPlus contains a free-standing TDD and a TDD call detector. The TDD contains a 48-character, two-line, tilted display and a 24-character thermal printer. It can communicate with ASCII or BAUDOT modems. Furthermore, it allows a user to answer a TDD call without interrupting the operation of the computer.

Silent Call Corporation manufactures the OMNI PAGE II personal pager system that can communicate any of 15 preset messages to a person who is hearing-impaired or deaf. Each of the 15 messages is assigned a number. The transmitter sends the number of the message. The receiver vibrates when it receives a signal from the transmitter and displays the message number. The device currently has a range of approximately 125 feet, but this range will soon increase to approximately 1,000 feet.

**Devices for Commercial Use**

In addition to the devices that are designed to facilitate communication with employees, there are devices designed to facilitate communication with customers. Several companies manufacture large area assistive listening systems for use in theaters, auditoriums, and conference centers, for example. One or more transmitters (inductive loop, FM, or IR systems) are connected to the sound system of the theater, auditorium, or conference center. Those wishing to use the system pick up receivers at the door. (For an inductive system, the user who wears a hearing aid can switch it to telecoil and not have to pick up a receiver.) These types of systems make it possible for many people who are hearing-impaired to listen simultaneously. Each of the three types of transmitters have advantages and disadvantages.

Large area inductive loop systems require a separate loop for each area (room). There may be interference between the two signals in parts of rooms that are adjacent, however. Large area FM systems can be set for different frequencies in each room to eliminate interference, but this strategy necessitates separate receivers for each room unless the receivers are adjustable. Large area IR systems have no interference between rooms, since the infrared light cannot penetrate the walls. Moreover, careful placement of strong transmitters can eliminate the line-of-sight problem.

Businesses that employ cashiers or tellers frequently need to communicate with customers who are hearing-impaired or deaf. This communication can be difficult, especially if sound is blocked by a glass partition separating the employee from the customer. One solution to this problem is to use an amplified intercom system. These systems usually consist of a nonamplified handset for the employee and a hearing aid–compatible, amplified handset for the customer. Another solution is to embed a loop in the glass or within the counter top so that the customer can use his or her hearing aid telecoil to listen to the teller.

Video monitors or microprocessor-controlled LED signs can be used to display visually information that is normally announced over a public address system.

For hotels and hospitals, assistive listening "kits" are available. These kits contain a variety of alerting and communication aids commonly used by guests or patients. An individual can check out a kit upon arrival and return it on departure.

### Devices for Classroom Use

Any of the personal communication systems mentioned earlier can be used in a classroom setting for students who are hearing-impaired. Because children move around within a classroom, however, they will have trouble maintaining the line of sight that an IR system generally needs. Therefore, most devices designed for use in the classroom use FM transmitters and receivers. Each student in the classroom has a receiver set to the same frequency. Other classrooms use different frequencies to prevent interference. The students' receivers should also contain a microphone with a separate volume control to pick up the voices of fellow students.

One system for classroom use consists of a transmitter that sends its signal to an amplified speaker. This system is not recommended, as amplified sound from the speaker will produce more echoes and background noise that will make listening more difficult for hearing-impaired students. If the classroom also contains non–hearing-impaired students, it will be difficult to adjust the volume to a level that is comfortable for everyone.

Table 7–2 is a summary of the capabilities and uses of assistive listening devices.

## EVALUATION PROCESS

The first step in evaluating assistive technology for a person is to determine its function. Is it to allow the individual to use the telephone, to perform vocational duties, to perform activities of daily living, or to function in a social setting? For which vocational duties does the user need auditory assistance? In what social settings will the user participate?

The second step is to identify the environment in which the assistive technology will be used. Will it be used at one location, or does it need to be portable? Is it to be used in wet or hazardous locations? How often and for how long will the device or technology be used?

The next step is to determine the capabilities of the user. Is the user hearing-impaired or deaf? If hearing-impaired, to what degree? Is there any residual hearing? Can the user understand speech with amplification, or is the technology intended to give the user primarily a greater awareness of environmental sounds? What is the personal attitude of the user toward the use of assistive technology? Can the individual properly care for whatever technology is chosen? Although family, employers, and counselors can contribute their insights or opinions, it is vital to determine the desires of the individual who will actually use the technology.

The information obtained in the first three steps is the basis for selecting devices or technologies that may be appropriate. Information on currently avail-

**Table 7–2** Summary of Capabilities and Uses for Assistive Listening Devices

| Device | For Hearing Impairment | For Deafness | Alert Modality | | | Transmission Modality | | |
|---|---|---|---|---|---|---|---|---|
| | | | Light | Sound | Vibration | IR | FM | Inductive |
| Hearing aid–compatible telephone | × | | | | | | | |
| Speaker telephone | × | | | | | | | |
| Amplified telephone | × | | | | | | | |
| "Clip-on" telephone amplifier | × | | | | | | | |
| Amplified telephone handset | × | | | | | | | |
| In-line telephone amplifier | × | | | | | | | |
| Text telephone (TT or TDD) | | × | | | | | | |
| Telephone ring detector | × | × | × | × | × | | | |
| Closed caption decoder | × | × | | | | | | |
| Television amplification system | × | | | | | | | |
| Pager | × | × | | × | × | | × | |
| Vibrating alarm clock | × | × | | | × | | | |
| Flashing alarm clock | × | × | × | | | | | |
| Smoke alarm | × | × | × | × | × | | | |
| Doorbell/knock detector | × | × | × | × | × | | | |
| Baby cry monitor | × | × | × | × | × | | × | |
| Hearing ear dogs | | × | | × | | | | |
| Personal communication device | × | | | | | × | × | × |
| Neckloop | × | | | | | | | × |
| Conference microphone | × | | | | | × | × | × |
| Large area assistive listening device | × | | | | | × | × | × |
| Video monitor | × | × | | | | | | |
| LED Sign | × | × | | | | | | |
| TDD computer keyboard | | × | | | | | | |

*continues*

**Table 7–2** continued

| *Device* | *Telephone Use* | *Telecoil Compatible* | *Television Use* | *Classroom Use* | *Personal Communication* | *Group Communication* | *Home Use* | *Business Use* | *Computer Use* |
|---|---|---|---|---|---|---|---|---|---|
| Hearing aid–compatible telephone | × | × | | | × | | × | × | |
| Speaker telephone | × | | | | × | | × | × | |
| Amplified telephone | × | Sometimes | | | × | | × | × | |
| "Clip-on" telephone amplifier | × | Sometimes | | | × | | × | × | |
| Amplified telephone handset | × | Sometimes | | | × | | × | × | |
| In-line telephone amplifier | × | | | | × | | × | × | |
| Text telephone (TT or TDD) | × | | | | × | | × | × | Sometimes |
| Telephone ring detector | × | | | | | | × | × | |
| Closed caption decoder | | | × | × | | | × | | |
| Television amplification system | | | × | × | | | × | | |
| Pager | | | | | | | × | × | |
| Vibrating alarm clock | | | | | | | × | | |
| Flashing alarm clock | | | | | | | × | | |
| Smoke alarm | | | | × | | | × | × | |
| Doorbell/knock detector | | | | | | | × | | |
| Baby cry monitor | | | | | | | × | | |
| Hearing ear dogs | | | | | | | × | | |
| Personal communication device | Sometimes | | × | × | | | × | × | |
| Neckloop | × | × | × | × | | | × | × | |
| Conference microphone | | | | × | | × | | × | |
| Large area assistive listening device | | | | × | | × | | × | |
| Video monitor | | | | | | × | | × | |
| LED Sign | | | | | | × | | × | |
| TDD computer keyboard | | × | | | | | × | × | × |

able devices can be obtained from many sources, such as professionals (engineers and therapists) working in the field of assistive technology, state rehabilitation and/or vocational agencies, and manufacturers. More often than not, the person with a disability is also aware of many products that are available to assist him or her. These devices should be explained to the potential user, and his or her feedback should be obtained. The user should test the devices under actual working conditions. Many times, it is necessary to repeat the process until there is a suitable fit between the technology and the capabilities of the user.

Finally, because an individual has a hearing impairment, many people mistakenly assume that he or she does not need to worry about exposure to loud and/or background noise. This is absolutely *FALSE*! A person with a hearing impairment is at a greater risk of noise exposure than a person with "normal" hearing. A person with a hearing impairment is often unaware of the noise level in the environment and, thus, does not take the necessary steps to limit exposure to the noise. This can lead to the loss of any residual hearing. It is *essential* to provide hearing protection for individuals with hearing impairments whenever other workers need hearing protection.

---

## REFERENCES

Guyton, A.C. (1976). *Textbook of medical physiology* (5th ed.). Philadelphia: Saunders, p. 829.

P.L. 101–336. (1990). The Americans with Disabilities Act.

Scherer, M.J., & Frisina, D.R. (1994). Applying the Matching People with Technologies Model to individuals with hearing loss: What people say they want—and need—from assistive technologies. *Technology and Disability, 3*(1), 62–68.

## *Chapter 8*

# Assistive Technology for Recreation

*Patricia E. Longmuir and Peter Axelson*

> When I got injured in a climbing accident at age 19, the last thing that I wanted to do was alpine skiing because I could only think of how I used to do it. A few years later someone talked me into trying to slide down a hill in a Norwegian pulk, which was kind of like a lunch tray going sideways on the snow. It was totally out of control, but then I realized that all skiers use adaptive equipment to ski on snow. By designing equipment specific to the activity I wanted to do, I could experience the same enjoyment of the sport of skiing even though I was doing it in a completely different way. I was still balancing and I was still sitting, but I was using my balance and the part of my body that was still functioning to ski. Through this experience, I learned that by designing activity-specific equipment I had the opportunity to enable myself and other people to enjoy outdoor leisure activity with family and friends or in competition. (Axelson, 1994)

Recreational participation by individuals with a disability has increased tremendously in the past two decades through changes in societal attitudes and technological innovations. In North America, there have been special government initiatives (e.g., Healthy People 2000, Active Living Canada) and formal mandates to ensure that persons with a disability have access to recreational activities. In the United States, the Americans with Disabilities Act of 1990 requires that all public and private recreation facilities and services be accessible to individuals with disabilities (Kalscheur, 1992; Seidler, Turner, & Horine, 1993). In Canada, accessibility of programs and services is a criterion for government funding. Nevertheless, many individuals with a disability remain unaware of the wide array of leisure pursuits available to them (Hamel, 1992).

Technology is an integral part of virtually all recreational activities. For example, the human hand is not designed to stop the flight of a hard, fast-moving object; thus, baseball players use a glove to compensate for the limited function of the hand. The technology used for recreational activities varies tremendously in complexity, cost, and necessity. Many people use simple types of equipment, such as running shoes, playing cards, or golf gloves, without thinking of them as "technology" for recreation. Radio-controlled model airplanes or cars, bicycles, and computers are examples of more sophisticated technology. For some recreational activities (e.g., scuba diving, rock climbing) the survival of the participant actually depends on technology.

Very few recreational activities require the use of "special" or extraordinary equipment in order for the person with a disability to participate (Seidler et al., 1993; Willard, 1978). In most cases, individuals with a disability can use the same types of recreational technology/equipment used by other participants. Consequently, they have the same range of recreational opportunities enjoyed by their able-bodied peers (Adams, Daniel, McCubbin, & Rullman, 1982; Hamel, 1992) and are no longer limited to swimming or wheelchair basketball. Limitations to involvement in physical activity are rarely necessary, except where there are specific medical contraindications; for example, individuals with brittle bones should not play contact sports, but can and should participate in a variety of recreational activities (Axelson & Zollars, 1992). Published information is readily available about the successful participation of people with disabilities in a wide variety of recreational activities (Exhibit 8–A–1 in Appendix 8–A).

Local sources of information about community recreational opportunities are sport clubs, recreation and park departments and facilities, instructional programs, and disability support groups. More general information and contact information for national, state, and provincial organizations may be obtained from the magazines, computer databases, publications, and national organizations listed in Appendix 8–A, Resources. Rehabilitation professionals must be aware of the "limitless" nature of the recreational pursuits that are now open to persons with a disability and must encourage their clients to seek out those activities of greatest interest to them. Indeed, there are appropriate leisure activities for all individuals, in any life circumstance (Loesch, 1981).

## IMPORTANCE OF INDIVIDUAL CHOICE

It is essential to consider individual interests, goals, skills, and functional abilities in identifying appropriate and satisfying leisure pursuits (Adams et al., 1982). Individuals must determine for themselves what they wish to gain from their leisure activities. Although professionals are often expected to define the individual's needs within their professional area of expertise (e.g., the physician recommends the medical treatment), individuals must use their own ideas and perceptions to identify the recreational activities that are a priority for them. To some people, recreational activities offer an opportunity for artistic expression; others seek risk and emotional exhilaration. Some people consider the opportunity for social interaction to be of greatest importance, while others seek solitude through leisure activities. Interests in competition, exercise, relaxation, or excitement can all motivate the choice of activity (Axelson & McCornack, 1983).

The most important factors in the selection of assistive devices for recreation are the interests of the individual (White, 1991). Recreation, when defined as what one does when not working or performing the activities of daily living (ADLs), covers an extremely broad spectrum of potential activities. Therefore, individuals should identify their own interests through either formal or informal assessments. Formal assessments require the individual to respond to standardized questions or statements, either during an interview or through a written questionnaire, and the responses are scored or categorized to determine the overall recommendations (Burlingame & Blaschko, 1990).

Such assessments are particularly appropriate for individuals, such as those with acquired disabilities, who may be unsure about their own skills or abilities. Formal assessments also benefit individuals whose previous experience with recreational activities is very limited, such as individuals with congenital disabilities who were unable to participate during childhood. Informal assessments suggest personal interests and priorities rather than specific leisure activities. Individuals must be aware of the full spectrum of potential recreational opportunities available to them before stating specific activity preferences. Otherwise, the stated preferences may represent what they would like best (or dislike the least) from among activities familiar to them, rather than their "ideal" interests. Therefore, caution is required in the use of informal assessments with individuals who have limited knowledge of, or experience with, recreational activities.

### Activity Characteristics

The identification of recreational interests should focus initially on the features or characteristics of different types of activity, rather than the "naming" of specific hobbies or sports. Activity characteristics may be categorized in a variety of ways, each with a continuum of potential responses (Table 8–1). A broad spectrum of potential recreational pursuits can meet the needs identified for each characteristic.

If a disability has been acquired, the individual may or may not be able to, or may or may not want to, return to previously enjoyed recreational activities. For example, a person whose recreational activities before a spinal cord injury were

**Table 8–1** Categories of Activity Characteristics

| *Activity Characteristics* | *Description* |
|---|---|
| **Competitive/recreational** | Does the person like to keep score (i.e., determine the winner/best performance), or is participating more important than the final result? |
| **Creative/defined** | Does the individual wish to have the freedom to pursue individual ideas and interpretations rather than being restricted to established rules/expectations? |
| **Individual/group** | Are activities with a large group of people of interest, or are activities alone or with a partner preferred? |
| **Organized/unstructured** | Is a class or organized program at a particular time and place preferred, or is an activity that can be done fairly spontaneously when time permits more appealing? |
| **Physically active/sedentary** | Does the person wish to be involved in strenuous physical activity, moderate physical activity, or sedentary activities? |
| **Segregation/integration** | Does the person with a disability prefer to participate with others who have a disability, with able-bodied individuals, or with both? |

dancing, tennis, and video games can resume all these activities if the person chooses to do so. If the primary recreational interest prior to the injury had been pole vaulting, however, a significant investment of time and expertise would be required to develop alternative techniques and equipment that would allow continued participation. In the latter case, the individual might choose to pursue alternative activities that provide similar types of rewards (e.g., individual, physically active, competitive). Professionals should be prepared to introduce new activities to those individuals who choose not to return to their previous interests.

### Match of Functional Abilities to Desired Activities

Once specific activities have been chosen, the individual's ability to perform the desired activity must be determined. A knowledge of the individual's diagnosis is not adequate for a functional assessment or the selection of appropriate assistive devices (Behrman, 1990; Enders, 1984). Gross and fine motor skills, muscular function, range of motion, balance, coordination, gait and mobility, endurance, posture, grip function, and strength are just a few of the factors that may need to be considered, depending on the type of desired activity (Axelson, 1985b; Bernhardt, 1984; Seaman & DePauw, 1989). The types of assistive devices regularly used by the individual, specific problem areas encountered, compensatory strategies employed, and both physical and mental skills should also be considered (Enders, 1984). For competitive athletes with a disability, the functional assessment of abilities is even more extensive in order to promote equitable competition (Meaden, 1991).

People have varying abilities to function and adapt to their environment; therefore, the functional assessment must focus on maximizing the individual's abilities, rather than accommodating the perceived or physiological limitations resulting from the disability (Seidler et al., 1993). Many "barriers" to participation can be overcome with enthusiasm, alternative ways of doing things, or technology (White, 1991). For example, it might be expected that individuals who have a visual impairment, who do not have the use of their arms, or who use a wheelchair cannot play tennis. A close examination of the features required for a tennis game (e.g., ability to move to the ball, return the ball to the opponent, coordinate the motion of the ball with the movement of the racquet to hit the ball) shows that, in fact, such individuals can (and do) participate successfully. Brightly colored balls that contrast with the environment can enhance the ability of an individual with a visual impairment to track the path of the ball. An individual without the use of his or her arms can attach a racquet to the body or shoulder, and a wheelchair can maneuver quite easily on asphalt or hard surface courts (Figure 8–1). Examining the specific skills/tasks required to play tennis highlights the abilities of such individuals and more clearly identifies additional needs for their successful participation.

The primary goal of selecting assistive devices for people with disabilities is to ensure their equal access and full participation in all desired activities, including recreation (Seidler et al., 1993). In many instances, the demands of recreational activities have enhanced the technology used for ADLs. For example, lightweight wheelchairs were initially developed for use during wheelchair sports (Crase, 1993; Kelly, 1990; Ragnarsson, 1990; Wilson & McFarland, 1990). Because standard wheelchairs were extremely heavy and difficult to maneuver, they did not meet the needs of athletes who required speed and agility. In addition, the back support and static position of the trunk in the sling-type wheelchair seat often limited movement or balance, resulting in muscular fatigue. The use of lightweight wheelchairs designed for maneuverability, back support shaping systems (Zollars & Axelson, 1993), and appropriate seating postures (Axelson, 1984c) can greatly enhance the individual's participation in active leisure pursuits. Thus, while a standard wheelchair would have been satisfactory for vocational and daily living tasks, it did not fulfill the requirements for recreational participation.

Physical fitness is an important component of all types of recreational activities, even if they are not strenuous, and should be part of the assessment. Although high levels of physical fitness are not a prerequisite to most recreational activities, the maintenance of adequate levels of endurance, strength, and flexibility ensure safe participation. Overuse injuries of the hand and forearm of-

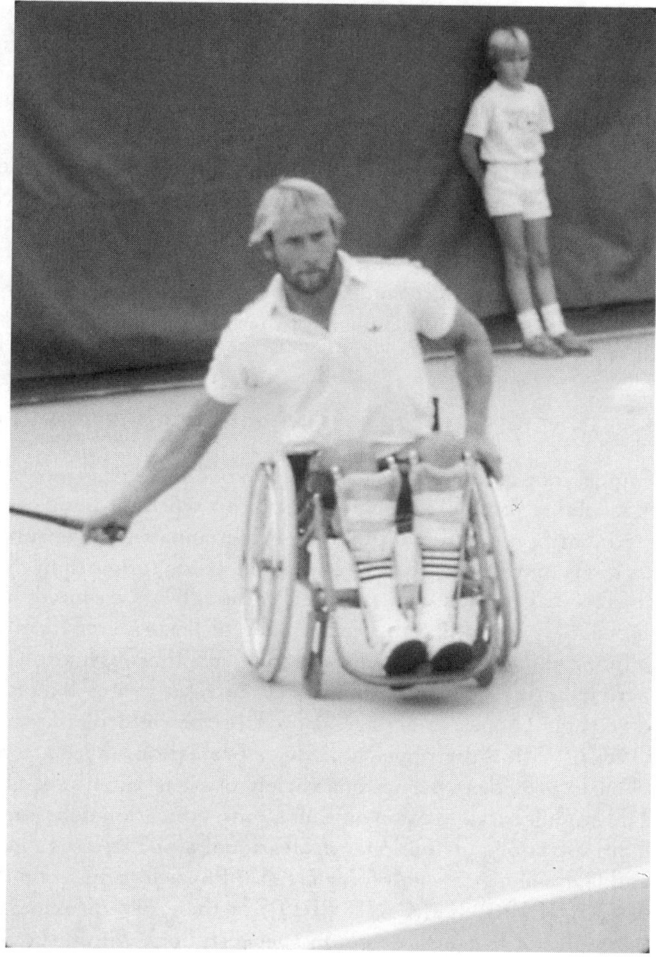

**Figure 8–1** Brad Parks, Director of the National Foundation of Wheelchair Tennis, promotes tennis for competition or recreation with family and friends.

ten occur among individuals who spend a great deal of time playing video games or using a computer mouse. The concentration required for lengthy games of chess can cause excessive fatigue for individuals who have been deconditioned by a lengthy period of immobilization. Fatigue, both physical and mental, can have particularly serious implications for participation in outdoor or adventure activities where poor judgment is extremely dangerous. Individuals with a disability should also carefully consider the impact of a potential injury on their independence and daily living skills. "Tennis elbow" may be an inconvenience for most people, but it can be a serious limitation for individuals, such as those who use crutches or wheelchairs, who rely on their arms for mobility and self-care. Standardized physical fitness assessments are available to measure a wide variety of individual skill levels and characteristics (American College of Sports Medicine, 1994; Bernhardt, 1984; Canadian Society for Exercise Physiology, 1995; Skinner, 1993). Certified fitness professionals, contacted either through the American College of Sports Medicine or the Canadian Society for Exercise Physiology, can recommend the most appropriate assessment techniques, conduct a formal fitness appraisal, or design an appropriate training program.

## PROFESSIONAL SPECIALIZATION FOR ACTIVITY SELECTION

As the importance of leisure has increased in our society, so too has the range of choices available for recreational pursuits. In working with people with a disability to identify recreational pursuits, professionals must ensure that these individuals focus on their own preferences and needs rather than their perceptions of what is "realistic" or "appropriate." Although it is essential that rehabilitation professionals recognize the importance of leisure activities for persons with a disability, they cannot be expected to have a thorough knowledge of the physical activity profession in addition to their own profession. Rather, they should refer their clients to a professional in the field of physical activity (Enders, 1984). Within the physical activity profession, there are many "specialists" who can provide expertise in a variety of areas. Such specialists may be contacted through local recreation organizations, educational institutions, sport clubs and organizations, or national professional associations (e.g., American Alliance and Canadian Association for Health, Physical Education, Recreation and Dance [AAHPERD and CAHPERD]) or their state/provincial affiliates. Selected examples of the most common specializations within the physical activity profession are provided in Table 8–2.

Each activity makes a different set of demands on the individual's physical, intellectual, and emotional abilities. The flexibility and necessity of each identified skill also varies with the type of activity and the level of performance; for example, elite competition usually requires greater skill and, therefore, has fewer opportunities for accommodating different abilities. A physical activity professional with expertise in the desired activity should be consulted to identify the requisite activity skills and recommended methods of training and assessment. It is not necessary for the physical activity professional to be familiar with individuals with disabilities or their involvement in the identified activity.

**Table 8–2** Fields of Specialization Within the Physical Activity Profession

| *Specialization* | *Description* |
|---|---|
| **Adapted physical activity** | Inclusion of persons with a disability in the physical activities of their choice (e.g., equitable access to opportunities, modifications when required) |
| **Coaching** | Teaching of sport skills and strategies to enhance the participants' caliber of play |
| **Exercise science** | Physical activity or exercise for the diagnosis or treatment of medical problems (e.g., exercise training for individuals after a heart attack) |
| **Fitness** | Enhancement of the efficiency and suitability of the body to perform physical work or activity |
| **Leisure** | Focus on all voluntary activities pursued during leisure time, including hobbies, travel, arts, crafts, physical activity, and recreation |
| **Physical education** | Education of participants about their physical health, fitness, skills, and capabilities |
| **Recreation therapy** | Recreational pursuits for the purposes of treatment or rehabilitation (e.g., teaching individuals with behavior problems to use physical activity as an outlet for aggression) |

Once the requisite skills for participation in the desired activity have been identified, the individual with the disability—together with the professional—can determine whether he or she already has the required skills or must acquire them.

## ADAPTATIONS TO ENSURE SATISFACTORY PARTICIPATION

When it becomes apparent that adaptations are necessary if a person with a disability is to participate in the leisure activity of his or her choice, it may be possible to make modifications to the individual, activity, and/or environment. Historically, the development of "disabled sports" (e.g., wheelchair basketball) has been the primary vehicle for providing recreational opportunities to individuals with a disability. Segregated activities enable persons with similar abilities to participate together but often preclude the participation of individuals with different abilities such as "nondisabled" family and friends (Axelson, 1985a). The desire to participate in recreational activities with family and friends may also require the individual with a disability to adapt to the activity, rather than vice versa. In most cases, modifications to the rules or techniques enable all interested individuals to participate. For example, allowing the person who uses a wheelchair to return the ball after two bounces instead of one enables equal participation in sports such as tennis and racquetball.

When rule/activity modifications cannot adequately provide for the participation of the individual with a disability, the use of assistive devices should be considered (Axelson, 1984d; Colston, 1991). A coordinated selection process helps to ensure the use of the simplest, most cost-effective solutions to the individual's needs (Behrman, 1990; Enders, 1984; Walker & Seidler, 1993). Given the importance of personal factors (e.g., age, size, interests) to the selection and use of recreational technology, the individual wishing to participate in the activity must be involved in all aspects of the selection process (Ozer, 1990).

The sport of sailing can illustrate the importance of information regarding the individual's interests before equipment selection. At its most basic level, sailing requires a boat and related safety equipment. The boat may be a small dinghy or an ocean-going yacht with multiple sails. Other types of technology (e.g., wetsuit, cooking facilities) may also be required, depending on the individual's interests and activity plans. In most cases, the individual with a disability can use the same equipment as all other participants without any additional modifications. Individuals with very limited or no limb movement can also sail, however, by using head, chin, or breath-controlled switches for the remote control of the sails and tiller (Wood, 1994).

> The sport of sailing can be done to one degree of difficulty or another. From a leisurely sightseeing tour under sunny skies and a light breeze, to competitive sailing in high winds and rough seas. I have been paralyzed since I was injured in a mountaineering accident in 1975 and so began to investigate a variety of options which would enable me to really experience sailing and meet its challenges. In order to identify the sailboat most suitable to my abilities, I went sailing with other people on a variety of boats. Through this experience, I found that moving from one side of the boat to the other was the biggest problem I encountered. I realized that additional padding would be required to prevent injury to my lower body, and I chose to pad myself rather than the boat. A custom designed wet suit and diving boots were activity-specific technologies which enhanced my safety. After testing several boats I decided that the Hobie 16 was most suited to my needs since I could easily slide from side to side on the soft "trampoline-like" deck [Figure 8–2]. I expected that I would have to modify the boat considerably to suit my needs but found that most of the necessary modifications were available to and utilized by any Hobie sailor (adjustable traveler, "easy righter" system for capsizing, mast hinge, etc.). With practice I developed methods that enabled me to counteract the forces of strong winds, sail the boat solo and launch the boat from either a dock or beach. (Axelson, 1978, pp. 5–6)

Equipment costs and the availability of funding for assistive devices can significantly influence an individual's access to appropriate recreational technologies. Some activities (e.g., horseback riding, auto racing) involve significant expenses for the participant by their very nature. Costs may increase if the individual with a disability requires assistance to participate and volunteers are unavailable. Many insurance programs cover the cost of assistive devices required for daily living and vocational activities wholly or partially, but exclude

---

A

**Figure 8–2** **A,** Peter Axelson sits on the trampoline deck of his Hobie-Cat sailboat for recreational sailing.

B

**Figure 8–2** continued **B,** uses a trapseat for better performance in competition.

recreational equipment from such coverage. It may take considerable creativity to identify sources of funding for the required recreational technology for an individual with a disability. Rehabilitation professionals must be challenged to consider the leisure and recreational needs and interests of their clients in the provision of assistive devices for daily living or vocational activities. For example, a number of wrist cuffs may enable an individual with limited hand function to hold a toothbrush; however, the selection of a cuff with additional gripping straps in the palm may enable the individual to use the same cuff for weight training, snooker, or tennis (Figure 8–3). Assistive devices should always be prescribed or designed to be as broadly applicable as possible.

## TYPES OF ASSISTIVE TECHNOLOGY FOR RECREATION

Assistive devices for recreation can be categorized as personal, activity-specific, or environmental technologies (Axelson, 1994, 1988a). A personal technology is equipment that individuals "wear" to enhance their ability to partici-

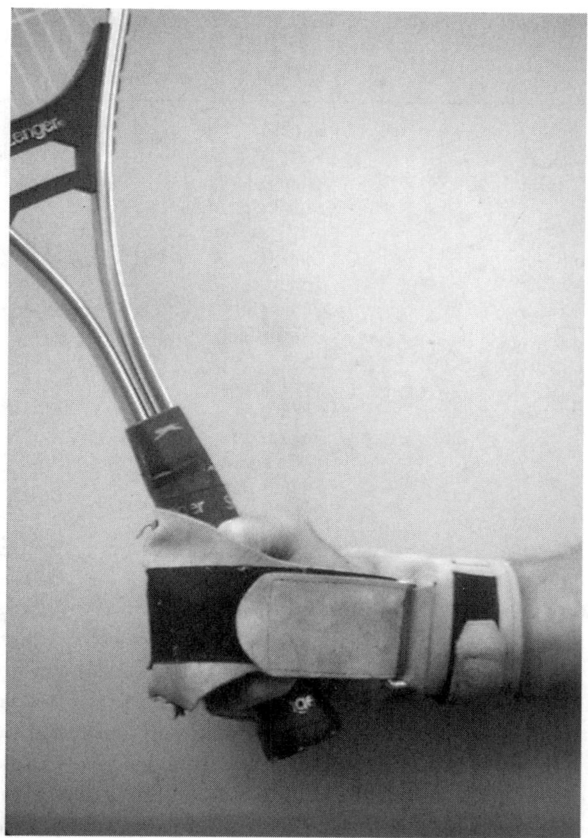

**Figure 8–3** Hand grip cuffs with an extra anchor strap in the palm can be used for both recreational and daily living activities.

pate in a desired activity (Table 8–3). Specialized personal technologies (e.g., racing wheelchair, dynamic prosthesis) are available to persons with a disability for a wide range of recreational activities. Through the selection of personal technologies suitable for both daily living and recreational pursuits, rehabilitation professionals can enhance the recreational participation of their clients without significantly increased investments of time (e.g., additional fittings) or resources (e.g., purchase of two wheelchairs).

Activity-specific technologies, which enable the individual to perform specific types of activities, often relate to the individual's need for transportation or

**Table 8–3** Personal, Activity-Specific, and Environmental Technologies

| *Category* | *Examples* | |
|---|---|---|
| **Personal** | Shoes<br>Wetsuits<br>Wheelchairs<br>Prosthetic limbs | Eyeglasses<br>Swimsuits<br>Braces |
| **Activity-specific** | Bicycles<br>Tents<br>Video games<br>Beep baseballs | Boats<br>Parachutes<br>Mono-ski |
| **Environmental** | Boat dock<br>Ski lifts<br>Textured floor services<br>Wide doorways<br>Hands-free shower facilities | Access ramps<br>Swimming pools |

communication (Table 8–3). For individuals with a disability, it is preferable to use "mainstream" activity-specific technologies or to modify these technologies, if required, because the development of a new type of technology requires a significant investment of time and resources. A back support attached to a seat (marketed to enhance user comfort) is mainstream technology that enables a person with a limited sitting balance to use a regular boat. Arm-powered cycles are "different" technologies that enable persons with a disability to cycle with their able-bodied friends. The Hand Bike is an arm-powered, accessible bicycle that enables individuals with good upper body function to cycle with family and friends (Figure 8–4). The Freedom Ryder Hand Cycle is an example of a three-wheeled arm-powered cycle (Figure 8–5). A wide variety of arm-powered cycles are currently available to people with a disability (Robbins, 1989).

Axelson (1984a, 1984b, 1986, 1988b) developed a chairlift-compatible, fully suspended mono-ski for use on challenging trails and in competition (Figure 8–6). The mono-ski uses a custom-molded seating system to give the user maximum control and connection to the ski. Custom-molded orthotics are used in a wide variety of assistive devices for recreation (e.g., mono-ski seats, tennis grips) to enable the user to "wear" and control the required technology as an extension of his or her body.

Environmental technologies most often function to provide for the daily living needs of people, such as shelter, food, and water. In general, these technologies do not move; the ramp that provides access to a recreational facility is an

**Figure 8–4** The Hand Bike, a two-wheeled arm-powered cycle, was developed by Doug Schwandt with support from the Palo Alto Veterans Administration Rehabilitation Research and Development Center. Photos courtesy of Doug Schwandt.

**Figure 8–5** Peter Axelson enjoys cycling on his Freedom Ryder Hand Cycle, one of many models of arm-powered cycles currently available.

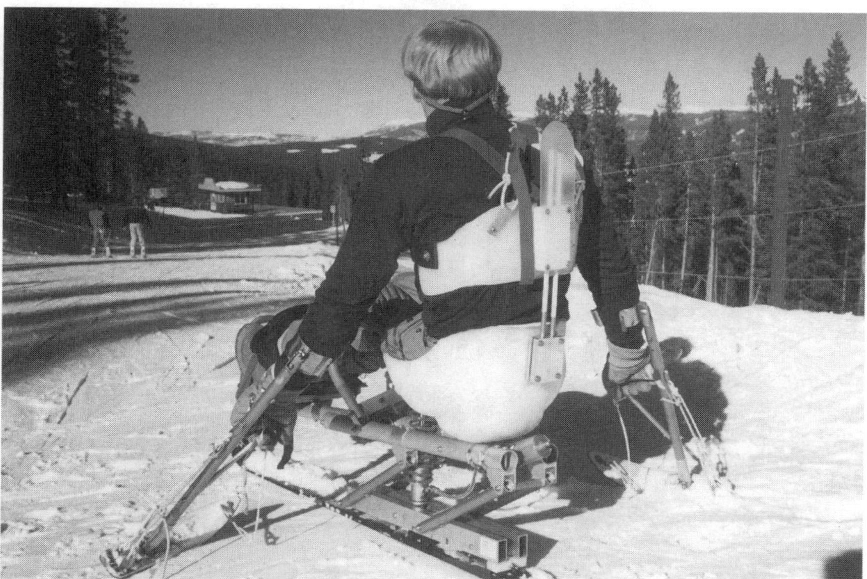

**Figure 8–6** Peter Axelson races downhill in the chairlift-compatible mono-ski that he designed with a custom-molded seat. A spring-loaded back orthosis replaces the function of the lower back muscles. Photos courtesy of Alan Siekman.

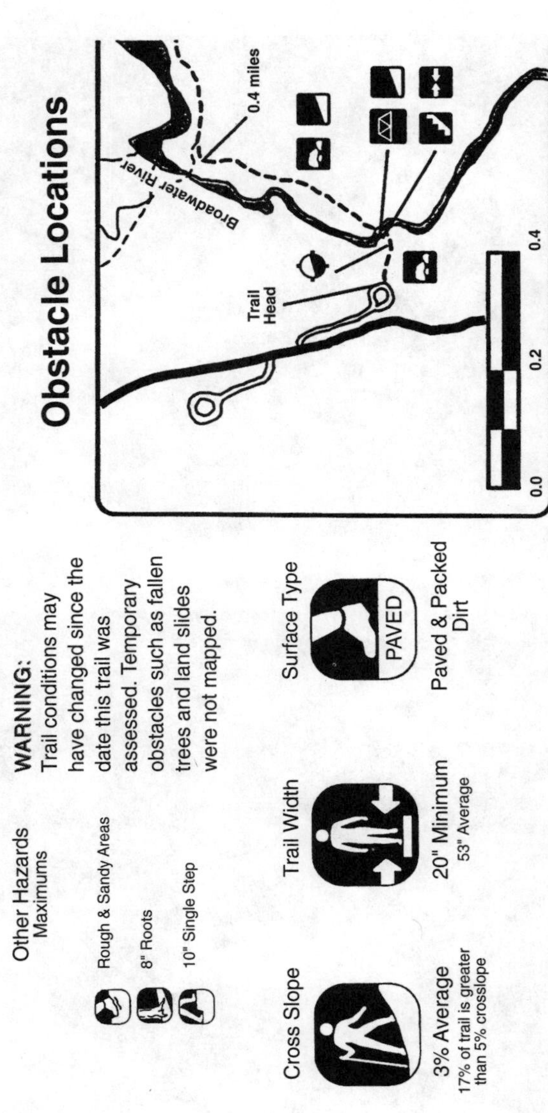


**Figure 8–7** Trail map

environmental technology, for example (Table 8–3). However, environmental technologies also include maps, signs, and other means used to communicate accessibility information for each environment. For example, objective measurements of trail characteristics can be combined with universal access information to facilitate the use of nature and hiking trails by people with a disability. Beneficial Designs has developed a Universal Trail Assessment Process that provides usage, mapping, maintenance, and access information (Axelson, Thomas, Chesney, Coveny, & Eve-Anchassi, 1994). This process is currently being implemented within various parks and forests in the United States. The development of technologies such as trail maps that incorporate universal access information enables those with a disability to make informed decisions regarding the conditions they will encounter during recreational activities and, thus, greatly enhances their use and enjoyment of public parks (Figure 8–7).

Architects and designers must be challenged to ensure that their designs are accessible to all members of the community and actively encourage their participation (Flynn, 1985; Galkowski, 1987a, 1987b; Thomson, Dendy, & de Deney, 1984). It is much more difficult to "retrofit" the environment after construction has been completed. The Phoenix Sportsplex (Crase, 1988), the Rick Hansen Centre (Clifford, 1989), and Variety Village (Bregman & Hamann, 1982–1983) are among many sport and recreation facilities designed specifically to be accessible to individuals with or without a disability.

## AVAILABILITY OF ASSISTIVE DEVICES FOR RECREATION

Recognition of the continuum of personal, activity-specific, and environmental technologies, and the differences and benefits of each type, is essential to the provision of assistive devices for recreation. For example, it may be better to modify a wheelchair to operate in sand than to build a boat that can move across the sand or a ramp over the sand to the edge of the water. Thus, in deciding on the type of technology that is best for the purpose desired, it is vital to consider the following questions:

- What information exists about the technology(ies) used for this activity?
- What information is available about the activity in the mainstream community, as well as in the disabled community?
- What are the functional capabilities of the individual?
- What are the characteristics of the environment (e.g., physical space, other participants) for the activity?
- Does this individual wish to participate independently or with assistance?

Once the technology most suited to the activity and the individual's needs has been selected, the next question is, how can the individual participate in the activity *right now*? A wide variety of modified recreational technologies are now readily available. Information about these devices can be obtained from a number of sources. Most companies that provide assistive technologies for daily living also carry a variety of devices for leisure activities (e.g., handgrips, playing card holders, book holders, page turners); the engineering departments in rehabilitation centers routinely modify switches and connections to provide access to powered devices (e.g., computers, model airplanes). Sporting goods manufacturers may have developed technologies suitable for individuals with a disability for the convenience or preference of able-bodied users (e.g., electric retrieve fishing reels, brightly colored tennis balls, lightweight basketballs, tennis racquets with enlarged hitting areas). Some companies consider making their products accessible to persons with a disability a priority and, therefore, provide consultation and instruction; for example, Shimano, a fishing equipment manufacturer, has a professional fisherman as a consultant to teach sport fishing to individuals with a disability. The recreation departments of rehabilitation centers can often provide information about available devices or access to magazines that publish information about recreational activities for people with a disability. National sport governing bodies and disability-specific organizations can also be potential sources of information.

Detailed information about assistive devices for recreation and relevant organizations can be obtained from *The International Directory of Recreation-Oriented Assistive Device Sources* (Nesbitt, 1986) and *Sports and Recreation for the Disabled: A Resource Manual* (Paciorek & Jones, 1994). Each of these books includes a detailed summary of adaptive technologies for more than 50 different leisure activities. Each listing includes a description of the technology, its use, and contact information for suppliers and manufacturers. In addition, many other directories of assistive devices include sections on recreation and leisure technologies. A few examples of the types of readily available devices for recreational activities, for a select number of leisure activities, are provided in Exhibit 8–A–3.

## CREATION OR MODIFICATION OF ASSISTIVE DEVICES

The development or modification of new assistive devices for recreation should be considered only as a last resort—after all avenues for using existing technology have been exhausted (Axelson, 1988a). When the desired activity is relatively unusual and, therefore, the number of participants is relatively small (e.g., mountaineering, hang gliding) or when the abilities of the individual are unique, there may be no suitable recreational technologies or designs. In this case, a new device or modification of recreational technology is required. The process begins with an analysis of what can be done by tomorrow, using materials on hand, in order to make the activity accessible. Existing assistive devices may have characteristics similar to those desired. For example, auditory signaling devices may be modified for use in an underwater environment by a person who is blind; enclosing the sounding device in a commercially available waterproof case may be satisfactory and is much easier than designing and building a new waterproof auditory signal. Similarly, hanging a garden hose from a rope above the swimming pool may help keep safe individuals who are deaf and blind (Figure 8–8). Holes in the hose allow the water to spray onto the surface of the pool, warning the swimmers when they approach the pool wall. The greater the similarity between the existing equipment and the desired technology, the easier, quicker, and cheaper the modifications. Although the initial efforts may not produce an ideal solution, attempting to solve the problem with a minimal amount of sophisticated technology will provide valuable information regarding the specifications for a more effective solution. Only after trying simpler measures should you seek to obtain or create more sophisticated types of technology.

When designing assistive technology, the following steps are recommended:

1. Specify the need.
2. Review available devices.
3. Identify specific design criteria.
4. Build a prototype.
5. Evaluate the prototype.
6. Use evaluation to revise prototype (repeat steps 3 to 5).
7. Publish completed design.

Specifying the "real" need is the first and most critical step in the development of assistive technology. If the need is not identified clearly enough or if it is identified incorrectly, considerable efforts can be wasted in trying to develop an inappropriate solution (Sobol, 1993). It is crucial that the "needs" for the assistive device (i.e., What function will this technology be required to perform?) be distinguished from the goals that the individual may have for participation (i.e., What is it that I want to be able to do?). For example, a person who uses a wheelchair may wish to try rock climbing. The goal may be to climb safely to the top of an indoor sport climbing wall, but the need may be for a device that ensures the safety of the legs during the climb or, depending on the individual's abilities, enables the legs to be used to support the body weight partially during the climb. If the goal of getting to the top of the wall is incorrectly identified as the need, solutions will focus on the use of ropes and pulleys

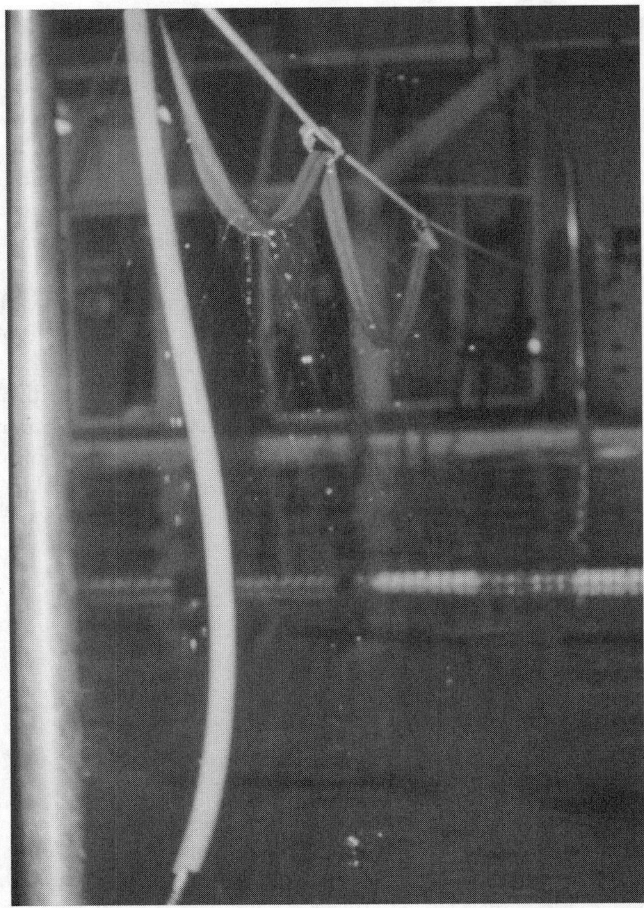

**Figure 8–8** A garden hose can be used as a simple warning device for deaf–blind swimmers.

to support or lift the participant or the design of the climbing course, and the individual will remain unable to climb independently or to climb on courses that are not specifically designed for his or her needs. In contrast, the development of technology that will enable the individual to support the body weight partially with the legs will encourage the development of the skills needed to get to the top of the wall independent of rope/pulley lifting devices and regardless of the course design.

Since new technology is being developed, the review of available devices should be expanded to include devices for nonrecreational pursuits that perform similar functions to the desired technology. For example, a rock climbing leg support may not be available per se, but a variety of braces are available that can support an individual's weight. The information previously collected and all of the new information obtained should be used to establish criteria for a satisfactory design. Just as the need must be clearly specified, so must the design criteria. Stating that a sailboard is to be modified for use by a person whose arms have both been amputated does not provide sufficient detail for the development of a prototype. It is essential to specify what the sailor is required to do and the ways in which the sailboard must be manipulated. For example, the individual must be able to pull the sail up out of the water when starting; move the sail forward and backward, as well as side to side relative to the board; hold the sail out of the water while moving around the mast to turn; and release or allow the sail to swing freely in order to stop. These actions require the ability to (a) hold onto the rope used to lift the mast, onto the mast itself, and onto the boom; and (b) continually change position or release the grip as required. In addition, the device used for grasping must function in water; be securely attached to resist wind, waves, and falls; and be light enough that it would not weigh heavily if the participant were in the water. Whether the device will be used in salt or fresh water affects the types of materials that can be used. The greater the detail of the design criteria, the more likely the success of the prototype. Individuals who are unfamiliar with different types of activity technology or those who wish to try a new activity should seek assistance from coaches, instructors, or more experienced participants in order to establish the design criteria.

Once the design criteria have been established, the first prototype can be developed. If the technology required is very sophisticated or expensive, the first prototype should be a working model or simulation. Many rehabilitation centers have engineers on staff who can assist with the prototype development. Using wood, wire, plastic pipe, or foam to build a model for preliminary evaluation can reveal required changes before an actual prototype is manufactured. For example, a prototype for a chair to enable individuals who use crutches or a wheelchair to participate in aquabics (water exercise) classes was easily produced in 2 to 3 hours using PVC (polyvinyl chloride) plumbing pipe and lawn chair webbing (Figure 8–9). The total cost of materials was approximately $20. Other potential sources of expertise are local fabrication shops that work with similar materials, manufacturers of similar devices, retail stores that sell and service recreational equipment, skilled tradesmen and/or related apprenticeship programs, or schools offering technical skills courses (Axelson, 1985b).

It is essential that the individual(s) for whom the design is intended evaluate the prototype. Only the individual with a disability knows exactly what his or

**Figure 8–9** Plumbing pipe and lawn chair webbing produce a simple, inexpensive functional prototype of a chair for water exercise classes.

---

her abilities are and whether the technology is satisfactory. Evaluations should take place on several occasions under several circumstances, particularly when the prototype involves parts that may change shape (e.g., leather, foam) or wear out (e.g., joints, fabrics). Every effort should be made to identify problems or changes in any aspect of the design that would improve the function of the device. Decisions can then be made on which changes can actually be incorporated into the revised prototype. In most cases, further revisions involve modifying the original prototype, although problems are sometimes significant enough to warrant a completely new design.

> The Arroya is a downhill skiing system for persons with disabilities [see Figure 8–10]. The user sits in the Arroya and controls the direction and velocity of the sled by shifting his or her weight and appropriate arm movements. The control surface of the Arroya features a central tunnel with four inward facing edges for maneuverability and control. The Arroya enables individuals with mobility limitations to ski with family and friends and also led to competitive skiing events. The development of the Arroya illustrates the significant investment of time and resources required to develop a totally new type of recreation technology.

**Figure 8–10** Rick Ruscio races downhill in the Arroya sit ski developed by Peter Axelson. Photo courtesy of Arne Folkedal.

The need for a new sledding device was identified in December 1977 when evaluation of a Norwegian Pulk indicated that improved directional and velocity control were required. The initial prototype, made of urethane foam and fiberglass, was tested in March 1978 both with and without a ski attached to the bottom. Evaluations of the prototype by individuals with a disability were completed and appropriate modifications incorporated into the design. Six prototypes were built and evaluated between March 1978 and December 1983 before the final product became commercially available.

The goal of the project was the development of an integrative sport in a winter environment. The need was identified for a skiing system which would enable people with lower limb disabilities to participate in the traditional downhill skiing environment. A review of previous research identified several existing skiing systems. However, these designs were limited in the user's ability to control the direction and velocity of the ski system and were not compatible with the ski lifts most commonly used in North America. Design specifications (length, width, weight, turning radius, etc.) were identified, evalua-

> tion sites were selected, year-round testing was established on glaciers, and user/instructor clinics were established prior to the prototype evaluation. Questionnaires and interviews of persons involved in the evaluation were used to obtain objective feedback on each prototype design. The researcher interacted with manufacturers of similar products, industries using similar technology and manufacturers of similar components to those used in the Arroya throughout the development process. Involvement of the manufacturers during the research and development process was crucial to the creation of a commercially viable product. Local industries were consulted regarding materials and manufacturing processes, and technical expertise was obtained through industrial and university sources. Legal expertise was sought for design patents and liability issues. Between 200 and 600 hours of time were invested in the research and production of each prototype, with the time increasing with the complexity of subsequent prototypes. Total resources utilized for the project (time and materials) exceeded $60,000. The development of the Arroya sit ski was supported by the Rehabilitation Research and Development Center of the Palo Alto Veteran's Administration. (Axelson, 1983)

The process of designing assistive technology is a lengthy and expensive one. The first prototype is not always a perfect solution to the problem. The development of the sit ski required 5 years and more than $60,000 (Figure 8–10). Depending on the type of device required, considerable resources are necessary to support the prototype development and revisions. Charitable organizations, service clubs, trade unions, sporting goods manufacturers, and private companies may provide financial support or donate materials or labor. The Adapted Sport Technology Research Association (ASTRA), coordinated through Variety Village in Toronto, is an international network of volunteers with expertise in the modification of recreation equipment for persons with a disability. Many other organizations (e.g., Tetra Society, Telephone Pioneers, Volunteer Medical Engineers), particularly those related to rehabilitation or medical engineering, also offer volunteer assistance for the creation of assistive devices for persons with a disability.

The final step in the design process is the publication of the finished product. If the product has broad applicability, "publication" may occur through the commercial manufacture and marketing of the product. Even if the developer does not think anyone else will require the same type of device, however, the project (including design information wherever possible) should be submitted to publications so that ideas and experiences can be shared. Most publications (e.g., *Sports 'N Spokes*, *Abilities*) directed toward individuals with a disability regularly include information on new products or do-it-yourself ideas. The growing interest in all types of recreational activities, as well as the disappearing biases regarding the types of activities in which people with a disability can participate, is creating an ever increasing demand for new types of recreational technology. The experience and knowledge gained through the development of a specific piece of equipment can greatly enhance the development of other types of technology for individuals with a disability.

---

## BIBLIOGRAPHY

Adams, R.C., Daniel, A.N., McCubbin, J.A., & Rullman, L. (1982). *Games, sports, and exercises for the physically handicapped* (3rd ed.). Philadelphia: Lea & Febiger.

Allen, A. (1981). *Sports for the handicapped.* New York: Walker & Company.

American College of Sports Medicine. (1994). *Guidelines for exercise testing and prescription* (4th ed.). Philadelphia: Lea & Febiger.

Axelson, P. (1978). Go for it. *Sports 'N Spokes, 3*(6), 5–6.

Axelson, P.W. (1983). *From research and development to a commercially available device: A case study on the Arroya Downhill Skiing System for persons with disabilities.* Paper presented at the 6th Annual Conference on Rehabilitation Engineering, Veterans Administration Medical Center, San Diego, CA.

Axelson, P. (1984a). Sit-skiing. *Sports 'N Spokes, 10*(5), 28–31.

Axelson, P. (1984b). Sit-skiing: Part II. *Sports 'N Spokes, 10*(6), 1–6.

Axelson, P. (1984c, November). *Positioning people with disabilities in active postures.* Paper presented at the National Symposium on the Care, Treatment and Prevention of Decubitus Ulcers, Arlington, VA.

Axelson, P.W. (1984d, October). *Facilitation of recreation through design.* Paper presented at the International Conference on Rural Rehab Technology, University of North Dakota, 98–104.

Axelson, P.W. (1985a, January). Facilitation of integrated recreation. *Paraplegia News, 39*(1), 26–29.

Axelson, P.W. (1985b, October). *Applying adaptive technology to recreation for people with disabilities.* Paper presented at the 5th International Symposium on Adapted Physical Activity, Toronto.

Axelson, P. (1986). Adaptive technology for skiing. *Palaestra,* 45–50.

Axelson, P. (1988a, June). *Technology as a continuum for recreation.* Paper presented at the 11th Annual Conference on Rehabilitation Engineering and International Conference of the Association for Advancement of Rehab Technology, Montreal.

Axelson, P. (1988b). Hitting the slopes. *Sports 'N Spokes, 14*(4), 22–34.

Axelson, P. (1994, March). The importance of recreation technology. Personal communication.

Axelson, P., & Castellano, J. (1990). Take to the trails. *Sports 'N Spokes, 16*(2), 20–22.

Axelson, P., & McCornack, J. (1983, September). Recreation: In pursuit of freedom, fulfillment, and balance. *Mainstream,* 8–10.

Axelson, P.W., Thomas, P.H., Chesney, D.A., Coveny, J.L., & Eve-Anchassi, D. (1994, June). *Trail guides with universal access information.* Proceedings of the 1994 Rehabilitation Engineering Society of North America Conference, Arlington, VA: RESNA Press, 306–308.

Axelson, P., & Zollars, J.A. (1992, September). *Assistive technologies for the seating and mobility needs of persons with osteogenesis imperfecta.* Presentation for the National Institutes of Health, Washington, DC.

Behrman, A.L. (1990). Factors in functional assessment. *Journal of Rehabilitation Research and Development* (Clin. Suppl. 2), 17–30.

Bernhardt, D.B. (ed.). (1984). Recreation for the disabled child. *Physical and Occupational Therapy in Pediatrics, 4*(3).

Blackwood, B. (1978). Flying: Changing your plane. *Sports 'N Spokes, 4*(4), 11.

Bregman and Hamann, Architects and Engineers. (1982–1983). Equal opportunity for the disabled and handicapped: Variety Village Sport Training and Fitness Centre—A place for all. *Coaching Science Update*, 38–41.

Burgess, E.M., & Rappoport, A. (1992). *Physical fitness: A guide for individuals with lower limb loss.* Baltimore: Veterans Health Administration.

Burlingame, J., & Blaschko, T.M. (1990). *Assessment tools for recreation therapy: Red book #1.* Seattle: Idyll Arbor.

Canadian Society for Exercise Physiology. (1995). *Leadership development initiative for persons with a disability.* Gloucester, Ontario: Author.

Clifford, L. (1989). Rick Hansen Centre, University of Alberta. *CAHPER Journal, 55*(3), 40–43.

Colston, L.G. (1991). The expanding role of assistive technology in therapeutic recreation. *Journal of Physical Education, Recreation and Dance, 62*(4), 39–41.

Cowin, L., Sibille, J., & O'Riain, M.D. (1984). Motor soccer: The electric connection. *Sports 'N Spokes, 10*(4), 43–44.

Crase, C. (1990). Mark Wellman. *Sports 'N Spokes, 16*(3), 39.

Crase, C. (1993). Choices, choices, choices . . . Wheelchair comparison. *Sports 'N Spokes, 18*(6), 33–40.

Crase, N. (1988). Pioneering a park for the disabled. *Sports 'N Spokes, 13*(6), 58–59.

Dean, R.C. (1976). Monoped bicycling. *Bicycling, 17*(10), 68–69.

Didon, M. (1987). Aviation de loisir et handicap physique moteur. *Agressologie, 28*(7), 751–753.

Douglas, G.R. (1986). Life beyond 20/200. *Canadian Journal of Ophthalmology, 21*(3), 77–78.

Duncan, S.J. (1986). Knitting device for bilateral upper extremity amputee. *American Journal of Occupational Therapy, 40*(9), 637–638.

Enders, A. (1984). *Technology for independent living sourcebook.* Bethesda, MD: Rehabilitation Engineering Society of North America.

Flynn, R.B. (1985). *Planning facilities for athletics, physical education, and recreation.* Reston, VA: American Alliance for Health, Physical Education, Recreation and Dance.

Forde, J. (1989). Dancing on wheels. *Nursing Times, 85*(33), 52–53.

Galkowski, A.E. (1987a). Architects supporting the integration of the disabled within the community. *International Journal of Rehabilitation Research, 10*(4 Suppl. 5), 220–224.

Galkowski, A.E. (1987b). Architectural design of appropriate facilities for leisure activities of disabled people. *International Disability Studies, 9*(2), 85–87.

Hamel, R. (1992). Getting into the game: New opportunities for athletes with disabilities. *Physician and Sportsmedicine, 20*(11), 128–129.

Hay, C. (1982). Wilderness travel on horseback. *Sports 'N Spokes, 7*(6), 6–8.

Hicklin, J. (1982). Sail towards health. *Nursing Mirror, 154 (Community Forum 5)*, xi–xii.

Kalscheur, J.A. (1992). Benefits of the Americans with Disabilities Act of 1990 for children and adolescents with disabilities. *American Journal of Occupational Therapy, 46*(5), 419–426.

Kegel, B. (1985). Physical fitness, sports and recreation for those with lower limb amputation or impairment. *Journal of Rehabilitation Research and Development* (Clin. Suppl. 1).

Kelly, L.E. (1990). Wheelchairs and assistive devices. In J.P. Winnick (Ed.), *Adapted physical education and sport* (pp. 109–118). Champaign, IL: Human Kinetics.

Kinney, W.B., & Coyle, C.P. (1992). Predicting life satisfaction among adults with physical disabilities. *Archives of Physical Medicine and Rehabilitation, 73*, 863–869.

Krag, M.H., & Messner, D.G. (1982). Skiing for the physically handicapped. *Clinics in Sports Medicine, 1*(2), 319–332.

Lais, G. (1985). Paddling the Yukon. *Sports 'N Spokes, 10*(6), 9–12.

Loesch, L.C. (1981). Leisure counselling for disabled older persons. *Journal of Rehabilitation, 47*, 58–63.

Madorsky, J.G.B., & Kiley, D.P. (1984). Wheelchair mountaineering. *Archives of Physical Medicine and Rehabilitation, 65*, 490–492.

Madorsky, J.G.B., & Madorsky, A.G. (1988). Scuba diving: Taking the wheelchair out of wheelchair sports. *Archives of Physical Medicine and Rehabilitation, 69*(3), 215–219.

McBey, M.A. (1985). The therapeutic aspects of gardens and gardening: An aspect of total patient care. *Journal of Advanced Nursing, 10*(6), 591–595.

McKinley, N. (1981). Wheels in the wilderness. *Sports 'N Spokes, 7*(1), 9.

Meaden, C.A. (1991). Assessing people with a disability for sport: The profile system. *Physiotherapy, 77*(6), 360–366.

Meyer, L., & Ruck, S. (1974). They too can shoot an arrow into the air. *Journal of Health, Physical Education and Recreation, 45*(1), 79.

Michael, J.W., Gailey, R.S., & Bowker, J.H. (1990). New developments in recreational prostheses and adaptive devices for the amputee. *Clinical Orthopedics and Related Research, 256*, 64–75.

Nava, L.C. (1986). Coupled bicycles for disabled and able-bodied to ride together. *Prosthetics & Orthotics International, 10*(2), 103–104.

Nesbitt, J.A. (Ed.). (1986). *The international directory of recreation-oriented assistive device sources*. Marina Del Ray, CA: Lifeboat Press.

Orr, R.E., & Sheffield, J. (1983–1984). Innertube waterpolo: More than just a non-swimmers' recreation. *Swimming Technique, 20*(3), 37–38.

Ozer, M.N. (1990). A participatory planning process for wheelchair selection. *Journal of Rehabilitation Research and Development* (Clin. Suppl. 2), 31–36.

Paciorek, M.J., & Jones, J.A. (1994). *Sports and recreation for the disabled: A resource manual* (2nd ed.). Carmel, IN: Cooper.

Petrofksy, J.S., Heaton, H., & Phillips, C.A. (1983). Outdoor bicycle for exercise in paraplegics and quadriplegics. *Journal of Biomedical Engineering, 5*(4), 292–296.

Ragnarsson, K.T. (1990). Prescription considerations and a comparison of conventional and lightweight wheelchairs. *Journal of Rehabilitation Research and Development* (Suppl. 2), 8–16.

Ranu, H.S. (1986). Engineering aspects of rehabilitation for the handicapped. *Journal of Medical Engineering and Technology, 10*(1), 16–20.

Robbins, S. (1989). Pedal power revisited: An updated survey of handcycle manufacturers. *Sports 'N Spokes, 15*(3), 32–36.

Rourke, L. (1985). Elements of archery: Part III. Instruction. *Sports 'N Spokes, 10*(6), 18–19.

Rubin, G., & Fleiss, D. (1983). Devices to enable persons with amputation to participate in sports. *Archives of Physical Medicine and Rehabilitation, 64*(1), 37–40.

Schwandt, D. (1980). Para-Bike. *Sports 'N Spokes, 6*(4), 18–21.

Seaman, J.A., & DePauw, K.P. (1989). *The new adapted physical education: A developmental approach.* Mountain View, CA: Mayfield.

Seidler, T.L., Turner, E.T., & Horine, L. (1993). Promoting active lifestyles through facilities and equipment. *Journal of Physical Education, Recreation and Dance, 64*(1), 39–42.

Skinner, J.S. (1993). *Exercise testing and exercise prescription for special cases* (2nd ed.). Philadelphia: Lea & Febiger.

Slagle, D.K. (1982). All terrain vehicles. *Sports 'N Spokes, 7*(6), 11–19.

Sobol, S. (1993, December). People with disabilities: Going my way. *Graduating Engineer,* 38–44.

Sol, N., & Zwiren, L. (1974). Fencing for quadriplegics. *Journal of Health, Physical Education and Recreation, 45*(1), 79–81.

Thomson, N., Dendy, E., & de Deney, D. (Eds.). (1984). *Sports and recreation provision for disabled people.* London: Architectural Press.

Walker, M.L., & Seidler, T.L. (1993). *Sports equipment management.* Boston: Jones and Bartlett.

Ware, M. (1982). Canoe racing. *Sports 'N Spokes, 8*(2), 13–14.

White, E. (1991). Leisure and Recreation. *British Medical Journal* 302 (6774):461–463.

Willard, D. (1978). *Becoming aware: A handbook for leaders working with disabled children.* Toronto: Ontario Ministry of Culture and Recreation.

Wilson, A.B., & McFarland, S.R. (1990). Types of wheelchairs. *Journal of Rehabilitation Research and Development* (Suppl. 2), 104–116.

Wood, D. (1994). A breath of freedom for quadriplegics. *Canadian Geographic, 114*(4), 10.

Zollars, J.A., & Axelson, P. (1993, June). *The back support shaping system: An alternative for persons using wheelchairs with sling back upholstery.* Paper presented at the Annual Conference, Rehabilitation Engineering Society of North America, Las Vegas.

# Appendix 8–A

## Resources

**Exhibit 8–A–1** Sample References for Additional Information on Selected Activities

| Activity | Selected References |
|---|---|
| Archery | Meyer & Ruck, 1974; Rourke, 1985 |
| Bicycling | Dean, 1976; Nava, 1986; Petrofsky, Heaton, & Phillips, 1983; Robbins, 1989; Schwandt, 1980 |
| Board Games | Nesbitt, 1986 |
| Canoeing | Lais, 1985; Ware, 1982 |
| Dancing | Forde, 1989; Kegel, 1985 |
| Fencing | Sol & Zwiren, 1974 |
| Flying | Blackwood, 1978; Didon, 1987 |
| Gardening | Kegel, 1985; McBey, 1985 |
| Golf | Burgess & Rappoport, 1992; Kegel, 1985 |
| Hockey | Burgess & Rappoport, 1992; Paciorek & Jones, 1994 |
| Hunting | Nesbitt, 1986; Ranu, 1986 |
| Lawn Bowling | Paciorek & Jones, 1994 |
| Martial Arts | Kegel, 1985 |
| Mountaineering | Madorsky & Kiley, 1984 |
| Needlecrafts | Duncan, 1986; Nesbitt, 1986 |
| Parachuting and Hang Gliding | Kegel, 1985; Nesbitt, 1986 |
| Racquet Sports | Burgess & Rappoport, 1992 |
| Rock Climbing | Crase, 1990 |
| Sailing | Axelson, 1978; Hicklin, 1982 |
| Scuba Diving | Kegel, 1985; Madorsky & Madorsky, 1988 |
| Skiing | Allen, 1981; Bernhardt, 1984; Krag & Messner, 1982 |
| Soccer | Bernhardt, 1984; Burgess & Rappoport, 1992; Cowin, Sibille, & O'Riain, 1984 |
| Wilderness Travel | Axelson & Castellano, 1990; Hay, 1982; McKinley, 1981; Slagle, 1982 |

**Exhibit 8–A–2** Magazines and Journal Publications

| Title | Focus |
|---|---|
| *Abilities* | People with disabilities accessing all aspects of life, including recreation and leisure (Canadian) |
| *Adaptive Physical Activity Quarterly (APAQ)* | Scientific publication of research on physical activity for people with a disability |
| *Disability Today* | Issues relating to people with a disability (Canadian) |
| *Disabled Outdoors* | Outdoor activities, programs, facilities, and technologies for people with a disability |
| *International Paralympic Committee Newsletter* | International competitive sport for people with a physical disability |
| *Mainstream Magazine* | A magazine written and published by people with disabilities covering all aspects of daily living, vocational, and leisure activities for all disabilities |
| *Palaestra* | People with disabilities accessing recreation and leisure (American) |
| *Paraplegia News* | Information for individuals with spinal cord injury on all aspects of life |
| *Sports 'N Spokes* | Sports and recreation for people who use wheelchairs (American) |
| *Technical Aid to the Disabled (TAD) Journal* | Scientific publication of assistive device research |
| *Wheeler's Choice* | Recreational and competitive wheelchair sports (Canadian) |

**Exhibit 8–A–3** Selected Leisure Activities and Assistive Devices

| Sport | Modified Equipment |
| --- | --- |
| All Terrain Vehicles and Snowmobiles | hand control<br>grip padding<br>extended backrest<br>cane/crutch racks<br>foot plates<br>modified seating and supports<br>foot and leg straps |
| Archery | trigger releases<br>wrist/elbow support<br>standing support<br>bow support<br>mouth pieces<br>prostheses<br>chest belts<br>bow sling |
| Baseball and Softball | beeper balls<br>wheelchair softballs<br>modified and audible bases<br>lightweight bats<br>prostheses |
| Basketball | adjustable hoops<br>netted hoops<br>sport wheelchairs<br>prostheses<br>banking backboard<br>spoke guards<br>standing platform |
| Bowling and Boccia | ball ramps and carriers<br>bowling sticks<br>ball carriers<br>handle balls<br>headstick or remote ball release<br>prostheses<br>bowling rails |
| Canoeing and Kayaking | custom seats and support<br>outriggers<br>enlarged cockpit<br>leg-powered paddles<br>seat belts/leg straps<br>tactile compass<br>prostheses<br>one-arm paddles |

*continues*

**Exhibit 8–A–3** continued

| Sport | Modified Equipment |
|---|---|
| Cycling | tricycles and recumbents<br>hand and row cycles<br>foot plates and straps<br>arm and leg gears<br>cycle wheelchairs<br>seat and back supports<br>tandem cycles<br>prostheses<br>hand and leg brakes |
| Fishing | rod holders/harnesses<br>prostheses<br>electric and electronic reels and casting devices<br>mouth switch control<br>grasp splint or hook<br>wheelchair accessible fishing boats<br>modified tackle |
| Fitness | exercise videos<br>wheelchair and arm ergometers<br>wheelchair rollers<br>grip splints for weights<br>accessible weight training equipment |
| Flying | hand controls<br>ultralight aircraft<br>single joy stick control<br>wheels or pontoons<br>parachutes<br>rear brakes<br>driving ring<br>prostheses |
| Golf | chairs and stools<br>customized and shortened clubs<br>prostheses<br>golf carts<br>putter with ball retriever<br>rotator golf shoe |

*continues*

**Exhibit 8–A–3** continued

| Sport | Modified Equipment |
|---|---|
| Hockey (Floor, Road, or Ice) | scooter hockey<br>ice picks and sledges<br>beep pucks<br>ringette<br>pillo polo foam sticks and ball |
| Horseback Riding | body harness or waist belt<br>modified saddles<br>modified reins<br>breakaway stirrups<br>Devonshire boots<br>prostheses<br>mounting blocks and ramps |
| Hunting and Shooting | variable gun sizes and designs<br>thumb hole stock rifles<br>shooting rests<br>trigger devices<br>gun loading press |
| Ice and Roller Skating | walkers<br>skate outriggers<br>ankle-foot orthoses<br>wheelchair runners<br>ice sledding<br>prostheses |
| Racquet Sports (Tennis, Squash, Badminton, Racquetball, etc.) | racquet sport wheelchairs<br>racquet control cuffs and grip aids<br>positioning straps<br>custom grip orthotics<br>extension handle |
| Reading and Board Games | book strap/holder<br>page turner<br>print magnifier<br>auditory reading machines<br>magnetic/Braille/Velcro games<br>card shufflers and holders |

*continues*

**Exhibit 8–A–3** continued

| Sport | Modified Equipment |
|---|---|
| Rowing | rowing catamaran<br>modified seating and supports<br>stationary seating<br>rowing mitts and wrist braces<br>prostheses |
| Running | shock absorbing crutch tips<br>track wheelchairs<br>running tethers<br>auditory direction guides<br>prostheses |
| Sailing | modified boat designs<br>"tacking" and specialized seats<br>prostheses<br>custom wetsuits<br>mast hinges<br>trapeze slings |
| Scuba Diving | modified wetsuits<br>purge valves<br>buoyancy compensator<br>vented fins<br>prostheses<br>diver propulsion vehicles<br>buddy tethers |
| Skiing | outriggers and angled poles<br>sit skis, bi-skis, mono-skis<br>ski bras and straps<br>walker and crutch skis<br>kayak poles<br>prostheses<br>boot wedges<br>ski weights |
| Sky Diving | tandem jumping<br>foot taping<br>water landings<br>blanket catches<br>prostheses<br>Wenger Cocoon body stabilizer |

*continues*

**Exhibit 8–A–3** continued

| Sport | Modified Equipment |
|---|---|
| Soccer | prostheses<br>electric wheelchair indoor version<br>crutch soccer<br>beeper balls<br>wheelchair ball bumper |
| Swimming | hand grip assists<br>arm and leg fins/paddles<br>pool lifts, ramps, and stairs<br>prostheses<br>auditory signaling systems<br>flotation devices |
| Table Tennis | audible balls<br>paddle grips, cuffs, and straps<br>table side guards and skirts<br>adjustable height tables<br>arm supports |
| Water-Skiing | ski rope harness<br>dual rope handles<br>ski trainer harness and ski bras<br>sit skis and saucers<br>ski boom and wide handle<br>hydro slide<br>stabilizer bar |

## *Chapter 9*

# It's Child's Play

*Doreen Brenner Greenstein*

> When I successfully adapted my first toy, I was empowered. Thus began an ongoing search for the next toy that would motivate my son. . . . But the more toys I adapted, the less interested [my son] became in using switches to simply turn toys on and off. I began to realize that there was much more to this play stuff than first meets the eye. Parents of typical kids simply buy them toys and they play with them. [My son] demanded a higher level of involvement, and I discovered that I didn't know how to play with him. I hit the books and started learning about the developmental levels of play. This knowledge gave me a whole new perspective on how to play with both of my children. (Isaacs, 1994, p. 4)

This was how one mother discovered that assistive technology and play were intricately involved. As Mrs. Isaacs became more sensitive, she learned that one of her son's favorite "switch activities" was turning on a flashlight installed in a shoe box with red cellophane and white construction paper; this device became a "fasten-your-seatbelts" sign and part of an imaginative game. Mrs. Isaacs started with assistive technology, but ended with—*play*.

Mark Twain defined *play* very well more than 100 years ago in *Tom Sawyer* (1875) when he wrote: "If he had been a great and wise philosopher, like the writer of this book, he would have now comprehended that Work consists of whatever a body is *obliged* to do and that Play consists of whatever a body is *not obliged* to do." Nowadays, it is common to consider play a child's work. Little is known about play and children with disabilities, however. In part, the problem has been that "the emphasis has been on helping the children compensate for and cope with their disabilities. . . . Much less attention has been paid to what was already there, and to make the most of the 'normal' aspects of special children's lives" (Hellendoorn, 1994a, p. 2).

A common factor in the research about the play of those children who have difficulty interacting with their immediate environment is an emphasis on active intervention by stimulating adults rather than on naturally occurring play behaviors. In fact, Hellendoorn (1994b) suggested that perhaps too much is "being done" to these children, and too little is being left for the children to do themselves. There is no simple alternative to this intervention mentality, especially when it is so easy for practitioners and therapists to turn play into therapy. So they are more apt to read about research in "play skills" (e.g., Berger, 1990), "play training" (de Moor, van Wasberghe, & Oud, 1994), "play behaviors" or "toy behaviors" (Black, Freeman, & Montgomery, 1975), than about play itself, which is defined as "self-initiated and intrinsically motivated activity, containing at least some spark of play pleasure" (Hellendoorn, van der Kooij, & Sutton-Smith, 1994, p. 220).

## MOTIVATION RESEARCH

In their research, Deci and Ryan (1982) developed the following definitions:

1. intrinsic motivation: doing something for the activity itself. There is no reward separate from the spontaneous feelings and thoughts that accompany the activity.
2. extrinsic motivation: working toward some external reward. The reward may be money, good grades, status, approval, or the avoidance of an unpleasant event.
3. amotivation: passivity and nonresponsiveness. Amotivation is sometimes linked with learned helplessness, a person's belief that he or she cannot have a meaningful impact on the immediate environment, leading to a feeling of helplessness and lack of self-initiated behavior.

Why is the phrase *play pleasure* preferable to the phrases, *play skills, play training,* or *play behaviors*? Looking at a child with a particular toy, the developmental psychologist observes that

1. she is playing with the toy because
   - she wants to (intrinsic motivation)
   - someone else wants her to (extrinsic motivation)
2. she is not playing with the toy because
   - she is not interested (amotivation)
   - she has failed before and has stopped trying (learned helplessness)
   - she wants to, but is physically unable to do so (needs assistive technology help)

More than 20 years ago, partially in response to behaviorists such as Skinner (e.g., 1938, 1954), a group of researchers began to look at some of the possible adverse effects of using rewards to encourage children to engage in an activity. After a considerable amount of research, it is clear that offering a reward for an enjoyable behavior is likely to decrease a child's subsequent interest in that behavior. Greene and Lepper (1974), two of the early motivation researchers, asked whether the provision of extrinsic rewards would turn "play" (an activity that will be engaged in for its own sake) into "work" (an activity that will be engaged in only with extrinsic incentives). Although challenged by reinforcement theorists (e.g., Feingold & Mahoney, 1975), the phenomenon has proven robust: even after one experience, children who are told they will get a reward for doing something that they like (such as coloring pictures, doing mazes) are much less likely to choose that activity voluntarily afterward. (Luckily, the negative effect disappears after several weeks.)

## PLAY INTERVENTION RESEARCH

In a study that examined a play training intervention with preschoolers with cerebral palsy and Down syndrome, researchers were trying to encourage developmentally more advanced patterns of play. They discovered, however, that the play training did not increase the frequency or duration of developmentally higher play levels; in fact, the control group of children with cerebral palsy made progress in achieving higher levels of functional-relational play, whereas the matched treatment group did not (de Moor et al., 1994).

One of the more persistent findings in research about play and children with special needs has been that mothers of children with disabilities are more directive than other mothers are in their interactions with their children. For example, Marfo (1984) and Jones (1980) found that mothers of children with Down syndrome were more likely to refer to interactive sessions with their young children as "teaching sessions" and believed that a "good interaction" was one in which their child had learned something while the mothers of nonhandicapped children felt that a good interaction was one in which both partners had shared a playful experience.

A study in imaginative play training for children with severe retardation showed that many of the children were able to learn new "play skills" in a laboratory setting and to demonstrate them to an adult. The children did not transfer the new skills to their natural living environment, however, leaving the researcher to caution that perhaps they were teaching and reinforcing the children's "tendency to repeat familiar acts, rather like tricks to satisfy the adults instead of intrinsically motivated action" (Hellendoorn, 1994c, p. 116).

When researchers brought severely developmentally delayed children into a laboratory setting, they found that these children did indeed play, even those who had not previously been encouraged to play. The children very quickly adapted to the new circumstances and played spontaneously. The children's play activities approximated the children's developmental rather than their chronological ages (Hulme & Lunzer, 1966).

## CHILDREN PLAYING AT HOME

The studies mentioned thus far were conducted in university or medical developmental psychology laboratories, although it is known that bringing parents and children into an artificial setting is likely to induce artificial behaviors (Bronfenbrenner, 1979). Natural family and at-home play (as opposed to play interventions) has been neglected as an area of interest and research for children with disabilities. With intervention frequently occurring at birth or shortly thereafter, professionals can enter the lives of families as "experts" very early on and can convert family interactions into therapies or educational activities, even—especially—at home. The natural strengths of families and the games and routines that families share are often overlooked when professionals "prescribe" activities. This is unfortunate because these family-initiated activities are less prone to elicit the feelings of inadequacy that "professional exercises" can arouse in families (Dunst, Trivette, & Deal, 1988).

McEvoy and McConkey (1983) found that mothers of moderately or severely handicapped children (like other mothers) viewed their children's play as an enjoyable and beneficial experience for themselves as well as for their child. They believed that the time spent playing with their child was an opportunity for positive and enjoyable interaction, a time (in comparison with activities such as dressing and shopping) when their child was able to control events.

A noteworthy, but unstudied, aspect of play activities and children with disabilities is that nowadays children generally spend more time in individual or private play than in group or social play. In fact, many of today's toys are designed to allow a child to play with them privately, since this is the century in which children spend more time than ever before in playing alone (Sutton-Smith, 1994). Family size and life style appear to be the underlying causes.

All these research findings lead to several common sense, applicable conclusions for parents who want to facilitate play for their child who needs some help in experiencing the world:

- Play is not work; play is not therapy; play is not education.
- Play should be an enjoyable activity; it is for fun—in and of itself.
- Play is not for rewards. Kids do not need to be given stickers for good playing.
- Training children in "play skills" does not seem to generalize to true play.
- Play style seems linked to "mental" rather than "chronological" age.
- A child's play passivity may be the result of boredom with the toy, an unwillingness to attempt to play, or even the lack of appropriate toys.

- Parents know their child best; *they* are the experts about *their* child, but they should use their child's therapists as resources.
- Most of all, parents should relax, enjoy themselves, and be joyful in play with their child.

Finally, it is important to keep in mind that "special needs" children sometimes have "special play needs." Miller (1994) pointed out that a child who has an overly structured life with therapies and special care needs unstructured time, both alone and with a parent, just to "see what happens." Miller advised parents:

- Your child may just want to sit and watch the fish swimming in the tank. She needs space and time to do nothing.
- If your child doesn't have much control over her life or feels weak and powerless, she may like to change the rules of games or make up special rules. Play can give her a chance to make herself feel big in a world where she feels very small.
- If she feels stressed, tired, or ill, or has been working really hard to master a skill, you may see her play in a way that makes you wonder if she is regressing. This isn't abnormal, it's a way children have of "catching their breath"—stepping back to a place of comfort and safety for a little while.
- You may feel you should be stimulating and teaching your child all the time, and you may feel compelled to improve on your child's play. . . . It's important to have play time where you don't criticize, don't correct, don't judge, and don't improve unless you're asked. And even then involve your child in deciding what to add or change.

## NUTS AND BOLTS OF ASSISTIVE TECHNOLOGY AND PLAY

Any device (homemade, custom-made, or commercially available) that helps a person with a disability do something that she or he could not do before, or do something more easily is assistive technology. Many "regular" toys can be adapted for children with a disability. The most recent Toys 'Я' Us catalog is a good place to start. Sometimes a small change can make all the difference. For example, it is possible to stabilize a toy by using nontoxic materials, such as nonslip carpet backing, double-faced carpet tape, clamps, or Velcro; even a big chunk of Play Doh stuck to the table top can be effective if the toy is embedded in the Play Doh. Handles can be built up with cellulose sponge, foam hair rollers, or cylindrical foam hot water pipe insulation. Switch and knob modifications can be very simple.

The ordinary light switch is seldom considered in terms of assistive technology but 5 minutes of adaptive effort can delight a child who may not have much control over his or her life. Small ($\frac{5}{64}$- or $\frac{3}{32}$-inch ) holes can be drilled through the light switch without even removing it from the wall and through the end of a $\frac{3}{8}$-inch dowel. The length of the dowel depends on the child's reach, but if the dowel is too heavy, the light switch may not stay in the "up" position. The dowel can be loosely fastened to the light switch using thin wire twisted into a loop with the ends tucked in (Figure 9–1). The dowel can be painted to match the wall, if desired. A lightweight ornamental handle (something fanciful like a bracelet or plastic vending machine charm) can be attached at the bottom end of the dowel for easier grasping.

A second, even simpler assistive technology device is likely to please a child who has problems in coordinating his hand movements or who has a visual impairment. The "cup" is spill-proof, fun to play with, and disposable. It can be used for holding freshly picked flowers, paint and paintbrush, a drink with a straw, and many other things. The label of a plastic soda bottle (any size) is

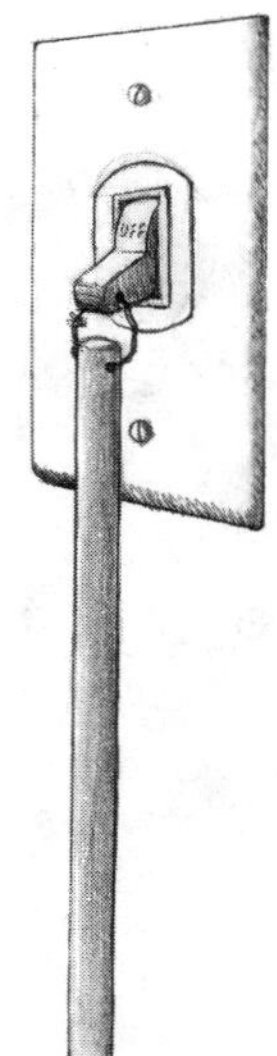

**Figure 9–1** Adaptation to light switch

removed, a sharp kitchen paring knife or single edge razor blade is used to cut the bottle carefully in two unequal parts, the bottom part 1 to 2 inches taller than the top part (depending on the size of the bottle). The top part is inverted into the bottom part of the bottle and the seam taped with adhesive, duct, or colored plastic tape (Figure 9–2). A wire handle can be added, or the cup can be fastened to a walker or wheelchair with tape. The secret is in filling the container with only an inch or so of liquid so that the top of the liquid is below the mouth of the bottle. If the cup is turned over, the liquid will not pour out.

Obviously, it is not necessary to become an engineer and make complicated assistive technology devices. The parent's most helpful contribution can be to know where to ask for help. Someone who loves to tinker and fix things is the type of person to cultivate as a friend and helper. Many assistive technology solutions are not complex, but they do require some specific steps.

1. Recognize the need for an adaptation. Sometimes parents are too busy even to notice the need for a change.
2. Think about solutions. While driving, waiting in line, and so on, parents can consider options. They can brainstorm with other parents, with therapists, and friends; they can look at specialty catalogs and magazines for ideas.

---

**Figure 9–2** Spill-proof cup

3. Talk to the child's therapist; share ideas; get the therapist's ideas.
4. Bring the person who will be doing the construction into the process, because materials are a big factor in making devices.
5. Build a prototype, and try it out. Make sure to involve the child's therapist in determining that it is appropriate.
6. Adjust the prototype, or build a final version.

Many specialty catalogs sell a variety of switches for toys. Many of them are relatively inexpensive, and many can be made at home by a clever person. Simply stated, there are ways to operate radios, televisions, tape players, battery-operated toys, and so on with any part of the body. Eyebrow wiggle, tongue pressure, head movement, breath, eye glance—the possibilities are endless. A therapist can purchase or build switches custom-designed for a particular child's needs. The child also needs to be in the best position to control the switch and play with the toy, and the therapist can help find the best functional position for the child to be while doing things.

Switches are just a starting point, however. There are adaptive riding toys and tricycles; there are "special" toys designed for children with "special" needs; there are adaptive large play structures and furnishings as well. These assistive technology solutions are no further away than the nearest occupational or physical therapist, who can use a clinical approach to determine what switch, tricycle, or piece of equipment is appropriate for the child. For nonspecific "special" toys and play things, the resources listed in Appendix 9–A are often helpful. There are also many everyday toys that can be simply adapted.

The battery interrupter is a useful device for many children (Kanor, 1994). Available from "Toys for Special Children," the battery interrupter is a gadget with a jack at one end and a disk at the other. The disk is placed on the battery nipple (positive terminal) between a toy's batteries, and then the jack is plugged into any special switch. The device is inexpensive and eliminates the need to modify an individual toy.

For children with physical conditions that limit their opportunities to explore play materials and their play possibilities, the purpose of intervention and assistive technology must be to bring the opportunities to them—not to direct their play, but to make "intrinsically motivated" activities and "play pleasure" possible.

### Indoor Play

Every child's bedroom and play areas start with the same four things: walls, floors, ceilings, and openings (doors and windows). The use of the space and the equipment within it depend on the needs of the child and the family. There are many ways to match an individual child's developmental needs with the home's physical environment. Most of the following ideas are simple, inexpensive, or free and are just a starting point to stimulate thinking. It is important to keep in mind the child's developmental changes, the family's life style, and the child's siblings and friends.

*Toy Storage.* Toy chests and drawers can be expensive. Because the drawers are often heavy and too deep, they can pinch little fingers as well. Children who use their hands to get around (e.g., scooting, crawling, using a wheelchair or walker) find it hard to carry toys and get themselves from place to place. For these children, some toys should be kept right where they will play with them. Other toys are best stored in easy-to-grasp shallow trays, bins, or small laundry baskets—within the child's reach. Shallow, small, cardboard boxes work well and can be covered with contact paper.

*Location of Play Areas.* Children may want to be near their parents while they play. The fanciest toys may not make them happy if the toys are in a room far away from where the parents are. A child may be more likely to play independently if he or she can see a parent, hear a parent, and be reassured by the parent's presence.

*Safety Hints.* Nontoxic paints and furnishing materials must be used in play areas. Venetian blind cords must not hang down to a point at which the child can become entangled in them. There must be a working smoke detector at the doorway of the child's bedroom. If the child falls frequently, corners on furniture should be padded or rounded, and there should be no sharp edges, table lamps, or other potentially dangerous room furnishings. Space heaters and radiators must be placed so that the child cannot touch or fall against them.

*Thinking Ahead.* For children who will be using a wheelchair, plans for long-term home modifications should include extra maneuvering space in bedroom and play areas, and windows low enough so that a child can see out. For all toddlers, windows must be escape-proof.

*Doorknobs.* It can be very hard for a child to grasp a doorknob, turn the hand, and pull the door at the same time. Twisting and holding the doorknob so that the latch is pulled in, then putting some strips of duct tape over the latch and door may make it possible for the child to open the door without assistance. A couple of thicknesses of tape are usually just right to rub a bit on the door frame so the door will stay closed if desired, but can be opened just by pulling the knob. Perhaps a child who cannot grasp a door handle or knob can hold onto and pull a ribbon or rope loop (big enough to slip a whole hand through, but not a head!) attached to the doorknob.

*Helping Mom Cook.* Children often love to "help" Mom or Dad in the kitchen. A play stove can be made out of an upside-down drawer or cardboard box. Very lightweight pots, pans, and grown-up cooking utensils can be fun to play with and easy to manipulate. Safe "cooking ingredients" can add fun to the process. It is essential to avoid items that are toxic or are small enough to choke the child if swallowed. The child must not play near the real stove or any place where hot liquids can be spilled. "Working" in the kitchen together can also be a time for a busy mom to share special time with a child.

*Water Play.* Kitchen floors are generally pretty forgiving when it comes to spilled liquids. A child who cannot get around to explore the environment can be positioned in a supporting seat and given a small dishpan or sturdy bowl of warm water and some easy-to-grip unbreakable pouring containers or floating plastic objects for play.

## Toys and Playthings

As noted earlier, it is often said that play is a child's work. Certainly, each child is unique and approaches this important developmental "work" in his or her own way. All children, however, need to have opportunities to make choices, manipulate objects, express curiosity, and solve problems. Offering choices is especially important if the child does not move around independently. A toy that fascinates today may be only somewhat interesting tomorrow and may be boring by the next day. Thus, it is vital to be sensitive to each child's interest (or disinterest) in a toy.

*Playhouse.* A large cardboard carton with a wide curtain door (taped on) and low window openings for a child to peek through makes an accessible playhouse.

*Cardboard Cylinder.* Fun to roll around in and fun to crawl through, a large diameter cardboard drum can provide hours of play. Many businesses use 55-gallon cardboard (or plastic) drums for shipping. It is necessary to make sure nothing harmful was ever stored in the drum before giving it to a child.

*Getting Exercise.* If there is room in the home, exercise equipment such as homemade balance beams, simple teeter-totters, small slides, and riding toys can be helpful in using up energy. Playing on these toys can help a child improve balance and coordination. Teeter-totters and some rocking toys can also offer cooperative play opportunities with siblings and friends.

*Riding Toys.* For a child who cannot sit independently on a riding toy or regular tricycle, there are many possible seating and handlebar modifications. There are also special tricycles and mobility toys with support seats, positioning belts, upright handlebars, and shoe holders on the pedals; however, these special toys are expensive. Therapists can help parents select the appropriate toy and modifications. A child should ride with seatbelts or shoe holder and caution is necessary in choosing a place for the child to ride, because the child cannot stop herself or himself from falling.

*Battery-Operated Toys.* The on/off switches on many battery-operated toys can be replaced so that a child can operate the toy using any part of the body. The cost of adapting toys can be minimal (or free.) In fact, parents can learn to make simple switches themselves.

*Swings and Rockers.* Even if a child cannot hold herself or himself up, swings and rocking toys can often be modified so that the child can be comfortably positioned and can enjoy the movement. The therapist should be consulted to see if swinging is an advisable activity for the individual child.

*Help in Walking.* A toy shopping cart, doll carriage, or other push-toy can be modified so that a child can use it to walk. Sometimes it is possible to modify one of the many commercially available toddler walking aids by making the handles higher, for example, or to construct a walking aid/toy based on the same idea. Stability and sturdiness must be primary considerations when choosing, modifying, or making a walking aid.

*Pretend Play.* Some children love "pretend" play, such as feeding a doll or driving a car. Pretend toys or lightweight real tools (e.g., kitchen utensils) can be modified so that a child can imitate and practice "grown-up" skills.

*Clutter.* Too many toys and too much clutter can confuse or discourage a child. Sometimes, toys keep a child's interest longer if the child cannot see all of them all of the time. Some toys should be put away and the available assortment changed periodically.

*Dress-Up Clothes.* Adding Velcro closures, keeping an assortment of easy-to-put-on accessories, and if the child uses a wheelchair, modifying garments so that they open in the back can make dress-up clothes accessible. It is important to include items that the child can put on independently.

*Remote Control Switch.* Some stores (e.g., Radio Shack) sell a receiver and transmitter that makes it possible to turn almost anything electrical on and off without having a direct wiring connection. For a child who cannot get around independently, this type of switch can be modified to control a radio, television, or tape player. An expert can help select the right "environmental control system."

*Small Knobs and Buttons.* Sometimes knobs, switches, and push buttons are too small for a child with a disability to use. Simple modifications can make control mechanisms bigger or easier to use. An occupational therapist can suggest appropriate materials to build up the controls. If there is some confusion about which button needs to be pushed, putting a bright paint mark or shape on the start button or on/off switch can be helpful. There are special hardening materials (sold in therapeutic supply catalogs) for building up knobs and handles, and similar materials are often found at crafts shops.

*Safety Hints.* As for any child, it is essential to avoid small toy pieces that can be swallowed, paint that may be toxic, pull strings that may get tangled around a toddler's neck. The toys selected must also be developmentally appropriate. Just because a toy's label says it is suitable for children of a certain age, does not mean that the toy is automatically appropriate for any particular child.

## Outdoor Play

Squishing mud between the toes, feeling sunshine on the face, smelling a flower, or touching a tree's bark . . . there are many ways to use assistive technology to make an outdoor play area fun for a child with a disability.

*Safety.* Outdoor play equipment can be dangerous. The swing set and other play structures must be checked to make sure there are no protruding bolts, no sharp corners, no rough splinters, no possibility of choking on a rope or chain. Playground safety guides are available to help in planning. If the child needs supervision, the outdoor play area should be planned so that the child is always visible through a window.

*Fences and Gates.* If the child is an "escaper," a fence and gate do not provide adequate security. Children can climb even chain link fences, and they can be very adept at opening gate catches. A fence offers some protection, but a motion detector or other alarm system, readily available in electronics stores, may be necessary as well.

*Water Play.* A wading pool, buckets, or tubs may be included in an outdoor area for playing with water. Tabletop water playing opportunities can be provided by placing a large dishpan full of water on a table. Lightweight, unbreakable cups and containers make simple toys; the handles can be modified, if necessary.

*Flowers and Vegetables.* Of course, it is important to make sure that there are no poisonous plants in the outdoor play area, but it is unnecessary to avoid growing flowers and vegetables just because the child is likely to pick them. Instead, vegetable or flower beds should be accessible to the child, for example, raised planting beds or containers if the child is in a stroller or wheelchair. Small gardening tools can be modified for use by the child.

*Fruit Trees.* Accessible dwarf fruit trees or berry bushes can be trained on trellises or a lattice fence for easy picking by a child in a wheelchair. Cooperative extension offices or garden clubs may have helpful suggestions.

*Pets.* The abilities of a child who is old enough to share responsibility for family pets should be kept in mind when setting up backyard housing for a dog or other pet so that the child can be involved in caring for the pet. Caring for rabbits in a backyard hutch can be rewarding and simple. The hutch can be at wheelchair height; knobs and catches can be modified for easy grasping.

*Slides.* Parents of a young daughter with cerebral palsy noted how their little girl loved to go down the slide, but could not climb the ladder. So they built a slide and ramp side to side, with a fenced-in platform at the top. They covered the ramp with outdoor carpeting. Now their daughter can crawl up and slide down, and all the neighborhood kids love the slide, too. More and more frequently in public playgrounds, slides are being built right into hillsides. An embankment in a backyard can be used in the same way for a plastic slide without a ramp or ladder.

*Sand Table.* For a child who cannot sit up alone or who plays while sitting in a wheelchair, an inexpensive sand table with a few inches of sand in it can be built. Drainage holes should be put in the bottom, and a cover for the table should be constructed to keep out the rain and to prevent cats from using it for their own purposes! Spoons, shovels, plastic pails, and all sorts of sand box toys can be made easier to grasp by building up the handles.

*Play Tent.* An accessible play tent can be constructed for a child to crawl in and out of by hanging a clothesline between two trees and draping a bedspread or large blanket over the clothesline. The bedspread can be anchored to the ground along both sides.

*Balance Beam.* A wonderful addition to a backyard play area is a balance beam. The plank does not have to be off the ground at all; as long as it is steady and well anchored, a wide board lying on the ground may be just as much fun for balancing. A brightly colored board is easier to see. Placing a stripe of bright yellow tape down the middle can turn the board into a play road.

*Commercial Play Structures.* The abilities of the individual child determine the appropriate plan for a swing set. There are many commercial kits available at lumberyards or home building centers. Components of these sets may be used, with modification if necessary. In addition, many styles of special swings are available for children who cannot support themselves on a regular swing seat. Some are like large toddler swings; others provide support for a child's entire body. There are even swing attachments that can be hooked directly onto a wheelchair so that the wheelchair becomes the swing seat. Such special swings can be incorporated into a regular swing set. The child's therapist should be consulted to decide what type of swing would suit the child and if swinging is an advisable activity at all.

**On the Go**

A trip to the supermarket, an hour in the laundromat, or a stroll around the block may be ordinary activities to an adult, but these everyday outings can be exciting adventures to a child. For some children, however, getting around the community can be a challenge. There are many ways to make trips into the community easier for a family.

*Special Car Seats.* If a toddler requires more support than a regular car seat provides or if an older child still needs to travel in a car seat, it may be possible to locate or create a specialized seating system. Many times, car seats are part of a total seating system—converting from car seat to stroller to high chair. The seat must be approved for use in a vehicle. Parents should talk with their child's physical therapist about purchasing a special seating system or car seat.

*Wagon with Support Seat.* An express wagon (i.e., a wooden wagon with slatted sides) can be a special way to take a child who does not walk on an exploratory walk. If the child cannot sit up, a supporting seat can be bolted in the wagon. The advice of a physical or occupational therapist about making a corner seat or other seat to support the child can be very helpful. Care is always necessary when pulling the wagon, especially on rough surfaces, hills, and around corners.

*Sled with Support Seat.* Just like a wagon, a sled can be modified with a support seat to take a child for a ride in the snow. It is important to make sure that the child is dressed warmly and that the path chosen is not going to capsize the sled.

*Electric Cars.* Toy stores sell battery-operated cars that can often be modified for young, nonambulatory children to drive. In fact, some children who cannot walk do just fine driving the cars around, and it gives them their first taste of getting around independently. The child's physical therapist may suggest using an electric car to teach wheelchair navigation skills. Conversion kits are available to modify the controls of some electric cars, if desired. A safety feature for a novice "driver" is to wire into the car's electrical system a long cable with a "kill switch" at the end so that a parent can shut the car off immediately in case of emergency. Of course, this means that the parent must remain relatively near the car.

*Walking and Standing Aids.* There are new styles of walkers for children. Some have bigger wheels, swivel wheels, and baskets in which to keep important supplies. There are new styles of standers as well, which allow a child to play while bearing weight in a natural standing position. Some of these standers are mobile; some are part of a flexible positioning system.

*Jogging Strollers.* Wheelchairs and regular strollers can be hard to manage on bumpy ground, grass, and anywhere "off the beaten path." Some new strollers have large, bicycle-sized wheels; these strollers are designed for parents who want to go jogging while pushing their toddler's stroller. It is not necessary to be a jogger, however. A stroller like this can be a way for a parent and a child who cannot get around independently to go exploring together.

*Positioning for Socializing.* The world view of a child who is in a car seat, stroller, or wheelchair is limited. For children who cannot get around on their own, strollers, car seats, and wheelchairs are their "window on the world." Rather than parked off to the side, the stroller should be positioned so that the child can interact with people and with the surroundings.

## INTERACTIVE PLAY

When a child has special needs, planning for play may require "assistive interactions" as well as "assistive technology." Miller suggested that families with children with developmental delays who have older brothers and sisters (who may be too busy, have too much homework, or may not be in the mood to include their younger sibling in their play) designate a specific time of day for "planned play." Each brother and sister selects a 10- to 15-minute time period to play one-on-one with the child with the disability. The parent sets a kitchen timer to measure the time, although the children can play longer if they want to do so. During planned play, the two children can play whatever they want. This is their special time together; there is no television, and none of the other children can interrupt. Miller noted that planned play accomplishes several goals. In families with several children, the special time gives parents a predictable break from supervising some of the children, it gives the child with special needs some concentrated, individual playtime with each brother or sister, and it gives the older brothers and sisters a chance to have a successful play experience with their younger sibling. Success comes from the brevity, the predictability, and the sense of cooperation and fun arranged by the parents.

---

### REFERENCES

Berger, J. (1990). Interactions between parents and their infants with Down syndrome. In D. Cicchetti & M. Beeghly (Eds.), *Children with Down syndrome: A developmental perspective* (pp. 101–146). New York: Cambridge University Press.

Black, M., Freeman, B., & Montgomery, J. (1975). Systematic observation of play in autistic children. *Journal of Autism and Childhood Schizophrenia, 5*, 363–371.

Bronfenbrenner, U. (1979). *The ecology of human development.* Cambridge, MA: Harvard University Press.

Clemens, S. (1875). *The adventures of Tom Sawyer*. New York: Grosset & Dunlap.

Deci, E.L., & Ryan, R.M. (1982). Curiosity and self directed learning: The role of motivation in education. In L. Katz (Ed.), *Current topics in early childhood education* (Vol. 4, pp. 71–85). Norwood, NJ: Ablex.

de Moor, J.M.H., van Wasberghe, B.T.M. & Oud H.H.L. (1994). Effectiveness of play training with handicapped toddlers. In J. Hellendoorn, R. van der Kooij, & B. Sutton-Smith (Eds.), *Play and intervention* (pp. 145–155). Albany, NY: State University of New York Press.

Dunst, C., Trivette, C., & Deal, A. (1988). *Enabling and empowering families: Principles and guidelines for practice*. Cambridge, MA: Brookline Press.

Feingold, B.D., & Mahoney, M.J. (1975). Reinforcement effects on intrinsic interest: Undermining the overjustification hypothesis. *Behavior Therapy, 6*, 367–377.

Greene, D., & Lepper, M.R. (1974). Effects of extrinsic rewards on children's subsequent intrinsic interest. *Child Development, 45*, 1141–1145.

Hellendoorn, J. (1994a). General introduction. In J. Hellendoorn, R. van der Kooij, & B. Sutton-Smith (Eds.), *Play and intervention* (pp. 1–2). Albany, NY: State University of New York Press.

Hellendoorn J. (1994b). Play for children with special needs. In J. Hellendoorn, R. van der Kooij, & B. Sutton-Smith (Eds.), *Play and intervention* (pp. 109–112). Albany, NY: State University of New York Press.

Hellendoorn, J. (1994c). Imaginative play training for severely retarded children. In J. Hellendoorn, R. van der Kooij, & B. Sutton-Smith (Eds.), *Play and intervention* (pp. 113–122). Albany, NY: State University of New York Press.

Hellendoorn, J., van der Kooij, R., & Sutton-Smith, B. (1994). Epilogue. In J. Hellendoorn, R. van der Kooij, & B. Sutton-Smith (Eds.), *Play and intervention* (pp. 215–224). Albany, NY: State University of New York Press.

Hulme, I., & Lunzer, E.A. (1966). Play, language, and reasoning in subnormal children. *Journal of Child Psychology and Psychiatry, 7*, 107–123.

Isaacs, J. (1994, October). Forrest Pumps: A sound-activated water gun works without adaptations. *Exceptional Parent*, pp. 40–41.

Jones, O.H.M. (1980). Prelinguistic communication skills in Down's syndrome and normal infants. In T.M. Field, S. Goldberg, D. Stern, & A.M. Sostek (Eds.), *High-risk infants and children: Adult and peer interactions* (pp. 205–225). New York: Academic Press.

Kanor, S.E. (1994, October). The battery interrupter, *Exceptional Parent*, p. 38.

Marfo, K, (1984). Interactions between mothers and their mentally retarded children: Integration of research findings. *Journal of Applied Developmental Psychology, 5*, 45–69.

McEvoy, J., & McConkey, R. (1983). Play activities of mentally handicapped children at home and mothers' perception of play. *International Journal of Rehabilitation Research, 6*, 143–151.

Miller, N.B. (1994). *Nobody's perfect: Living and growing with children who have special needs*. Baltimore, MD: Paul H. Brookes.

Skinner, B.F. (1954). *Science and human behavior*. New York: Macmillan.

Skinner, B.F. (1938). *The behavior of organisms: An experimental analysis*. New York: Appleton–Century–Crofts.

Sutton-Smith, B. (1994). Paradigms of intervention. In J. Hellendoorn, R. van der Kooij, & B. Sutton-Smith (Eds.), *Play and intervention* (pp. 3–21). Albany, NY:State University of New York Press.

# Appendix 9–A

## Resources

- **RESNA Technical Assistance Project**
  1700 North Moore Street
  Suite 1540
  Arlington, VA 22209
  (703) 524-6686
- **Toys for Special Children**
  385 Warburton Ave.
  Hastings-on-Hudson, NY 10760
  (914) 478-0960
- **Exceptional Parent Magazine**
  P.O. Box 5446
  Pittsfield, MA 01203-9321
  (800) 247-8080
- **Council for Exceptional Children**
  1920 Association Drive
  Reston, VA 20901
  (703) 620-3660
- **National Therapeutic Recreation Society**
  2775 South Quincy Street
  Suite 300
  Arlington, VA 22206
  (703) 820-4940

## *Chapter 10*

# Home and Worksite Accommodations

*William A. Peterson and Anita Perr*

Home and worksite accommodations increase the potential for people with disabilities to live independently. Accommodations may be very simple, such as rearranging furniture in the home or workplace, or quite complex and expensive, such as structurally remodeling a bathroom to accommodate someone in a wheelchair or purchasing expensive electronic equipment to control the environment. Whether the accommodations are simple or complex, the process by which they are determined is similar.

The needs and abilities of one person typically do not match those of other people. Furthermore, the home environment of each individual differs from the worksite of that individual. Adding the simple facts that people's needs change over time as their abilities change and that everyone has distinct likes and dislikes, one can begin to see the complex nature of performing home and worksite evaluations. With a comprehensive evaluation and careful planning, however, it is possible for a person with a disability to function at home and/or work successfully.

## THE EVALUATION

Before a person with a new disability can return to his or her home and work, it is important to look at the entire picture. The evaluator must have a good sense of the person's functional level. Some performance components to be evaluated include strength, coordination, endurance, balance, sensation, task planning, problem solving, and safety judgment. Furthermore, the evaluator needs to determine exactly what the person will be expected to do, in what environment, and what the goals of the accommodations are. For example, are they to ensure that the person with a disability will be capable of performing the activities in question independently, or are they to make the job easier for a caregiver or colleague? It is necessary for evaluators to ask many questions about the person's life style and occupation. A good open relationship with the individual is critical to a successful outcome.

An evaluation can range from a few well worded questions to a simulation in which the person actually uses specifically recommended devices or modifications while performing the necessary tasks. Appropriately worded questions are helpful, but answers to those questions may change according to activities; an individual may be capable of performing certain aspects of a task independently, but may require assistance for others. The most reliable evaluation of the person's abilities occurs in the setting where the activity will usually take place and with the tools and equipment that the person will use for the task. If this is not possible, simulating the activity gives an indication of the actual performance. Trials and simulation may not be possible due to time constraints or the necessity to rely on information learned through interviews with family members, loved ones, caregivers, supervisors, and/or others familiar with the disability and home/worksite situations.

Whether the information is learned through simulation or interview, the individual with a disability must be included in the process of determining appropriate accommodations. Depending on his or her familiarity with the disability, the individual may or may not have an understanding of the type(s) of accommodations that are necessary. The evaluator also needs to get a feel for the individual's comfort level regarding specific accommodations. Some people, for example, simply will not use high-technology devices even if it would mean greater independence.

The results of a thorough evaluation should include a list of the problem areas, along with a list of possible solutions. Factors such as space limitations and high costs may affect decisions. Therefore, it may be necessary to prioritize the importance of various accommodations and shuffle them somewhat to achieve the greatest results. Some accommodations may be low on the priority list, but may cost little or nothing to execute; in this case, they can be moved up in the hierarchical scheme of things.

## HOME ACCESSIBILITY

There are many aspects to home accessibility. It includes access to and through the actual structures of the home, such as getting in and out of the front door, getting into the bathroom, and reaching into the kitchen cabinets. It also includes getting to and utilizing electrical appliances and controls for the environment, such as heating, air conditioning, and lighting. Furthermore, home accessibility includes caring for the home and its contents through such activities as vacuuming and washing dishes.

Every home is different. Every person's needs and abilities are different. Additionally, needs may change over time, as interests and abilities change. Thus, the process of making home modifications is circular in nature. Information learned early becomes the basis for later decisions. Information learned later can change decisions made earlier. Successful decision making usually comes down to performing a comprehensive evaluation and making changes in an orderly process rather than through the hit-or-miss approach:

> Bob recently had a stroke. Because Bob needed to use a wheelchair for most ambulation activities at home, Mary, Bob's wife, enlisted the help of Roger, Bob's business partner, to make the home more accessible. Another of Roger's friends had recently had a stroke and required changes to his home to make it more accessible. Being a good friend, Roger made all of the changes that were made for his other friend; he assumed that, because both people had experienced strokes, their needs were the same. Roger and Mary were quite happy with the results until Bob was discharged from the rehabilitation hospital. Some of the home modifications worked well for Bob, but other modifications actually made things more difficult; still others had little or no impact. Bob and Mary eventually made modifications to the modifications—some to change them further and others to return them to their previous state. In the end, the home was modified to meet Bob's needs. It took more money, time, and energy than was necessary. Some of the problems may have been avoided if a comprehensive evaluation had been completed to determine Bob's abilities and needs prior to making the modifications.

The hit-or-miss approach can be effective if the first guess is the best choice or if the person adapts to the modifications made. It is more likely, however, that the hit-or-miss approach will increase expenses, waste time, and frustrate the people involved.

When a caregiver is involved, his or her abilities should also be evaluated. Home modifications should be made not only for the benefit of the person with a disability, but also for the benefit of the caregiver. For instance, the use of a mechanical lift may make it easier, or possible, for a caregiver to move an individual from the bed to the wheelchair. Again, performing the actual task is the best way to evaluate a person's abilities, but simulation and verbal report are sometimes necessary (Exhibit 10–1).

### Evaluation of the Physical Structure of the Home

The simplest way to determine whether pathways, appliances, and furniture are accessible is to take measurements of the home. Once the measurements have been taken, it is possible to determine whether alternate routes are available or if reorganization or remodeling is necessary to resolve the problems

**Exhibit 10–1** Common Household Activities

- **Self-care.** Self-care includes activities of toileting, bathing, and grooming. It includes getting to and using the bathroom fixtures; grooming aids, like hair brush, razor, and blow dryer; and toiletries like cosmetics, soaps, and lotions. Accessibility issues related to these activities include, firstly, where the activities will occur. Since many of these activities usually occur in the bathroom, and most others in the bedroom, accessibility in these areas is paramount.
- **Homemaking.** Homemaking activities include meal preparation and clean-up, laundry, vacuuming, and dusting. Homemaking activities also include sending and receiving mail and managing finances. Child care activities would also be included in this category.
- **Work.** If work activities are done at home, the usual locations should be addressed. This might include access to a computer work station, a desk, or a myriad of other locales and appliances.
- **Recreation.** Accessibility to the location and use of the objects should be addressed. This might include such things as access to a porch or deck, use of a television and/or stereo system, getting to a wood shop and using the tools, utilizing a garden, or participating in any other familiar or new activity.

identified. In many instances, a rehabilitation therapist, often an occupational therapist, evaluates the home and takes the measurements. If the person's needs are complex or if the home modifications are expected to be elaborate, it may be wise to consult a rehabilitation engineer or a building contractor, architect, or interior designer with experience in home modifications.

When the therapist or other experts cannot perform the home accessibility evaluation, family members or friends should take the measurements. If they are unable to complete a full evaluation, they should investigate especially problematic areas, such as entrances, stairways, doorways, and bathrooms. Drawing a floor plan of the rooms evaluated can provide a sense of the layout and space constraints, especially if it includes a record of the measurements. Many people have difficulty using a tape measure correctly. An alternative method is to cut a piece of string that is the same length as the required width, such as the width of a wheelchair. The family member or friend can then stretch out the string and pass it through the doorway being measured. Any doors through which the string cannot pass pose an obstacle to the person using the wheelchair.

If the individual with a disability uses a wheelchair in the home, measurements should relate to that specific wheelchair. The width of the wheelchair should be measured at its widest part, usually at the outside of the push rims on either side of the rear wheels. If the person propels the wheelchair with his or her hands, additional space may be required so his or her hands don't scrape against the walls or doorways. If the person uses a power wheelchair, the joystick box may protrude further than the wheels and, thus, should be taken into account in overall width measurements. The overall length is measured from the tip of the foot plate (or the person's foot) to the furthest posterior aspect, usually the back edge of the rear wheel, but occasionally the backrest or headrest, ventilator tray, or other added component. Combined with the width and the wheelchair configuration, the length affects the navigation of the wheelchair around turns and corners.

If the person uses an ambulation aid, such as a cane or a walker, or walks with a gait deviation, the key space requirements are (1) the space required to take a step and (2) the minimum space in which a step can occur (even for short distances of no more than a few steps).

In performing a home accessibility evaluation, it is helpful to use a framework or format that outlines the areas to investigate (Exhibit 10–2). The framework should be adapted to meet each individual's needs by duplicating sections when there is more than one similar area (e.g., stairs to second floor and stairs to basement) or by omitting sections if that area does not exist in the home (or will not be accessed by the person). It may be helpful to perform the survey in the order in which the person is most likely to encounter the areas. One such pathway may be driveway, front entrance, foyer, living room, kitchen, stairs to second floor, bedroom, and second floor bathroom.

An organized framework can also be used to determine the extent of the modifications that will be necessary. Following is a hierarchy of performance that uses questions to determine the level of modifications required:

- Can the person perform the desired activity in the usual manner in the location where it is usually performed?
- Can the person perform the desired activity in the usual manner in a different location, OR can the person perform the desired activity using an alternative procedure in the usual location?
- Can the person perform the desired activity if the appliances are modified?
- Can the person perform the desired activity with the addition of assistive technology?
- Can the person perform the desired activity if the appliances are replaced with different models?

Usually, but not always, the least costly and least invasive options are preferred.

## Common Household Accessibility Problems and Possible Solutions

When determining solutions to accessibility problems, a hierarchy of change can be followed to ensure that simple solutions are considered before elaborate

**Exhibit 10–2** Framework for Home Accessibility Evaluation

**Garage or parking area**
- Sizes of spaces
- Pathway

**Driveway**
- Slope
- Terrain

**Walkway to entrance**
- Slope
- Ground cover
- Curbs

**Public areas (such as in apartment buildings)**
- Elevator controls
- Mailbox

**Doorways (outdoor and indoor)**
- Width
- Direction of door swing
- Door sill
- Type of door knob
- Locks

**Bathroom**
- Doorway
- Shower/tub
- Faucets/handles/drain
- Under sink space
- Toilet

**Bedroom**
- Bed
- Dresser
- Closet

**Kitchen**
- Refrigerator
- Stove
- Dishwasher
- Microwave

**Living room/den/dining room/stairway**
- Turns
- Landings
- Handrails
- Rise, run, nosing

**Special purpose area** (patio, pool area, work shop, laundry facilities)

solutions are considered. This approach helps to prevent unnecessarily complicated solutions. Exhibit 10–3 lists these levels of change, ranging from most simple to most complex, with examples of solutions at each level.

### *Safety*

In addition to determining which activities the individual with a disability wants to perform, it is essential to address home safety. Every home should have at least two emergency evacuation routes so that if one route is blocked, the alternate can be used. For people with mobility impairments, it may be necessary to build ramps at two entrances or to arrange a system that allows the person to call a neighbor for help with an emergency evacuation. It is also wise to inform the local police, ambulance, and fire departments when a person with a disability lives in their area so that they can react accordingly in an emergency.

**Exhibit 10–3** Hierarchy of Change with Examples of Possible Solutions

| | |
|---|---|
| Change or eliminate the task. | Move the person's bedroom from the second floor to the first.<br>Have groceries delivered.<br>Hire a housekeeper. |
| Remove obstacles. | Move the telephone table that blocks access to the stairs and handrail.<br>Remove throw rugs from the living room floor. |
| Use adaptive equipment. | Add knob turners to door knobs.<br>Add loop to refrigerator door handle.<br>Install hair dryer mount to wall at optimal height and facing in optimal direction. |
| Modify the current situation. | Mark high, low, medium, and off positions on stove's burner knobs with correction fluid, nail polish, paint, or tape.<br>Remove door from frame. |
| Buy different mainstream device; adapt, if necessary. | Change from top loading to front loading washer and dryer.<br>Change from dial telephone to push-button telephone with capacity to program numbers. |
| Buy specialty equipment; adapt, if necessary. | Buy stair glide.<br>Buy environmental control unit.<br>Buy commode to use over toilet. |

For instance, if there is a fire in an apartment building where firemen know that a wheelchair user lives on the third floor, they can arrive with a gurney or stretcher to evacuate the person. Of course, smoke detectors and other warning devices must be in good working order. If additional security is needed, closed circuit television systems or other surveillance systems can be installed.

The individual with a disability should also be able to contact the police, ambulance, and fire department in an emergency. A telephone should be within the person's easy reach in all locations. If the person is mobile and frequents many locations, a cordless telephone may be appropriate. Any problems in dialing the telephone and communicating effectively may be resolved by such telephone options as auto-dialing and such services as return calling.

A person who is unable to communicate effectively may find a recorded message system helpful. It may also be useful to designate a specific individual who knows the circumstances and knows that, if the person with a disability calls, there is a potential emergency situation. Commercially available emergency systems offer easy communication. These systems usually require the press of a button to activate the system in some manner and relay a message automatically. Some systems automatically trigger an emergency response, while others trigger a call-back to determine the nature of the emergency.

### *Lighting*

Proper lighting is essential throughout the home. The general rule is that there should be "enough" lighting to see the activity easily, but not so much that it causes glare. General room lighting should be bright enough so that objects in the room, such as furniture and other objects that may block passage, are clearly visible.

Switches for overhead lights should be in easily reachable locations. Multiple lights can be re-wired so they are controlled by a single switch, or switches can be relocated so that they are clustered around the person. If the person with a disability cannot reach the light switch (e.g., because the person uses a wheelchair and cannot reach high enough to flip the switch), the attachment of a switch extender may solve the problem without any permanent changes to the home. Otherwise, it may be necessary to install switches at different locations or to connect the lighting to another mechanism, such as an environmental control unit (Exhibit 10–4).

Activities requiring close attention, such as reading, writing, and sewing, often require particularly good lighting. This may be provided through the use of stronger overhead lighting or by adding lamps. It is important to make sure that the cord for any lamp used is not a hindrance to safe passage. If it is impossible to place the cord out of the way, it can be taped down along the floor or base of the wall. If the lamp is to be plugged and unplugged repeatedly, the outlet must be accessible.

Lamps have some type of switch to turn them on and off. The knobs, dials, or pins on some lamps are so small that their operation requires a significant amount of finger dexterity. Still others can be turned on and off merely by touching them. Adapters are available in home centers and in some medical supply stores and catalogs to convert lamps into "touch" lamps, requiring only that a metal part of the lamp be touched to turn them on or off. Lamps can also be controlled by an environmental control unit, if necessary or preferred.

**Exhibit 10–4** Environmental Control Unit (ECU)

Sometimes called an environmental control system (ECS), an environmental control unit is a device that is used to control electrical appliances when a person is unable or unwilling to control them in the usual manner. Among the reasons may be limitations in movement or an excessive expenditure of effort and time required to control the device in the usual manner. Different types of ECUs are available, ranging from simple to complex and inexpensive to expensive. Environmental control units are frequently used to control appliances such as lamps, televisions, and radios. They can also be used to control computers, fans, window air conditioners, and specialty devices such as electric door openers.

An ECU usually consists of four parts: the input, the central processing unit, the feedback, and the output. The input is the method used to turn on the device, usually a switch that is hit with the hand or other body part. The switch can be remote or attached to the central processing unit. If the person is unable to activate this type of switch, other controls (e.g., a sip-and-puff control and voice activation) are available.

The central processing unit is the "brains" of the system. It receives the message from the input and translates it into a language that the device can understand. It sends another message to the device.

There are usually two types of feedback. One tells the person the status of the device, whether it is off or on. Sometimes, this feedback comes directly from the device, such as the sound of a television that is on in the same room. Other times, the status of the device is monitored remotely. For instance, if the ECU controls an electric door opener, the user should know whether the door is open or closed even if not in the same room. This commonly occurs when the person is relatively immobile, such as a person who spends a portion of each day in bed, but still needs to know the status of the objects that he or she controls, such as an electric door opener at the front entrance to the home.

The second type of feedback regards the status of the ECU itself. Some units work by scanning through a menu of options, and the user selects the option desired at the appropriate time. If feedback were not provided regarding the options available at any given time, the user would be required to memorize the sequence, or select options randomly and hope the desired effect occurred.

The output is the effect on the device. The appliance may turn on or off, the volume may change, a telephone number may be dialed, or any other function of the device regulated by the ECU may occur.

### *Obstacles*

People are much less likely to trip or lose their footing in areas that are free of obstacles such as foot stools, end tables, throw rugs, and electric cords. Small pieces of furniture should be moved to a different location or removed altogether if they impede passage. If they must remain in place, however, they should be clearly visible or marked.

It is usually more difficult to traverse carpeting because the friction between the feet and a carpet is higher than the friction between the feet and a firm, smooth surface such as linoleum or hard wood floors. Friction also makes it more difficult to propel a wheelchair over soft surfaces such as plush carpeting than over harder surfaces such as wood floors, linoleum, or even low-pile, tightly woven carpet.

Area rugs pose another threat. They may slide when stepped on, throwing the person who steps on them off balance. Carpets, area rugs, and throw rugs can also roll or fold over, creating a lump or obstacle that can trip someone. The best solution may be to remove the carpet or area rug altogether. If this is not possible, there are measures that can be taken to lessen the risk of accidents. Wall-to-wall carpeting that is loose or wrinkled can often be re-pulled. Area rugs and throw rugs can be secured to the floor with double-sided tape or by a nonskid underlay between the floor and the rug.

### *Stairs and Stairways*

Ambulation up and down stairs is difficult for many people, and soft or loose carpeting makes it even more difficult. Thus, special care should be taken to ensure that carpeting on stairs is secure. Extra care should also be taken to ensure that there is sufficient lighting in the stairwell so that the person can use his or her vision for maximal advantage.

People with ambulation difficulties often have impaired sensation, making it more difficult to "feel" where they are stepping. When steps are of differing heights or widths, these individuals may falter because they cannot count on a familiar pattern for foot placement. To amend problems with the riser height and tread width, modifications and/or replacements are necessary.

Nosing is the front edge of the tread that hangs over the riser. The front part of an individual's foot can easily catch on this lip, causing a fall. Cutting the front edge of the step, smoothing it, and refinishing it to match the rest of the stairs may remedy this situation.

If there are only a few steps or if there is sufficient space, a ramp, either temporary or permanent, can be put in place. The recommended slope of ramps is 12 inches of length for every inch of height, although individuals vary in the angle that they can negotiate. Outdoor ramps should be covered to protect the users from weather conditions. A textured surface reduces the likelihood of slipping. Secure handrails and curbs at the edges of a ramp are usually recommended for the added safety of the individual (REquest, 1993).

It is frequently necessary to add handrails so they are present on both sides of a staircase. This arrangement allows a person who has good use of only one arm to hold a handrail both while ascending and while descending the stairs. It is also helpful if the handrail extends past the end of the steps at both the top and the bottom of the stairs.

Some people have great difficulty navigating stairs while carrying an ambulation aid. Usually, the person climbing the stairs carries the device in the hand that is not holding the handrail. If this is not possible, a second ambulation aid can be purchased so that a device can be kept and used on each level of the home. Another solution is to attach a loop to the cane near the hand grip. When placed around the wrist, the loop allows the person to drag the cane along with one hand while holding the handrail with the other. Many canes already have these loops, but they can be added, if necessary. Care should be taken to ensure that canes hanging from the wrist do not interfere with safe navigation on stairs.

Specialty devices are also available for use on stairs. For a person who is unable to climb the stairs, but still needs access to other levels of the home, there are stair glides, wheelchair lifts, and elevators. Stair glides usually consist of a chair attached to a track that runs along the staircase. The person transfers to the chair, which then carries the person up or down the stairs. A wheelchair lift allows the individual to remain in the wheelchair while being carried, on a platform, up or down the stairs. Both of these devices require activation of a control. The control switch may be on the device itself, where the rider activates it, or at a remote location, where an assistant activates it. If the rider is to activate the control switch, it is important to ensure that it is within easy reach. For example, some stair glide controls are under the edge of the seat and require the rider to reach down to activate them. Such a configuration is problematic for those who are unable to reach down to their side without losing their balance (REquest, 1992a).

### *Doors*

People with disabilities have a variety of problems with doors; they may be unable to turn the knob, to push or pull the door open, or to fit through it. Because round door knobs are more difficult to grasp and turn than levers, they are often removed and replaced with commercially available levers. As an alternative, knob turners can be attached to round door knobs to transform them into levers. If these solutions are insufficient, the doorknob and latch can be removed altogether, or the door itself can be removed and replaced with a curtain.

Some doors have tension closures that make them feel heavy to push open. These doors are more commonly found in multiple family dwellings, such as apartment buildings. The tension on these devices can usually be adjusted to make the door easier to push.

If the door is so narrow that the person in a wheelchair cannot fit through it, there are a few solutions to the problem. The removal of the door can add approximately 1 inch of clear width to the space. If the door must remain, replacing the door hinges with offset hinges makes the door flush with the edge of the door frame when opened 90 degrees. Another possible solution is to remove the lower portions of the door stop (i.e., the strip of wood that surrounds the frame and stops the door from swinging through) up to the height of the top of the wheelchair's wheels, allowing the chair to roll through while the upper portion of the door stop remains effective. If none of these solutions work, it may be necessary to enlarge the doorway.

Door sills or thresholds that hinder access can be removed and replaced with thresholds that are flush with the surface of the floor. Thresholds on doors to the outside often have weather stripping attached to prevent air and rain from blowing into the home. If the sill of an outside door must be removed, weather stripping can be added to the bottom edge of the door to provide the same protection.

It may not be necessary to modify the door at all. Some wheelchairs are available in narrow models that are a viable solution, provided they meet the person's needs for positioning. Sometimes the wheels and/or push rims can be moved toward the center to narrow the wheelchair. There are also wheelchair-narrowing devices that draw the two sides of a wheelchair closer together as a crank is turned. This is effective only if the seat is soft (i.e., upholstery versus solid seat).

### *Air Temperature*

Sometimes, a disability impairs a person's ability to regulate body temperature, making that person vulnerable to changes and extremes in temperature. For instance, individuals with multiple sclerosis may find that heat or hot environments exacerbate their condition. Additionally, an individual may be unaware of changes and extremes in temperature because of a sensory perception impairment.

Issues of temperature control can be addressed in modifying or remodeling the home. Thermostats can be lowered or added in accessible locations. Some small appliances (e.g., space heaters, fans, air conditioners) can be controlled by an environmental control unit (see Exhibit 10–4). Of course, the usual safety measures must be followed when using any electrical appliance. Windows can be adapted or changed to different styles so that people with a variety of abilities can adjust them.

### *Appliances/Furniture*

Any appliance/furniture to be used by an individual with a disability should be easy to reach and easy to use. If the individual will not use the appliance/furniture and its presence hinders performance of other activities, it should be removed or relocated.

*The Bathroom.* If access to the bathroom is just not possible, alternate facilities must be arranged. There are tubs that can be used in bed, shampoo trays for use at the sink, and a variety of bedside commodes, for example. If the person with a disability has a problem getting through the bathroom door, changes to the door and/or doorway are essential. Manual and electrical lifts and track systems are also available for small areas.

Once in the bathroom, access to the toilet, tub/shower, and sink areas are at issue. People who have difficulty standing from and/or sitting on low surfaces may use taller toilets or raised toilet seats. Some bedside commodes can be placed over conventional toilets to raise the seat and to provide arm supports. Installing grab bars can also provide arm supports.

The person who has difficulty managing hygiene following toileting may find a bidet helpful. Fixture bidets, which require a move from the toilet, and add-on models, which are added directly to the toilet, are both available. The bidet is hooked to a water source and sprays water to clean the perineal area.

The need to step over the side of the tub commonly hinders access to the shower and tub. Clamp-on grab bars or floor-to-ceiling bars may suffice for those who require assistance while stepping into a tub. When grab bars are used, care must be taken to ensure that they are installed safely and satisfactorily. Towel rods and other wall-mounted fixtures should not be used for support, as they are not designed or installed as a weight-bearing surface.

Once in the tub, a seat or shower chair allows people with impaired standing balance or insufficient endurance to sit down. Available seats range from small, hard plastic seats without backs to elaborate shower chairs that double as commodes and have wheels, padded seat backs, footrests, armrests, and positioning straps. People who have severe disabilities, such as quadriplegia, and are usually unable to get into a bathtub commonly use the more elaborate shower/commode chairs. Roll-in showers, both commercially available and custom made, eliminate the need to climb over the side of a tub or stall shower sill. The size requirements for a roll-in shower depend on the space available and the size and maneuverability of the wheeled seat.

People who bathe in the seated position often use a hand-held shower. Connected to the water source by a hose, it can be mounted in various locations; several mounts can be installed so that the shower can be moved. Some hand-held showers have the on/off and temperature controls on the handle, making it unnecessary for the user to reach for controls. Some devices have a diverter valve that allows the water to flow either to the conventional shower head or to the hand-held shower.

Using the sink and vanity involves getting to the faucet, handles, and mirror. It also involves retrieving articles used for grooming. Removing the vanity to provide space under the sink may be necessary to allow a person in a wheelchair to reach the faucets. If this is done, exposed hot water and drain pipes should be insulated to prevent accidental burns. Once at the sink, some people find that a high, arching faucet provides easier access to the water. Control knobs that are round and difficult to turn can be replaced with levers or knob turners. An automatic water control system can also be installed; in such a system, placing the hands under the faucet turns on the water (REquest, 1992b).

Towels and grooming articles should be kept in easy reach. If the person has difficulty removing caps and lids, adaptations should be made or alternate products that require different motor skills should be used.

*The Bedroom.* If the person with a disability is unable to change position in bed independently or the caregiver has difficulty moving the person, a hospital bed may be appropriate. It is possible to raise and lower the entire bed, the head of the bed, or the foot of the bed separately. Some hospital beds have manual control, while others have electric control. Guard rails and bed-mounted lifting rails can be used with either hospital beds or conventional beds.

Clothing and other articles that are used frequently should be kept accessible. Drawer pulls can be adapted with easier to manage handles or with loops. Clothing rods in closets can be lowered for easier reach.

*The Kitchen.* Access in the kitchen involves getting to the refrigerator, stove and oven, dishwasher, small appliances (e.g., toasters, microwave ovens), pantry, cabinets, and drawers. Commonly used kitchen ware, small appliances, and food items should be kept on the counter or on low shelves in the cabinet. Less frequently used items can be kept out of the way. It is usually easier to slide heavy objects along a counter than to lift them. If the kitchen is large and it is not possible to slide items along the counter, a rolling cart can be used to carry items around the kitchen, as well as to and from the dining area. If the person has difficulty reaching and lifting objects from high or low shelves, a reacher is helpful. The type of grasp and amount of hand strength required to squeeze the trigger, the length of the shaft of the reacher, and the amount of weight it can lift must all be considered, however.

If cabinets or drawers are difficult to open, the knob or handle can be changed. Loops can be added to drawer pulls and to the handle of a refrigerator door so that arm strength can be used, making hand strength and coordination less important.

Impairment of safety judgment and/or memory increases the risk of fires caused by the failure to turn off appliances. Small appliances such as coffee makers come with automatic shut-off mechanisms. Specialty timers are available to shut off electric stoves and burners. An automatic shut-off should be considered for the iron as well.

*The Dining Room.* The use of the dining room table is a special concern for people who use wheelchairs at the table and do not transfer to typical chairs. Wheelchairs are generally higher than typical chairs, and some dining tables are too low to roll under easily. Removing the sash from the table edges, having the person sit where the table legs do not block access, or placing the table on blocks may solve the problem. Sometimes the wheelchair can be adapted; for example, removing the armrests may enable the wheelchair to roll under the table.

*The Living Room and Den.* In living areas, the person who uses a wheelchair and does not transfer to other furniture needs space to place the wheelchair near such things as tables, lamps, and furniture where other people may sit.

Many people with mobility problems in the home are able to use conventional furniture. Higher seats are generally easier for them to use than lower seats. If a higher chair is not available, low chairs can be placed on blocks or on a platform. In addition, it is easier for many of these individuals to stand from firm cushions than from soft cushions.

Small electrical appliances, such as televisions, radios, and stereos, may be difficult to manage. Many solutions are possible:

- Use a magazine style compact disc player that can be loaded with several favorite discs, limiting the need to manage changes.
- Use a remote control for television and stereo. Remote controls are available with large buttons or easy-to-read labels.
- Use an environmental control system (see Exhibit 10–4).
- Leave television or radio on the desired station to eliminate the need to turn it on/off or change channels.

Electrical outlets in living areas are historically placed low and out of the way so that furniture will hide them. Attempting to reach such outlets may cause people with mobility impairments to fall, however. Therefore, it may be necessary to have additional outlets installed. If this is not possible, extension cords can be used, but care must be taken to ensure that these cords are not placed where they can cause tripping. It is also important to follow the manufacturer's recommendations regarding the safety of using one plug for multiple devices.

## ACCOMMODATIONS IN THE WORKPLACE

Under the Americans with Disabilities Act (ADA) (P.L. 101-336), employers are prohibited from discriminating against individuals on the basis of disability. To ensure nondiscrimination, the ADA requires employers to focus on the essential functions of a job to determine whether a person with a disability is qualified.

### Essential Functions of a Job

Those fundamental duties that help define the job are its essential functions. For example, a surgeon must be capable of performing surgery, a data analyst must be capable of conducting complex statistical analyses, and a machinist must be capable of using a metal lathe. Employers determine the essential functions of a job.

The ADA does not require employers to conduct a job analysis in order to identify the essential functions of a job. Anyone who does conduct a job analysis, however, should concentrate on the end result, or outcome, rather than on the way that the job has traditionally been performed. If an employee needs a full grasp of information contained in technical assistance manuals, for example, the job description may be written to require that the person holding the job have the ability to read technical manuals—although what is important is that the person have the ability to "learn" technical material. People with visual and other reading impairments can perform this function through other means, such as audiotapes. As indicated by this example, there are many alternative ways of doing the same task.

### Qualified Individual with a Disability

Title I of the ADA is very clear in its language stating that only qualified employees with disabilities must be considered for employment. In order to be qualified, a person with a disability must have the skills, education, experience, and certifications necessary for the job. If a person with a disability cannot perform one or more essential functions of a job because of his or her disability, but is otherwise qualified, the employer must consider whether modifications or adjustments could allow the individual to perform the essential functions of the job successfully. Such modifications or adjustments are called "reasonable accommodations."

### Reasonable Accommodations

There are 48.9 million Americans with a disability, roughly 19.4 percent of the total population in the United States. Of these, 29.5 million are between the ages of 15 and 64, the age when most people are likely to work. Of these individuals, 13.2 million have a severe disability that can impact their ability to successfully find a job (Job Accommodation Network, 1994). Making reasonable accommodations for qualified applicants or employees with a disability are generally regarded as key to the successful employment of persons with severe disabilities. Employers must consider reasonable accommodations when determining whether an individual with a disability is qualified to perform the essential functions of a job and when making other decisions regarding employees with disabilities. Individuals with disabilities have a right to enjoy the benefits and privileges of employment enjoyed by their nondisabled counterparts (e.g., benefits, staff meetings, break rooms, fitness rooms, etc.). Exhibit 10–5 provides some specific examples of accommodations.

A worker with a disability may request an accommodation in order to perform specific tasks of a job. It is a widely held misconception among employers that accommodating workers with disabilities is expensive. In 1995, the Job Accommodation Network (JAN) conducted a survey to determine the costs of accommodating workers with disabilities in the workplace. The results indicate that 81 percent of all accommodations cost $1,000 or less. Of these, 69 percent cost $500 or less, and a full 19 percent cost absolutely nothing (Exhibit 10–6). Accommodations that have no dollar value include such things as moving workers to a different location, rearranging furniture, or making a schedule change.

## An Employer's Reasonable Effort

Once a qualified employee with a disability has requested a reasonable accommodation, the employer must make a reasonable effort to determine the appropriate accommodation. The process should be informal and interactive; it should involve the employer, the employee's supervisor(s), *and* the employee requesting the accommodation (Peterson & Ross, 1994). Following are the steps that should be taken.

*1. Analyze the specific job, and determine its essential functions.* In order to determine the appropriate accommodations, everyone involved must have a clear understanding of what the job entails. Several questions should be considered:

- What aptitudes are necessary to do the job?
- What knowledge is necessary to do the job?
- What methods, techniques, procedures, and tools are typically used to do the job?
- How much physical exertion is required?
- Does the job require lifting, standing, bending, reaching, twisting, or crawling?
- What skills are necessary?
- Are dexterous movements required?

**Exhibit 10–5** Specific Examples of Accommodations

| | |
|---|---|
| Physical accessibility | Parking spaces with access aisles<br>Wider doorways<br>Bathrooms with adequate floor space<br>Elevator controls with appropriate signage<br>Accessible work stations<br>Accessible drinking fountains<br>Visual and audio fire alarms<br>Signage with braille and raised lettering |
| Job restructuring | Flex time off<br>Job sharing<br>Focusing on outcomes rather than traditional methods of doing the job |
| Work station modifications | Modified equipment<br>Ergonomic furniture and equipment<br>Special jigs and fixtures to provide better access |
| Provision of assistive devices | Telephone headsets and speaker telephones<br>TDDs (telephone devices for the deaf)<br>Assistive listening devices<br>Braille printers<br>Computer peripherals |
| Environmental changes | Changes in lighting<br>Better ventilation<br>Noise abatement |

- Does the job have visual and audio demands?
- How much time is allowed to perform each function of the job?
- Is the pace consistent?
- How often is each function performed?
- Are the functions that are performed less frequently as important to success as those that are performed more frequently?
- How is success measured?
- What happens if a task is done improperly?
- What are the psychological, physiological, and environmental considerations for each task?
- How frequently is supervision required?
- What standards are employees required to meet independently?

**Exhibit 10–6** Statistics on Job Accommodations Costs

- 19% cost more than $1,000
- 81% cost $1,000 or less

*Of these:*

- 19% Cost Nothing
- 50% $1–$500
- 12% $501–$1,000
- 3% $1,001–$1,500
- 4% $1,501–$2,000
- 9% $2,001–$5,000
- 3% Greater than $5,000

Mean–974
Median–200

*Source:* Reprinted from Job Accommodation Network, 1995.

2. *Consult with the employee who has a disability to determine how that disability will affect the employee's ability to perform the essential functions of the job.* If the job has audio requirements, for example, deafness would have a significant effect. Noting such limitations does not necessarily mean that accommodations cannot be found to help the individual with a disability to overcome those limitations.

3. *Consult with the individual who has a disability about potential accommodations, and jointly assess the effectiveness each would have on the individual's ability to perform the essential functions of the job.* Employers should always include the individual being accommodated throughout the process. Too often, employers make decisions on "appropriate" accommodations without consulting the individual with a disability. The individual may have a better feel for the type of accommodation that is necessary than does the employer, however. Furthermore, the individual may have previous employment with a particular device that has given him or her some insight about its appropriateness for this particular job. Finally, it is important to understand the individual's tolerance and preference for specific accommodations.

4. *After consulting with the individual and determining his or her preference, consider which accommodation would be the most appropriate for both the employee and the employer.* The employee's preference is not necessarily the best for the entire operation. This is where the employer must consider the cost and overall ramifications, if there are any, for providing a particular accommodation.

In some cases, neither the person who needs the accommodation nor the employer can readily identify the appropriate accommodation(s). If this happens, it is wise to consult a professional who can help with the process (i.e., vocational specialists, occupational therapists, or rehabilitation engineers). Such a professional can help to ensure that the employer avoids the most common mistakes:

- neglecting to include the individual with the disability in the design process
- failing to consider alternative ways of providing accommodations
- making incorrect assumptions about a particular disability with respect to work performance
- exaggerated or poorly documented cost estimates
- failing to give the individual with the disability a fair chance

Taking everything into consideration, however, it is the employer who decides whether an accommodation is reasonable or not.

### Undue Hardship

Employers have the right to refuse an employee's request for an accommodation, even if the employee feels the request is reasonable. Employers have the right to claim that a specific accommodation would cause them an "undue hardship." Workers who feel that they have been discriminated against (based on the ADA) may file a complaint with the Equal Employment Opportunity Commission (EEOC). In determining whether a particular accommodation would cause an undue hardship, the EEOC considers a number of criteria: (1) the nature and net cost of the accommodation in question, (2) the overall financial resources of the site or sites involved, (3) the overall financial resources of any parent companies, (4) the type of operation involved, and (5) the impact that the accommodation would have on the operation.

### Fundamental Principles

In trying to determine the appropriate accommodations for qualified individuals with disabilities, certain fundamental principles should be followed:

- Form a partnership between the employer and the individual with a disability to be accommodated. This is probably the most important step; yet it is often the most neglected. The most successful accommodations occur when the employee with a disability is involved in the process from the beginning.
- Focus on the individual's ability, not on the disability. Too often, employers look at a person with a disability and assume that he or she is incapable

of doing the job. These opinions are often based on uninformed judgments about certain types of disabilities.

- Individualize the solutions. Since no two disabilities are alike, it is reasonable to suggest that no two solutions will be exactly alike.
- Keep it simple. Simplicity minimizes cost, facilitates repair, and does not disrupt the workplace.
- Apply the least invasive approach. No one wants a neon sign flashing on and off saying, "I have a disability." Therefore, an accommodation should blend in well with the surroundings.
- Be holistic in approach. It is always essential to look at the entire picture when considering an accommodation, including how the accommodation will affect the rest of the operation.
- Consider the preference of the individual with a disability.
- Whenever possible, have the person being accommodated try out a particular device before purchasing it, preferably within the setting where it will be used. Many companies now allow users to try a device before ordering it, especially expensive, computer-related equipment.

## Assistive Technology Intervention

As stated earlier, reasonable accommodations in the workplace can be simple and inexpensive (e.g., rearranging office furniture), complex and expensive (e.g., structurally remodeling a bathroom to make it wheelchair-accessible), or anything in between. In any case, there is a "common sense" approach to determining appropriate accommodations for qualified individuals with disabilities. The following hierarchical strategies provide a guide from simplest to most complex solutions:

1. Find an alternative way to do the task. It is far simpler to modify or adapt the task whenever possible.
2. Use commercially available products whenever available. It is usually easier and cheaper to buy an assistive device already on the market than it is to develop something new.
3. Use commonly available products in creative ways. Probably some of the most creative people around are those who have disabilities. They are always finding dual purposes for common household items. One lady uses an old-fashioned potato masher as an extension device to turn the knob on her dryer; the s-shaped masher fit perfectly over the dryer knob.
4. Modify and adapt commercially available devices already on the market. It is usually cheaper and less difficult to modify an existing device than it is to fabricate something from scratch.

5. If all else fails, design and fabricate custom devices as needed. This is by far the most costly of all the strategies and is usually saved for those times when nothing else works.

Accommodating persons with disabilities in the workplace is very much a dynamic process. During post-accommodation visits, it is not uncommon to find the employee doing things in unanticipated ways. Usually, the employee can articulate what works and what does not work. Simple adjustments may be necessary. It may also be determined that several more follow-up visits are required. With appropriate planning and regular follow-up visits, costly mistakes can be avoided.

## CONCLUSION

Independence in the home and ability to work are two of the most fundamental values for most of us. Not only for those of us with a disability, but also for those of us who are aging and likely to have functional limitations, being able to stay in our homes and to keep our jobs is critical. It is important that we all consider how we can make our lives easier, safer, more comfortable, and more productive. Adaptations and accommodations at home and work can benefit us all.

---


### BIBLIOGRAPHY

Bain, B. (1993). Assistive technology. In *Willard and Spackman's Occupational Therapy*. Philadelphia: J.B. Lippincott.

Job Accommodation Network. (1994). *The new facts about disability*. The President's Committee on Employment of People with Disabilities. Morgantown, WV: West Virginia University.

Job Accommodation Network. (1995). *Accommodation benefit/cost data summary*. The President's Committee on Employment of People with Disabilities. Morgantown, WV: West Virginia University.

Peterson, W., & Ross, D. (1994, May). Working it out . . . reasonably. *Team Rehab Report, 5*, 23–29.

P.L. 101–336, Americans with Disabilities Act (ADA). (1990).

REquest Rehabilitation Engineering Center. (1992a). *Stairlifts*.Washington, DC: National Rehabilitation Hospital and ECRI.

REquest Rehabilitation Engineering Center. (1992b). *Independence in the bathroom*. Washington, DC: National Rehabilitation Hospital and ECRI.

REquest Rehabilitation Engineering Center. (1993). *Prefabricated ramps*. Washington, DC: National Rehabilitation Hospital and ECRI.

*Stairlifts*. (1992). Washington, DC: REquest Rehabilitation Engineering Center.

*Chapter 11*

# Computer Access and Use by People with Disabilities

*Gregg C. Vanderheiden*

The computer, by its very nature, is an extremely flexible tool that can be used in many different ways. It can be especially helpful to people with disabilities.

## USES OF COMPUTERS BY PEOPLE WITH DISABILITIES

One of the problems in understanding computers and their use by people with disabilities stems from the fact that computers can be used in a variety of ways. There are three distinct and different roles that computers can play for people with disabilities:

1. for special education/therapy
2. in assistive technology
3. as a standard computer

Each of these uses may involve different computers or types of components, and each has different constraints. Finally, the funding of the computer is also often handled differently for each type of use.

### For Special Education/Therapy

When people with disabilities use computers as a special educational or therapeutic tool, the school or clinical program usually owns the computer and the special disability-related software running on the computer. The person with a disability generally uses the computer either at the school or at the clinic. Because the special software programs running on the computer are designed specifically for use by people with disabilities, they have built-in access features. The programs are designed either to evaluate or to develop skills such as reading, spelling, and language. Once a person has developed those skills, he or she no longer uses that particular computer and software. Funding of the computer and software are handled by the school or clinical program.

### In Assistive Technology

Computers used as an assistive technology by people with disabilities are purchased by or for those individuals and become their property in the same way that a pair of glasses or a wheelchair would. The computer provides the individual with a way to carry out activities that people who do not have that disability carry out in other ways. For example, people can use a computer to read (if they are blind), to manipulate documents (if they have a physical disability), to supplement or enhance their memory or sequencing abilities on a daily basis (if they have a cognitive impairment), or to communicate over telephones (if they are deaf). In general, computers used in assistive technology have special software that is written specifically to allow people with disabilities to carry out these functions while circumventing their particular disabilities. Because the computer that has been programmed to serve as these assistive technologies remains in the possession of the individual, he or she can use it to carry out these activities in all environments. The technologies may be paid for either by the individuals themselves or by some funding agency.

### As a Standard Computer

In many cases, people with disabilities need to operate the same computers for the same reasons as anyone else. Computers are now so integrated into all educational levels and most employment situations that people with disabilities must be able to use them along with everyone else in order to participate and compete effectively in these environments (e.g., education, employment, daily living). The person with a disability must be able to access not just a computer, but the specific computer that is found in the school or job site. Moreover, that person must be able to access the standard software programs that everyone else at the site is using.

Sources of funding for these standard computers and this standard software are the same for an individual with a disability as for anyone else. If anyone employed at a particular company in a particular job needs to use a computer, for example, that company usually provides the computer and the software for the employee. Similarly, an employee with a disability receives the computer needed to carry out the job. The only difference in this case is that, in order to use the computer effectively, the employee with a disability may need some adaptations. These adaptations either may be built into the computer or may take the form of an assistive technology to be used in conjunction with the computer.

## TRANSPARENT ACCESS

To achieve full access to standard computers and standard software, an individual with a disability needs some form of transparent access to the computer; that is, the individual must be able to interface with the computer in such a way that the computer cannot tell that the individual is not using a standard technique (e.g., keyboard, mouse, lightpen). In other words, the special access technique must be transparent, or invisible, to the computer. When an interface technique is truly transparent, the individual with a disability is able to access and use all of the standard software that is written for a computer that any user without a disability could use.

Some transparent access adaptations are hardware-based, such as a keyguard or mechanical latches that hold down the shift and other modifier keys. In these cases, as the individual is actually using the standard keyboard, the transparency of the modification is generally very good. Individuals who cannot use the standard keyboard or display screen (even with modifications), however, need a mechanism that allows them to use a different interface.

### Types of Adaptive Devices

#### *Keyboard-Emulating Interface*

An individual who is physically unable to use a standard keyboard, even if it is modified, may be able to operate an alternate keyboard or a communication aid by such means as sip and puff, head pointing, eye gaze, or speech. A device that can take input from these different interface techniques and make the input look as if it comes from the standard computer keyboard is called a keyboard-emulating interface. This type of adapter is able to emulate exactly the signals from the computer's standard keyboard, and therefore, its output cannot be distinguished from that of the standard keyboard. (See Figure 11–1.)

Newer computer systems also make extensive use of the mouse. It is, therefore, necessary on these systems to be able to emulate both the keyboard and the mouse. A device, called a General Input Device Emulating Interface (GIDEI), was developed for this purpose. The Trace Transparent Access Module (T-TAM) is one example of such a device (Figure 11–2).

#### *Alternate Interfaces with Built-in Emulating Interfaces*

In the case of the T-TAM, the emulator is a separate module that can be used with a variety of different communication aids or special interfaces. If an individual is going to work only with a single interface, the keyboard and mouse emulating functions may be built directly into the interface. The different types

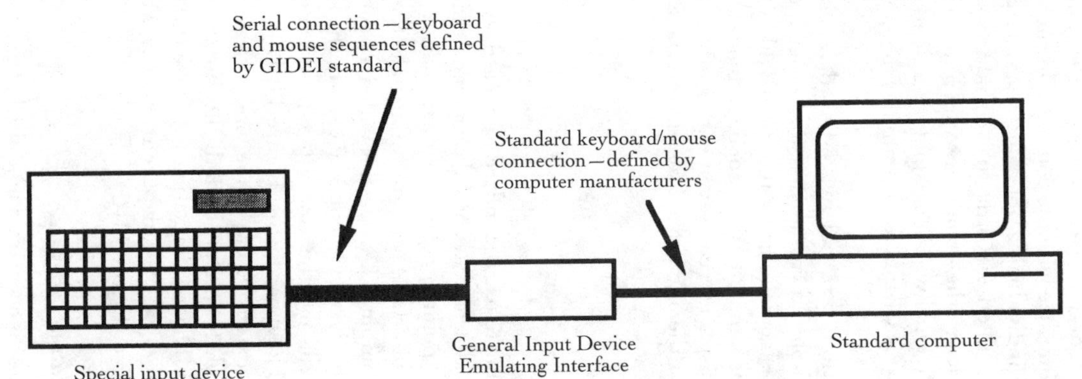


**Figure 11–1** The General Input Device Emulating Interface (GIDEI), which does both keyboard emulation and mouse emulation, is connected between a keyboard and a computer. It passes on any signals from the keyboard or mouse to the computer (so that the computer can still be used by individuals without disabilities). However, it also passes on signals from other devices to the computer, as if they came from the keyboard and/or mouse. The General Input Device Emulating Interface plugs into the same jack as the keyboard/mouse used to, and sends the exact same signals that the computer's keyboard and/or mouse do. As a result, the computer cannot distinguish between keystrokes and mouse actions coming from the keyboard and mouse, and those coming from the special input device.

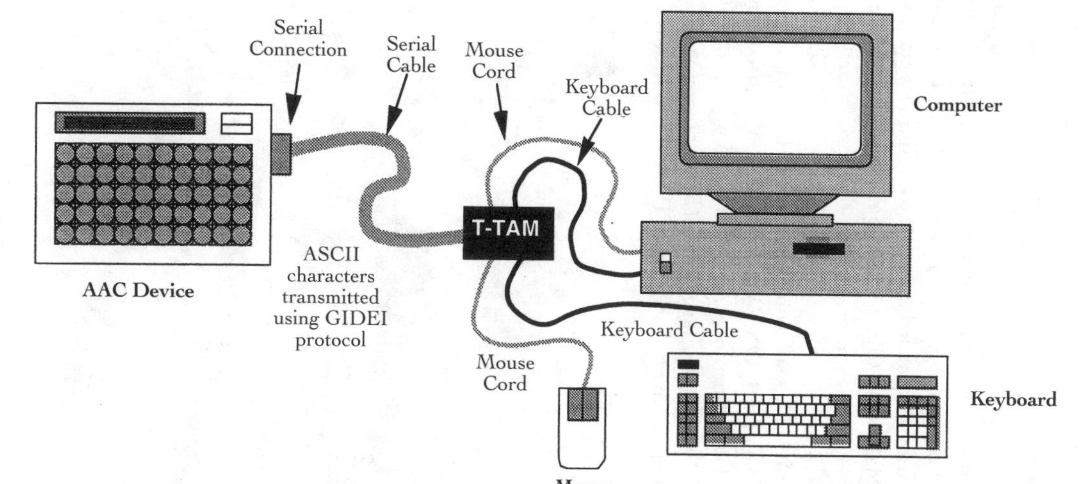


**Figure 11–2** The T-TAM allows a communication aid to create both keyboard and mouse action. Because this is a hardware keyboard and mouse emulating interface, it works independently of operating systems. This device has now been largely replaced by software extensions to Macintosh OS, DOS, Windows, and OS/2. ASCII, American Standard Code for Information Exchange. AAC, Augmentative/Alternative Communication. GIDEI, General Input Device Emulating Interface.

of such alternate interface systems shown in Figures 11–3A through 11–3F can all be used as a substitute for or in parallel with the standard keyboard and mouse on a computer.

### *Software Keyboard and Mouse Emulation*

With advances in software and operating systems, it is also now possible to build the keyboard- and mouse-emulating functions directly into the computer itself. Dubbed SerialKeys, this capacity is currently available as an add-on for DOS, Windows, and Macintosh, and it is built into Windows 95 and future generations of UNIX and Macintosh OS. SerialKeys allows the user to connect communication aids or other special interfaces to the serial port of the computer; then it converts commands sent to the serial port into standard keystrokes and mouse movements. This software eliminates the need for hardware emulators such as the T-TAM for DOS, Windows, and Macintosh users, except in the most unusual of circumstances. For DOS computers, it is part of AccessDOS, which is available free of charge from IBM or from Microsoft. For Windows 3.1, it is available as a part of the Access Pack for Windows 3.1, free

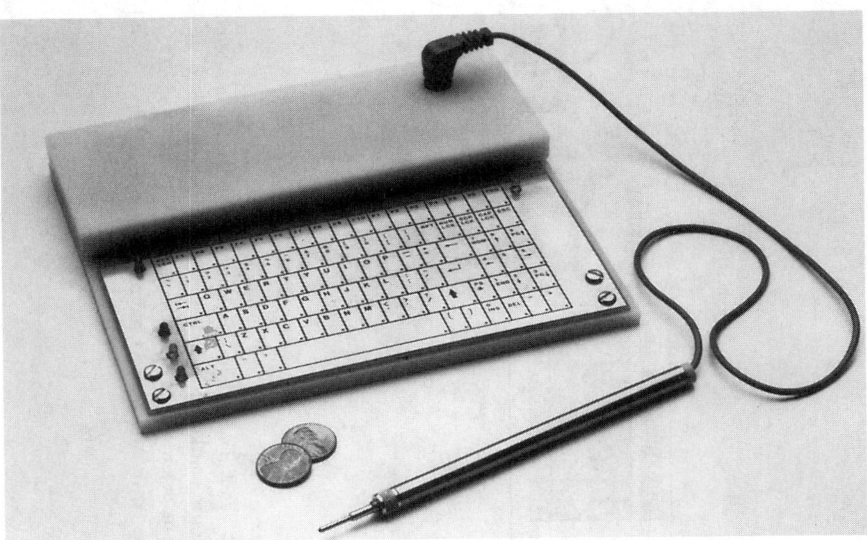

**Figure 11–3A** Magic Wand Keyboard (In Touch Systems): a miniature computer keyboard with zero-force electronic keys that require no reach, strength, or dexterity. Operated with a hand-held wand or mouthstick, the device provides full keyboard and mouse capability.

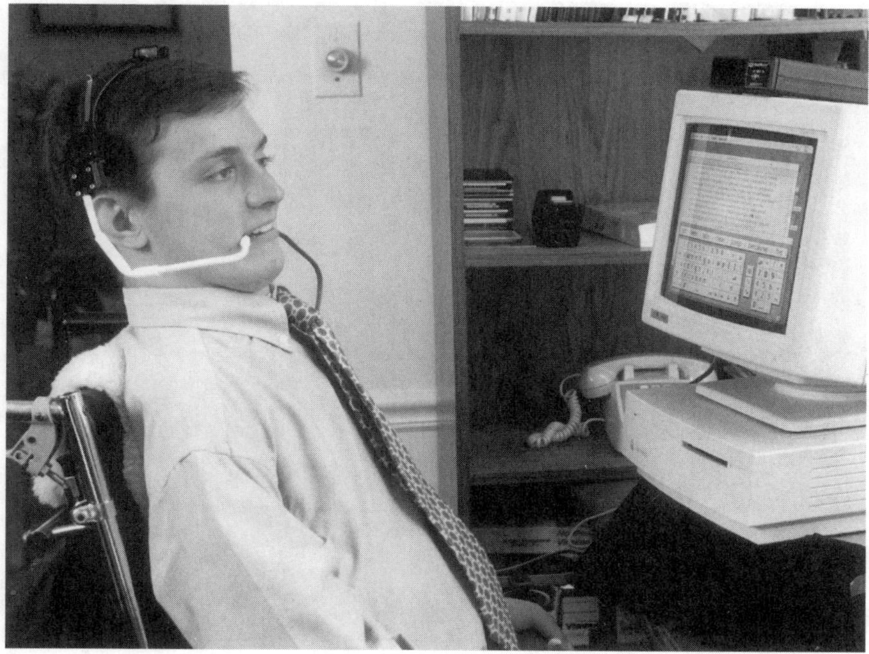

**Figure 11–3B** Headmaster Plus (Prentke Romich Company): a head-pointing system. HeadMaster translates changes in the user's head position into changes in the cursor's position on the screen; lightly puffing into a tube connected to the headset is equivalent to pressing the mouse button. On-screen keyboards can also be purchased with the HeadMaster to allow access to the keyboard.

---

of charge. For Windows 95, SerialKeys is a standard part of the default install and should be available automatically on almost any computer running Windows 95. As computers become more powerful, building disability access into the base hardware and operating system becomes more feasible and is an important trend in computer accessibility.

### Built-in Versus Adapted Access

There are basically four different strategies for making computers more accessible to people with disabilities:

1. *Built-in (Universal Design)*, building features directly into the computer, operating system, or application programs that make them directly

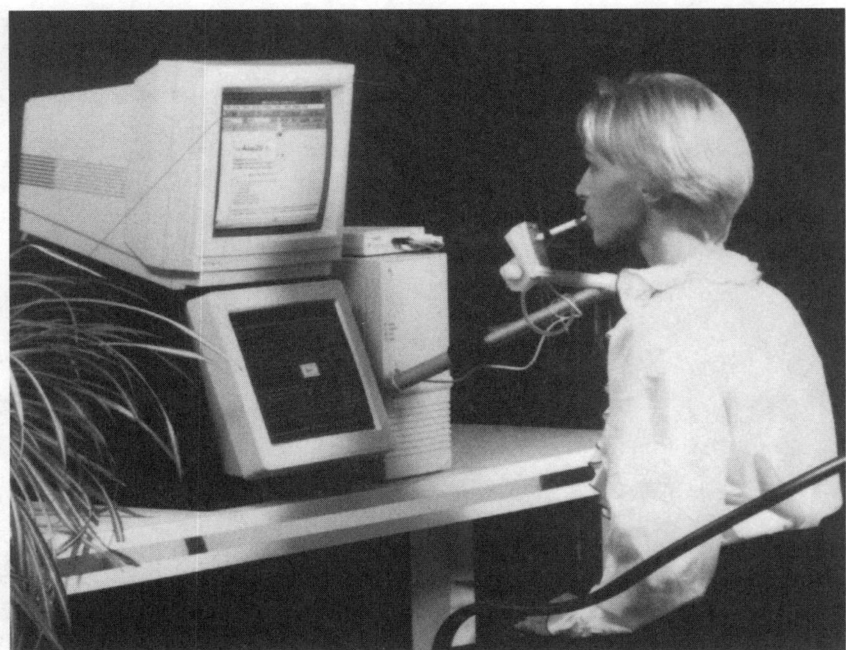

**Figure 11–3C** Adap2U (AdapTek Interface): an alternate input interface system that allows transparent access to standard IBM-compatible computers and DOS and Windows application programs. It provides control of dynamically interchangeable menus, such as custom keyboard layouts, which are then displayed on a separate monitor. Access can be by direct pointing and selection from menus, scanning, Morse code, or user-definable time codes.

---

usable by people with disabilities without requiring any further modification.

2. *Adaptive Interfaces,* standard software or hardware products that provide modifications or alternate interfaces that are installed on a computer to make it accessible to people with one or more types of disabilities.
3. *Connectability to Personal Assistive Devices,* provision of a mechanism for allowing individuals to connect their own personal assistive device(s) (communication aids, interfaces, braille displays, etc.) to computers they encounter and need to access.
4. *Custom Modifications,* custom adaptations (which are not available off the shelf) to computers to meet the needs of a particular user.

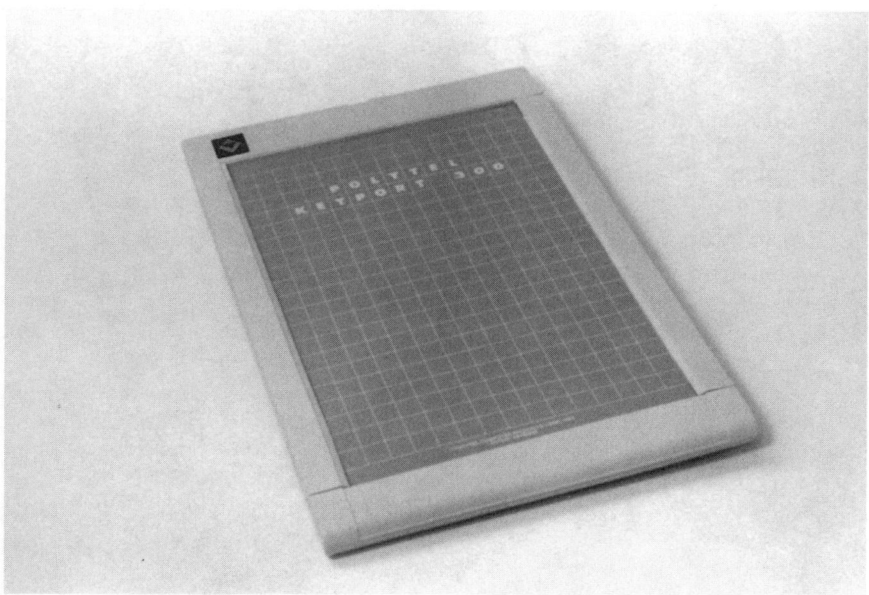


**Figure 11–3D** Keyport 300 (Polytel Computer Products Corporation): a 300-key alternate keyboard for the IBM PC. It allows any series of commands or characters to be mapped to any key on the Keyport 300's membrane surface. Larger keys can be created by assigning several adjacent keys with the same value. The user can place different overlays on the Keyport to correspond to the key assignment patterns.

---

### *Built-in (Universal Design)*

Wherever possible, it is desirable to have the disability access features built directly into the product as an extension of its standard human interface. If the features are truly integrated, people with disabilities can use the computer in the same manner as their peers who do not happen to have disabilities. A design that attempts to be usable by everyone, or by as many people as possible, usually by having built-in flexibility, is often referred to as a "universal" design.

Having access built in as part of the standard human interface has a number of advantages. First, it provides access for people with disabilities at no additional cost, putting them on a par with their colleagues without disabilities. Second, it removes the stigma of needing a "special" computer at the worksite, school, or community. It allows those who are older to use computers that they might not be able to use because of failing vision, hearing loss, or decreased

**Figure 11–3E** Maltron Keyboard (International Management Services, Inc.): specially curved and arranged keyboard to best suit single-handed (left or right hand; right hand shown here) or mouthstick use.

---

physical abilities, especially if they are unwilling to recognize or admit that they have disabilities. Products that are easy for people with disabilities to use are also easier for people with reduced abilities (due to aging, circumstance, temporary injury, etc.) to use. A third advantage is compatibility. Often, access adaptations are incompatible with particular software programs or standard computer accessories. When adaptations are built directly into the operating system, third-party vendors who are installing additional software can identify and accommodate any incompatibilities immediately. Special add-on access options are usually not even known to, and almost never tested by, application manufacturers, and they are therefore much more likely to result in conflicts. This problem is exacerbated by the fact that there are hundreds of different adaptations, which may be used singly or in combination, that would have to be tested. Most important, built-in access allows an individual to use computers in public and shared environments where it may not be practical or permissible to install custom hardware and software in order to make the system accessible.

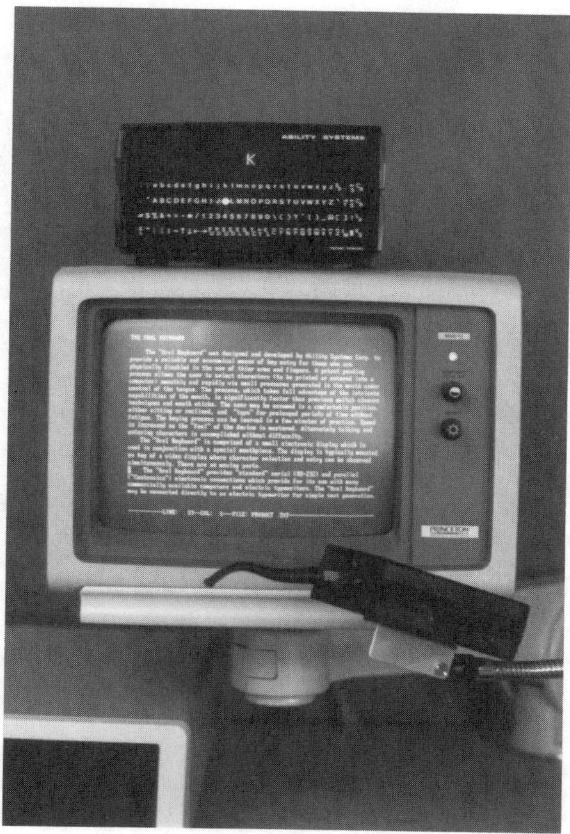


**Figure 11–3F** Proportional Keystroke Scanner (Ability Systems Corporation): operated by scanning characters at a rate proportional to the air pressure the user applies to the puff tube. Each of the four rows can be scanned horizontally by sipping; characters are selected by puffing gently, which sends that character to the computer as a standard keyboard character.

---

Apple Computer was the first to build disability access features directly into every computer they sold and to have the features automatically installed as part of the standard software. IBM not only built special features into the hardware of its computers, but also included some access features directly in OS/2. Windows 95 contains more than a dozen disability access features as part of its standard install. These features allow individuals with a wide range of type, degree, and combination of disabilities to use computers that they would previously have needed to modify.

### *Adaptive Interfaces*

Some individuals with a disability cannot use a computer as it comes out of the box, either because the particular computer lacks any built-in accessibility features or because the type and degree of disability require an adaptation that is too expensive to build into each computer (e.g., a dynamic braille display or special head pointer). In these cases, adaptive interfaces that can make the computer accessible may be available from the computer company or from third-party vendors. This add-on approach has the advantage of allowing the incorporation of more expensive hardware or more varieties of software than is possible to package with every computer sold. On the other hand, it requires the individual with a disability to pay or secure additional funds to cover the costs of these adaptations. Furthermore, it may be difficult to carry these adaptations about and install them on public and shared computers as they are encountered in employment, education, or daily life. Thus, the user may not have access to many public computers, such as automated transaction machines (ATMs).

### *Connectability to Personal Assistive Devices*

In some cases, individuals with disabilities can carry with them their own personal assistive technology that can act as an alternate interface to other devices. For example, it may be possible to use an augmentative communication aid as an alternate keyboard or mouse control device for a computer. Similarly, an individual who is blind or deaf-blind may have a braille note-taking device that can also serve as an alternate display and input device. These devices can be used with computers if they can be connected so as to substitute for the computer's standard input or display devices.

Although SerialKeys, as noted previously, allows users to connect some personal assistive devices, there is currently no similar standard connection mechanism for braille or portable audio displays for standard computers. An interconnection standard is under development to allow such systems to be used with public kiosks, information terminals, ATMs, and so on. The use of infrared (IR) links could allow individuals who are physically disabled to walk or roll up to a computer and use it without needing someone to hook and unhook them each time they come and go (Figure 11–4).

### *Custom Modifications*

In some instances, the circumstances, abilities, and constraints of the individual with a disability are unique, requiring custom modifications to the computer system. This approach has the advantage of providing a maximal fit between the user and the computer, but it generally is much more expensive—

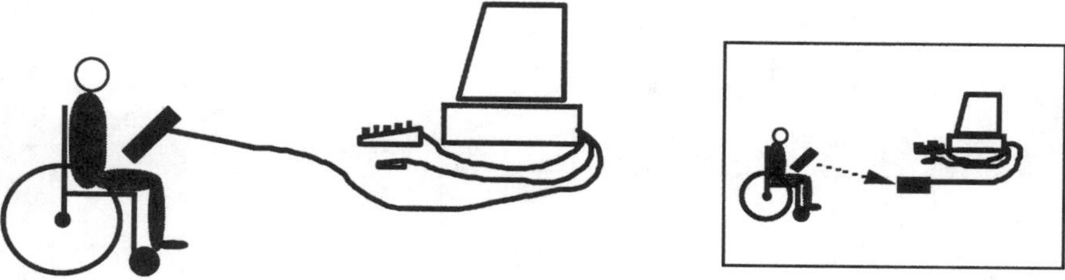

**Figure 11–4** With appropriate transparent access connection points, individuals with special input or control systems have access to standard computers and other electronic devices, either by connecting to their serial port or via infrared link.

sometimes as much as 10 to 20 times more expensive—as the same modification would be if it were commercially available. Also, a custom modification is usually more difficult to repair or replace if it should break. The individual who fabricated the original version may have moved, or the parts used may be difficult or impossible to find. Furthermore, because such modifications are specific to one type of system, they are useless in other (e.g., public) systems.

#### *Combination of Techniques*

Often it is necessary to combine techniques to ensure broad accessibility. The goal is generally to maximize the number of people who can use computer systems without assistive technologies, while still allowing those who have personal assistive technologies to connect and use them easily. Again, modern computers and operating systems have both very flexible and very adaptable interfaces. As more and more computers are incorporating built-in speech output capabilities and infrared links, the range and options available will only increase.

## COMPUTER USE WITH VARIOUS DISABILITIES

### Physical Disabilities

People with physical disabilities have a variety of problems with computer access. For example, they may have problems in using the standard input devices (e.g., keyboard, mouse) and in handling media (e.g., disks, tapes). Users with physical disabilities may also have trouble with latches on portable computers and with power switches and other controls on all computers.

#### *Built-in Accessibility Features*

At the present time, there are six disability features or extensions to the human interface that are being built into various computers to make them more usable by people with physical disabilities (Table 11–1):

**Table 11–1** Built-in Accessibility or "Universal Access" Features

| *Computer/OS Model* | *Apple IIGS* | *Macintosh OS* | *DOS* | *Windows 3.1* | *OS/2* | *UNIX* | *Windows 95* |
|---|---|---|---|---|---|---|---|
| *Model/Extension Package* | *1 megabyte* | | *Access DOS* | *AccessPack* | | *X11R-6* | |
| *Developer* | *Apple* | *Apple* | *Trace Center* | *Trace Center* | *IBM* | *Sun, DEC* | *Microsoft* |
| **Access Feature** | | | | | | | |
| Stickykeys | • | • | • | • | • | • | • |
| MouseKeys | • | • | • | • | | • | • |
| RepeatKeys | • | • | • | • | • | • | • |
| SlowKeys | | • | • | • | • | • | • |
| BounceKeys | | | • | • | | • | • |
| SerialKeys | | * | • | • | | | • |
| ToggleKeys | | N/A | • | • | | • | • |
| SoundSentry | † | † | • | • | | | • |
| ShowSounds | | | | | • | | • |
| Screen enlargement | • | • | | | | | ? |
| High contrast mode | | ‡ | | | | | • |
| Adj. system fonts | | • | | ? | • | • | • |

† Indicates partial functionality; menu bar flashes for system beep when set to zero.
‡ Black and white mode is standard.
* Currently available as separate utilities.

1. StickyKeys
2. MouseKeys
3. RepeatKeys
4. SlowKeys
5. BounceKeys
6. SerialKeys

*StickyKeys.* Some individuals who use a headstick, a mouthstick, or only one finger to type are unable to use a standard keyboard because it is sometimes necessary on a standard keyboard to hold down multiple keys at the same time (e.g., a shift and an 8 to type an asterisk; a control, an alt, and a delete to reboot the computer). On a computer with the StickyKeys feature, simply tapping on the shift key five times makes the shift, control, and alt (option and command on a Macintosh) all go "sticky." The user can then press the shift key, release it, and then press the 8 key in order to type the asterisk—rather than having to hold both keys down at the same time.

*MouseKeys.* Many individuals do not have the fine motor control necessary to accurately point with the mouse or to move the mouse around and press the buttons. MouseKeys allows such a person to use the number keypad on the keyboard to move the mouse cursor around on the screen. A three-key sequence activates the MouseKeys feature, turning the number keypad on the keyboard into a mouse control pad (Figure 11–5).

*RepeatKeys.* Individuals who have slow response times can get unwanted extra characters if they are not able to remove their finger from the keyboard in time. RepeatKeys extends the rate for the key repeat function on the keyboard. It also allows the individual to turn the repeat function off completely.

*SlowKeys.* Individuals with cerebral palsy or other conditions that interfere with their motor control often find it difficult to use the standard keyboard because they accidentally bump and activate unwanted keys when they try to type. Many of these people use a physical keyguard with holes over each key to provide stability. The SlowKeys feature allows some people with this type of disability to operate the keyboard without such a keyguard. The user can adjust the period of time for which a key must be held down before it is accepted. By setting SlowKeys to a half second or so, an individual is able to move the hand across the keyboard and hit large numbers of extraneous keys before settling on the target key. Pausing on that key for a half second activates it, while all the other keys that were depressed on the way to the target key are ignored. The delay period can be adjusted to accommodate an individual's abilities, keeping the amount of time for key acceptance to the minimum required for that individual.

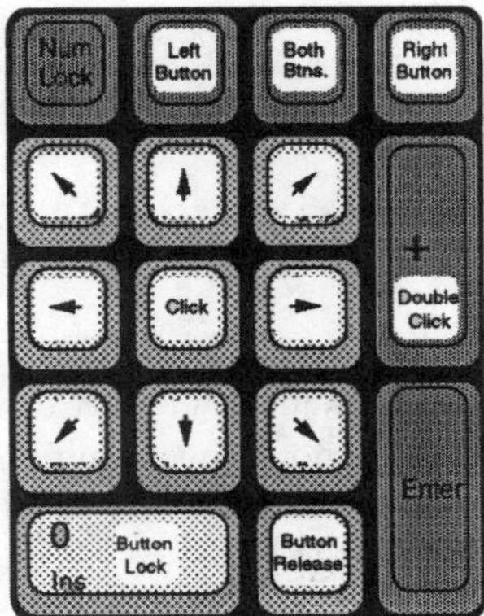


**Figure 11–5** The MouseKeys feature allows the individual to move the mouse about on the screen, click its button(s), and carry out drag functions. The standard mouse is active throughout, allowing users to combine the use of the standard mouse or trackball with the MouseKeys feature for single-pixel positioning accuracy. Graphic artists and others who do not have disabilities, but who require very precise, single-pixel positioning that is difficult to achieve for anyone using just the mouse, also use the MouseKeys feature.

*BounceKeys.* Individuals with tremor may not press the wrong keys, but they may get a double key when trying to press and release a key. The BounceKeys feature prevents the typing of these extraneous characters while the key is being either pressed or released. It is possible to set the BounceKeys so that such bounces would be ignored, while deliberate double pressings of the same key (such as the double *t* in button are accepted if they occur in a specific fraction of time (more than *x*/100ths of a second).

*SerialKeys.* As discussed earlier, SerialKeys is a function that allows individuals to connect their personal assistive devices to a computer and use them instead of the keyboard or mouse. The most common use of SerialKeys is to replace the computer's standard keyboard and mouse with an augmentative communication device.

### Hardware Design Features

Other features have been incorporated into the hardware design of computers to make them more accessible for individuals with physical disabilities. IBM had the ejection system on the floppy disk drives improved so that the disks protrude farther when ejected, making them easier to grasp (e.g., with tongs, fists). They also repositioned the on/off switch to the front of the case and changed to concave buttons for the disk drives and power to facilitate use with headsticks, mouthsticks, and so on. Although caddy-less CD ROM drives are slightly less expensive and seem to be preferred by many users, the ability to put each CD into a separate caddy makes it much easier for people with physical limitations to handle and change CDs safely themselves.

### *Adaptive Interfaces*

The number of different adaptive interfaces that can be used with computers is enormous. Both the ABLEDATA* database, which lists 20,000 assistive technology devices of all types, and the TraceBase† database, which lists communication, control, and computer access aids, contain a wide range of adaptations: arm supports; copy holders; keyboard trays; monitor-mounting systems; paper loaders; wheelchair interfaces; disk-loading systems; eye-controlled input systems; scanning, encoding, and direct selection input systems; cursor control interfaces (more than 50); Morse code input systems; optical pointer interfaces, which can be held in the hand or mounted on the head; voice input interfaces; and 100 to 200 expanded, miniature, modified, one-handed, or remote keyboards and keyboard modifications. In addition, there are software adaptations for speeding up the input using abbreviation–expansion, word prediction, and word-and-phrase dictionary approaches that allow individuals to type out full words and sentences using only one or a few keystrokes.

A wide variety of special switches and transducers are also available to be used in conjunction with these adaptive interfaces: chin, eye, foot, posture, and tip switches; bite, eyebrow, glove, pull–push, touch, rotate, squeeze, thumb, tongue, and lightbeam switches; joystick switches; switches that operate by means of electrical muscle or eye movement signals; and switches that simply detect any movement or sound.

Most of these techniques are designed to allow the individual to use the techniques with any standard software on the computer. The interfaces shown in Figures 11–6A through 11–6H are only a few of the wide variety of techniques that are available.

### *Special Applications for People with Physical Disabilities*

The list of computer applications possible for people with physical disabilities is almost limitless (Figures 11–7A through 11–7C). (For an overview of the types of application programs available, see the ABLEDATA and TraceBase databases.) A sampling of special functions or applications that a computer may provide to a person with a physical disability includes

- augmentative communication aid
- a means for writing, handling, and storing paperwork

---

*Macro International, 8455 Colesville Road, Silver Spring, MD 20910-3310.

†Trace R & D Center, S-151 Waisman Center, 1500 Highland Avenue, Madison, WI 53705.

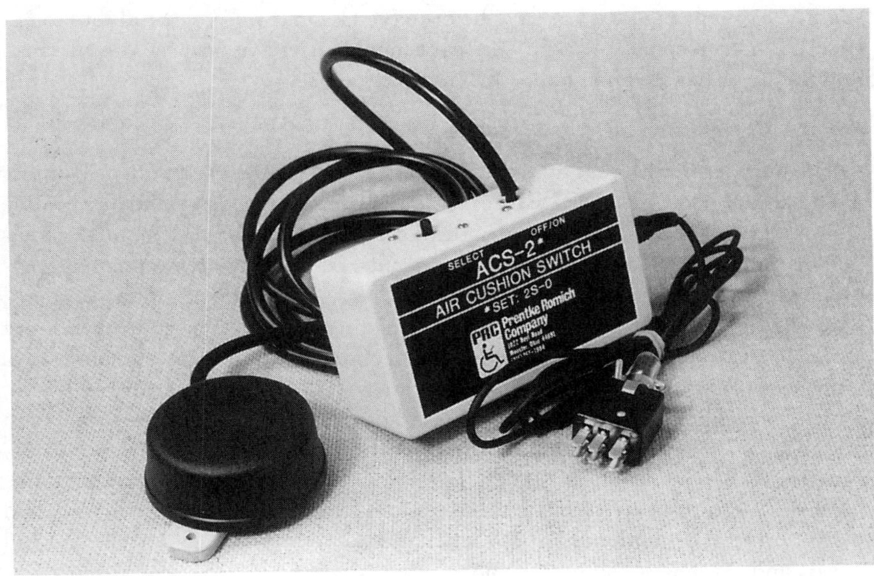


**Figure 11–6A** Air Cushion Switch (Prentke Romich Company). A light touch on the bellows sends air pressure to the switching unit, where the change in pressure activates a switch.

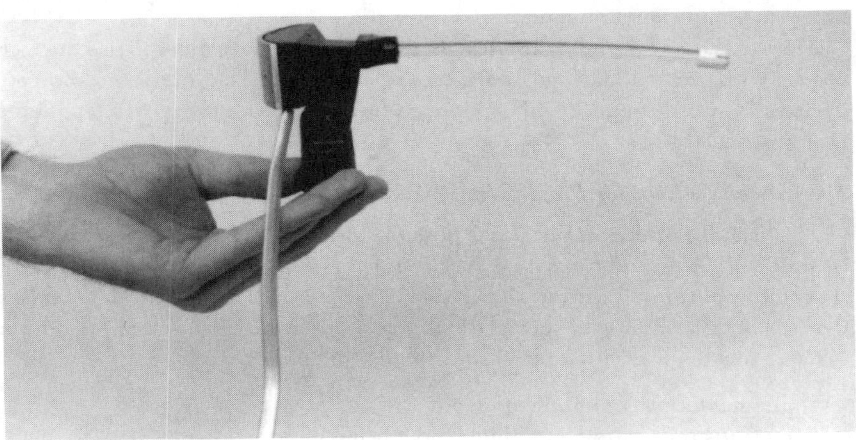

**Figure 11–6B** Breath Input Device (Neil Squire Foundation). A change in air pressure caused by sipping or puffing on the switch activates these switches.

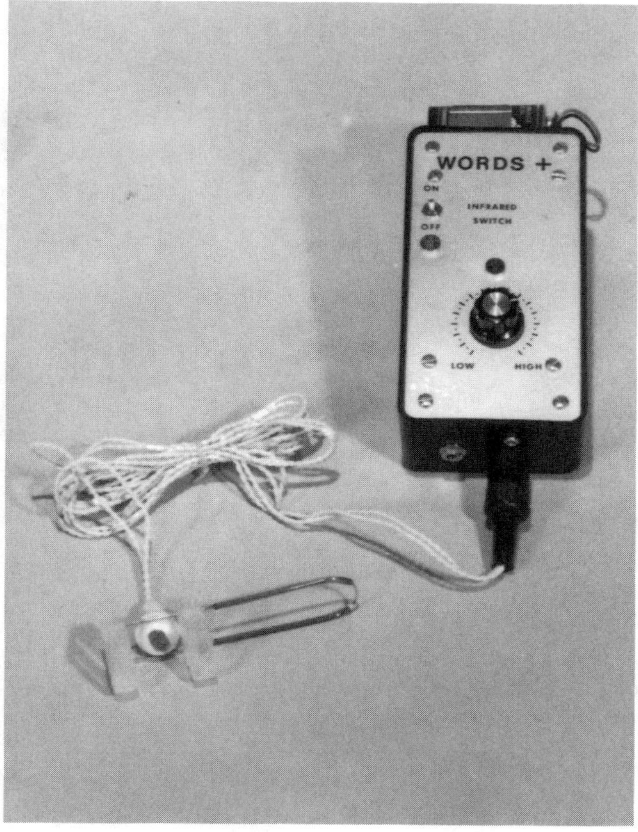


**Figure 11–6C** IST Switch (Words+, Inc.) This zero-force switch can be used with virtually any body movement and can be activated via infrared, sound, or touch.

---

- control of a power wheelchair
- control of various appliances in the home or work environment
- a means for drawing accurately and with detail
- a means for working from a distance
- electronic attendance at meetings when it is difficult to travel
- "travel" to inaccessible locations (e.g., pyramids, caves)
- manipulation of scientific instrumentation (e.g., microscopes, chemical analyzers)

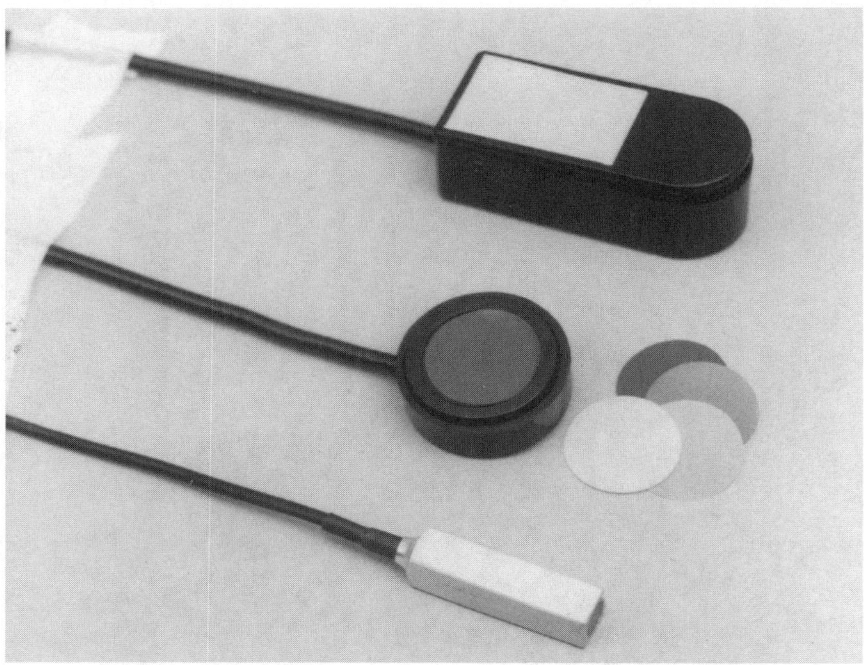

**Figure 11–6D** Tip Switch (Tash, Inc.): a mercury switch. A change in vertical orientation allows the mercury to slide away inside the switch.

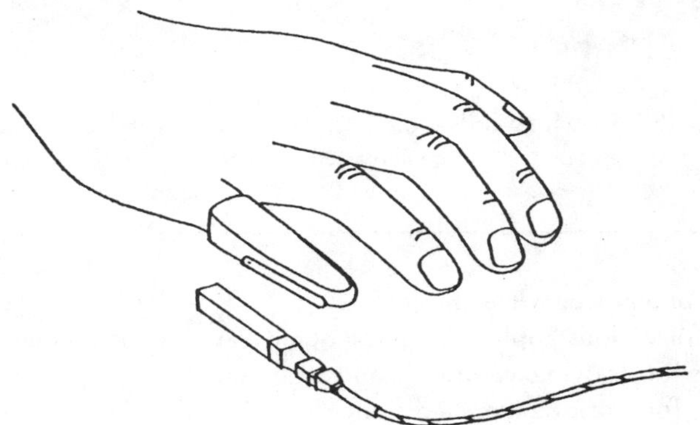

**Figure 11–6E** Magnetic Finger Switch (Luminaud, Inc.): a finger sleeve containing a magnet, plus a small external switch unit. A small movement of the finger toward the switch unit activates the switch.

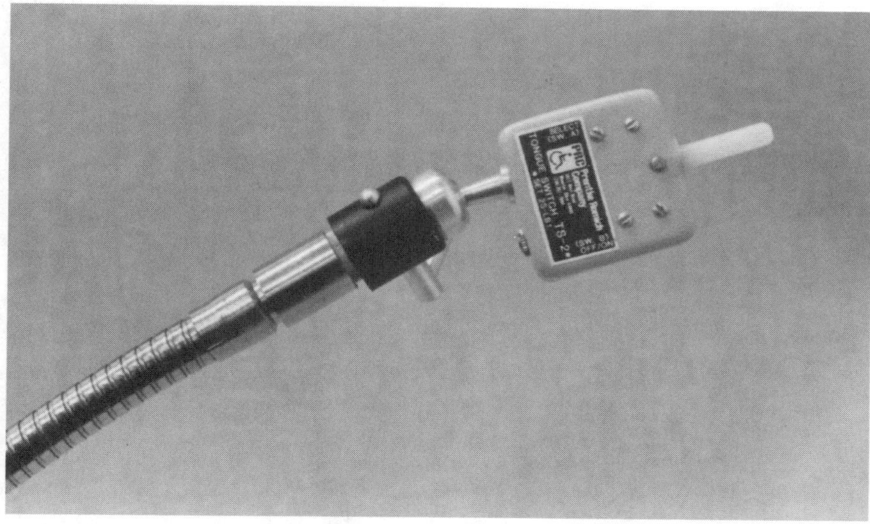


**Figure 11–6F** Tongue Switch (Prentke Romich Company). Pushing up or down on the short lever activates the dual switches. This switch can be mounted for easy access by other body parts besides the tongue.

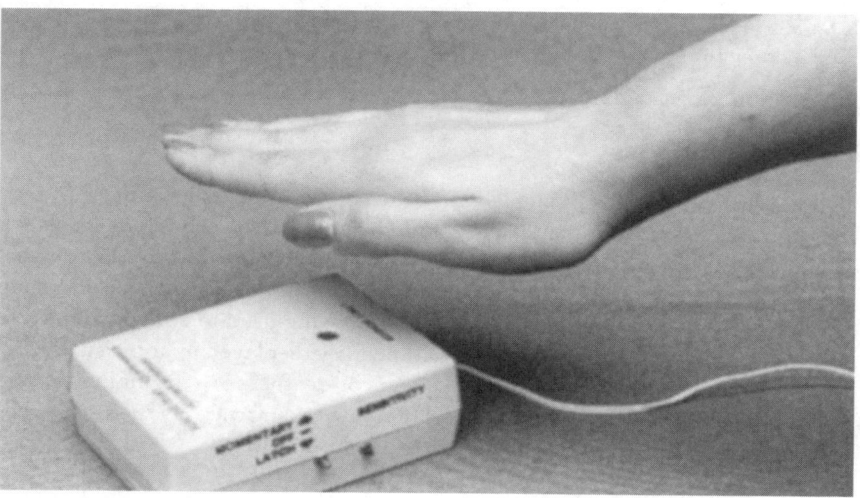


**Figure 11–6G** Shadow Switch (Crestwood Company). Moving any body part to create a shadow over the photocell activates the switch.

**Figure 11–6H** Self-Calibrating Auditory Tone InfraRed (SCATIR; Artificial Language Laboratory): switch activated by the movement of any body part from a distance of up to 3 inches from the sensor.

---

## Hearing Impairments

Up to this point in time, people with hearing impairments have not had serious problems using computers. The computer interface has largely been visual; even the occasional warning beep has usually been accompanied by some visual event. The current shift toward multimedia and sound, however, is producing drastic changes. Sound effects and speech are being used to convey important information that is not necessarily simultaneously displayed in any visual form. As a result, people with hearing impairments or deafness are beginning to have problems with access to computers and multimedia software. Access strategies are beginning to appear both in built-in and add-on form.

### *Built-in Accessibility Features*

At the current time, there are basically four types of built-in accommodations for people with hearing impairments and deafness:

**Figure 11–7A** Sensei (Safko International): an integrated environment control, augmentative communication, and computer input system for the Macintosh. Not only does it allow alternate input to the computer but it also gives the user the ability to write and send faxes, communicate via e-mail, and talk on the telephone. Applications such as word processing, graphics, spreadsheets, and databases are included.

---

1. controllable volume
2. headphone/speaker jacks
3. SoundSentry features
4. ShowSounds features (including captions)

*Controllable Volume.* First appearing in the Macintosh, controllable volume is now becoming increasingly common even on laptop computers. Combined with a headphone/speaker jack, controllable volume allows people with a hearing impairment to hear and understand many sounds that would otherwise go undetected.

*Headphone/Speaker Jack.* Macintosh was the first to offer a headphone/ speaker jack, but it is now available in most desktop and portable computers.

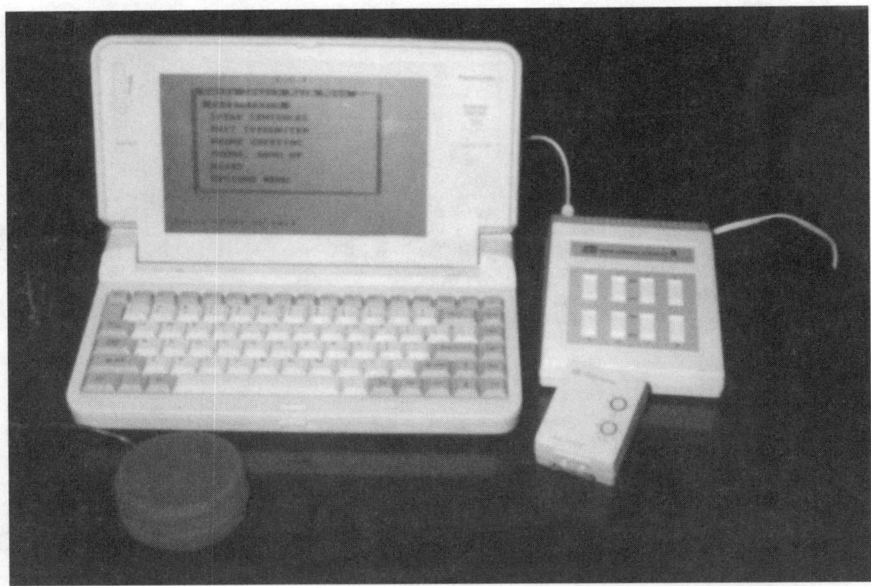

**Figure 11–7B** CCT Environmental Control (Consultants for Communication Technology): a hardware/software environment control system. Up to 16 electrical switches and outlets can be controlled from the screen. Also has an infrared control that can provide full access to any device that uses an infrared control.

---

The headphone/speaker jack allows the user to connect to the computer a number of devices that can help to amplify the sounds from the computer and eliminate background noise.

The output from the headphone jack can be fed into small amplifiers that can, in turn, be connected to either a headphone or speakers to increase the computer's sound levels. Similarly, inductive loops that can work with the t-coil in the individual's hearing aid can be connected to help deliver clearer, less distorted sound to the individual while at the same time essentially eliminating background noise. Finally, a small light-emitting diode (LED) device that is connected via the headphone jack and lights whenever a sound is emitted from the computer is an inexpensive mechanism for providing visual indications that simple beeps are being emitted. (This strategy, however, has now been replaced by the SoundSentry feature.)

*SoundSentry.* Built directly into the operating system, the SoundSentry software adaptation provides a visual on-screen indication (e.g., a marker, reversal

**Figure 11–7C** Eyegaze Computer System (LC Technologies, Inc.): a communication system controlled by the use of one eye. Using a camera and an infrared light source, the computer interprets where the eye is focused on a computer screen. Nothing needs to be attached to the user's body. Various extra options allow the user to turn on lights and appliances, dial and receive telephone calls, and run IBM DOS-compatible software.

---

of the title bar window, change in the color of the border around the screen) whenever the computer speaker emits a sound. SoundSentry is good for detecting simple beeps or warnings, but it does not indicate what type of signal is being sent out to the speaker and, of course, is not useful if the signal is speech or some other complex wave form. A form of the SoundSentry has been available on the Macintosh since its inception. SoundSentry has been available as an add-on for DOS and Windows 3.1 (originally titled ShowSounds) and is a standard feature in Windows 95 (see Table 11–1).

*ShowSounds (Including Captioning)*. The ShowSounds feature is a system level software flag or switch, usually contained in the computer's control panel, that allows the user to have any important sounds that are created by the computer shown in some visual way on screen. Application programs that are ShowSounds-compatible would then provide a redundant visual presentation of any important information being presented auditorily. Purely decorative music, speech redundant with text that is already on screen, and sounds that are not important to the operation of the computer can be ignored. Where speech or other important sounds occur, however, the ShowSounds-compatible program presents captions, adds text to the screen, or presents the information in some other appropriate way so that it can be received by someone unable to hear. In addition to being useful to individuals with hearing impairments or deafness, this feature is useful in noisy environments (e.g., airplanes, shopping malls) and in environments where sound is not appropriate (e.g., libraries, nursing stations in hospitals at night). The ShowSounds feature is standard in Microsoft Windows 95. The same function, labeled Captioning, is available in the OS/2 multimedia system.

*Caption Display Tools*. There is an increasing trend for schools, groups, and individuals to create their own multimedia materials. These may be distributed on disk, CD, or very commonly, over the Internet. New tools are making it easy for people, even those with no programming experience, to create these materials. Unfortunately, few if any of these tools presently incorporate easy mechanisms for captioning and other visual displays of auditory information as a simple integrated part of the multimedia tools. With efforts from a number of groups (notably the CPB/WGBH National Center on Accessible Media, 125 Western Avenue, Boston, MA 02134), it is hoped that this situation will soon change. Until then, however, the accessibility of educational materials is likely to remain a function of the availability of these tools and the number of times that teachers or school systems request ShowSounds-compatible or captioned materials in ordering multimedia materials.

### *Special Applications for People with Hearing Impairments or Deafness*

In addition to the use of standard computer software programs and accessories, there are special uses of the computer for individuals with hearing impairments or deafness:

- to capture and translate spoken speech into text for visual display, a use that will expand very rapidly as speech recognition continues to improve.
- to provide real-time captioning for speakers at public events and in private meetings. Both speed typing and stenographic techniques are currently

being used to input information to be projected to a large screen at public presentations or displayed on the personal computer screen.

- to learn finger spelling and sign language.
- to control home signaling and security systems.
- to provide multifunction telecommunication devices that allow the individual to communicate via TDD/TT (telephone device for the deaf), ASCII, speech recognition, speech synthesis, and touchtone keypad to text translation. Such systems allow the individual who is hearing impaired to communicate with people who can hear and who are communicating at the other end with nothing but a standard telephone.
- to carry on communication via e-mail as well as on-line chat sessions on bulletin boards and the Internet.

Figure 11–8 shows an example of these applications.

### Visual Impairments

Access to standard computer software for individuals with visual impairments or blindness was fairly straightforward for many years, when the primary

**Figure 11–8** BookWise (Xerox Imaging Systems, Inc.): a PC-based reading and tutoring system. BookWise scans books or other printed materials, recognizes the characters, and simultaneously displays the text on the computer screen and reads it aloud in synthesized speech.

operating systems (Apple II and DOS) were character-based. Screen enlargement, large print programs, and screen readers were relatively quickly developed for these systems and grew in sophistication over the years. The appearance of pop-up windows and drop-down menus caused some problems, but screen readers adapted for the most part to these developments.

With the advent of the graphic user interface (GUI) first on the Macintosh and then in Windows, OS/2, and the X Window system, the problem became considerably more complex. Although some of the structured aspects of these new operating systems have actually made them more accessible, the new difficulty of determining exactly what text was where on the screen and the increased use of graphics have resulted in a net loss of accessibility to the computers and to the information presented through them to people with visual impairments. Screen readers are steadily improving, but the movement toward even greater use of graphics, animation, and movielike interfaces is presenting continual challenges.

### *Built-in Accessibility Features*

Building accessibility directly into computers for people with visual impairments or blindness basically takes four forms:

1. screen magnification features
2. font enlargement features
3. speech-enabled applications
4. screen reader support

*Screen Magnification Features.* Available both as add-on products from third parties and as a built-in feature of some operating systems, many people with visual impairments find screen magnification helpful. Apple Computer has included its CloseView program as part of the standard operating system since approximately 1989. Screen magnification is a standard feature of OS/2 and Microsoft Windows 95. Screen magnification features allow the user to enlarge part of the screen to up to 16 times its normal size. The user can then move around on the screen, magnifying different portions, much as if using a large magnifying glass. Because the user can see only a portion of the screen at any time, the effect is somewhat like viewing the computer screen through a small tube. The user can move the tube around and see different portions of the screen, but cannot get a view of the entire screen at one time. Other third-party screen enlargers provide additional features, including the ability to enlarge the full screen, a part of the screen, or just a line.

*Font Enlargement Features.* Rather than enlarging the entire image on the screen, some systems allow the user to adjust the size of the fonts used to display information. Thus, there are simply fewer words per line and fewer lines per page visible in any one scrolling field. The individual can, however, see the full text information that is on the screen and can scroll down through the field to read additional lines. Most of the current graphic operating systems include this feature. Also, many programs have this capability, although it may be limited to certain fields and is not always available in help files, controls, and other important parts of the program.

*Speech-Enabled Applications.* Some programs have a built-in speech output mode that enables an individual to control the program entirely from the keyboard using only a voice synthesizer. Menus, controls, on-line documentation, and information on the screen can all be controlled through the keyboard and the voice synthesizer output. There are no speech-enabled operating systems, but there are a number of speech-enabled application programs, particularly in the area of public information systems and programs that are specifically designed for use by people with visual impairments or blindness. An example of a speech-enabled program as well as one with font enlargement capabilities can be found on the cooperative Electronic Library software on the CO-NET CD available from the Trace Center and attached to the inside of this book. Both the Trace Document Browser and the Publication, Media, and Materials directories on the CD provide these features for both Macintosh and Windows.

*Screen Reader Support.* Screen readers are software programs that can read the text on the computer screen and present it to the user, either as speech or on a dynamic braille display. Because there are so many conventions (many of them mutually exclusive) used for controlling and using screen reader programs, there are no computers or operating systems that have built-in screen reading capability. However, if the operating system can provide support to the screen reader program, through provision of built-in voice synthesizer, or provision of an off-screen model of the information being presented on the screen (the most difficult technical part of a screen reader), it is much easier for the manufacturers of screen reader programs to keep their product current as new computers and operating systems appear. Apple Computer has provided a built-in voice synthesizer as a part of its standard Macintosh computer for several years, and built-in speech will soon be a standard part of most operating systems. Microsoft Corporation is in the process of building an off-screen model for their Windows 95 and future GUI operating systems in order to facilitate the development and availability of screen readers for their systems.

### *Limitations of Speech-Enabled Applications and Screen Readers*

Both speech-enabled applications and screen readers have little difficulty in reading text (unless it is part of a picture or graphic, rather than being drawn on the screen through the standard text-drawing routines of the operating system). Both technologies can also work fairly well with icons and other standard graphic constructs in the operating system. Neither type of system can do a very good job of presenting information that is inherently graphic in nature, however. For example, neither can present the information in a photograph. Similarly, most charts and diagrams, schematics, and drawings cannot currently be automatically presented to the user by the software. The only way that this information can be made accessible is if the documents contain text descriptions of this information:

1. The information in the picture can be redundantly presented in the text.
2. A caption below the picture can be expanded to provide not only an orientation to the diagram, but also a complete description of the item.
3. Hidden text can be embedded in the document to describe the item. One strategy that has been suggested is simply to write the description in an invisible color directly over the graphic item on the screen. Although a sighted user would not see such writing, the screen reader could pick it up via the off-screen model mechanism and present it to the user when the graphic item (with the invisible text over it) is encountered. An alternate method would be to provide a mechanism for attaching the text description to the graphic object. When the screen reader encountered the graphic object, it would query the operating system, which could, in turn, supply the description of the object to the screen reader for presentation to the user.

### *Special Applications for People with Visual Impairments*

Among the special uses of the computer for individuals with visual impairments or blindness are the following:

- speech-enabled training programs
- braille training programs
- braille translators
- special braille, voice, and large print writing and note-taking systems
- speech-output calculators
- accessible interfaces for other equipment, including laboratory, educational, job-related, and audio and radio equipment
- orientation and mobility, including portable systems that use satellite-relayed information about precise location and directions to other locations
- access mechanisms for electronic books
- special nonvisual electronic games
- dynamic braille display of electronic documents (for those who are deaf-blind)
- translation of print documents into electronic documents that can be read aloud via synthesizer, displayed on dynamic braille displays, or printed on a braille printer (for those who are deaf-blind)

Probably one of the most exciting future uses of computers will be to help display graphic information to individuals who are blind. A number of computer-based techniques that are currently being explored combine audio and tactile information to help provide access to graphic information (e.g., line drawings, charts, diagrams, floor plans, and eventually, pictographic information). One such technique, called Nomad, combines raised line tactile images with a touch tablet and voice output. In this case, a tactile image is prepared as a raised line drawing, and information about the image is hand-programmed in advance. The two items are then packaged as a set. Users place the raised line drawing on the special touch tablet. As they feel the image, they hear the pre-prepared audio from the computer.

Another technique, which allows access to graphic information as it is encountered (versus preprogrammed or specially programmed information), is called Systems 3. A vibrating tactile array of 100 pins is mounted on a special puck/mouse. As the mouse is moved around on the tablet, the tactile representation of the information on the screen corresponding to that location on the tactile tablet is provided to the individual's fingertip. Coupled with voice output screen-reading features, the system allows the individual to feel the image on the screen and to have any text read aloud while touching the text on the virtual tactile tablet.

The Tactile Snapshot is similar to the Nomad, except that it is designed to be used with graphic information as it is encountered. The information is displayed on the computer screen (scanned from a printed image, if necessary) and then printed out on either a raised line wax jet printer or onto special paper that can create a raised line image of the contents of the screen. This is then placed on a touch tablet. As the individual moves the hand around on the tablet, feeling the raised line image, the computer can track the movements and read aloud any words encountered.

Other experimental techniques include those that would automatically recognize and verbally describe stereotypic information presentation formats such as pie charts and bar graphs (see Figure 11–9). As computers and image-processing software advance even further, computers will provide even more detailed information about even more complex images to users who are blind.

### Cognitive Impairments

Recently, the possibility of making standard computers and computer software more usable by individuals with cognitive impairments has been receiving increased attention. This is, in part, because computer applications have expanded from spreadsheets and databases to include communication, information, and now daily living activities. The greater emphasis on public access to computers has also facilitated access by people with cognitive impairments. The

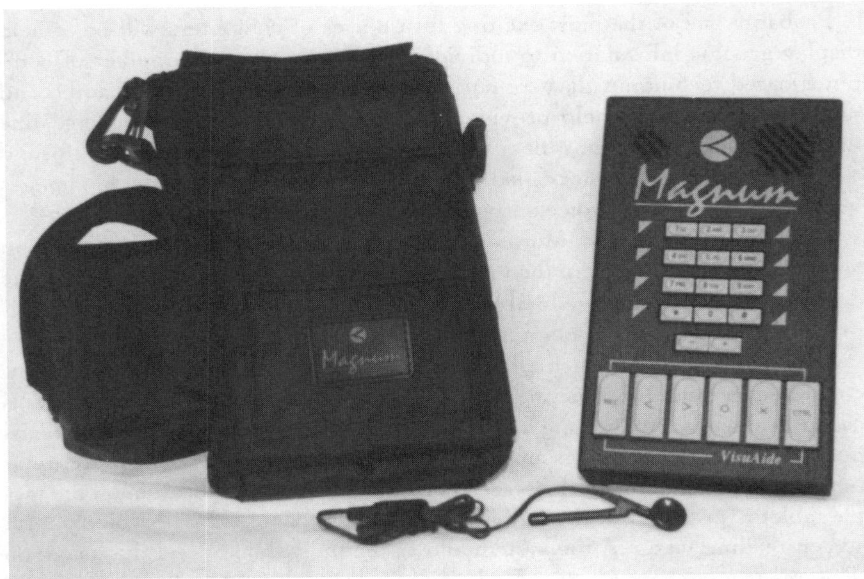


**Figure 11–9** Magnum (VisuAide): a speech-driven personal digital assistant that stores recordings on floppy disks. The note-taking feature allows messages to be marked and reached through a table of contents. Other features include an agenda and reminder function, an address book, various utilities, and braille keyboard entry.

same strategies that make computers easier for everyone to use and to learn also make them easier for individuals with cognitive impairments to use. Thus, a good design for everyone tends to create better designs for people with cognitive impairments. The reverse is also true; the incorporation of features to make computer use easier for people with cognitive impairments tends to increase the usability and learnability for everyone. Finally, a number of strategies that were initially developed for those with other disabilities benefit individuals with cognitive impairments. In particular, the voice input and voice output techniques developed for people with physical and visual impairments can be helpful to someone who has difficulty reading text on the screen.

### *Accessibility for Individuals with Cognitive Impairments*

In general, the strategies that help to make a product simpler to use fall into six general areas. These are good principles to keep in mind when designing or selecting software for an individual with a cognitive impairment (as well as many other computer users):

1. simple layout, appearance, and operation
   - Important elements should be distinct from background.
   - Avoid text over patterns.
   - Use a layered design, where only the most obvious or the most used choices are presented, with more complex or more unusual options and features buried deeper.
   - Keep language as simple as possible.
   - Minimize the number of options presented at one time.
2. obvious, intuitive operation
   - Make things to be acted on distinct from the background.
   - Highlight key information.
   - Group items together that belong together.
   - Avoid attaching multiple functions to a single control (unless very obvious, like four directions on a joystick).
   - Avoid simultaneous activations.
3. built-in cuing
   - Provide on-screen instruction.
   - Establish automatic cuing if the user just waits.
   - Include contextual help (not just a full hierarchical help file buried under a single button).
4. allowance for error recovery
   - Provide clear feedback to the user whenever an action or change takes place.
   - Make it possible to reverse any action (unless there is a clear warning in advance).
5. alternate forms for presentation of information
   - Use pop-up labels for icons
   - Make it possible to have any text on screen read aloud.
   - Present information in multiple (redundant) forms, or provide display options.
6. simple, direct selection
   - Pick from among choices versus entering from memory.
   - Point directly to choice with mouse or, better yet, use touchscreen versus keyboard navigation, "hot keys" (key combinations that can activate menus or commands), or numbers.

### *Special Applications for People with Cognitive Impairments*

Most of the software that has been written specifically for people with cognitive impairments falls into the rehabilitation, education, and training areas. Special programs have been developed across a broad range of topics, including

- academic topics
- money management
- personal skills development
- behavioral training
- cognitive skills tutorials
- memory improvement
- problem solving
- time concepts
- safety awareness
- consumer tutorials
- cognitive rehabilitation/retraining
- speech and language therapy
- evaluation and testing
- telephone usage
- full range of daily activities (e.g., cooking, toileting, cleaning)
- recreation and games (both for therapy and entertainment)

Although there have been few computer applications intended to serve directly as assistive technologies for people with cognitive impairments, the number of such applications is now growing. The number of different types of cognitive disabilities for which they are effective is also growing, as systems become more powerful and more "intelligent." Among the applications of computers to assist individuals on a daily basis are

- grammar and spelling checkers
- word prediction and other writing aids
- communication aids, especially for individuals who are unable to speak
- memory aids and reminder systems (e.g., for individual events, regular schedules, medication)
- personal reference/notebook
- wayfinding
- procedure cuing
- reading

One hypothetical device, called the Companion, brings together many of these concepts to show how a personal assistive technology could assist people with cognitive impairments in the future. The device would provide the following functions:

- calendar reminder system that could wake an individual up, remind the individual of appointments and schedule for the day, alert the individual to items on the schedule that are different from the normal routine (e.g., doctor appointment or a regularly scheduled event that does not occur on this day)

- cuing system that could help the individual follow the correct sequence through the morning routine (e.g., dressing, simple meal preparation)
- artificial intelligence system to adapt the above functions to what is actually going on, to help detect when the individual appears to be having a problem, to help the individual problem-solve when it detects a problem or when the individual indicates a problem by pressing a Help button
- GPS system that would use satellite information to pinpoint the individual's location at any time
- access system that could provide maps to the city and major buildings so that user could receive directions on request
- camera and optical character recognition system that the individual could point at any sign or text, press a button, and have the sign or text read aloud
- infrared link that would communicate with similarly equipped computers, kiosks, information systems, ATMs, and so on
- electronic smart card/debit card that would permit cashless money transactions
- communication link to a central resource service that would have complete information about the user and could link the user to a live human resource person for more serious problem solving and for all of the situations in which the limited artificial intelligence system could not help

The use of such a system could best be exemplified through a short scenario.

> Tim is awakened in the morning by his Companion, which reminds him what day it is and what he needs to do first. It also reminds him that he has a meeting tonight with his counselor and that he is supposed to appear at the alternate worksite this morning. Tim has worked out a routine with his Companion in which he sort of mumbles what he is doing as he is going through his morning routine, and the Companion notes whether any important activity seems to be missing or out of order and asks him simple questions as reminders. Tim walks out to the bus stop. As the buses pull up, he aims the Companion at the name on the bus windshield display and pushes the trigger; the Companion reads the name of the bus to Tim and also tells him whether the buses seem to be ahead of or behind schedule. Tim's Companion also knows exactly which bus stop they are standing at (from the satellite GPS), whether Tim is where he should be, what time it is, and when to expect the bus.
>
> When the correct bus arrives, Tim gets on board, authorizes his smart card by voice to transfer the proper fare to the bus, and takes his seat.

> On his way home from the meeting with his counselor, Tim is very tired, falls asleep on the bus, and rides past his normal transfer stop. The Companion detects this and tries to wake him; it is tucked between Tim and the side of the bus, however, so it is muffled and Tim does not hear the signal over the noise of street construction. When Tim wakes up, he finds himself in an unfamiliar neighborhood. He panics and gets off the bus, which drives away. He further panics and presses the Help button on his Companion. The Companion runs through a standard set of questions and comments to calm Tim and help him apply his own problem-solving skills. Tim aims the Companion at a number of street signs, pushing the button to have them read to him. The Companion realizes where they are, but does not have any information about the safety or potential resources for Tim in this neighborhood. It advises Tim to call in, so Tim pushes the button to contact the central resource point. A specially trained resource person appears on the Companion's screen; by using the Companion's camera, the resource person can also see Tim. All of Tim's information is displayed directly on the screen in front of the resource person, along with whatever information the Companion can provide on the situation, including Tim's exact location. The resource person directs Tim to a local building that will be safe and calls a cab, since there are no buses that will easily get Tim back home from that location at this time of night.

Such a system might benefit those individuals who could live independently if they had some mechanism for helping them when problems arise. Great care must be taken, however, in designing these systems to ensure that they function in the form of a benevolent companion who supports the natural decision-making skills of the individual and who operates in either facilitative or suggestive mode rather than directing the individual. While many disabilities can be facilitated through the use of a prosthetic device which replaces the lost function with an artificial version (e.g., an artificial arm, an artificial ear, artificial vision), trying to replace an individual's cognitive abilities with an artificial brain risks a situation where we are providing an artificial intelligence with a body, rather than providing an individual with intelligence. A device that helps to strengthen or maximize the abilities of individuals with a cognitive impairment while minimizing the impact on their free will and decision making (or perhaps enhancing it) could significantly facilitate their functioning and enhance their opportunities in life.

Although there are no devices such as the Companion today, many of the components are available. Also, the same principles apply in terms of applying the assistive technologies and setting up the daily routines and support structures of individuals with cognitive impairments. Further, with the rate at which technology, miniaturization, and artificial intelligence is progressing, it is likely that all of the capabilities described here will be available early in the next century long before it is possible to program and apply them effectively.

## THE FUTURE

The field of computers and computing is evolving rapidly, and there are likely to be dramatic changes over the next 10 years. Four trends in particular bear watching.

First, the cost of portable computers will continue to drop, and miniaturization will continue. Fairly sophisticated and complicated software will be handled easily by these computers, which will also have large storage capacities and built-in speech and speech recognition features. They will all also have infrared data links that will allow their connection to stationary devices, environment controls, and public information systems. Small credit card–sized PC cards will pop into the side of these computers and provide additional capabilities. Already today, there are cards with miniature half-gigabyte hard drives and wireless cellular telephones and modems. Thus, there will be a tremendous amount of capability at a relatively low price.

Second, more dedicated information appliances will evolve and will assume duties currently carried out by (and used in conjunction with) general purpose computers. These information appliances will be friendly and will allow people to write and send mail, make telephone calls, leave messages, look up just about any kind of information, read books, and watch movies. Families will often own multiple versions of these information appliances. A large screen version may hang on the wall of the family room, a small screen version may rest on the counter in the kitchen, and several family members may carry pocket versions.

Third, there will be an increasing number of public information systems and kiosks. Building directories, fare machines, service kiosks, ATMs, and electronic stores will appear everywhere—both to provide convenience and to make public information systems available to those without computers.

Fourth, the line between computer and display, between personal computing power and network computing power, will blur. Computers and information appliances will all be connected to each other in a wireless fashion, and they will exchange information and resources as required. An individual using a pocket computer to run a routine that requires very heavy computing power may offload this function to some central computer, which would then return the result. In this fashion very small, compact devices would have tremendous computing power and storage capability. Furthermore, all individuals could access all of their personal information basically from any computer or information appliance.

The following two examples illustrate what this might mean to people with disabilities.

> David, who is blind, buys a frozen dinner, but is unable to read the back of the package to find out how to cook it. He takes a picture of the package with his portable information appliance, which has a miniature electronic camera, and sends this as a fax to himself. He routes it through a service at the telephone company that will automatically translate any fax into an electronic text file, which then shows up in his e-mail box. He simply picks it up from his e-mail box, has it read to him by his voice synthesizer, and proceeds to cook his meal. He uses the service provided by the telephone company, not only because the service is inexpensive, but also because it uses a very sophisticated optical character recognition program on a mainframe computer that does a much more accurate job and can handle much more complicated arrangements of text and graphics than anything he could afford to own himself. He also takes advantage of storage systems and backup services that are available on the network, thus allowing the device that he carries to be small, light, and inexpensive. Furthermore, the consequences would be less drastic if he were to lose or damage his system.
>
> Ruth is deaf. She carries a small device that has built-in speech recognition software for use with friends in quiet environments. If her friends speak somewhat carefully and there is not much background noise, it works quite well. When Ruth finds herself in noisier environments or is speaking with less familiar or careful speakers, she simply switches to a networked speech recognition algorithm provided by another network-based service company. Essentially, she pipes the voice signal over an audio data line to the network service provider, which applies a highly sophisticated and powerful speech recognition program to the signal. Originally developed for use by the army and law enforcement agencies, this particular speech recognition program does an excellent job of deciphering the speech and providing Ruth with a real-time electronic transcript of what the person she is talking to is saying. The transcript is transmitted back across the same data link that the voice signal was sent on and displayed on her hand-held device, or, at her preference, on her glasses so that the words appear to be floating in space wherever she is looking. As a result, Ruth can look directly at the person she is communicating with and see the words being spoken displayed directly in front of her.

Thus, computer access and use may be dramatically different in the future. Many of the basic principles regarding accessibility and usability will remain the same, but the special uses to which people with disabilities will put these technologies will continue to evolve, and new access systems will be required.

## IMPLICATIONS FOR PROFESSIONALS AND CONSUMERS TODAY

Technology will continue to evolve rapidly. Miniaturization and the increased power and connectivity will provide new opportunities for creating affordable and effective assistive technologies for people with disabilities. Unless we have a better understanding of exactly what these systems need to provide and unless we have the skill development programs in place, however, these new technologies will be little more than fancy toys. We need to anticipate the capabilities these new products will provide, understand the different environments in which the individuals will live and potentially work, and begin to develop the skills—both in ourselves and in our clients—to take advantage of these tools and environments. Without such intervention and guidance, these wonderful technologies will lack certain functions or capabilities necessary to meet the needs of people with disabilities.

As new information systems evolve, the needs of people with all types, degrees, and combinations of disability must be kept in mind. As wonderful as these new technologies are and can potentially be, they can also inadvertently create new barriers. For example, an early video compression technique used to send movies over telephone lines inadvertently stripped out the closed captions for people with hearing impairments in the process. Selecting a seat on an airplane sometimes involves pointing to the seat desired on a picture of the airplane displayed on a screen. This method would be completely inaccessible for a blind person unless some nonvisual alternative were provided.

Computers are rarely, if ever, a solution in and of themselves. In order to be effective, the computer must be applied within a general intervention program. For example, simply providing access to a computer at a worksite seldom makes an individual employable. Other components that are usually important include modifications to the worksite, telephones, and other equipment; strategies for manipulating and accessing paper, books, and other materials; and accommodations in the job design. The situation is similar for individuals using computers in educational situations or as communication systems. Clearly, however, different strategies and technologies can be used, each of which has different advantages and limitations. As a result, it is highly recommended that an evaluation by an appropriate assistive technology specialist be carried out before any investment in particular technology.

## FOR MORE INFORMATION . . .

In the few pages provided here, it is not possible to detail the vast and myriad aspects of computer applications. Therefore the focus has been to provide some examples and to highlight some of the issues and principles involved in computer access and use by people with disabilities. The Closing the Gap Product Directory probably has the best coverage of educational software. A CD-ROM reference bibliography is provided at the end of this text. This CD-ROM library contains extensive compilations of resources on assisted technology, disabilities, and reference materials including:

- Hyper ABLEDATA—more than 19,000 products
- Cooperative Services Directories—eleven directories of services
- Publications, media, and materials—books, videos, and REHABDATA
- Text-document library—full text of 34 key documents

*Chapter 12*

# Interactive Technologies

*Anthony J. Vitale*

According to recent statistics from the National Institute on Disability Rehabilitation Research (NIDRR), 20 percent of all noninstitutionalized individuals age 15 and over (nearly 40 million people) have some limitation in physical function. Such limitations include the inability to read newsprint even with corrective lenses, the inability to hear normal conversation, and the inability to have speech understood. Under this definition, 12.8 million people have some visual limitation; 7.7 million people, a hearing problem; and 2.5 million, a speech problem. As much as 0.6 percent of the school-age population (ages 6 to 22) are nonspeaking. In addition, some 14.3 million people have some other functional limitation. These demographics are usually surprising to the uninitiated and underscores the vital need for assistive technology.

## COMMUNICATION AND LEARNING

If cultural anthropologists from another planet were to visit Earth on a mission to research the way in which the information revolution has affected communication, they would immediately realize that the standard paradigm of listening–speaking as primitives and reading–writing as derivatives has been inverted. That is, in all languages, the tasks of listening to what is being said and speaking are universals and the first things a child learns. Reading and writing skills are not nearly as common; much of the world can neither read nor write.

Although liberating on some fronts, computers are extremely constraining on others. For example, most require writing (e.g., typing on a keyboard or using a mouse or other physical input device). The extraterrestrial anthropologists would discover that the fastest typist types at 80 to 100 words per minute, whereas speakers can produce 200 to 300 words per minute. The restrictions of reading and writing, of course, are extremely constraining for those who either cannot see words displayed on a screen or who are unable to use their hands or fingers to operate a keyboard or other device. Several enabling and interactive technologies are available, however: distance learning, electronic mail (e-mail), facsimile, and speech.

## DISTANCE LEARNING

As defined by the U.S. Office of Technology Assessment (Moore, 1989), distance learning is the "linking of a teacher and students in several geographical locations via technology that allows for interaction". Distance learning is simply a form of telecommuting (i.e., working by computer from some remote location, such as home). Thus, professors and students have the opportunity to overcome the boundaries of time and space. It is the way of the future. It saves time, money, and logistical difficulties.

Distance learning replaces the traditional teacher–student physical interface with electronic (i.e., computer) conferencing. Because no one has to be at the same place at the same time to participate in the conference, this pedagogical approach provides a maximum of schedule flexibility for students and teachers alike. Moreover, distance learning is available 24 hours per day, every day. Finally, students are likely to have greater self-confidence and not worry about stereotypes of ethnicity, appearance, or disability.

### Enhancement of Independence

Numerous universities are now experimenting with distance learning. Rochester Institute of Technology (RIT), for example, is using distance learning in an experiment that includes some students who have a disability. Electronic distance learning makes such disabilities invisible. Experience at RIT with distance learning by Professor Norman Coombs, a blind professor of history, has shown definitively that working at the computer instead of interfacing directly with other students can help these students overcome shyness and diffidence. Furthermore, they feel less "disabled," more individual, and freer to share thoughts and feelings about such sensitive topics as racism, welfare, and other sociopolitical issues.

### Development, History, and Future

There is a growing realization that focusing on the needs of the average student and adhering rigidly to a particular curriculum have a negative impact on the diffident student, the shy student, and the student with a disability, as well as the very bright student. Consequently, computer networking and distance learning are spawning a revolution in education. As Coombs (1992) observed, the teachers of the future will be guides for students; they will help students learn which questions to ask and where to find the information that they need.

Educators are beginning to realize that students learn differently and that their minds are not "empty slates" waiting for the teacher to write on them. For the first time in history, extremely large databases, encyclopedias, popular books (both fiction and nonfiction), dictionaries, thesauruses, library catalogs, and the like are available on the worldwide computer network. People who cannot be physically present for personal reasons (e.g., shyness, disability) should not be denied access to a high-quality education.

Early experiments in distance learning by telephone and hard copy mail showed that this approach was inadequate. There was an absence of group discussions, and students were, in essence, isolated from one another not only in terms of sharing ideas and opinions, but also in terms of measuring their progress against one another. The development of computer networks began to solve this problem. It allowed students, especially students with disabilities, to work from their home or office and to tailor the course to their individual needs. Moreover, they could work at their own pace. One other advantage to distance learning over a computer network is that a teacher can respond to an individual student without making a special appointment or, worse, providing the feedback in front of 20 other students.

Since 1985 RIT has offered its faculty productivity grants that focus on developing new strategies for distance learning. The initial target audience was made up of students who lived in the Rochester area, worked full-time, and found commuting on-line an appealing option. Early on, a proposal was submitted to explore the uses of computer conferencing in education. Coombs began requiring his students to submit their term papers through e-mail. This allowed him to cut back dramatically on the need for readers, because the speech synthesizer hooked to his computer converted the ASCII text into speech. This was an innovation at the time, at least in academic circles. Although industry had for years been using e-mail as a tool for communication, computers in academic circles then were typically used for programming, word processing, and the like.

The first course that was adapted for teleconferencing was a course in modern American history, taught by Coombs. The original course contained videotapes and reading texts, but group discussion was at its core. As such, the course lent itself quite easily to distance learning. E-mail replaced office visits, and teleconferencing via networked computers replaced the classroom discussion. User manuals contained explanations and instructions about the use of e-mail and the conferencing system itself. Modems were loaned to students with access to a personal computer (PC) at home or work. Students without PCs or other home computers had to access the large computer on campus.

According to Coombs (1988), the relative anonymity of this approach (i.e., people were not confronting each other face to face in one room) made it easier for many of the students to share personal thoughts, opinions, and even anecdotes about their personal lives. At the time, there were a number of students with disabilities in class, including a student who was deaf who, for the first time, did not require a sign language interpreter. More than a year later, another student who had only recently become deaf and did not understand sign language very well participated easily and expeditiously in group discussions.

Later, Coombs (1987) developed a course that combined computer conferencing with captioned video and text readings as a delivery system exclusively for a group of hearing-impaired students. A set of discussion questions was prepared and posted in the conference. Each topic was restricted to one screen, and there were typically several topics per week. The one-screen format itself forced the teacher to make questions concise and succinct, which is not dissimilar to captioned text, and thus, the approach was beneficial and familiar to the hearing-impaired students.

Kinner and Coombs (1995) reported on an experiment conducted with distance learning in which one course was taught from RIT and the other was taught from Gallaudet University in Washington, D.C. Some students were hearing-impaired, and one teacher was blind. Evaluation results and the success of this course is reported in McKee and Scherer (1992). Videos and movies were used, but most communication (i.e., class discussions and meetings between a student and a teacher) took place with computer telecommunication through the Internet. Personal contacts between students and between student and teacher occurred over e-mail. Therefore, direct face-to-face contact between a professor and student was minimal. There is, of course, no reason that such learning cannot include potential students from anywhere with an Internet access.

Alternative Approaches to Learning (Altlearn; Wissick, 1994) at St. John's University in Jamaica, New York, deals with different techniques in teaching, especially those that relate to students in special education. This program encourages discussion among academics and classroom teachers. Today, this institution has more than 20 lists devoted to education and disability located at a single Internet node.

**Beneficiaries**

Distance learning is now being used in courses on PCs, which will open new avenues of communication with distance learners. Computers both bridge the gap between the teacher and distance learner, and ease the difficult logistics of physical disabilities in the pedagogical process. A person with disabilities need only be able to sit at a computer to enjoy the benefits of an education.

This distance learning system proved particularly beneficial for four groups: (1) off-campus continuing education students who no longer had to commute; (2) students who had been taking mainly television or correspondence courses and who claimed that the facile exchange of information between themselves and their teacher, as well as between themselves and other students, replaced the traditional educational process; (3) regular day students with scheduling problems or adults who were attempting to juggle work, family, and school; and (4) students with disabilities for whom it would be logistically difficult or physically impossible to get to a classroom.

**Consumer Feedback**

In one of the most seminal courses in distance learning conducted at RIT, both the professor and some students felt that this technique led to "more than the usual interaction between professor and student." Furthermore, one-to-one conversations (via computer) occurred quite frequently. One student noted that, as a result of being able to use distance learning, "this professor was the most helpful she had encountered at college" (Coombs, 1987). Students were much less diffident about issues of race, ethnicity, and, of course, disability. One student in a Black history course said that what he liked about conducting class discussion on a computer network was that no matter what sex, color, ethnic group, or disability group a person belonged to, his or her comments were accepted for their own worth and not judged by a stereotype. One deaf student claimed that this had been the most valuable course in her college experience because she could share in the discussions so completely and facilely. Another student was blind; he took home handouts that his teachers had stored on a VAX in ASCII and then ran them through a word processor and screen reader.

Students interact differently on a computer network than they do in a classroom. According to Coombs (1992), one student claimed that "people have the ability to write their feelings in a somewhat anonymous way, leaving the person with the ability to say how they really feel." According to this teacher, "I do not think people would respond in the same way if this were a face-to-face, in-class discussion." Hauptmann and Rudnicky (1988) noted that people react differently when they knowingly speak to a computer than when they speak to another person. An examination of variables such as attitude, communication rate, word density, vocabulary, errors, and syntax showed that, in contradistinction to what is claimed in much of the literature, human-to-machine communication has a simpler structure than human-to-human discourse. It has also been observed that speech is both qualitatively and quantitatively simpler when speaking directly with someone (including a facial video) than when responding to a verbal or written message in non–real time (e.g., e-mail message).

Other students are not good speakers in public, and a computer discussion may help them articulate their thoughts better. Several students reported sharing more in the computer network course than they had in normal classes. Others said that sometimes they hesitated to speak openly in classrooms. These students felt freer to express their thoughts openly because the environment was "less threatening."

### Auxiliary Considerations

Student demographics and academic backgrounds have changed dramatically over the last 25 years. It is estimated that 45 percent of all college enrollment now consists of part-time students (Jacobson, 1994). There is a variety of ethnic groups. Individuals with disabilities are more likely to enter college, and most students come into undergraduate institutions with much more knowledge of computers than those in previous generations ever had. One way to utilize the electronic information superhighway to its greatest advantage is through distance learning. A teacher in distance learning can establish the curriculum, monitor topics, and set ground rules for the course by computer, thus minimizing any misunderstanding that may occur in the written medium.

There is a downside to distance learning. First, a student must have self-discipline. Second, computers, especially PCs and similar small systems may be ubiquitous among the middle class, but many students do not have the means to purchase or even rent a PC with a modem. Also, graphic on-line data are not usually accessible for a blind person, because graphic user interfaces (GUIs) and touch screens are not yet reliable enough. Furthermore, only about 10 percent of blind individuals know braille, and this makes speech that much more important.

## ELECTRONIC MAIL

More popularly known as e-mail, electronic mail represents the ability to transmit memoranda, letters, announcements, and the like by computer. Millions of people worldwide, ranging from the average person with a home PC to the President and Vice President of the United States (*president @whitehouse.gov* and *vice.president@whitehouse.gov*), are currently using e-mail. The public can even comment on network newscasts (e.g., *nightly@nbc.ge.com*) or market news on National Public Radio (e.g., *market@usc.edu*) via e-mail. Even newspapers are soliciting letters from readers via e-mail (e.g., *ask@globe.com* for the *Boston Globe*). Numerous books devoted to the Internet and e-mail (e.g., Gilster, 1993) are available in most bookstores.

The origins of e-mail go back to the 1960s when Western Union developed its computer-based messaging system (CBMS). In 1969, the U.S. Government initiated the Advanced Research Projects Agency (ARPA) to develop an electronic mail system to facilitate communication among researchers around the world, both in academia and elsewhere. E-mail systems have blossomed in the past 5 years, and tens of millions of people now regularly use e-mail.

E-mail commands vary according to the operating system being used, but typically commands are easily manipulated. For example, if I receive a message from a colleague at Monash University in Melbourne, Australia, I can reply immediately with a simple command such as *reply*. My colleague's e-mail address and the subject will all be written out for me. I simply type out the reply and send the message. Alternatively, I can type the message on an editor and send it as a file. I can choose to send it to several or even hundreds or thousands of people all over the world by a command that references another file of e-mail addresses. If the computer belonging to the person(s) receiving the message is not available, the message will be sent as soon as possible. The many commercial systems may contain different commands, but they work in essentially the same way.

Subscribers can use e-mail to communicate with others all over the world. If the message does not reach its destination, the sender receives a speedy response to that effect (e.g., *Unable to deliver message for the following reason . . .*). If successfully delivered, the message goes into the addressee's *in-basket* to be read the next time he or she checks the mail.

E-mail is extremely efficient across time zones. For example, a person who sends a message from the East Coast to the West Coast in the morning will probably have an answer by noon or whenever the correspondent first reads the mail. In the afternoon, e-mail sometimes works better than a telephone for European correspondence. With a 5- to 8-hour time difference, it is usually too late to telephone Europe by mid-afternoon, but sending an e-mail message is likely to produce a reply first thing the next morning. Those who are still at a computer or terminal at 6 P.M. or later can contact colleagues in the Far East since it is the next day there and receive a timely reply.

E-mail can transmit not only text, but also binary files and bit-mapped graphics files. An increasing amount of software is being written to allow the transmission of video and voice. Moreover, e-mail transmission is now becoming PC LAN (local area network typically utilized for intra-organization communication) and, thus, will reach more and more people as time goes on.

The primary problem with e-mail, perhaps the only major problem, is that it requires an ability to write. The user needs a modicum of spelling expertise, not to mention a certain amount of manual dexterity. A person who is blind can send e-mail by listening to the characters typed via a speech synthesizer, however. Similarly, a person who is mobility-impaired or has a neurological disease that limits or prevents hand movement can now use a speech recognizer or even an eye gaze system.

Intonation, which plays a vital part in the semantics of messages, goes undetected in written text except for a small number of symbols, such as the exclamation point. Even humor often needs to be signaled so as not to cause inadvertent offense or confusion. For example, a current convention is to use a sideways smiling face such as :) or :-) to indicate that facetiousness. A blind person using a synthesizer to read the mail will hear the punctuation spoken or can even choose to define it as a sequence of spoken words (e.g., *ha ha* or *only kidding*).

**Enhancement of Independence**

E-mail opens up the entire world to the person with disabilities. There are numerous discussion groups available on the Internet or on other commercial services that deal with correspondence and medical breakthroughs on multiple sclerosis, ALS, and various other diseases. Professionals in the field often contribute to these bulletin board systems (BBS). For example, there is a newsgroup on ALS to which individuals from all over the world, ranging from the patients themselves to neurologists and neurosurgeons, contribute information about the latest breakthroughs or experimental drug protocols. Individuals on the distribution list for this newsgroup can also receive a regularly published newsletter. The person with a disability who has hobbies can find discussion groups for aficionados on everything from electric trains and beer to computers and the Internet itself. Thousands of such files are accessible to any person with a modem and network connection. The World Wide Web (also known as WWW, W3, or simply the Web) and Mosaic is essentially a "browser" that helps users to locate material on the Internet.

To use the Internet efficiently, it is necessary to find out which discussion groups are available from a particular site. A utility called Listserv can provide such a list. Some subscriptions can be obtained automatically by typing a particular message. Others require simply a request to be added to the list; removal from a list works in the same way.

Many newsletters are stored in archives, which means that the subscriber can go back months to read older notes, bulletins, or newsletters. Many types of searches are possible, depending upon the system. For example, some systems allow the subscriber to search by author, date, or subject.

The person who is blind or vision-impaired can "read" messages via a speech synthesizer (one of the most common uses of speech synthesis) and can type a reply, again using a synthesizer that will read out the characters typed letter by letter so as to minimize typographical errors. The mobility-impaired person can use large vocabulary speech recognition to dictate e-mail messages into the computer. Many recognizers include a macro capability that allows the user to expedite the process by defining large phrases, clauses, or even long lists by using only one word.

**Beneficiaries**

E-mail is perhaps the most central of the Internet applications. Unlike regular (hard copy) mail—known in popular computer jargon as *snail mail* (often abbreviated s-mail)—e-mail is speedy, efficient, and cost-effective. Access to e-mail via speech synthesizer is in great demand by individuals who have vision impairments and use computers on a regular basis.

Among the beneficiaries of e-mail systems are those who cannot see a computer screen or type on a keyboard. E-mail offers more, however, even to able-bodied people. It is much faster than regular mail, which may take days to weeks. Messages can be stored in an electronic "filedraw" and "folder," edited, or forwarded to someone else. These features overcome the difficulties that a person with a vision or motor impairment may have in replying to a letter. Under normal circumstances, the person must have another person read the original letter to him, write the reply for him, add the destination address and stamp to the envelope, and then travel to a mailbox or post office.

E-mail can also be scanned very quickly. Experiments have shown that experienced persons using e-mail can comprehend speech at nearly twice the normal speaking rate when using speech synthesizers in screen-reading applications for the blind (Schmandt, 1993). Some visually impaired people can comprehend synthesized speech at faster than 550 words per minute, more than three times faster than the normal speaking rate. This is corroboration that the listening–speaking form of communication is much more effective, facile, and accessible than the reading–writing form.

Perhaps the most important thing about e-mail (and voice mail as well) is that communication is asynchronous. The mode of communication is not the give and take of normal conversation. Rather, some time may go by between the sending of a message and the reply to that message. The sender of a message never gets a busy signal, however. Moreover, the respondent who is not at the computer terminal or workstation (or telephone) can easily reply later when he or she receives the message. As Gilster (1993) claimed, the rate of return on replies from e-mail vastly exceeds that of voice mail.

### Selection of Devices

A number of commercial systems allow an individual to interact with others on the same or different systems. E-mail is available for most, if not all, common operating systems (e.g., UNIX, VMS, OSF, Windows). Large (noncomputer) corporations such as General Electric are now beginning to use the Internet with customers; in the near future, the purchase of commodities from automobiles to dishwashers will come with a diskette that will help connect consumers to their company via the Internet.

Clearly, e-mail requires certain equipment, such as a PC, a modem, a telephone line, and some communications software. Funds are often available for such systems for individuals with disabilities. Perhaps more important are the people who volunteer their time and expertise to assemble computers for use by individuals with disabilities. One such person is Robert Ambrose, who started The Enabling Support Foundation, a nonprofit group, and is a full-time volunteer there. Working in an office donated by the United Cerebral Palsy Foundation in midtown Manhattan, he and other volunteers find, pick up, and fix outdated and sometimes broken computers that large companies are discarding. Ambrose also takes old computers that such places as banks and brokerage houses were discarding. So far, Ambrose has helped place 50 computers with people with disabilities who would otherwise be unable to afford one; 100 people are on a waiting list. The foundation has also helped another 70 people learn how to use the Internet.

### Consumer Feedback

Bob Zenhausern (personal communication) from St. John's University, one of the pioneers in the use of the Internet for individuals with disabilities, cites many examples of consumer feedback. For example, Randy Horwitz, a blind 18-year-old computer science student at the RIT says, "The Internet makes everything so accessible for us," and uses it to talk with friends at other universities. He uses a speech synthesizer and a special pad that spells out in braille the characters on the screen. Randy also taps into a collection of more than 4,000 special interest discussion groups available to most Internet users, including one that provides basketball scores.

Chris Bell, 41, of Aurora, Canada, learned 3 years ago that he has ALS. Since then, he has lost most of his ability to speak and type. Using a special program on his computer that projects a standard QWERTY keyboard in a window on his screen, Bell is still able to communicate effectively. "I firmly believe that computer communications, along with the continuing abilities of writing and synthesized speech that computer technology provides, is a vital opportunity to extend lives otherwise swamped by frustration and loss. . . . I'm convinced this technology can and will extend lives of folks battling life-threatening illnesses such as ALS," Bell writes. "Without an ability to continue meaningful output, life's purpose would quickly erode, creating melancholy and despair" (personal e-mail communication).

Peter Boulay is a 24-year-old double amputee. "I don't know what I'd do without this," he says of the Internet and e-mail. "I think I'd be a totally different person without these connections. I'd be bored . . . boredom can lead to alcoholism and despair." Not only does he have no legs, but also he was born with only one finger on each hand. Boulay, who types up to 4 hours each day, claims that he types "faster than most people with ten fingers," however. Boulay gets approximately 200 pieces of e-mail each day, most from special interest lists devoted to disability issues. One list is concerned with ramifications of the Americans with Disabilities Act (ADA).

Polio has necessitated a wheelchair and a respirator for Robert Mauro, age 47. As the moderator of an e-mail list called Mobility-L, Mauro has been active in getting people with disabilities on-line ever since he got his first modem in 1985. "I got involved with different bulletin boards and commercial services like CompuServe, . . . I wasn't interested in games or downloading software, just communicating with people. . . . For someone like myself whose mobility is very limited, it's a great way to meet people. . . . I sometimes get forty letters a day that I respond to. If I were doing that with first-class mail, you know how much that would cost?" Mauro has managed to publish two books about on-line communicating and the disabled. "Without the computer, for me to go to the library, forget it . . . No way would my little library have this information. I was able to do hours of research from home."

In conclusion, a blind person can use e-mail for many reasons, ranging from business to total frivolity. When writing is a chore (e.g., hard copy), however, the user will not write as creatively or humorously. Before he got into computers, inaccessible equipment stood in the way of Joe Lazzaro's writing. As he puts it, he "burned out easily" and had "no stamina for the mechanics of putting the text on paper." Essentially, he needed all of his energy for his creative thoughts. Utilities such as e-mail now take away the drudgery of writing.

### Auxiliary Considerations

E-mail is extremely useful in a work situation; for example, internal office e-mail permits communication with co-workers in a timely manner. Some individuals with disabilities may not be able too communicate naturally without e-mail. Lazzaro provides an excellent example here. He has a co-worker who is deaf. Prior to using e-mail, they communicated primarily by patting each other on the back. Now they can communicate easily and get to know each other as individuals and fellow human beings.

## FAX MACHINE TECHNOLOGY

Either a PC with fax/modem hardware or a specially dedicated machine can be used to send images of documents over a telephone line. The former, of course, is a much less expensive option and requires nothing more than a card and software that run on a PC. The original copy can be sent from a dedicated fax (short for facsimile) machine to the PC, which can then send the file to a printer.

### Enhancement of Independence

The personal opinion of a few individuals with disabilities is that e-mail is better than fax in terms of flexibility. Nevertheless, fax is obviously useful to send letters to people who do not have e-mail. A dedicated fax machine requires no specific computer skills. Fax can be as useful as e-mail, and the reach is much broader than e-mail since there are currently more fax machines than e-mail boxes. If certain word processing programs are used to write the fax, the fax program dials out, links with the remote fax, and sends; the sender can still retain the original document on disk to which both parties can then refer in a subsequent discussion.

Fax is particularly useful for people who are deaf and have little access to devices such as teletypewriters (TTYs) and telecommunication devices for the deaf (TDDs). For example, if a deaf person (or even a person with a speech or language problem) wishes to order a pizza, call for a taxi, or order items from a catalog, the pizza parlor, taxi stand, or catalog company is not likely to have a TDD or a computer hooked to the Internet, but may indeed have a fax machine and can fax back questions, confirmations, etc.

The downside of fax technology is that a fax is not quite as accessible as e-mail, because incoming faxes have to be scanned in order to be read. An incoming fax can be either paper (i.e., hard copy) coming out of a fax machine or printer, or a file on a PC (e.g., a bit-mapped graphic file) that can then be printed. Bit-mapped graphic files can be very large, however. For example, a one-page document may be as large as 250K bytes of memory, but may shrink to 2K bytes once that file has been scanned into ASCII. Moreover, an incoming fax must be good enough in quality to be scanned by an unsighted individual using an OCR (i.e., 200 dots per inch), which means that it must be sent in *fine resolution mode*. Some programs convert documents automatically into ASCII, but the machines involved would have to be fairly powerful.

### Selection of Device

Fax machines can now be found not only in most businesses, but also in people's homes. A Gallup poll indicated that fax transmissions account for 36 percent of all telephone expenses at 500 of the largest companies in the United States. Now, typical users fax more than 10 pages per day, and that number is expected to double in the next 4 years. As the number of faxes increases, the number of busy signals that senders will encounter is also likely to increase—since the receiving machine sends out a busy signal whether it is sending or receiving faxes. There are ways to obviate this problem. One is to connect a number of different fax machines to different telephone lines. This may be used in business, but is hardly practical for the user with disabilities. Another method is to install automatic redialing so that the fax machine keeps trying at intervals. Still another approach is alternate number dialing where, if the first number is busy, the fax machine tries a second, and so forth.

The trend of the future in both PCs and faxes is toward portability. There is no reason why portable fax machines (including battery-powered machines) cannot be taken on trips. In addition, fax machines will incorporate speech synthesis so that individuals who are blind or visually impaired can "hear" the fax as it comes out of the machine. Again, little has been done as yet in terms of integrating speech output with graphics.

Fax machines, as explained earlier, come as either dedicated devices or cards with software that can be used with PCs and the fax itself is output to a printer. The former are more expensive, but the latter can be useful for more general use.

A dedicated fax machine can use the same line as the home or office telephone and can instruct the caller to leave a fax by pressing some numbers on the keypad; for example, "If you would like to leave a message, please wait for the tone. If you would like to send a fax, please press 1-1."

### Consumer Feedback

Text tends to be sent via e-mail, but graphics generally tend to be sent via fax. Graphics, of course, cannot yet be read by a reading machine with OCR technology. There is increasing interest in adding voice capability to fax, however, so that a synthesizer can read fax (sans graphics) as it is coming out of the machine or printer. Although this is already being implemented in industry, it is currently fairly expensive.

## SPEECH TECHNOLOGY

Human beings have no problem learning to speak at a very early age. It is infinitely easier to teach a person to speak a language than it is to teach a computer. Scientists have not yet succeeded in algorithmically producing computer-generated speech that is indistinguishable from natural speech, nor have they programmed machines to "understand" the wide variety of human utterances. It is not for want of trying, however. It is now approximately 283 years since the first mechanical attempt to reproduce human speech and 53 years since the first electrical attempt. Each year brings us a bit closer to realizing these objectives, and in spite of the current imperfections of the technology, speech input and output can now be used for people with disabilities in ways that were not possible just a few years ago.

It is more than mere optimism to suggest that assistive applications and commercial technologies will influence and advance one another. Assistive technologies used by able-bodied people include descriptive video and closed-captioning. Descriptive video, originally developed by the Public Television station WGBH in Boston, allows unsighted individuals to enjoy a movie through the use of elaborate descriptions that are recorded on a separate audio channel and spliced into the movie. Currently, the manufacture of descriptive videos is extremely time-consuming, but the use of speech technology has the potential to make the production easier and such applications more widespread. In addition to its usefulness for those who are visually impaired, this technology enables able-bodied people to listen to a television while performing a totally different task. Closed captioning, now a standard feature on all new television sets, allows people to watch television without the sound on.

Conversely, commercially produced technologies are now being used to assist individuals with disabilities. The information superhighway will assist people who cannot leave their homes because of mobility impairments. Electronic newspapers available online, when used in combination with screen-reading software, can now make a world of information available to people who are visually impaired and would not otherwise have access even to an object as common as a newspaper. Sightless people, for instance, can for the first time read a newspaper on the day that it is published; previously, they had to wait a week for a braille version. Deaf people, using a TDD, can talk with anyone without a human interpreter. Individuals who are confined to their homes now feel less lonely and isolated.

## Types of Devices and Services

There are two main speech technologies: speech input, also called automatic speech recognition (ASR), and speech output. The latter comes in a variety of types from audio tape, to more sophisticated digitized (i.e., recorded) speech and the unlimited vocabulary of text-to-speech (TTS) synthesis.

ASR is a technology that enables a speaker of a language to dictate words into a microphone and have those words converted into machine-readable text (e.g., ASCII). An abstract term, ASR encompasses many different approaches and implementations of one technology with a single objective. These various approaches may be described in such terms as type of fundamental units (e.g., phonemes), size of vocabulary, method of input (discrete vs. continuous), degree of speaker adaptation required, utterance type (e.g., word spotting), and bandwidth limitations. The technology has received great media attention in recent years for several reasons: (a) voice technology is visible and acceptable; (b) the technology has been shown to work for a variety of practical applications (e.g., the automation of collect and third-party calls); and (c) the technology is now becoming an integral part of the personal computer/workstation. Most important, ASR is now being used effectively by individuals with disabilities to participate more actively in the workplace.

A method of translating normal ASCII text into highly intelligible speech, TTS can be used in a variety of assistive applications. Voice output communication aids (VOCAs), for example, can be used in a variety of assistive applications by individuals with dysarthric or otherwise dysfunctional speech to enable them to communicate by voice or by individuals who are blind or visually impaired to enable them to hear the contents of databases such as telephone books via voice. E-mail now becomes accessible to the individual who is blind or visually impaired.

**Enhancement of Independence**

Voice input and output make the entire world of speaking and listening available to individuals who cannot see a screen, cannot communicate with their own voice, or cannot type or write. The population of these groups numbers in the tens of millions in the United States alone. There are, however, certain obstacles that the person with disabilities faces when confronted with the selection of such devices. The cost of speech input/output devices must be brought within the reach of the average user with disabilities. This is beginning to happen; the cost of devices utilizing OCR technology, coupled with speech synthesis, for users who have visual disabilities has declined 80 percent in recent years. Within the next 2 years, these devices will in all likelihood cost less than 2 percent of their price just 10 years ago. The cost of scanners themselves are now already under 2 percent of the original price of a full-functionality OCR. Similarly, the highest quality synthesizers have also decreased in cost by 80 percent, and attempts are being made to reduce the cost even further. The most important factor that a user should consider, however, is speech quality. A person who has a vision impairment and uses a screen reader or OCR scanner for much of the day or a person with a vocal impairment who depends on this device to communicate effectively with others needs the highest quality technology that he or she can afford.

Hardware vendors are now beginning to offer their technology in software, which was impossible until recently because of a lack of processing power. In fact, many vendors are going to software to distance themselves from the responsibilities of hardware or, conversely, in order to sell their hardware and are putting much more functionality on the board for a small increase in cost. Fortunately, the availability of fast microprocessors is allowing speech technology, both input and output, to run in software.

**Development, History, and Future**

Mechanical speech synthesizers have been around since the time of the Hungarian scientist and inventor Von Kempelin, who invented such a device in 1711. Electromechanical attempts at synthesizing human speech have been documented as far back as the 1930s; in fact, such a system was shown for the first time at the 1939 World's Fair in New York (Dudley, 1939) with many significant achievements along the way (Klatt, 1987). High-quality TTS has existed commercially for only 10 years, however.

The size of speech input/output devices needs to be reduced in order to make them more portable and less conspicuous. There is already an effort under way to accomplish this. For example, one of the highest quality speech synthesizers has been reduced from a weight of 16 lb and the size of a very large attaché case to a weight of 15 oz and a size that fits into a pants pocket or pocketbook; furthermore, the newer device can be attached to a PC, Macintosh, or notebook or laptop computer with Velcro. More important, it can be transported from site to site (e.g., from work to home) with no more effort than placing a datebook in a briefcase. Although this reduction has taken 10 years, advances in microchip, memory, and speaker technology will continue to decrease the weight and size of these devices.

The intelligibility of speech synthesis is constantly being improved, and a great deal of interesting research has been done in this area. In the highest quality synthesizers, intelligibility is now very close to that of humans. Because so many people will be using speech synthesis as a prosthesis for vocal dysfunction, however, technologists must achieve a greater degree of naturalness (i.e., those qualities that make the synthesizer sound "human") so that listeners will understand easily. It is in this area that a great deal of improvement is possible. The quest for naturalness in formant speech synthesis is really the quest for "acceptable" naturalness—that is, a level of naturalness that does not claim to replicate the linguistic behavior of a native speaker, but rather one that lacks those aspects of synthesized speech most noticeable to the novice, annoying to the user, or distracting to the listener. This is especially important when the synthesized voice becomes the voice of the user. Although experiments have shown that there is a high cognitive load on the listener of synthetic speech, similar experiments have shown that the listener can accommodate and adapt linguistically and perceptually to even low-quality synthesis with as little as 8 hours exposure. Furthermore, synthesized speech can in some respects be considered simply that of a nonnative speaker with an unusual accent.

Naturalness also plays a significant part in ASR. Currently, people can speak naturally to recognizers only with very small vocabularies—at most a few dozen words. Most recognizers with large vocabularies (e.g., more than 1,000 words) with unconstrained syntax require a person to pause after each word. Thus naturalness in speech input, like output, is still some years away. Allowing users a choice of a small set of emotion-specific intonation contours has become important. Linguists well understand that prosodics (i.e., the intonation of an utterance) may carry as much or more information about emotional content than the actual words themselves. In fact, it is believed that semantic differences conveyed by intonation contours are one of the earliest contrasts perceived by children.

***Voice Quality***

Most speech synthesizers offer no female voice. Those that do often create a "female" voice simply by altering the male voice; as a result, the voice sounds extremely unnatural and, thus, less intelligible. Females who have a vocal impairment are justifiably dissatisfied with having to speak using a male voice. Klatt (1987) cited the case of a nonvocal 16-year-old Arizona girl, the victim of an auto accident, who refused to use a synthesizer because it offered only a male voice.

Recent research (Klatt & Klatt, 1990) suggests interesting paths for improvement of the female voice in formant synthesizers. High-quality diphone synthesizers, of course, can offer a female voice as a separate entity and may be a temporary advantage in this regard. Ultimately, however, they may be less natural because of the concatenation techniques used by digitized voice and the variation of sounds associated with the context. Experiments have shown that speech made up of recorded sounds chained together are often not as intelligible as sounds that are generated entirely by computer. One of the reasons for this is that dramatic variation can occur in two similar sounds in different contexts. The first sounds in the words *kill* and *cool* are clearly different, even though both of these sounds are considered to be a /k/, for example.

In ASR, occasionally some voices are more difficult to understand. There are currently no empirical data that a female voice is any more difficult to understand than a male voice, although anecdotal data suggest that nonnative speakers of certain source languages have a difficult time with speech recognition systems. Similarly, there are no empirically based studies suggesting that certain dialects have lower comprehension than others within the same language family, but there is plenty of anecdotal evidence and perhaps some studies that suggest that speech recognizers do not work very accurately with certain types of nonnative speakers.

New voices must be created to emulate more closely the qualities of the voices of children and adolescents, as the only choice currently among most format synthesizers is the voices between adult and preadolescent children. The flexibility of a high-quality formant synthesizer is that it allows the user to modify acoustic characteristics for voices of individuals of various ages, both male and female. This is crucial, because even a rough matching of the general characteristics of a voice (in age and sex) to a particular user is extremely useful and will promote the use of the technology among individuals with disabilities of different ages.

***Functionality***

Technologists must increase the functionality of various voice-related assistive technologies because of the diversity of the client base and the immediate need of this population. Individuals who have some speech impairment need to summon attention, participate in a conversation in a reasonably rhythmic manner, or speed up communication when required. They also need to be able to maintain eye contact while speaking, communicate with nonreaders (e.g., very young siblings or children), and talk to others over the telephone or in another room. These are issues that have not been adequately addressed by existing functionality of speech input/output devices. For example, Scherer (1979) showed that in conversational turn taking, increase in amplitude (i.e., loudness) is an efficient method of defending or reclaiming one's turn in a dyadic conversation (i.e., a person tends to talk louder when he or she wishes to interrupt or to avoid interruption).

As synthesized speech becomes more natural, it should also become more widely used. The individual with severe speech and language problems will be able to communicate more intelligibly and effectively as high-quality speech output systems and synthesizers become less expensive and more portable. Improved speaker technology will also help downsize these systems and make them more portable. More important, speech characteristics will be customizable by the user. The next few years should also see more natural sounding voices for both men and women, as well as for young children and adolescents; easier manipulation of the voice characteristics; and a closer coupling with predictive dialogue algorithms to increase the speed and efficiency of dyadic communication. The speech synthesizers of the future will provide users with the ability to convey various emotions by allowing the prosodics to match the semantics of the utterance.

## Beneficiaries

The chief beneficiaries of speech technology, as mentioned earlier, are individuals who are blind or visually impaired. They can use TTS in conjunction with screen reader software to read the contents of a computer screen, to hear what they have typed character by character, and to allow the computer to read back what is on the screen. More than one blind individual has written entire books by means of screen-reading technology with TTS. People with visual impairments can use scanning technology with TTS to read books and papers. High-quality scanners with high-end TTS systems embedded within them can generally read most character fonts; thus, books and newspapers become readily available to those who are visually impaired.

Individuals with vocal impairments now can discard the primitive communication boards, dismiss the assistants spelling out the alphabet to them in the most laborious fashion, and do without communication facilitators. People with motor dysfunction—paraplegics, quadriplegics, people with cerebral palsy, multiple sclerosis, and even ALS—can make use of TTS technology and can learn to function extremely well even under these adverse conditions.

Individuals with motor dysfunction can also use ASR technology. Writers who are confined to bed in a prone position can dictate into a speech recognizer. People who are paralyzed from the neck down can use ASR to write letters and papers on their computer. People with vocal impairments, provided that they have a certain threshold of linguistic consistency, can learn to use a speech recognizer to communicate with others. This large group includes patients with cerebral palsy, as well as people with dysarthric speech due to hearing impairments (especially prelingual deafness).

There are currently a number of other interesting ASR applications for users who are motor-impaired. For example, to obviate the necessity of around-the-clock monitoring of hospital patients, a voice-activated hospital bed has been developed that responds to such commands as *call nurse*. Lights on the control console provide visual feedback, although speech output could be added for the visually impaired. The console also has a screen with menus. There are also voice-controlled wheelchairs, home appliances, VCR remotes, cellular phones, car utilities (e.g., wipers, headlights, radio), and even remote control of a mouse.

## Selection of Devices

Being "fitted" for a speech device should be no different from being fitted for a brace or artificial limb. It requires analysis of the patient by a competent professional who understands the particular person's needs and the availability of state-of-the-art technology. Information on speech devices is available from each vendor of such a device, of course, and there are a number of centralized databases that can provide information. The TRACE Resource Center at the University of Wisconsin–Madison has a large catalog containing information on devices, prices, functionality, and the addresses and telephone numbers of vendors. Furthermore, this TRACE database is available on CD-ROM, and is included with this book.

There are many speech input/output devices on the market today. These are differentiated by quality (i.e., intelligibility and naturalness) in the case of TTS and accuracy in the case of ASR. Furthermore, some are integrated devices, while others are peripheral devices or cards that can be attached to or inserted into a computer. For the VOCA market, the intelligibility (i.e., quality) of the device is of primary importance, as communication with a first-time listener can be vital. VOCA users have available to them both peripheral devices attached to laptop and notebook computers (which can be easily mounted on a wheelchair) and integrated devices. For those who are blind or visually impaired, the typical architecture is a PC, a laptop with a peripheral synthesizer attached to the PC, or a PC containing a voice card. With the faster microprocessors and the current tendency of many of the well-known computer manufacturers to include digital signaling processors on the motherboards, speech synthesizers are beginning to appear in software in the form of a 3½-inch diskette. A speech synthesizer without specialized software to read text on computer screens in a variety of formats is not useful. Many screen-reading companies sell their software along with a variety of speech synthesizers as a turnkey package. For individuals with motor impairments as well as speech or language problems, ASR technology can be helpful; typically, these persons need large vocabulary systems that are available from a number of companies.

### Auxiliary Considerations

There are speech synthesizers that are very inexpensive, but are limited in intelligibility; some are more expensive, but are highly intelligible and sound like a nonnative speaker of English. The person who is blind should take into consideration the fact that he or she must listen to the synthesizer for many hours per day. Nevertheless, feedback has shown that speech quality is still a lower priority than responsiveness and indexing. The person who is vocally impaired should remember that the listener will often be an individual who is hearing synthetic speech for the first time and that high intelligibility and naturalness are critical to a reasonably fluid dialogue.

Any initiative to broaden functionality should focus on adults who need augmentative and alternative communication. The adult population (i.e., those over 22 years of age) has been less served by professionals. In a survey done some years ago by Blackstone in *Augmentative Communication News*, only 8 percent of professionals claimed to work with people over 65 years of age. This trend will be exacerbated in the near future, since older individuals (those over 65) will represent a very large portion of the population as the baby boomers near retirement.

## CONCLUSION

Each of the technologies discussed will improve during the next few years, and many will be combined with each other. For example, blind users are already "reading" and distance learning with a speech synthesizer. In the not-too-distant future, fax will be combined with voice to take out the middle (and somewhat unnecessary step) of scanning hard copy fax into a reading machine. The future is brighter for individuals with disabilities because of these and other services, the dedicated technologists who make them possible, and the assistance of legislation such as the ADA, which now allows people with disabilities to insist on equal opportunities and access in transportation, communication, education, and other essential aspects of life.

---

### REFERENCES


Conroy, D.G., Vitale, A.J., & Klatt, D.H. (1986). *DECtalk DTC03 text-to-speech system owner's manual.* Nashua, NH: Educational Services, Digital Equipment Corporation.

Coombs, N.R. (1987). Modern American history on VAX Notes. *Edu* (Spring): Digital Equipment Corp.

Coombs, N.R. (1988). Using distance education technologies to overcome physical disabilities. In R. Mason & A. Kaye (Eds.), *Mindweave: Communication, computers and distance education.* New York: Pergamon Press.

Coombs, N.R. (1992). Teaching in the Information Age. *EDUCOM Review, 27*(2),

Dworkin, C. (1989). *FAX for home and office: The guide to buying and maintaining fax machines.* Greensboro, NC: Chilton.

Dudley, H. (1939). The vocoder. *Bell Labs Rec.,* 122–126.

Fishman, D., & King, E. (1990). *The book of fax: An impartial guide to buying and using facsimile machines.* Chapel Hill, NC: Ventana Press.

Fromkin, V., & Rodman, R. (1978). *An introduction to language.* New York: Holt, Rinehart & Winston.

Gilster, P. (1993). *The Internet navigator.* New York: John Wiley.

Goodglass, H., & Hunt, J. (1958). Grammatical complexity and aphasic speech. *Word, 14,* 197–207.

Greenspan, S.L., Nusbaum, H.C., & Pisoni, D.B. (1985). Perception of synthetic speech: Some effects of training and attentional limitations. In *Proceedings of the American Voice I/O Society.*

Hauptmann, A., & Rudnicky, A. (1988). Talking to computers: An empirical investigation. *Journal of Man-Machine Studies, 28,* 583–604.

Jacobson, R.L. (1994, July). Extending the reach of "virtual" classrooms. *Chronicle of Higher Education.*

Kanavetsy, D., Dnis, C.M., Gopalakrishman, P.S., Hodgson, R., Jameson, D., & Nahamoo, D. (1990). A communication aid for the hearing-impaired based on an automatic speech recognizer. In L. Torres, E. Masgrau, & M.A. Lagunas (Eds.), *Signal processing V: Theories and applications.* Amsterdam: Elsevier Science.

Kinner, J., & Coombs, N. (1995). Computer access for students with special needs. In Z.L. Berge & M.P. Collins (Eds.), *Computer-mediated communications and the online classroom: Overview and perspectives* (Vol. 1). Cresskill, NJ: Hampton Press.

Klatt, D.H. (1987). Review of text to speech conversion for English. *Journal of the Acoustical Society of America, 82* (3), 737–793.

Klatt, D.H., & Klatt, L.C. (1990). Analysis, synthesis and perception of voice quality variations among female and male talkers. *Journal of the Acoustical Society of America, 85*, 820–857.

Ladd, D.R. (1980). *The structure of intonational meaning.* Bloomington: Indiana University Press.

Lazzaro, J.J. (1990, August). Opening doors for the disabled. *Byte*, 258–268.

Lazzaro, J.J. (1993). *Adaptive technologies for learning and work environments.* Chicago: American Library Association.

Levitt, H. (1994). Speech processing for physical and sensory disabilities. In D.B. Roe & J.E. Wilpon (Eds.), *Voice communication between humans and machines*. Washington, DC: National Academy of Sciences.

Liberman, M., & Prince, A. (1977). On stress and linguistic rhythm. *Linguistic Inquiry, 8*, 249–336.

Logan, J.S., & Pisoni, D.B. (1986). *Preference judgements comparing different synthetic voices. Progress Report No. 1; Research on Speech Perception 2.* Bloomington, In: Indiana University.

Logan, J.S., Greene, B.G., & Pisoni, D.B. (1989). Segmental intelligibility of synthetic speech produced by ten next-to-speech systems. *Journal of the Acoustical Society of America, 86*, 566–581.

McKee, B.G., & Scherer, M.J. (1992). *A fomative evaluation of two Gallaudet University/Rochester Institute of Technology courses offered via teleconferencing.* Paper presented at the annual meeting of the American Educational Research Association, New Orleans. ERIC document #ED377213.

Mason R., & Kayne, A. (Eds.). (1988). *Mindweave: Communication, computers and distance education.* New York: Pergamon Press.

Mirenda, P., & Buckman, D. (1990). A comparison of intelligibility among natural speech and seven speech synthesizers with listeners from three age groups. *Augmentative and Alternative Communication, 6*, 61–68.

Moore, M.G. (1989). *The effects of distance learning: A summary of literature.* Paper presented at Office of Technology, May 31, Washington, DC.

Morrison, R., & Ellsworth, J.H. (1994, May). Internet resources for distance education. *C&RL News*, 256–258.

Nusbaum, H.C., Dedina, M.J., & Pisoni, D.B. (1984). Perceptual confusions of consonants in natural and synthetic CV syllables. *Technical Note 84-02,* Speech Research Laboratory, Department of Psychology, Indiana University.

Nusbaum, H.C., & Pisoni, D.B. (1985). Constraints on the perception of synthetic speech generated by rule. *Behavior Research Methods, Instruments, & Computers, 17*, 235–242.

Nusbaum, H.C., Schwab, E.C., & Pisoni, D.B. (1984). Subjective evaluation of synthetic speech: Measuring preference, naturalness, and acceptability. *Research on Speech Perception Progress Report No. 10,* Speech Research Laboratory, Department of Psychology, Indiana University.

Olson, R.K., & Wise, B.W. (1990). *Reading whole text with computer speech feedback.* Paper presented at the American Educational Research Association in a Symposium entitled Using Computer-Generated Speech to Teach Reading Skills: Current Research and Future Directions.

Pisoni, D.B., Nusbaum, H.C., & Greene, B.G. (1985). Perception of synthetic speech generated by rule. In *Proceedings of the IEEE 73* (pp. 1665–1676).

Roe, D.B., & Wilpon, J.G. (Eds.). (1994). *Voice communication between humans and machines.* Washington, DC: National Academy of Sciences.

Scherer, K.R. (1979). Personality markers in speech. In K.R. Scherer & M. Giles (Eds.), *Social markers in speech* (pp. 147–210). Cambridge: Cambridge University Press.

Scherer, M.J., & McKee, B.G., (1993). The Views of Adult Deaf Learners and Institutions Serving Deaf Learners Regarding Distance Learning Cooperative Arrangement with NTID/RIT: The Results of Two Surveys. Paper presented at the annual meeting of the American Educational Research Association, Boston. ERIC document #ED377214.

Schmandt, C. (1993). *Voice communication with computers.* New York: Van Nostrand Reinhold.

Schwab, E.C., Nusbaum, H.C., & Pisoni, D.B. (1985). Effects of training on the perception of synthetic speech. *Human Factors, 27,* 395–408.

Selkirk, E.O. (1984). *Phonology and syntax: The relation between sound and structure.* Cambridge, MA: MIT Press.

Silverman, K.E.A. (1987). The structure and processing of fundamental frequency contours. Unpublished doctoral dissertation, Cambridge University.

Slowiaczek, L.M., & Nusbaum, H.C. (1985). Effects of speech rate and pitch contour on the perception of synthetic speech. *Human Factors, 27,* 701–712.

Sproat, R. (1990). Stress assignment in complex nominals for English text-to-speech. In *Proceedings of the ECSA Workshop on Speech Synthesis* (pp. 129–132).

Tetschner, W. (1992). *Voice Processing* (2nd ed.). Norwood, MA: Artech House.

Warrick, A., Nelson, P.J., Cossaltor, J.G., Cote, C., McGillis, J., & Charboneau, J.R. (1977). Synthesized speech as an aid to communication and learning for the nonverbal. In *Proceedings of the Workshop on Communication Aids for the Handicapped* (pp. 120–135).

Wise, B.W., & Olson, R.K. (1991a). Remediating reading disabilities. In Obrzut & Hynd (Eds.), *Neurophysiological foundations in learning disabilities: A handbook of issues, methods, and practice.*

Wise, B.W., & Olson, R.K. (1991b). What computerized speech can add to remedial reading. In A. Syrdral, *Behavioral aspects of speech technology: Theory and applications.* Boca Raton, FL: CRC Press.

Wissick, C. (1994, February). On-ramp to the information highway. *The TAM Newsletter.*

*Chapter 13*

# Technologies of the Future

*Joel N. Orr*

Technology—especially computer technology—is both an equalizer and a differentiator. Some technologies enhance or amplify different human abilities; text-processing systems, for example, allow us to explore enormous volumes of written material very quickly. Because computer technologies can work with visual, auditory, or tactile output, they can equalize information-processing opportunities for people with sensory limitations. Other technologies (e.g., the graphical user interface) rely heavily on a particular modality (e.g., vision). However, it is difficult for people with visual disabilities to use these technologies.

The current explosion in computer-based technologies will produce more equalizers and more differentiators. As computer-based environments become more realistic, they will require the same abilities that reality does; meanwhile, specific assistive and compensatory technologies are being developed to enable persons with disabilities to deal effectively with the new digital environments. Ultimately, that is, in 20 years or more, technologies that are already under development hold out the promise of almost total equalization between those with and those without disabilities.

As promising as these technologies are, there is yet more hope on the horizon. From the point of view of assistive technology, extrapolating to the future involves understanding basic computers and related infrastructure; powerful tool level developments, such as object-oriented technology, knowledge-based systems, and neural networks; and interesting applications, like virtual reality (VR) and nanotechnology.

---

*Note:* Brief portions of this chapter appeared previously in Joel Orr's articles in Miller-Freeman's *AI/Expert VR Supplement* magazine and Penton's *CAE* magazine, and are used here with the kind permission of both publishers.

## COMPUTERS AND NETWORKS

The architecture of computing systems has undergone an interesting sequence of developments over the almost half-century history of commercial computing. The first systems were approachable only by the most knowledgeable of experts, who were able to translate their problems into terms meaningful to the arrays of relays and, later, vacuum tubes that constituted the computers of the 1940s and early 1950s. These machines were little more than enormous calculators, performing arithmetic at speeds measured in seconds and large fractions thereof.

The information explosion, so wonderfully described by Toffler (1980) and others, made itself felt in the 1970s through the refinement of computer networks and interactivity, and the addition of rudimentary computer graphics capability. The enormous quantities of resources required to generate and transmit pictures, as compared to text, began to give planners an inkling of the computational power that would be needed to fulfill their long-term visions.

In the 1980s, workstations and personal computers came on the scene—complete systems designed for personal use, with their own operating systems and peripherals. In the path of computer development, they represented a helical loop back to individual computers, but now under individual control. The interconnection of these individually powerful systems into networks occupied the computing world for most of that decade, and the process is continuing as standards are worked out in the midst of accelerating technologies.

The client–server model is the architectural model for cooperating software and hardware in these systems that has emerged as most popular. It is a generalization of the computer–terminal model beyond the bounds of hardware. The "client" uses some service that is provided by the "server." Clients and servers can be hardware devices or software processes.

Client–server systems have been characterized as fast, powerful, and out of control. They must provide the individual user with a high degree of interactivity; in addition, they must be functionally independent of one another, yet able to cooperate. An extreme example of cooperation appears in the programs sold by a number of vendors that make it possible to apply all the idle resources on a network to a single large problem, such as the rendering of a complex animation sequence or a highly involved engineering computation.

Today, anyone who wants to use a computer must acquire some knowledge of the operating system. This is a burden and an obstacle, particularly to the disabled person, for whom the computer may be a tool of critical importance. It will take at least 10 more years, but in the future operating systems, the programs that give computers their basic functionality, will be completely invisible to users.

Integrated circuits, chips, are at the heart of all computer progress. Today's processors have as many as 3 million transistor equivalents on a single chip; miniaturization doubles approximately every 3 years. Current semiconductor technology, based mostly on silicon, can accommodate approximately four orders of magnitude more miniaturization; that is, devices that are one ten-thousandth the size of present ones can be made from silicon. Gallium arsenide and other materials offer the prospect of even denser circuits. Recently, the idea of protein-based computers that are much smaller and faster than those based on semiconductors has been put forth in as reputable a publication as *Scientific American* (Birge, 1995).

Even if there are no completely different innovations, computers are almost certain to be small enough and cheap enough to be everywhere. They will be woven into clothing, embedded in furniture, integral to building parts. By radio and other communication means, they will "talk" to one another to coordinate the details of human lives. Thus, an elevator will be "told" by a blind person's processors of that person's need for auditory floor numbers; a building will "hear" a wheelchair approaching and activate appropriate ramps and doors.

An important prerequisite to this "ubiquitous computing," as it has been called by scientists at the Xerox Palo Alto Research Center (Weiser, 1993) is an extensive infrastructure of networks. The Internet, the oddly anarchical structure that is incorporating more and more of the world's computers, suggests what universal networking might be like. Once it more fully integrates telephone and cellular networks, almost any device will be able to communicate with almost any other device on the face of the planet. Between now and the day of the universal network, there will be an increased use of infrared and other forms of wireless communications, as well as rapid spread of amazingly high bandwidth optical fibers, and new kinds of communication satellites.

## OBJECT-ORIENTED TECHNOLOGY AND COMPONENT SOFTWARE

Because the market for software to be used by disabled persons is not very large in commercial terms, the cost of software research and development has simply been too high to encourage commercial investment. All that is about to change, thanks to object-oriented programming and component software. These technologies will make it possible to write very small programs and have them "plug in" to existing applications.

OpenDoc is likely to become the dominant component environment; it is supported by all the leading software companies. OpenDoc is a new plug-in software architecture that lets you extend the usefulness of your applications by easily adding new functionality. OpenDoc uses software components—called parts—

that can be dragged-and-dropped into documents created by any OpenDoc-aware application. Since OpenDoc is a cross-platform technology, documents created with OpenDoc can work across different computer platforms, including Mac OS, Windows, UNIX, and OS/2. Because OpenDoc-compliant programs integrate at the document level, any additions required to make documents accessible to persons with particular disabilities will be purchased as small, inexpensive modules and simply added to general purpose programs.

Procedural programming is like building an apartment building with ten apartments on each floor, while object-oriented programming resembles the construction of a development with 100 individual houses. The apartment building has centralized utilities; units share walls, and the ceiling of one level is the floor of the next. The individual housing development is more expensive to construct than the apartment building, because each house has its own utilities and more walls per dwelling unit. On the other hand, adding a dwelling unit to the apartment building is difficult and expensive, while an additional house in the development costs no more, in principle, than any of the first 100.

Procedural methods require the programmer to become involved immediately in implementation details; object-oriented techniques encourage the programmer to think about *what* needs to be done, rather than *how* to do it. The creation of a good model of the problem is paramount. This is why procedural programs are verb-oriented, while object-oriented programs focus more on nouns.

In object-oriented programming, objects, which can be almost anything, are grouped into classes and have methods associated with them. An object belonging to a class is said to be an instance of that class. All actions are the result of events, such as mouse clicks and key entry. Events generate messages, which activate objects. For example, a mouse click could generate a message that would activate a method associated with a button object in a graphical user interface program.

To be formally considered object-oriented (a term developed at Xerox's Palo Alto Research Center ([Want, Schilit, Adams, Gold, Petersen, Goldberg, Ellis, & Weiser, 1995] along with the first object-oriented language, SmallTalk), a programming environment must support four behaviors:

1. inheritance, meaning that new objects in a class inherit the characteristics of the class (although the programmer can modify those characteristics)
2. encapsulation, meaning that objects contain both data and methods, behaviors that are triggered under certain conditions
3. information hiding, meaning an encapsulation in which certain details are not visible
4. polymorphism, meaning the ability of a single message to represent different things to different objects

Programming in an object-oriented environment consists of the creation of classes of objects that will collaborate to produce the desired effects. Debugging object-oriented programs can be very simple, or terrifyingly complex, depending on how well the programs are written.

Object-oriented programming is not harder than procedural programming, but it is very different; many programmers find it difficult to "unlearn" the procedural approach. "The object-based approach promises to make software easier to reuse, refine, test, maintain, and extend," said Brian Wilkerson of Apple (Wirfs-Brock, Wilkerson, & Wiener, 1990), "but simply implementing an application in an object-based language does not guarantee these benefits. They can only be achieved if the implementation is based on a sound object-based design."

Adding capabilities to properly designed object-oriented programs is much easier than enhancing procedural programs, for many of the same reasons that it is easier to add another house to a development than to add an apartment to an apartment building. Houses and objects are largely self-contained; apartment buildings and procedural programs are completely determined by their original plans.

The qualities of object-oriented programs make possible the creation of software components that can be used in many programs with little integration effort. More than any other, it is this promise that has attracted adherents to object-oriented programming. For example, object-oriented database management systems (OODBMS) store items as objects, rather than hierarchically associated records or rows in tables. Thus, new data types (classes) can be added at any time, without affecting the pre-existing structure or methods.

The topology of the object metaphor—the way in which its components are interconnected—is very simple; in fact, relational and hierarchical structures can be emulated or embedded in it. The self-contained nature of objects is responsible for this strength. Moreover, this topology is well suited for implementation in client–server networks, which represent an important trend in modern systems. Like such networks, OODBMS are extensible and modular; they can grow or shrink to adapt to new demands.

The power of objects is in their robustness, extensibility, flexibility, and modularity. Actually, it would be better if no user had to know or care about objects; except as interesting metaphors, they are not useful to any but computer professionals. We are not yet able to reach that level of information hiding, however.

## KNOWLEDGE-BASED SYSTEMS

A computer scientist asked a computer, "Do you compute you will ever be able to think like a human?" The computer responded, "That reminds me of a story. . . ." There is a broad cultural assumption of some kind of equivalence between human minds and computers. Yet even the most casual acquaintance with computers is enough to make one aware of how *un*like people they are.

One of the obvious differences between people and computers is that the former use knowledge as the basis for their interaction with the world, and the latter use information. An important step in the humanization of computers is presently being taken by Noyes, who has developed and patented a system called Cogito in which knowledge can be represented. Any required stylized pictorials or linguistic representations of that knowledge (e.g., engineering drawings of one form or another) are automatically generated by Cogito. Therefore, they are always consistent with their source and with each other.

"Knowledge can be represented by a network, with ideas at the nodes, and the relationships among them as the connectors. Here is an interesting point: Each idea is completely defined by its connections," declared Noyes (personal communication, 1995). Thus, while computer-aided design (CAD) systems maintain the geometry and some topology of physical objects as the basis of their world representation, Cogito has the knowledge of the represented system as its heart. Cogito also learns, adding to its knowledge base with every interaction it has. So as work proceeds, the system becomes more and more efficient.

External expressions of Cogito's knowledge are in the form of languages. New ones can be added at any time to meet demands for new expressions of the knowledge. For example, the program's first commercial application has been in the generation of drawings for process plants. "Data entry is simple. We teach the data-entry people Cogito's six commands, and how they must be applied to the information to be entered" (personal communication, 1995). Different types of drawings and textual documents can then be generated automatically. Each drawing or document type requires a peculiar language; Cogito learns new languages easily.

The development of knowledge-based systems reflects a general trend in information management: getting real. Throughout the realms of computer science, products, and applications, there is a movement away from the abstract and toward the concrete. The move toward object orientation, for example, is a move away from the purity of the Spartan verbs of FORTRAN and other procedural languages to the messy, baggage-laden nouns of SmallTalk and event-driven systems.

Complete deterministic analysis of complex systems is just not possible, chaos tells us, because very small changes in initial conditions can lead to arbitrarily large changes in end conditions. A miss might be as good as a mile. In the absence of deterministic solutions, a system designer must model in order to understand the effect of changes. And the key to modeling is the representation of knowledge. If would-be practitioners of knowledge-based systems start with the old tools and methods, however, they will mistake signal for noise. In order to make use of the computational resources at our disposal, we must learn to model knowledge.

It is easy to picture ways that knowledge-based systems will benefit persons with disabilities. For example, such systems could learn common miscommunications from the user and compensate for them.

## NEURAL NETWORKS

The study of the brain and the study of computers have influenced each other. Initially, brain researchers tried to understand the human brain as an extremely complex computer. Later, computer designers began studying the brain to attempt to model its structure. Although still very young, this latter study has yielded a powerful new computing model: that of the neural network.

Neural networks are computational structures made up of many simple interconnected processing elements. Like the neurons and synapses of the brain, they operate in parallel and exchange information among themselves. Neural networks can be implemented in either hardware or software. They map a given set of inputs onto a desired set of outputs and learn by example. For complex pattern matching, for example, a neural network does not need to be programmed to seek specific features; instead, it can be "shown" a range of examples and given a "tolerance" within which to declare a match. These devices are ideally suited for incorporation into systems that "observe" the user's actions and produce the desired results, even in the absence of explicit commands. They will also make possible computers that "see" or "hear" the user and identify gestures and speech in natural ways.

There are already neural network chips on the market. They will be able to serve as controllers for relatively inexpensive eye-tracking devices for paraplegics, for example. Such chips may also be used in systems to decode idiosyncratic speech for speech-impaired people.

### Virtual Reality

At the 1994 conference on virtual reality (VR) and persons with disabilities, a gentleman in the audience from the University of Oregon described a power wheelchair training facility that he had built so that new users of power wheelchairs could make their mistakes in a simulated environment, rather than out on the street. That almost-VR activity known as telepresence, in which the participant's senses are technologically extended over space and possibly magnified, will give disabled people access to places and things from which they are kept by their disabilities. VR's greatest promise may be in the improvement of communications, however. As Blanchard, a founder of VPL, a pioneer VR company, and a wheelchair user, noted,

> VR will replace the telephone, not the television. It will make it possible for people to gain empathy with others by modeling different bodies, for one thing. People have trouble communicating because they can't put themselves in the other person's shoes. Well, one of the demos we had at VPL was a lobster persona. You put on this wired body suit, and became a lobster. But a lobster has six legs! That seemed to be an insurmountable mapping problem, but we worked it out. And if you can give someone the experience of being a lobster, you can give an amputee the experience of legs, somehow—and a fully-limbed person the experience of an amputee. That will improve communications. (personal communication, 1995)

Life is full of communication problems; VR has the potential to help solve them. Among the first beneficiaries should be people with sensory limitations, because they need communicational equality.

VR offers a place of mediation, a space in which computers control access to our senses and receive our outbound communications. Mediation offers tremendous flexibility for modifying the communications—amplification, attenuation, even synesthetic transformation of a stimulus in one modality into another (e.g., turning sound into tactile stimuli, sights into sounds). The Smith-Kettlewell Eye Research Institute Rehabilitation Engineering Research Center grew out of a sensory substitution project. The Center has explored ways to have touch and hearing function in place of sight for people who are blind. "It's beginning to look as if we can go beyond sensory substitution," noted Gilden, associate director of the Center. "But first we have to explore the issue of brain plasticity; that is, can the parts of the brain that deal with the missing sense accept the substitute information in a meaningful way? Perhaps VR can provide a milieu in which such explorations can be profitably made" (personal communication, 1995).

Moravec has written for years about the "uploading" of human personality into computers (Regis, 1990). While such a concept raises serious philosophical and even spiritual questions, by its very statement it emphasizes the essential sameness of able-bodied (some say, "temporarily able-bodied") and disabled people. Perhaps bodies are not essential.

As long as it is necessary to deal with bodies, it is good to note that therapeutic applications of VR will directly address some disability issues. A company called AquaThought is documenting the health benefits of spending time in the company of dolphins (which seems to powerfully reduce or eliminate stress and its effects), and is building a VR system that will simulate the experience so that it can be widely distributed. Cole, president of AquaThought, described the project:

> The AquaThought Dolphin Encounter Immersive Platform will transport the point of perception of its user into an underwater location populated with friendly and inquisitive dolphins. State-of-the-art virtual reality and neurotechnology will be employed. . . . A stereo visual/aural recording will be used to drive the various sensory output modalities of the platform. The platform is based on a VibraSonic ACV-8000 Total Sensory Stimulation Device. The participant will lie with his/her back on a liquid-crystal filled mattress. The mattress is designed to distribute stress evenly against the body, closely approximating the feeling of floating in water. The patented Liquid Crystal Floating Transducer Platform will "bass drive" the participant's entire body with the stereo hydrophone audio signal. To simulate the feeling of the massive acoustic energy of echolocation perceived while underwater with a dolphin, a neurophone will be employed to transduce the incoming stereo hydrophone audio signal directly onto the participant's nerve pathways.
>
> Here's what you will experience: You lie down on the table and wait while an attendant adjusts the stereo-optic display and attaches the neurophone electrodes. The bed begins to gently undulate as a 3D underwater scene fills your vision. Suddenly, you hear and feel an intense explosion of sound sweeping around you and through you. As you try to orient yourself to the direction of this strange and wonderful sound, a dolphin darts by you, giving you a comforting glance. You playfully encounter each of the six dolphins and join their pod in a high-speed race around a beautiful reef. The five-minute experience ends with a grand and triumphant farewell as the six dolphins form a circle around you, then skyrocket out of the water in a synchronistic movement. (personal communication, 1995)

So VR holds out to people who are disabled—as well as to those who are merely stressed—the hope of a way out of their limitations and a way into more complete participation in work and social environments.

### Nanotechnology

"The principles of physics, as far as I can see, do not speak against the possibility of maneuvering things atom by atom," said Feynman (1990), 1965 Nobel laureate in physics. Maneuvering atoms gives us unimagined abundance, undreamed of power, and the promise of immortality. Charles Platt said it well in *Wired* magazine:

> Instead of smelting steel, making molds, stamping out components, and fitting everything together on an assembly line, we can have robots tiny enough to assemble molecules one by one. This way, a gadget should be able to grow itself from a chunk of raw material, much as human beings grow by absorbing nutrients, turning them into useful compounds, and fitting them together according to instructions stored in our DNA.
>
> Stacking atoms individually is obviously going to be a time-consuming business. But suppose you tell your microminiaturized robot arm to build a copy of itself. Then you get the two arms to make two more, and you get those four to build another four . . . until, in a short space of time, this exponential growth gives you billions upon billions of arms ready to do whatever you want.
>
> Now suppose each arm has an equally tiny onboard computer controlling it, so that it can be quickly reprogrammed in a way that DNA never could be. Result: You have an entire factory of microbe-sized machines capable of building just about anything you want, including drugs, televisions, homes, highways, or microscopic repair robots that could run around in the human blood stream, rejuvenating tissues and zapping cancer cells.
>
> Our tiny helpers can be told to create whole new cities (and disassemble the old ones), eat up pollution, and remake the world as a neat, clean, postindustrial paradise. Along the way, they can bring us immortality by arresting the aging process.
>
> This is the promise of nanotechnology, the prefix "nano" meaning on the scale of a nanometer, which is a billionth of a meter (a typical virus might be about 100 nanometers long).

Nanotechnology will make it possible to build robots small enough to repair tissue damage that causes disabilities or to construct sensory or motor prostheses that are as good or better than the original. Drexler, who coined the term *nanotechnology,* has made two "conservative" estimates about the timing: "If you want to rely on it happening, it is conservative to plan on twenty years. If you are concerned the competition is going to get it first, it is conservative to plan on ten years."

There are two approaches to nanotechnology: bottom up and top down. Machines designed by believers in the bottom-up approach are made of individual atoms and molecules. "The three paths of protein design (biotechnology), biomimetic chemistry, and atomic positioning are parts of a broad bottom-up strategy: working at the molecular level to increase our ability to control matter," said a recent report from the Foresight Institute, the premier nanotechnology education and policy group (Hall, 1995). Nobody can build the machines yet, because the tools are still too gross.

Eigler (Eigler & Schweizer, 1990) attracted global publicity when he used a device called a scanning tunneling microscope to arrange individual xenon atoms on a piece of chromium so that they made the world's smallest billboard and spelled out IBM—the name of his employer. More recently, Eigler has been trying to create carbon dioxide by pushing carbon and oxygen atoms together. Both the scanning tunneling microscope and another device, the atomic force microscope, can move atoms around in the plane, but they cannot build three-dimensional objects. Using these devices to attempt to build molecules "is like trying to build a wristwatch with a sharp stick," said Merckle (1995). Nevertheless, progress is being made.

The top-down school is represented by Wolf, spokesman for the National Nanofabrication Facility (NNF) at Cornell University (personal communication, 1995). According to Wolf, it will be necessary to build small things, which will build smaller things, which will build yet smaller things, and so on. Among other projects, the NNF is working on a chip with a very tiny motion sensor built right into it—a kind of submicroscopic pea in a tube—that will be used in car seat belt interlock systems.

In fact, standard semiconductor manufacturing techniques such as electron-beam lithography best typify the top-down approach. These have achieved submicron constructions, but are still far from producing the wonders envisioned by Drexler and others. Drexler described himself as "agnostic" with regard to the bottom-up/top-down controversy, and expressed hope that both work.

There is no question; we are learning to make things smaller. Although no one knows how close nanotechnology really is, it is clear that only engineering problems remain to be solved. There are no fundamental scientific or philosophical matters to be confronted.

As for the commercial, social, and personal implications, Drexler has predicted that "the first high-payoff applications are likely to be in information. First, molecular sensors that provide special information about compounds, perhaps in home medical-test kits. Second, molecular devices that do what silicon does now, but better, perhaps providing terabyte RAM chips."

In considering the danger of nanotechnology running amok, Drexler asked:

> Should we be concerned about runaway replicators? It would be hard to build a machine with the wonderful adaptability of living organisms. The replicators easiest to build will be inflexible machines, like automobiles or industrial robots, and will require special fuels

and raw materials, the equivalents of hydraulic fluid and gasoline. To build a runaway replicator that could operate in the wild would be like building a car that could go off-road and fuel itself from tree sap. With enough work, this should be possible, but it will hardly happen by accident. Without replication, accidents would be like those of industry today: locally harmful, but not catastrophic to the biosphere. Catastrophic problems seem more likely to arise though deliberate misuse, such as the use of nanotechnology for military aggression.

## APPLICATIONS TO COME

Technology is progressing at its own accelerating pace; assimilation of technology is moving forward, too, but it is constrained by the inertia and friction of the human component. Inertia, the tendency of a system to continue in the direction and at the velocity at which it is going, is evident in the fact that people resist change. The movement of adjacent systems at different speeds or in different directions causes friction, which wastes energy.

The advent of comprehensive computerization in the business world bodes well for people with disabilities. The more sophisticated the computers, the more extensive the networks, the more easily they will accommodate adaptive devices and programs. Many attention-grabbing technologies will be in the most modern offices before the turn of the millennium. For example, color printing and fax will be common. Its integration with more completely electronic communications will be total within 5 years. Optical character recognition (OCR) programs will not only read machine-generated text perfectly, but also they will "understand" page layout. So, even if a person scans a paper document and faxes it, it will end up in the recipient's mailbox as if it had been prepared within the computer with a word-processing or page layout program. This is important, of course, for people with visual impairments.

Video input will be everywhere, and most machines will have video cameras built-in or available as inexpensive options. Short video messages (v-mail?) will clog the wires of in-house networks, ensuring the rapid replacement of copper by optical fiber.

Speaker-independent voice recognition systems at reasonable prices will just be coming on the market in 1999. These programs will truly take dictation, allowing people with disabilities to control their computers by voice. These systems will include such subtleties as spatial location of sound, so that if the user turns away from the screen to talk to someone who appears at the door of the office, the system will know that the user is talking to someone else. Moreover, speech will replace pens and keyboards as the main form of interaction with personal digital assistants.

Wireless communications will be everywhere. It is already possible on some flights to hook a portable computer's modem into the airplane's telephone system. By 1999, even the connection between the computer and the airplane's switch will be wireless—infrared, most likely, but perhaps spread-spectrum low-power radio frequency.

"Ubiquitous computing," wherein all the many computers in homes, cars, offices, and airplanes talk to one another and to simple tiny devices that we wear on our wrists or carry in our pockets, will be around. It will deal mostly with very simple environmental functions, however, such as control of lighting, air conditioning, and heating. Later, this innovation will extend its sensorium so that rooms will know not only who entered them, but also will adjust to that individual's personal preferences.

One factor that greatly impedes the spread of technology today is the difficulty of trying out new software and hardware. By 1999, the Compaq/Microsoft "Plug 'n' Play" standard should be in wide use so that computer users will have simple peripheral and software installation.

Multimedia will disappear by becoming part of all computing. Most new PCs are already shipped with CD-ROM drives and sound boards. CD-ROM will be the most common medium for retail software distribution, although its growth will flatten as broad-bandwidth communications become universal. Within corporations and other organizations, software distribution and maintenance will take place over the network.

The most striking impact of technology on the "office" of the late 1990s is that it will obviate the need for a physical gathering place. This will have major importance for people with disabilities. People collect in one place to do business because they need to talk to each other, to refer to the files (e.g., corporate information, forms, all kinds of records), and to share office equipment (e.g., copiers, printers). Of course, there is also the matter of control: the boss wants to see employees, at least occasionally, to "really know what's going on." Telephone, videoconferencing, e-mail, and v-mail are already replacing face-to-face meetings, however. As imaging and OCR systems improve, the need for physical access to files goes away. Personal copiers, fax machines, shredders, and the like are already quite common. Employers are adapting to results-oriented measures of work that can easily be gauged at a distance.

Amway, Mary Kay Cosmetics, and other multilevel marketing organizations have proven that substantial businesses can be built and run without having offices. Television and computer network shopping are burgeoning, demonstrating that customers do not have to actually handle the merchandise in order to make a purchase. Face-to-face meetings with colleagues and sales prospects are hard to give up for other reasons. Frankly, we still need to observe the unintentional communications of people. The downside of meetings in virtual reality is that everything a person presents is conscious; people can hide the bags under their eyes, the run in their stocking, the throbbing vein, the body language that reveals so much. This is one reason that businesses resist letting their employees work from home or that salespersons insist on personal meeting with prospects.

There is more to the problem of inertia, however. Blind habit works against progress. Most people try to implement technology without changing anything in the flow of work or in the nature of the organization. As a result, they realize only a fraction of the benefits that technology offers. This situation is most likely to develop when employees do not envision themselves in a favorable position in the proposed new order of things and resist the new technology. In fact, this resistance is so common that it is the principal impediment to the spread of automation in business.

How best to deal with this obstacle to organizational prosperity? By being open, and planning the changes with the participation of all who will be around to implement them. By showing the participants the roles they are to play in the revised organization, and offering them explanations, if not compensation, for any real or apparent loss of status they must suffer. And by convincing all that the survival of the organization depends on making the proposed changes.

Perhaps the greatest boon granted by computers is the ability to make choices and to see their consequences quickly. There are no formulas or algorithms that produce optimal outcomes for a given set of requirements. We design them by trial and error. What the computer offers is a place in which to make many more trials and record the effects of many more errors than we can without it. Moreover, it is a protected place in which the trials can be made. There is no need to get a wheelchair onto a factory floor or go without sight into dangerous environments. Instead, we can create those environments on a computer and run the experiments there.

There are two important ways in which computers make it possible to examine alternatives: modeling and simulation. Things are explored through modeling; processes and interactions are researched by means of simulation.

Modeling can be as simple as representing the edges of an object in a wire frame, or as complex as a parametric feature-based solid with information built in on material and finish. The less abstract the model, the closer its features to reality, and the better the results.

Simulation is one of the most powerful and least exercised capabilities of computers. On mainframes, the creation of simulations required arcane, mathematically oriented languages that took months or years to master. Today, PC-based graphically oriented simulation systems, such as ithink and Extend, allow the user to create simulations by dragging, dropping, and drawing. Most business professionals are simply not aware of them, but they can simulate work flow, economics, material movement—any process or interaction.

The bottom line is that computers may well be the most important ally of the disabled person in tomorrow's world. Computer technology will bring about environments tailored to individuals in ways that diminish or neutralize the significance of their particular disability.

---

## REFERENCES

Birge, R. (March 1995). Protein-based computers. *Scientific American,* 90–95.

Eigler, D.M., & Schweizer, E.K. (April 5, 1990). Positioning single atoms with a scanning tunnelling microscope. *Nature.*

Feynman, R. (February 1990). *There's plenty of room at the bottom: An invitation to enter a new field of physics.* Presented at annual meeting of the American Physics Society, California Institute of Technology, Pasadena, California.

Hall, J.S. (1995). Overview of nanotechnology (not "Just the FAQs"). (Adapted from papers by R.C. Merkle and K.E. Drexler).

Regis, E. (1990). *Great mambo chicken and the transhuman condition: Science slightly over the edge.* Addison-Wesley.

Toffler, A. (1980). *The Third Wave.* New York: Bantam.

Want, R., Schilit, B.N., Adams, N.I., Gold, R., Petersen, K., Goldberg, D., Ellis, R., & Weiser, M. (March 1995). *The ParcTab ubiquitous computing experiment.* Xerox PARC Computer Science Laboratory Tech Report CSL-95-1.

Weiser, M. (October 1993). Hot topic: Ubiquitous computing. *IEEE Computer,* 71–72.

Wirfs-Brock, R., Wilkerson, B., & Wiener, L. (1990). *Designing object oriented software.* Englewood Cliffs, NJ: Prentice Hall.

*Chapter 14*

# Assistive Technology-Related Legislation and Policies

*Jan C. Galvin and Rachel A. Wobschall*

The potential of technology to help individuals with disabilities achieve maximum independent functioning is well recognized among those in the field of rehabilitation. Several pieces of legislation, notably the 1986 Amendments to the Rehabilitation Act (P.L. 99–506), the Americans with Disabilities Act (ADA) (P.L. 101–336), the Individuals with Disabilities Education Act (IDEA) (P.L. 101–476), and the Technology-Related Assistance for Individuals with Disabilities Act (P.L. 100–407), have placed significant emphasis on the use of assistive technology as part of the continuum of services and have mandated that assistive technology services become more consumer-responsive. Although this heightened awareness of the benefits of assistive technology is encouraging, it requires a concurrent increase in awareness of *what is* appropriate technology and how to deliver appropriate assistive technology services.

Assistive technology (AT) as defined in the Technology-Related Assistance for Individuals with Disabilities Act of 1988 (29 U.S.C. Sec. 2202(S)) includes two components: "assistive technology device" and "assistive technology service." An AT device is defined as "any item, piece of equipment, or product system whether acquired commercially off the shelf, modified or customized, that is used to increase, maintain, or improve functional capabilities of individuals with disabilities. AT service means any service that directly assists an individual with a disability in the selection, acquisition, or use of an assistive technology device." This includes

- evaluating the needs of an individual with a disability, including those functional needs that arise in the individual's customary environment
- purchasing, leasing, or otherwise providing for the acquisition of assistive technology devices by individuals with disabilities
- selecting, designing, fitting, customizing, adapting, applying, maintaining, repairing, or replacing assistive technology devices

- coordinating and using other therapies, interventions, or services with assistive technology devices, such as those associated with existing education and rehabilitation plans and programs
- training or providing technical assistance to an individual with a disability or, where appropriate, the family of an individual with a disability
- training or providing technical assistance to professionals (including those who provide education and rehabilitation services), employers, or other individuals who provide services to, employ, or are otherwise substantially involved in the major life functions of individuals with disabilities

The concept of the rehabilitation engineering process is closely related to assistive technology and its application. This process is the application of scientific knowledge to practical purposes. It makes use of devices and techniques or strategies to remove or reduce barriers or obstacles to physical, behavioral, or cognitive performance confronted by individuals with disabilities.

Some researchers make a distinction between high technology and low technology. High technology usually refers to complex electrical and electronic devices, such as computers, augmentative communication boards, and environmental control systems. Low technology generally refers to simpler interventions, such as custom-designed hand tools; work station modifications; and simple, easy to use, inexpensive devices. "Often, low technology involves the application of 'ergonomics' or human factors in which the workplace or home is designed to fit the person instead of making the person fit into a fixed design" (McFarland, 1989, p. 2). When considering the issue of technology, people tend to think of talking computers, robots, laser optics, and spy satellites—not door levers, canes, and telephone headsets. It is often assumed that bigger, newer, and more sophisticated means better; however, "low technology alternatives can be just as effective and more easily integrated into a person's lifestyle" (Galvin & Phillips, 1990, p. 1).

Although there are few outcomes data reflecting the cost benefits of assistive technology, individuals and families who received devices and services reported that assistive technology is cost-effective in that appropriate devices can increase the functional capacity of both children and adults with disabilities in the home, workplace, and community (National Council on Disability, 1993):

- About 75 percent of children who received assistive technology were able to remain in a regular classroom, and about 45 percent were able to reduce school-related services.
- About 62 percent of working age persons with disabilities were able to reduce their dependence on their family members, and 58 percent were able to reduce their dependence on paid assistance.

- About 80 percent of older persons were able to reduce their dependence on others, and about half were able to avoid entering a nursing home.
- About 90 percent of employed persons reported that assistive technology helped them to work faster or better, 83 percent indicated that they earned more money, and 67 percent reported that assistive technology helped them to obtain employment.

Despite these positive outcomes and the apparent cost benefits of assistive technology, major problems remain in evaluating, selecting, and applying assistive technology. For example, who is going to fund both the device and the related services? A major part of the evaluation is identifying appropriate funding source(s). Many service providers and consumers have become frustrated over the years because of all the red tape involved in funding. Some agencies pay for this, but not for that; others pay only a certain amount and take up to a year to approve even that amount. Therefore, improving consumer responsiveness requires better ways to conduct the business of evaluating, selecting, and purchasing assistive technology devices and services. It is necessary not only to ensure that there is an appropriate linkage between the technologies and those who need them, but also to understand the many pieces of legislation, regulations, and funding systems that make it possible to provide the appropriate technologies and related services. Understanding the laws, regulations, agencies, and programs that serve individuals with disabilities is critical to the better utilization and improvement of available services.

## FEDERAL LEGISLATION AND REGULATIONS AFFECTING CHILDREN AND ADULTS WITH DISABILITIES

Children and adults with disabilities make up one of the largest minority populations in the United States. Approximately 49 million U.S. citizens have disabilities. Some are born with a disability. Others develop a disability because of environmental factors, accidents, illnesses, or war. Still others develop age-related disabilities. Unlike other minority groups, people with disabilities are not set apart by demographic categories. Disabilities transcend age, sex, race, culture, and socioeconomic group. Everyone is a potential member of this minority population.

Like all people, those with disabilities need quality health care, good nutrition, appropriate education, employment opportunities, affordable housing, adequate income, and reliable transportation and communication. For too many years, however, the majority of individuals with disabilities have been unable to realize those rights and opportunities that other citizens take for granted. Millions are without access to comprehensive health care. Furthermore, people with disabilities have one of the highest rates of unemployment and underemployment in the United States.

As of 1995, there are more than 60 pieces of legislation and/or regulations, as well as many programs and activities, that affect individuals with disabilities. The areas covered include education, health, rehabilitation, transportation, housing, employment, training, research, and entitlements. Not all relate directly to assistive technology devices and services, but a knowledge of the wide range of services and options available for persons with disabilities is essential to initiate and implement systems change activities and coordinate services between agencies and organizations serving these individuals. The Consortium for Citizens with Disabilities (CCD; 1994), a working coalition composed of consumer, provider, and professional organizations that advocate on behalf of people of all ages with physical and mental disabilities and their families, and the Office of Special Education and Rehabilitative Services (OSERS; 1992) provide a great deal of information about the relevant laws, regulations, and the agencies that administer them, as shown in the following discussion. Laws and regulations will change, however, through amendments, sunset provisions, budget cuts, the move toward state block grants, and many other considerations dependent on congressional policy changes. In addition, state regulations for implementing many federal programs differ. Therefore, it is important to keep abreast of congressional changes and state implementation plans. One of the best means of keeping up-to-date on legislation, regulations, and programs is through the publication of the United Cerebral Palsy Associations, called *Washington Watch*. For $25.00 per year, subscribers receive regular updates (by mail, Internet, fax, or disc) about all that is happening in Congress as it pertains to disability- and rehabilitation-related legislation. Other means of finding relevant national, state, and local information include

- local library
- local congressional office
- databases
- bulletin boards
- local disability-related organizations
- state technology act programs
- state protection and advocacy programs

**Children**

*Children's Mental Health Services Program—Department of Health and Human Services (DHHS).* The Children's Mental Health Services Program authorizes federal grants to states and communities to stimulate the development of interagency, community-based systems of care for children and adolescents with mental, emotional, or behavioral disorders. Recipient states match federal dollars and use the resources to establish interagency systems of care among mental health, child welfare, education and special education, and juvenile justice agencies. This program is based in the Community Mental Health Service.

### *Children's Civil Rights*

*Developmental Disabilities Act, Basic State Grant Program—DHHS.* The developmental disabilities basic grant program provides assistance to states to plan, monitor, evaluate, coordinate, and promote comprehensive services for people with developmental disabilities through 56 state and territorial Developmental Disabilities Councils. The councils' mandate is to advise federal, state, and local policymakers on ways to encourage independence, productivity, and integration into the community for all people with developmental disabilities and to invest in activities that effect long-term policy change and state-of-the-art services. The 1994 amendments to the Developmental Disabilities Act increase council responsibility to enhance cultural diversity and competence among consumers of services and within the programs themselves, and make grants available to American Indian consortiums to provide protection and advocacy services. The Administration on Developmental Disabilities (ADD) is responsible for the management of all developmental disabilities programs.

### *Direct Services for Children*

*Maternal and Child Health Block Grant—DHHS.* The university-affiliated program block grants awarded through the Special Projects of Regional and National Significance support interdisciplinary training for assessments and diagnosis research, genetic screening and counseling activities, and service coordination of community-based providers. They provide family-focused direct clinical services to children with severe disabilities and their families. Among the unserved and underserved populations for whom there are new outreach initiatives are children from minority backgrounds, children of substance-abusing parents, children infected with the human immunodeficiency virus (HIV), and at risk children who live in foster care.

*Head Start—DHHS.* A 25-year-old nationwide program, Head Start provides a wide range of educational, social, nutritional, and health services to 3- to 5-year-old children from low-income families. Ten percent of enrollment opportunities in each state must be available to children with disabilities. Head Start is the largest U.S. program for preschool children in which children with disabilities are integrated with their nondisabled peers. Studies have shown that the sooner intervention services are provided to children with disabilities, the more effective they are.

### *Education Programs for Children*

The Individuals with Disabilities Education Act (IDEA), administered by the Department of Education (DOE), establishes a state and local grant program (Part B) to initiate, expand, and improve educational programs for children and youth with disabilities. The federal government maintains a partnership with states and localities to provide appropriate education for children who require special education and related services. The relative count of children with disabilities being served within the state determines each state's allocation of funds.

*Preschool Grants, Part B, IDEA—DOE.* Included in the IDEA in 1987, the preschool grant program extends the requirement of free appropriate public education to eligible preschool children. The program is intended to ensure that all preschool children with disabilities receive special education and related services.

*Early Intervention State Grants Program, Part H, IDEA—DOE.* The early intervention program authorizes grants to states to support statewide, comprehensive, family-centered early intervention systems for infants and toddlers from birth through age 2 and their families. The program serves infants and toddlers who meet the eligibility criteria for "developmental delay." Children at risk for substantial developmental delays may also, at a state's discretion, be eligible for services. The 1991 IDEA amendments included new provisions to strengthen the role of families in service delivery, improve the transition from early intervention to preschool programs, increase participation of underserved populations, enhance services to the at risk population, and ensure the delivery of early intervention services in integrated settings.

*Early Childhood Education, Part C, IDEA—DOE.* Part C of the IDEA supports demonstration outreach and research activities that (1) address the special problems of infants, toddlers, preschoolers, and young children with disabilities (birth through age 8) and their families, and (2) assist state and local entities in expanding and improving early childhood programs and services. Amendments in 1991 expanded the scope of this program to include projects that

- serve children at risk for substantial developmental delays if early intervention is not provided
- improve outreach to low-income, minority, inner-city, rural, and other underserved populations eligible for assistance under Parts B and H

- promote the use of assistive technology devices and services to enhance the development of infants and toddlers with disabilities
- address the early intervention and preschool needs of infants and toddlers prenatally exposed to maternal substance abuse
- change the delivery of early intervention and preschool services from segregated to integrated environments

In addition, the program authorizes up to five states to establish an interdisciplinary, interagency, coordinated system for identification, tracking, and referral to appropriate services for all categories of children biologically and/or environmentally at risk for developmental delays.

*Centers and Services for Deaf–Blind Children, Part C, IDEA—DOE.* Part C of the IDEA assists states and local agencies to provide appropriate services more effectively to deaf–blind infants, children, and youth, many of whom require highly specialized assistance. The law authorizes the provision of special educational programs and related services, as well as vocational and transitional services. Such transitional services may include assistance related to independent living and competitive employment.

*Secondary Education and Transitional Services, Part C, IDEA—DOE.* Part of the IDEA provides for grants to support projects that develop and improve programs and services for youth with disabilities in the transition from school to work, to postsecondary education, and to adult life.

*Postsecondary Educational Programs, Part C, IDEA—DOE.* The purpose of postsecondary educational programs is to enable individuals with disabilities to continue their formal education beyond high school and to widen the choices of educational and vocational preparation available to them. These programs support the development, operation, and dissemination of specially designed model programs of postsecondary, vocational, technical, and continuing education. Contracts and grants are awarded to state education agencies, institutions of higher education, junior and community colleges, vocational and technical institutions, and other appropriate nonprofit education agencies.

*Special Education Technology, Part G, IDEA—DOE.* The purpose of Part G of IDEA is to support the development and use of technology, media, and materials in the education of children and youth with disabilities. Program-funded activities include projects to (1) design and adapt technology, assistive technology, media, and materials to facilitate the education of students with disabilities; (2) assist the public and private sectors in the development and marketing of such; and (3) increase access to and use of such in the education of infants, toddlers, children, and youth with disabilities.

*Program for Children with Severe Disabilities, Part C, IDEA—DOE.* States and local agencies can obtain federal assistance in developing innovative, best practice educational strategies for students with disabilities whose disabilities are determined to be "severe." Since its inception, the Program for Children with Severe Disabilities has emphasized exemplary practices in inclusive settings. The most effective use of these funds is in the statewide systems change projects, competitive grants to states that focus on the collaborative efforts of all stakeholders in the state (e.g., state education agencies, local education agencies, parents, universities, other service delivery systems) to develop and implement successful inclusion practices for students with the most severe disabilities.

*Program for Children and Youth with Severe Emotional Disturbance, Part C, IDEA—DOE.* Created in 1990, this discretionary Program for Children and Youth with Severe Emotional Disturbance awards grants to school districts to increase the availability of community services for these children and their families. Children with severe emotional disturbance are one of the most underserved groups in special education. Of the total number of children served in special education in the United States, close to 400,000 have serious emotional disturbances.

### Vocational Education

The Carl D. Perkins Vocational and Applied Technology Education Act authorizes funding for vocational–technical programs through the DOE. The funding is targeted to school systems serving the largest numbers of disadvantaged students and students with disabilities. Supplemental services under this act include curriculum modification, equipment modification, classroom modification, support personnel, and instructional aids and devices. Schools must also provide counseling and instructional services designed to facilitate the transition of students with disabilities from school to post-school employment and career opportunities. New initiatives under the 1990 reauthorization include the Business–Labor–Education Partnership for Training program and the Tech–Prep Education programs.

### Research Programs That Focus on Children

*Developmental Disabilities Projects of National Significance—DHHS.* As part of a federal discretionary authority, Developmental Disabilities Projects of National Significance provides funding for cutting edge research and development in the developmental disabilities field. These projects are giving the Administration and the nation information affecting national policy, models for appropriate supports, and opportunities to resolve interagency and interstate issues.

**Children and Adults**

*Social Security Disability Insurance (SSDI)—Social Security Administration (SSA).* The SSDI program provides monthly cash benefits for 5 million workers who have contributed to Social Security trust funds under age 65 who have become unable to engage in substantial gainful activity because of a disabling physical or mental impairment. In addition, the Old Age and Survivors Insurance program provides benefits to approximately 663,000 adults disabled before age 22 and approximately 73,000 widows and widowers who are disabled. After 2 years of benefit payments, beneficiaries are eligible to receive Medicare coverage.

*Supplemental Security Income Program (SSI)—SSA.* The SSI program provides federally financed and administered cash benefits to 5.4 million persons of limited incomes and resources who are aged, blind, or disabled. Children in low-income families with disabilities of "comparable severity" to those of adults are eligible for SSI benefits. According to the Social Security Administration, currently 4.4 million individuals who are disabled or blind, including more than 770,000 children, receive SSI monthly payments.

***Direct Services for Children and Adults***

*Developmental Disabilities University Affiliated Programs—DHHS.* In 1995, there is a network of 58 programs located at major universities and teaching hospitals throughout the United States focusing on activities to support the independence, productivity, and integration into the community of individuals with disabilities and their families. University-affiliated programs provide training for personnel in the field of developmental disabilities, including technical assistance and community training for state and local service providers, and may provide direct services to individuals with disabilities and their families. There may be special training initiatives in such areas as aging, early intervention, assistive technology, direct care, and positive behavior management.

***Health Care for Children and Adults***

*Medicaid—DHHS.* More than 34 million low-income or otherwise medically needy individuals receive health care benefits through Medicaid (CCD, 1994, p. 32). States currently have flexibility in structuring their Medicaid program, although the federal government has established broad guidelines. For example, a state's Medicaid program must cover all beneficiaries of Aid to Families with Dependent Children (AFDC); most beneficiaries of SSI; pregnant women, infants, and children born after September 1983 in families with incomes under 100 percent of poverty level; and children up to age 6 in families with incomes under 123 percent of poverty level. By the year 2000, all children under the age of 19 living in families with incomes below the poverty level will be covered by Medicaid.

States have the option to cover people with higher incomes who are institutionalized; low-income pregnant women and infants in families with incomes up to 185 percent of the poverty level; and people with incomes below the poverty level who are aged, blind, or disabled. States may also offer Medicaid coverage to children with severe disabilities or medical conditions who are living at home without considering family income. Fewer than 20 states have chosen this option under the Tax Equity and Fiscal Responsibility Act of 1982, however.

The Medicaid program has long been a mainstay of health care rehabilitation services and long-term care for people with disabilities. For instance, Medicaid provides nearly 75 percent of the federal funding for services to persons with mental retardation and other developmental disabilities.

### *Advocacy for Children and Adults*

*Technology-Related Assistance Grants—DOE.* The Technology-Related Assistance for Individuals with Disabilities Act was created in 1988 to increase access to assistive technology devices and services for individuals of all ages with disabilities. Under Title I, states have competed for 5-year grants to develop consumer-responsive statewide assistive technology service programs. The 1994 reauthorization of the act places new emphasis on systems change through the use of protection and advocacy services, in the states, and through interagency coordination in the delivery of assistive technology devices and services. Title II of the act focuses on critical issues such as financing of assistive technology devices and services, training and public awareness projects, and model demonstration and innovation projects.

*Protection and Advocacy System—DHHS.* Congress mandated the protection and advocacy system for persons with disabilities in response to public outcry against abuse and neglect in mental health facilities. The system operates in 50 states and six territories. Although agencies within the system may bring legal action on behalf of their clients, they have developed a tradition of successful negotiation, settling more than 95 percent of their cases without litigation (CCD, 1994, p. 12). Now, protection and advocacy agencies also represent children with developmental disabilities in areas that include special education, child abuse, and neglect. Adults with developmental disabilities receive protection and advocacy services related to abuse, neglect in institutions, access to community services, income benefits, transportation and housing, guardianship, employment discrimination, and accessibility to public structures. Special emphasis is placed on outreach to minorities.

Funds are provided under a formula to existing systems to protect and advocate for persons with mental illness and to investigate complaints of abuse and neglect in mental health facilities. In 1988, services to persons in jails and detention centers were added. The program also includes services to individuals in facilities administered by the Department of Veterans Affairs.

*Protection and Advocacy for Individual Rights—DOE.* The Rehabilitation Act Amendments of 1978 authorize protection and advocacy for services for persons with severe disabilities. This program is intended for those who are not eligible for other advocacy programs, but who are in need of advocacy services with legal representation.

### Adults

*Title XX Social Services Block Grant—SSA.* A major source of financing for noninstitutional, community-based services for persons with disabilities, the Social Services Block Grant is designed primarily to encourage self-support, promote self-sufficiency, and avoid inappropriate institutionalization. Funds obtained through Title XX are critically important for many states in financing group and independent living initiatives. Title XX also provides 23 percent of the extremely limited federal funding for personal care assistance services.

*Special Recreation Programs—DOE.* Programs and activities under Section 316 of the Rehabilitation Act are designed to demonstrate ways in which recreation and leisure skills assist in maximizing personal independence and community integration. Programs must be provided in settings with nondisabled peers whenever possible.

### *Adults' Civil Rights*

*Americans with Disabilities Act (ADA).* Signed into law on July 26, 1990, the ADA is the single most important piece of civil rights legislation since the Civil Rights Act of 1964. This landmark law prohibits discrimination on the basis of disability in private sector employment, public accommodations, transportation, state and local government operations, and telecommunications. Section 506 of the ADA calls for the federal agencies with implementation responsibilities—the Department of Justice, the Equal Employment Opportunity Commission, the Department of Transportation, the Federal Communications Commission, and the Architectural and Transportation Barriers Compliance Board—to render technical assistance to both covered entities and individuals with disabilities. The act mandates reasonable accommodations in the workplace for qualified individuals with disabilities and readily achievable modifications in public accommodations to ensure equal access to employment opportunities, goods, and services.

### *Employment for Adults*

*Vocational Rehabilitation State Grants—DOE.* The 74-year-old Vocational Rehabilitation State Grant program is the cornerstone of the efforts of the United States to assist its citizens with mental and/or physical disabilities to become gainfully employed and self-reliant. Comprehensive services are provided by and through State Rehabilitation Agencies, often through cooperative agreements with other public and private, nonprofit, community rehabilitation programs and facilities.

*Supported Employment Services for Individuals with Severe Disabilities—DOE.* Federal funding is available to assist states in the development of collaborative activities that will support and maintain individuals with the most severe disabilities in competitive work settings. Individuals eligible for supported employment, by definition, are those (1) for whom there is no tradition of competitive employment, (2) for whom employment has been interrupted or intermittent as a result of a severe disability, and (3) who, because of the nature and severity of their disability, need intensive and/or extensive supports in order to become and remain competitively employed.

*Job Training Partnership Act—Department of Labor (DOL).* Grants obtained through the Job Training Partnership Act are administered on a state and local level by Private Industry Councils (PICs), which plan, fund, and administer training programs for those persons who have experienced difficulties in the labor market. The 1992 Job Training Reform Amendments encourage longer and more comprehensive education, training, and employment services targeted to low-income individuals who must overcome barriers to employment, including people with disabilities. Although the amount of employment and training for persons with disabilities is limited under this act, seven national programs providing training and job placement to people with epilepsy, blindness, mental retardation, and other disabilities are currently funded.

*Innovation and Expansion Grants, Rehabilitation Act—DOE.* Under the 1992 Rehabilitation Act Amendments, states must prepare a statewide strategic plan for developing and using innovative long-term approaches to expand and improve vocational rehabilitation services. These new requirements are to ensure that each state develops a systematic, open, participatory process for identifying and articulating the appropriate future directions of vocational rehabilitation and supported employment services. This is crucial to achieving systems change and improvement.

*Projects with Industry—DOE.* As part of the Rehabilitation Act, the Projects with Industry program authorizes the DOE to fund cooperative arrangements for rehabilitation agencies and private employers to develop job placement programs in competitive employment. Its purpose is to create and expand job and career opportunities for individuals with disabilities in the competitive labor market by engaging the talent and leadership of private industry as partners in the effort; to identify competitive job and career opportunities and the skills needed to perform such jobs; to create practical job readiness, career readiness, and training programs; and to provide job placements and career advancement opportunities.

*Special Demonstration Programs, Rehabilitation Act—DOE.* Among the special demonstration programs authorized by the Rehabilitation Act are projects that hold promise of expanding or improving rehabilitation services to individuals with disabilities; applying new types or patterns of services or devices; making recreational activities fully accessible; meeting the special needs of isolated populations, particularly Native Americans; preparing youth with disabilities for entry into the labor force; and providing for supported employment.

*Extension Program Assisting Farmers with Disabilities—Department of Agriculture.* The AgrAbility Project initiated in 1991 brings assistance to farmers, ranchers, and agricultural workers with disabilities and their families. More than 500,000 of these individuals have physical disabilities that limit them in their work. In addition, about 140,000 people are injured in farm-related accidents annually (CCD, 1994, p. 90). Rural isolation, gaps in rural service delivery systems, and rural professionals' lack of familiarity with ways to accommodate disability appropriately are among the barriers confronting farmers with disabilities. The AgrAbility Project encourages State Cooperative Extension Services and nonprofit disability organizations to work together in providing education and assistance to accommodate disability safely in agriculture work and rural community life. Seventeen projects currently serve people with disabilities working in agriculture in 19 States. State level activities are supported by a national program of training, technical assistance, and information dissemination services.

*Handicapped Assistance Loan Program—Small Business Administration.* The Handicapped Assistance Loan program provides direct loans to (1) nonprofit organizations operating in the interests of and employing individuals with disabilities and (2) small independent businesses wholly owned by individuals with disabilities. Financial assistance (a maximum of $350,000) is available only if credit cannot be secured from commercial sources or from other federal, state, or local sources.

### Health Care for Adults

*Medicare—DHHS.* The Medicare program is a federally managed and financed health insurance program for people who are 65 years of age and older, as well as for some individuals under age 65 who have disabilities or end-stage renal disease (CCD, 1994, p. 31). The program covers more than 36.8 million individuals. Of this number, about 3 million qualify for benefits on the basis of disability. Part A, hospital insurance, is financed through Social Security payroll taxes and pays for inpatient hospital care, skilled nursing facility care, home health care, and hospice care. Part B, supplementary medical insurance, is financed partly by general revenues and partly by premiums paid by beneficiaries. It helps pay for physician services, outpatient hospital services, comprehensive outpatient rehabilitation agency or other facility-based services, laboratory services, independent physical and occupational therapy, audiology, speech–language pathology, durable medical equipment, treatment for end-stage renal disease, and other medical services and supplies. Individuals who qualify for Medicare on the basis of disability are eligible to receive both Part A and Part B benefits after a 24-month waiting period.

### *Independent Living*

*Independent Living Services, Parts B and C of the Rehabilitation Act—DOE.* The 1992 Amendments to the Rehabilitation Act authorize federal funding for independent living services and centers. The purpose of these services and centers is to promote the philosophy of independent living through consumer control, peer support, self-help, self-determination, equal access, and individual and systems advocacy in order to maximize the leadership, empowerment, independence, and productivity of individuals with disabilities. Part B authorizes financial assistance to provide independent living services to individuals with severe disabilities; to demonstrate ways to expand and improve independent living services; to support the operation of centers for independent living; and to increase the capacities of nonprofit agencies and organizations, as well as other entities, to develop comprehensive approaches or systems for providing independent living services. Part C, under the 1992 Amendments, provides grants for the establishment and operation of community-based centers for independent living for persons who have significant disabilities. Centers are required to be "consumer controlled"—that is, 51 percent of their board and staff must be made up of people with disabilities—and to serve all disability populations without focusing services on any one primary disability group. They must deliver four core services: (1) peer counseling, (2) information and referral, (3) independent living skills training, and (4) individual and systems advocacy.

*Independent Living Services for Older Individuals Who Are Blind—DOE.* Title VII, Chapter 2 of the Rehabilitation Act as amended authorizes a program for independent living services for older blind individuals. First funded as a competitive grant program for states, Title VII provides services such as low-vision aids, orientation and mobility training, medical treatment, training in activities of daily living, and other services to assist older persons who are blind to live independently. This is now a formula grant program in which all states and territories are eligible for funding when the appropriations level reaches a trigger amount of $13 million.

### *Advocacy for Adults*

*Client Assistance Program, Rehabilitation Act—DOE.* A state's governor must designate a public or private agency to conduct the client assistance program. The agency must be able to assist by informing and advising all clients and client applicants of all available benefits under the Rehabilitation Act. Furthermore, when asked, the agency must be able to assist clients in their relationships with the programs and projects funded under the act, including any necessary pursuit of legal, administrative, and other appropriate remedies to ensure the protection of clients' rights. The 1992 Amendments to the Rehabilitation Act give client assistance programs permissive authority to provide advocacy services with respect to issues that are directly related to facilitating the employment of eligible individuals.

*Older Americans Act—DHHS.* The Administration on Aging, created by the Older Americans Act, develops new programs and improves current programs to help older people remain independent. The 1987 Amendments to the act include provisions to assist aging individuals with developmental and other disabilities or mental health care needs. Title III provides grants for supportive services (e.g., nutritional services) to help individuals in the community avoid institutionalization and individuals in long-term care institutions return to their communities. It addresses the integration and coordination of community services from client assessment through case management. Title III also includes the provision of assistive technology to overcome the barriers confronted by older individuals with functional limitations.

### *Housing*

*Community Development Block Grant—HUD.* Some grants to state and local governments are intended to fund neighborhood revitalization, economic development, and improved community facilities and services. Individuals with disabilities benefit through the acquisition or rehabilitation of buildings used for group living arrangements and other community-based services, shelters for persons who are homeless, programs to remodel homes for accessibility, and assistance to low- and moderate-income families for direct home ownership.

*Congregate Housing Services Programs—HUD.* For people living in HUD Section 202 (low-income housing for elderly and people with disabilities) and public housing units, the congregate housing services program provides assistance within the home to low-income people with disabilities or the elderly. These services include meals, transportation, personal care, and housekeeping.

*Supportive Housing Program—HUD.* The supportive housing program consists of three components: transitional housing, permanent housing for homeless persons with disabilities, and innovative housing to meet the needs of homeless persons. Through this program, homeless persons with mental illness and other disabilities can obtain community-based long-term housing and supportive services.

*Shelter Plus Care—HUD.* Authorized under the Stewart B. McKinney Homeless Assistance Act, Title IV, as amended by the National Affordable Housing Act, the shelter plus care program combines housing and support services to homeless persons with mental illness, dual mental illness and substance abuse disorders, and acquired immunodeficiency syndrome (AIDS).

*Incremental Rental Assistance—HUD.* Section 8 of the United States Housing Act of 1937 is a rent subsidy program that assists low-income households. Because they make up much of the low-income population, people with disabilities can benefit from this generic HUD rental assistance program. Tenants pay no more than 30 percent of their adjusted income, 10 percent of their gross income, or the portion of welfare assistance designated to meet housing costs.

### *Transportation*

*Rural and Small Community Transit Grants—Department of Transportation (DOT).* Section 18 of the Federal Transit Act authorizes the apportioning of funds to each state for public transportation projects in non-urban areas. In the form of matching federal grants, these funds allow states to increase the access of people in non-urban areas to health care, shopping, education, employment, public services, and recreation. These grants are also used to respond to the rising demands for accessible transportation in non-urban areas.

*Federal Transit Grants—DOT.* Section 9 of the Federal Transit Act makes federal resources available to urban areas for mass transit planning, implementing, and operating activities. Assistance is in the form of federal matching grants. The federal share can be as much as 95 percent of the total grant for projects devoted exclusively to enhancing the mobility of elderly individuals and people with disabilities, or the accessibility of various facilities for these individuals.

*Vehicle Purchase—DOT.* The Federal Transit Act authorizes the provision of capital assistance to private nonprofit organizations for the purchase of vehicles and equipment to provide transportation services to people with disabilities and the elderly. The program is administered at a state level.

### *Training*

*Parent Training Centers, IDEA—DOE.* Grants under IDEA are awarded to nonprofit organizations formed by parents to provide training and information to parents of children with disabilities and volunteers who work with these parents so that they can participate more effectively with professionals in meeting the educational needs of their children. In the spring of 1993, the number of parent centers grew to 68, including 4 experimental centers funded to serve parents in dense urban and remote rural areas (CCD, 1994, p. 47).

### *Personnel Development*

*Special Education Personnel Development, Part D, IDEA—DOE.* Because of the need for qualified special education personnel, Part C of IDEA authorizes grants for three main purposes: (1) the preparation of qualified special education, related services, and early intervention professionals; (2) the continuing education of such professionals; and (3) the training and support of parents of children with disabilities. Grants are also available for the development and demonstration of effective ways for resource training programs to prepare traditionally trained educators to work with children and youth with disabilities.

*Rehabilitation Training, Rehabilitation Act—DOE.* Rehabilitation training grants are made to states and public nonprofit agencies and organizations, including institutions of higher education, to help ensure that adequately skilled personnel are available to provide rehabilitation services to persons with disabilities.

*Special Demonstrations and Training Activities, Rehabilitation Act—DOE.* Section 803 of the 1992 Rehabilitation Act Amendments authorizes training activities that include distance learning through telecommunications, braille training projects, parent and consumer information and training programs, training for impartial hearing officers, and the recruitment and retention of professionals in urban areas.

*Technical Assistance for Community Rehabilitation Programs, Rehabilitation Act—DOE.* Section 302(g) of the 1992 Rehabilitation Act Amendments authorizes the Commissioner of Rehabilitation Services Administration to provide technical assistance to state and community rehabilitation programs directly or indirectly through contracts with state vocational rehabilitation agencies or nonprofit organizations. Technical assistance can be provided to address such community rehabilitation provider needs as in-service training for personnel on recent innovations in assistive technology, job coaching, and consumer choice; meeting the needs of underserved populations; and coordination of vocational rehabilitation with related services (e.g., special education, Social Security).

## AGENCIES AFFECTING CHILDREN AND ADULTS WITH DISABILITIES

### Federal Agencies

*National Institute on Disability and Rehabilitation Research (NIDRR).* Authorized by Title II of the Rehabilitation Act of 1973, the NIDRR was established to coordinate the administration and conduct of research and demonstration programs, training, information dissemination, and related activities concerning the vocational, social, and medical rehabilitation of persons with disabilities. The NIDRR also supports the ten regional disability and technical assistance centers created to foster awareness and implementation of the ADA; the Technology-Related Assistance for Individuals with Disabilities Act grants, rehabilitation engineering research centers, and research training centers.

*Architectural and Transportation Barriers Compliance Board.* The only federal agency focusing exclusively on the accessibility needs of people with disabilities, the Architectural and Transportation Barriers Compliance Board develops accessibility guidelines under the ADA. It also sponsors research in a broad range of accessibility-related fields, including new technologies for accessibility in housing, employment, recreation, health care facilities, and transportation.

### Independent Agencies

*National Council on Disability.* Not only is the National Council on Disability responsible for reviewing all laws, regulations, policies, and programs of the federal government affecting individuals with disabilities, but also it gathers information about the implementation and effectiveness of the ADA.

*President's Committee on Employment of Persons with Disabilities.* The mission of the President's Committee on Employment of Persons with Disabilities is to facilitate the communication, coordination, and promotion of public and private efforts to enhance the employment of persons with disabilities. The committee provides technical assistance, information, and training to business leaders, organized labor, rehabilitation service providers, advocacy organizations, families, and individuals with disabilities. In response to the ADA, the President's Committee has developed a network of disability community leaders in all states.

## ROLE OF THE INDIVIDUAL OR SELF-ADVOCATE

### Involvement at the Grassroots Level

Assistive technology includes computers, lever door handles, and other gadgets that make life easier or more independent for individuals with disabilities.

These devices are "tools" in the task of writing a thesis or opening a door. In the public policy arena, there are also "tools" that facilitate the achievement of technology policy objectives. One of the most critical tools in this area is self-advocacy—self-representation in an effort to obtain the rights provided under the law. Self-advocates must

- believe in themselves
- know their rights
- let others know their needs to the best of their ability
- defend their position
- be assertive
- find out things for themselves instead of just taking someone's word for it (The library is a good place to ask for help with this.)
- work with others (agencies, case managers/counselors, and any other organization or individual) to get the help needed

Nowhere is self-advocacy more important than in public systems where the issue of access to technology cuts across all major funding sources (e.g., federal programs, private insurance) and civil rights protections (e.g., the ADA, the IDEA, the Amendments to the Rehabilitation Act, Medicaid, Medicare). Ideally, the goal of statutes is to improve access to assistive technology and to enhance individual rights to a range of services. In a perfect world, these statutes would provide direction for action of agencies and individual people. In reality, however, they generate regulations that further define the implementation of the law and finally guide practices. In the end, the practice may or may not bear a resemblance to the original concept of the statute. To ensure that what policymakers envision actually becomes practice for the individuals affected on a personal level, it is important for individuals to watch and advocate . . . from the beginning to the end of the process.

There are many ways in which a self-advocate can affect the policy process. Golden (1995), director of the Missouri Assistive Technology Project, described the accomplishment of policy change as an "up and down proposition." There are two distinct approaches: working directly with policymakers to change policy on a broad conceptual issue (top down), or using an individual case to create policy change (bottom up).

If the concern involves an existing federal law, such as the ADA, the first step is to obtain a copy either through a congressional representative or through a public or law library. If it is a state law, such as the building code, a copy is available through a state legislator, the legislature's information office, or the statute books. Reading the legislative history and the committee reports shows if and when the statute was amended, what was the intent, and which agency or entity is responsible for its implementation or enforcement. In addition, the NIDRR has established disability technical assistance centers in each Rehabilitation Services Administration region; these centers assist all affected entities with implementation of the various requirements of the ADA.

Often, federal agencies issue directives to clarify or help agencies implement policies and practices. For example, recent directives have addressed the role of assistive technology in special education, including a child's right to take devices home; the right to assistive devices, including hearing aids, when included in a child's individualized education plan (IEP); and the critical role that assistive technology can play in determining eligibility for rehabilitation services and in ensuring successful job placement. Issuing a policy directive is a top-down approach to the state and local agencies affected, even when the policy is in response to a single query, but there are a number of action steps that the self-advocate concerned about program implementation can take. First, it is necessary to determine if a policy directive has been issued by contacting the appropriate federal agency (e.g., the Rehabilitation Services Administration, the Office of Special Education Programs), the state technology act program, or a disability advocacy organization (e.g., United Cerebral Palsy Associations). If so, the state Director of Education or Director of Vocational Rehabilitation, counselors, educators, administrators, parents, protection and advocacy organizations, therapists, and other individuals should see the letter.

Second, the self-advocate should arrange a meeting with the appropriate administrators of the program to determine the following:

- What steps will the agency take to ensure compliance with the right to assistive technology?
- Will guidelines or best practice scenarios be available to help agencies comply with the right to assistive technology?
- How will individuals and families be notified regarding the right to assistive technology?
- Can agreement be reached on practices that would allow greater access to assistive technology?
- Can the public participate in developing a written policy if one does not exist?
- Who will be involved in determining the need for assistive technology interventions?
- Who will determine if assistive technology is provided to the full extent of the law?
- How will disputes be resolved?
- Who will be responsible for ongoing training of professionals, individuals, and parents to keep all up-to-date on the latest technological and policy developments?

Finally, if interaction with local and state agencies proves unsuccessful, the self-advocate can contact the federal agency responsible for the program regarding assistive technology.

As a result of the 1994 Amendments to the Technology-Related Assistance for Individuals with Disabilities Act, individuals with disabilities have recourse to legal action if they are denied access to the assistive technology devices and services to which they are entitled under federal or state law. Successful case law in the areas of augmentative communication provision, computer access, powered mobility, and access to environmental control is already affecting state funding streams and policies.

**WAYS TO BE YOUR OWN ADVOCATE**

1. Know your rights.
2. Remember that rights are *not* favors.
3. Be polite when you ask for help or share ideas.
4. Remember that your ideas are important.
5. Remember that you are a unique and special person.
6. Always ask "why" when you do not get the service you want.
7. Keep all important papers about services together in a safe place (e.g., notebook, file).
8. Never give your *only* copy of important papers to others. Let them make a copy, if necessary.
9. Know that you have a right to have the records in your file explained to you.
10. Know who can help you get services (e.g., advocate, parent, teacher) and ask that person to attend meetings with you.
11. Do not give up asking for help until you have been helped.
12. If you call someone for help who does not return your call, call back.
13. Go to the next person in charge if you do not get the help you need from the first person.
14. Practice what you will say before a meeting.
15. Be ready to explain why you need a service.
16. Write down your most important points and questions before the meeting so you will not forget.
17. Follow up requests in writing, and keep a copy of the letter.
18. Listen to ideas shared by others.
19. Know what your body language is saying.
20. Dress neatly and be well-groomed.
21. Keep your cool.
22. Always show up for meetings, and always be on time.

### Problem Prevention

Although some disagreements are almost inevitable, many problems can be prevented. The following suggestions may decrease the number of problems that arise.

**Communicate.** It is vital for people with disabilities to maintain communication with the agencies working with them or their family members. They should attend meetings or, if that is not possible, discuss the progress by telephone. The contact person at the agency should be aware of the concerns and the desire of a person with a disability to be informed.

**Speak up.** The person with a disability who is dissatisfied with a service or does not understand an agency policy should ask about it immediately. It is better to talk about each problem when it arises rather than waiting until there are numerous grievances.

**Give positive reinforcement.** People with disabilities should let the agency know when they feel that the services are good. Recognizing the agency's past accomplishments may increase the staff's willingness to listen to future concerns.

**Know the rights of people with disabilities.** A knowledge of agency policies and procedures is helpful if there is any disagreement with their proposals.

**Be flexible.** It is essential to listen to the agency's position, understand the reasons for the decision, and consider the possibility of compromise.

These steps should make it possible to maintain friendly relations between the agency and the person with the disability—even if they disagree on a particular issue. Good relations should help to resolve any problems while they are still small and to head off others before they arise.

## SYSTEMS CHANGE

Under the Technology-Related Assistance for Individuals with Disabilities Act of 1988 as amended (P.L. 103–218), "systems change and advocacy activities mean efforts that result in laws, regulations, policies, practices, or organizational structures that promote consumer-responsive programs or entities that facilitate and increase access to, provision of, and funding for, assistive technology devices and assistive technology services on a permanent basis in order to empower individuals with disabilities to achieve greater independence, productivity, and integration and inclusion within the community and the workforce." In a period of scarce resources and competing demands for those resources, vigilant efforts at systems change are particularly important to ensure access to the assistive technology promised by recent public policy developments. Not surprisingly, many individuals engage in systems change activities to secure devices and services primarily for themselves; however, successfully advocating for and using assistive technology often motivates them to work on broad-based systems change. True to the adage "nothing breeds success like success," these individuals are effective models for other consumers and persuasive advocates with policymakers.

Increasing awareness and rising expectations about what people with disabilities can achieve raise a collective conscience; it is necessary continually to reevaluate the community and its institutions to make sure that they are accessible for all people. The enthusiasm that surrounds a success is critical because systems change takes time and sustained effort. Most people are willing to commit to long-term efforts, however, when they realize how many people benefit from the results.

Table 14–1 represents public policy developments related to assistive technology devices and services. Many of these developments came about through direct advocacy by individuals with disabilities, family members, practitioners, and educators.

## CURRENT ISSUES IN ASSISTIVE TECHNOLOGY DELIVERY

The assistive technology field is just over 20 years old, and progress in the field has been significant. Despite recent policy advances in the provision of assistive technology devices and services, however, a number of issues challenge truly effective access to these tools by all individuals with disabilities. The 1994 Amendments to the Technology-Related Assistance for Individuals with Disabilities Act addressed many of these issues. Following are the definitions as included in the act and some state experiences in addressing these issues.

### Awareness

In spite of the existence of technology-related assistance projects in most states, Congress found that individuals with disabilities and their family members, guardians, advocates, and authorized representatives; individuals who work for public agencies or private organizations that have contact with individuals with disabilities; educators and related service personnel; technology experts; employers; and other appropriate individuals still lack information about the availability and potential of technology for people with disabilities. Therefore, Congress, in the 1994 Amendments, provided financial assistance to states to support systems change and advocacy activities designed to increase the awareness and knowledge of the efficacy of assistive technology devices and services among all appropriate individuals.

**Table 14–1** Public Policy Developments Contributing to Assistive Technology Access for Persons with Disabilities (1986–1994)

| Year | Action | Contribution |
|---|---|---|
| **1986** | **Action:** Amendments to Rehabilitation Act. Added definition, expanded program requirement. | **Contribution:** Clarified and expanded program benefit of major public program. |
| | **Action:** Early Intervention. Created new entitlement, expanded program benefits. | **Contribution:** Established new major public program. |
| | **Action:** Section 508, Rehabilitation Act Amendments. New guidelines for federal procurement of computers. | **Contribution:** Changed procurement practices, impacted manufacturer expectations of accessible design standards at lower cost. |
| | **Action:** Social Security Amendments. | **Contribution:** Permitted tax sheltering of income to purchase technology. |
| | **Action:** Temporary Child Care for Children with Disabilities and Crisis Nurseries Act. | **Contribution:** Provided grants to states for respite, emergency or planned supports for families with disabilities including assistance in accessing assistive technology resources. |
| **1987** | **Action:** Amendments to Development Disabilities Act. Expanded program requirements. | **Contribution:** New priority within existing public program. |
| | **Action:** Older Americans Act Amendments. Created new provision of assistive technology within existing program; defined assistive technology. | **Contribution:** Expanded program benefit. |
| **1988** | **Action:** Medicaid Amendments. Clarified funding options and mandates. | **Contribution:** Clarified and expanded existing program benefit. |
| | **Action:** Tech Act. Created statewide systems of technology assistance. | **Contribution:** Created new funding, new public program. |
| | **Action:** Telecommunications Devices for the Deaf Act. | **Contribution:** Established new telecommunications law with access requirement within federal agencies. |
| **1990** | **Action:** Americans with Disabilities Act. Employment, transportation, public accommodations, telecommunications. | **Contribution:** New access requirements of private sector, access technology by expanding concept of civil rights. |
| | **Action:** ADA Tax Credit for Small Businesses. | **Contribution:** Created tax incentives to expand access to assistive technology. |
| | **Action:** Decoder Circuitry Act. Design standard for televisions. | **Contribution:** Required new manufacturer standard for access. |
| | **Action:** Policy Letter, Special Education. | **Contribution:** Clarified rights under existing major public program. |
| | **Action:** Policy Memo Rehabilitation. | **Contribution:** Clarified rights under existing major public program. |

*continues*

**Table 14–1** continued

| Year | Action | Contribution |
|---|---|---|
| | **Action:** Amendments to IDEA adding definitions of assistive technology devices and services. | **Contribution:** Clarified rights under existing major public program. |
| | **Action:** Amendments to Vocational Education Act. Created integrated quality and equity requirements. | **Contribution:** States must provide special population students (including students with disabilities) with equal access to vocational programs and provide assistive technology. |
| **1991** | **Action:** Amendment to Part H of IDEA adding definitions of assistive technology services and devices. | **Contribution:** Clarified rights under existing public program. |
| | **Action:** Policy Letter, Special Education. | **Contribution:** Clarified right to take technology home from school. |
| **1992** | **Action:** Rehabilitation Act Amendments of 1992. | **Contribution:** Expanded use of rehabilitation technology; widened scope of services and allowed choice of provider, including those for assistive technology. |
| **1993** | **Action:** National and Community Service Trust Act of 1993. | **Contribution:** Included a set-aside of from $5–8 million to make necessary accommodations, including assistive technology. |
| | **Action:** New rules for Part 1308 of the Head Start Act for children with disabilities. | **Contribution:** Ensured coordination of assistive technology provisions in children's IFSPs are carried over into IEPs. |
| **1994** | **Action:** National Information Infrastructure Advisory Council formed by U.S. Secretary of Commerce. Includes national disability advocate. | **Contribution:** Industrial leaders must review legislative and regulatory reforms impacting the electronic communications industry, including disability access provisions. |
| | **Action:** Reauthorization of the Technology-Related Assistance for Individuals with Disabilities Act. | **Contribution:** Included set-aside and focus on assistive technology advocacy. |
| | **Action:** Human Services Reauthorization Act of 1994. | **Contribution:** Ensured expansion of access to assistive technology through coordination of Head Start services with activities for children with disabilities. |
| | **Action:** School-to-Work Opportunities Act. Established national network of transition systems from school-to-work. | **Contribution:** Aid to states to establish state and local partnerships between school and the workplace; presumes systems of support for students with disabilities, such as assistive technology. |

IFSP, Individual Family Service Plan
IEP, Individualized Education Plan

Courtesy of Michael W. Morris, Executive Director, and Christopher Button, Director of Community Services Division, United Cerebral Palsy Associations, Washington, D.C.

Each state's agenda includes a variety of awareness activities. One innovative approach involves the states of Arkansas, Iowa, Maine, Minnesota, and Nebraska in collaboration with the American Medical Association (Schwartzberg & Kakavas, 1994). In response to repeated requests from consumers, the states approached the American Medical Association to help primary care physicians increase their skill in detecting functional limitations among their patients and their awareness of the assistive technology devices and services available. The goal of the physician training is to ensure that patients can obtain assistive technology information from the source where they are most likely to seek it—their family physician.

### Outreach to Underrepresented Populations

A key concept in the 1994 Amendments is outreach to traditionally underserved individuals with disabilities, such as minorities, the poor, and persons with limited English proficiency. State technology-related assistance projects have selected a variety of ways to provide technology devices and services to these individuals.

In Iowa, for example, the Small Changes, Big Differences program provides low-technology kits containing items such as button hooks, jar openers, reachers, and card holders to county agencies on aging and trains older adults to give demonstrations and assistance to their peers. Mobile service delivery programs are another avenue to individuals in rural areas. Typically, these programs employ vans to transport equipment, tools, and professionals to remote sites for the assessment, evaluation, demonstration, fabrication, and repair of devices. Two models of these mobile programs have transportable, self-contained shops or mini-vans stocked with carts full of equipment that can be easily unloaded at a nursing home or community center.

### Consumer Involvement

The Technology-Related Assistance for Individuals with Disabilities Act defines consumer involvement as "the active participation of individuals with disabilities, their families, guardians or advocates in all phases of service delivery" (Section 101(b)). Consumers should be involved in the establishment of personal goals and objectives of a technological application or intervention, the selection of delivery methodologies, the assessment of the effectiveness of the device or service, the long-range planning required for self and ongoing services, and the evaluation of service delivery at regular intervals.

Amy Goldman, Director of Pennsylvania's Initiative on Assistive Technology (PIAT), noted that people with disabilities are competent not only to participate in, but also to direct the process of technology acquisition; "rather than focusing our efforts exclusively on advocating on behalf of others, we have realized that if we share our knowledge with those who have the greatest investment, and help them develop skills that result in effective advocacy, systems will change faster and with better results" (Goldman, 1995, p.1). PIAT Partners, an adaptation of Partners in Policy Making (a product of Minnesota's Governor's Planning Council in Developmental Disabilities) with an Assistive Technology Focus, trains individuals with disabilities and parents on policy issues, advocacy skills, and the technology assessment process so that consumers can be truly effective in their involvement.

### Consumer Satisfaction

The Technology-Related Assistive Technology Act defines consumer satisfaction as "achievement of desired outcomes expected from the selection of appropriate service options designed to meet specific individual needs." Focus groups, individual interviews, surveys, periodic follow-up queries, and number of voluntary return visits or repeat use following the provision of services can all indicate the degree of consumer satisfaction with assistive technology services. Those who provide services can increase the likelihood of consumer satisfaction by increasing consumer opportunities for self-determined decision making. Typically, this involves a process of mutual education between consumer and provider. The greater the consumer's awareness of choices, options, and processes of acquisition and the provider's knowledge and respect for consumer preferences, life style, environments, receptivity to technological intervention, and ability to maintain and use an assistive device, the greater the likelihood of consumer satisfaction.

### Qualified Service Providers

There is a scarcity of qualified assistive technology service providers. First, those who are providing assistive technology services are not easy to find, as they can work in almost any setting and under almost any job title. Second, the demands on their time are great, because there are so few with expertise (Langton, 1991).

There are few training programs for rehabilitation engineers and few technology specialization training programs for other clinicians. Currently, there are only 13 academic programs in the United States that offer degree or certificate programs in some aspect of assistive technology—special education, rehabilitation engineering, occupational therapy, and vocational rehabilitation. Opportunities for continuing education programs on various aspects of assistive technology are increasing, however. Federally funded regional rehabilitation continuing education programs may offer such training. In addition, NIDRR and the Rehabilitation Services Administration periodically fund projects to develop and implement training modules.

**Credentialing**

The field of assistive technology is one without the professional licensure or accreditation standards commonly found in rehabilitation and related fields, such as occupational therapy, speech–language pathology, and physical therapy. Most programs, whether medical, vocational, or community support, have accreditation, however. RESNA, Rehabilitation Engineering and Assistive Technology Society of North America is presently investigating the establishment of a standards/credentialing program for assistive technology providers that hopefully will improve consumer safeguards, ensure quality assistive technology services, and, thus, increase consumer satisfaction.

Historically, there has been no way to judge a provider's qualifications. To facilitate appropriate outcomes of assistive technology interventions and to decrease product abandonment, the service delivery process must meet two critical requirements. First, devices must meet consumer needs; this is possible only if the service delivery process becomes more consumer-responsive. Second, consumers, providers, and payers must have access to valid data on

1. qualified services providers
2. assistive technology devices and services available
3. outcome measures that identify the expected outcome of specific technology interventions (RESNA, 1995)

**Funding**

Like the health care system as a whole, assistive technology services are driven by third-party payer coverage. The system is controlled by what Medicaid, private insurance companies, or rehabilitation agencies will approve, or by what the family can afford. Consequently, there is insufficient and inconsistent funding for devices (Governor's Advisory Council, 1989). With the support of the Technology-Related Assistance Act, states are trying to develop consumer-responsive systems. Funding specialists from each state are involved in a collaborative effort to increase access to funding.

**Fragmentation**

The service delivery system for assistive technology is fragmented and compartmentalized. There are many individuals involved, each with a separate agenda, and there is little coordination or integration of services provided through different agencies (Corthell, 1986). As a result, services are duplicated, and the delivery of technology to the consumer is delayed. Again, the Technology-Related Assistance Act is designed to encourage the development of comprehensive statewide services with an emphasis on facilitating transitions between agencies.

### Support Services

There are few ongoing or follow-along support services for individuals using assistive technology. Often, technology is a lifelong need, but only limited resources are available in the community for repair and maintenance, upgrading, or replacement of devices. Agencies and vendors seldom promote these services, because they are costly, time-consuming, and rarely reimbursed by payers. However, data are proving that without these services, people with disabilities often abandon technology with concomitant loss of function, learning capacity, employment, or quality of life.

## CONCLUSION

Each state is endeavoring to address these issues. However, both state and federal programs are facing budget cuts and many of these issues may not easily be resolved. You can make a difference to the current situation by becoming an advocate and being well informed on important issues and how your state is dealing with these issues.

---

### REFERENCES

Consortium for Citizens with Disabilities. (1994). *The impact of the President's FY 1995 budget on programs for people with disabilities.* Washington, DC: Author.

Corthell, D.W. (1986). *Rehabilitation technologies: Thirteenth Institute on Rehabilitation Issues.* Menomonie: University of Wisconsin–Stout Research and Training Center.

Galvin, J., & Phillips, E. (1990). *What is appropriate technology?* Washington, DC: REquest REC, National Rehabilitation Hospital, p. 1.

Golden D. (1995). *Policy work: An up and down proposition.* Independence MO: Missouri Assistive Technology Project.

Goldman, A. (1995). *Empowerment, advocacy and self-advocacy for assistive technology.* Philadelphia: Pennsylvania's Initiative on Assistive Technology (PIAT), p. 1.

Governor's Advisory Council on Technology for People with Disabilities, State of Minnesota. (1989). *Barriers to effective use of technology as identified by people with disabilities: A hearings report.* St. Paul: Author.

Langton, A.J. (1991). *Critical issues impacting on the use of assistive technology.* Columbia, SC: Center for Rehabilitation Technology Services.

McFarland, S. (1989). *REquest REC on the evaluation of assistive technology: Annual report year I.* Washington, DC: National Rehabilitation Hospital, p. 2.

National Council on Disability. (1993). *Financing of assistive technology.* Washington, DC: Author.

Office of Special Education and Rehabilitative Services, U.S. Department of Education. (1992). *Summary of existing legislation affecting people with disabilities* (Publication No. ED/OSERS 92-8). Washington, DC.

P.L. 99-506. (1986). Amendments to the Rehabilitation Act of 1973.

P.L. 100-407. (1988). Technology-Related Assistance for Individuals with Disabilities Act.

P.L. 101-336. (1990). The Americans with Disabilities Act.

P.L. 101–476. (1991). Individuals with Disabilities Education Act.

P.L. 103–218 (1994). Amendments to Technology-Related Assistance for Individuals with Disabilities Act of 1988.

RESNA. (1995). Outline for developing a credentialing program in assistive technology. Arlington, VA: RESNA.

Schwartzberg, J., & Kakavas, V. (Eds.). (1994). *Guidelines for the use of assistive technology: Evaluation, referral, prescription.* Chicago: Department of Geriatric Health, American Medical Association.

United Cerebral Palsy Associations (UCPA). *Washington Watch* (weekly publication of the United Cerebral Palsy Association, Inc., 1660 L Street, N.W., Suite 700, Washington, D.C. 20036).

# *Chapter 15*

# Funding Assistive Technology

*Steven Mendelsohn*

For those who have come to appreciate the capacity of assistive technology to enhance the education, employment, and quality of life for all persons with disabilities, few barriers to its full utilization are more perplexing or intractable than cost. Although important low-technology devices and even some high-technology equipment are far less costly than generally assumed, all too many individuals and families continue to confront the harsh truth that the lack of adequate funding erects an all but insuperable barrier to their acquisition of the technology that will, often dramatically, improve their lives. Like the wheelchair rider sitting at the bottom of a steep flight of unramped stairs, they feel frustration and despair.

Just as there is no single criterion for evaluating devices and no single source of comprehensive information on the range of technologies that are available for meeting various functional needs, there is no single source or strategy for funding assistive technology. Indeed, it is fair to say that the United States has yet to develop a clear public policy or a societal consensus on how, when, or to what extent public or private sector resources should be committed to the funding of assistive technology devices or services for use by individuals, schools, or other institutions. Few can doubt that the articulation of clear public policy, the designation of specific sources, and the formulation of clear eligibility criteria would greatly simplify the funding puzzle. As the increasing numbers of people who have obtained funding now know, however, addressing the problem with thoroughness and determination can many times uncover resources. The day may come when the major options are clearly articulated and widely known, but until then, effort, resourcefulness, knowledge, and attention to detail represent the most effective and rewarding tools available to penetrate the funding morass.

Accordingly, the first principle of assistive technology funding is to gather information. The collection of data, the evaluation of trade-offs, and many other elements of the overall equipment evaluation and selection process have distinct parallels on the funding side of the equation. Just as there is no need to be an engineer or a computer expert to select and use appropriate technology, there is no need to be a financial wizard or sophisticated manipulator of bureaucracies to obtain funding. Anyone with the capacity, commitment, and resources needed to identify, evaluate, and select appropriate assistive technology devices also possesses the resources necessary to pursue its funding with a reasonable prospect of success.

There are never any guarantees that the funding barrier can be overcome. When the need is time-sensitive, such as funding for equipment that would make it possible to accept an immediate job offer, the fact that persistence will eventually pay off in the vast majority of cases may not be encouraging. If the timeframe is extended or needs have been anticipated somewhat in advance, however, the rapid changes in the nature and cost of available technology and in the pattern of funding resources make it likely that some or all of the funding needed can be obtained.

## DEFINING THE PROBLEM

"I need *X* dollars to buy assistive technology." What could be simpler than that? A careful examination of that statement proves it to be anything but simple, however. First, there is the question of amount. Is the full amount needed all at once, upfront, or over a period of time (e.g., in installments)? Second, if the technology configuration in question consists of more than one component, must all the components be obtained simultaneously, or can they be acquired gradually over some period of time? Third, if phased payment or gradual acquisition is possible, will the acquisition of the early items have any impact (such as permit the start of a job that will itself yield wages or obligate the employer to provide further components as "reasonable accommodations" under the Americans with Disabilities Act, P.L. 101-336) on future ability to pay or to acquire the rest of the technology?

Such questions matter because they bear directly on appropriate funding sources and strategies. They ultimately highlight the critical distinction between cost and cash flow. The actual cost of an item or system may not change, but a person's ability to pay for or to find funding for it can vary greatly, depending on the person's current cash flow. For example, a $5,000 item that must be paid for all at once may prove far less available than a $10,000 device that can be paid for over a period of years or can be financed through a loan.

For individuals who plan to pay for assistive devices themselves, the variables that affect timeframes and, hence, ability to pay may include matters as mundane as the willingness of one vendor to accept credit cards, the existence of a specialized loan program, or the fact that a local organization or another consumer happens to have a serviceable device that is no longer needed. For those who seek outside funds for assistive technology, the variables may be a good deal more complicated and bureaucratic. For instance, a state vocational rehabilitation or independent living services program may buy technology from a list of items pre-approved for purchase by the state's general services or other centralized procurement agency. In that case, not only the cost, but also the timeframes and justification requirements may be far less onerous for the approved than for the nonapproved item, even though the reasons for the state's choice may be less than obvious to the prospective user. Similarly, a particular model of wheelchair may be approved for Medicaid purchase and, therefore, more readily available in your state than another.

In many instances, a used, but still serviceable, device can meet a particular need, either for an indefinite period of time or for long enough to permit the development of other resources or to avoid the loss of some time-sensitive opportunity. A recycling program, a public or nonprofit agency, or a local user who happens to have no further need for the particular item may be able to supply a used device at a bargain price. A device vendor may have items from a discontinued line available at a substantial reduction from their previous cost. If the person who seeks the device has the flexibility to accommodate temporary use of what is available through any of these sources, the cost savings can be dramatic.

Finally, there is the issue of ownership versus access. Does the person with a disability need to "buy" or only to "use" the equipment? If it is necessary to "possess" it, short-term rental is sometimes an option while more permanent options are being explored. A dispute in the special education system has dramatized the access question. Many schools and school districts have taken the position that assistive technology devices provided under student individualized education plans (IEPs) cannot be taken home. The Department of Education, in the exercise of its authority to interpret and administer the special education program under P.L. 101-476, the Individuals with Disabilities Education Act (IDEA), has made it clear that no such generalized restriction is permissible, however. Knowing this, a family may be able to avoid buying a duplicate device for home use.

## IDENTIFYING POTENTIAL FUNDING SOURCES

Conceptually, there are three kinds of funding: (1) self-funding, in which the user or user's family somehow manages to pay for the necessary devices; (2) third-party funding, where some other entity pays; and (3) mixed funding, which involves a combination of self-funding and third-party funding. Where loans, the effective reduction of costs for assistive technology through tax benefits, or the use of Social Security work incentives are involved, the line between self-funding and third-party funding inevitably blurs. Some people perceive a tax deduction or credit as nothing more than a means for allowing people to keep more of their own money; others feel that such indirect subsidies logically fall within the sphere of third-party resources. (The tax credit amounts to a third-party subsidy in the sense that the government forgoes revenue by granting the tax credit.)

The process of identifying, evaluating, and prioritizing potential funding sources requires answers to three basic questions:

1. What are the individual characteristics of the prospective technology user that may be relevant?
2. What kind of equipment is needed?
3. What is the purpose or use for which the equipment is intended?

Issues of geographical location, of ethnicity, of community affiliations, and of particular disability are primary considerations. For instance, consumer groups, service organizations, and other informational resources designed specifically for or by persons who are blind or visually impaired represent the most logical starting point for a person with a visual impairment. Community affiliations through religious congregations or civic groups suggest themselves, if not as a direct source of funding, as a point of departure for the information-gathering processes that are indispensable to ultimate success. Community involvements should be defined as inclusively as possible. Members of almost any group—a trade union, a health maintenance organization (HMO), an unrelated support or self-help group, a reading club, a computer users group, or even a bowling league—are likely to have a new suggestion about where to start, to know something or to have a relative or acquaintance who got this "nifty device" from somewhere, who got some special training some place, or who "is doing real great now." This sort of networking resembles that which experts recommend for job searching.

For any particular device or category of equipment, there are vendors, possibly user groups, and sometimes specific funding sources that are device- or category-specific. Thus, if an individual who is deaf needs a text telephone to access and use the telephone system, contacting the manufacturers of such devices and the various deaf-oriented organizations in the community may locate a program for the distribution of such equipment at greatly reduced or no cost.

Perhaps the key dimension in the search for funding is the purpose of the assistive technology. If the objective is to find equipment needed for use by a child in education, for example, the educational system is the likeliest place to begin. Similarly, as far as public sector entities are concerned, if the issue is entry into or return to work, the employment sector resources of the state and community are the obvious starting points.

Because no one seeks funding without some prior contact with assistive technology, its providers, or users, most people have some idea where to begin. The more significant problem may be how. The response to a sudden telephone call to ask the local school superintendent if the school system will provide an adaptive keyboard for a student who needs it may be one of incredulity or of reflexive negativity. If, on the other hand, the question asked was whether a student with a motor impairment, whose IEP includes a commitment to computer access in the classroom, can possibly expect to receive an adaptive keyboard as the means for achieving that agreed upon access, the response may result in a referral to the district's director of special education or a comparable official.

As this illustration suggests, the way in which a question is formulated and the person to whom it is posed can often determine the response of a given service system to any request. For this reason, the ordinary person who knows roughly what agency to call, but is uncertain of the appropriate subunit or official to contact and uncertain of the proper technical terms to use, may fail to penetrate to the potential that the given service system actually offers. To avoid such problems, it is wise to consult with experts before launching inquiries.

## NETWORKING RESOURCES

Every state currently has a technology assistance program, operating under various names and under various agencies, with funds appropriated under P.L. 100-407, the Technology-Related Assistance for Individuals with Disabilities Act. Most of these state-run programs maintain and disseminate information on assistive technology funding. Generally, they can be located through the governor's office, governor's council, or office on people with disabilities. Otherwise, Rehabilitation Engineering and Assistive Technology Society of North America (RESNA) in Alexandria, Virginia, which provides technical assistance to all these state projects, should be able to give contact information.

Every state operates a vocational rehabilitation program pursuant to Title I of the Federal Rehabilitation Act, P.L. 93-112. In the majority of states, one agency operates the program for all people with disabilities. In approximately 20 states, however, a general agency and a commission or division for the blind share the responsibility for program management.

Centers for independent living represent an invaluable source of information, advocacy assistance, and hands-on exposure to a range of assistive technology devices. If general networking does not lead to such a center, the state independent living council or such national sources as the Independent Living Research Utilization Project in Houston, Texas, or the National Council for Independent Living may be helpful contacts.

Perhaps more important than any resource list is an understanding of exactly how these or other resources can help, once they are located and contacted. Of course, many individuals and organizations can provide specific resource information on the who, what, and where of assistive technology funding.

## FORMULATING REQUESTS

As noted earlier, the United States has no "system" for assistive technology funding. Various programs and sources do offer funding assistance, but they do so to specific people, in specific contexts, based on specific eligibility criteria and documentation requirements. Moreover, no major service system, whether in the vocational, educational, health, or income maintenance areas, has the provision of assistive technology devices or services as its primary purpose; an individual must first qualify for the services of the program in general and then demonstrate eligibility for assistive technology in particular. Unless the individual has some sense of where assistive technology fits along the continuum of services defining each program, the prospects of formulating a request appropriately and of making it in the most appropriate procedural context may be small.

An examination of three major and diverse service systems—vocational rehabilitation, special education, and Medicaid—can clarify the meaning of this fact. Vocational rehabilitation involves the provision of a broad range of services, ranging from assessment to training to job placement, for individuals with disabilities who qualify for the services in terms of their potential employability or related positive outcomes. Assistive technology comes into the process at three key points: as a tool in the evaluation of vocational potential, as a training modality in the acquisition of competitive job skills, and as a service that the vocational rehabilitation agency provides to enable an individual to enter into or continue in employment.

If someone has a vocational goal that would be feasible with the use of appropriate technology, then the eligibility assessment or evaluation cannot be adequate without a consideration of this technology. Once that person has been declared eligible for services, the content and timing of those services is established through a document known as the Individualized Written Rehabilitation Program (IWRP). If technology is appropriate either as a training tool or as a component of the goods and services to be provided, then the IWRP should set forth clearly the details of its use and provision. Accordingly, the vocational rehabilitation service recipient should generally request the inclusion of assistive technology provisions in the service plan.

Special education services are available for students with disabilities that create barriers to their educational performance. The availability of such services arises from the IDEA's requirement that these students be provided with a "free and appropriate public education" in the "least restrictive environment" possible (P.L. 101-476, 20 U.S.C. Sec. 1401(a)). As with vocational rehabilitation, however, establishment of eligibility is only the beginning so far as assistive technology is concerned. The law explicitly includes assistive technology devices and services among the range of goods and services that can be provided, but their provision in any given case is a function of the individualized needs assessment and goals-setting process for the particular student.

The mechanism used for identifying needed services in the special education system is the IEP. For assistive technology devices or services to be available as a component of special education services, their need must be noted in the IEP. The inclusion of technology in the IEP, in turn, depends on the underlying assessment of needs and potential. For present purposes, then, the key point to bear in mind is that students with disabilities and their families should request assistive technology in the context of inputs to the IEP planning process; their inputs should document the needs to which technology would be responsive and should identify the equipment that would meet those educational needs.

Medicaid is a federal program of medical assistance for those who meet eligibility standards based on income, including persons with disabilities who receive payments under the Supplemental Security Income (SSI) program. As with the vocational rehabilitation system, states operate the program with a combination of federal funds and their own matching funds, and they have some discretion in the range of services that they provide and in the definition of those services. Accordingly, the first step in determining the availability of assistive technology under Medicaid is to determine the range and the definitions of "optional services" in the particular state. If the state has no appropriate category or definition, the next step is to look to the core services, those that all states are required to provide. Among these core services, the two most frequently used to justify the provision of assistive technology are the provision of "durable medical equipment" and "early periodic screening, diagnosis and treatment," which applies exclusively to children (Medicaid Title XIX of the Social Security Act as amended, P.L. 101-508).

Thus, the request for assistive technology arises after eligibility for Medicaid has been determined and under circumstances in which the technology would represent an appropriate and arguably a medically necessary response. Medical necessity becomes important because it conditions the availability of any goods or services and because the procedures for assessing it in relation to any request may be complex and protracted. Generally speaking, prior authorization is required before such a request can be approved, and the selection of particular devices may prove every bit as complex as the determination that a device is appropriate.

Clearly, timing, context, and procedure are all critical variables in ensuring that the major service systems live up to their potential as assistive technology funding sources. Nomenclature is also crucial. For example, although the term *assistive technology* is included in the range of services potentially available under vocational rehabilitation or special education, agency personnel may not be familiar with it. In vocational rehabilitation, assistive technology may be a component of a broader service such as "rehabilitation technology," or it may fall into a category such as "sensory aids." Under Medicaid, the term *assistive technology* has no currency at all, so those seeking it must understand that their choice of terminology will heavily influence the response to their requests.

## JUSTIFYING TECHNOLOGY REQUESTS

As reflected in their diverse purposes and target populations, service systems make technology and other goods and services available under very different conditions. Therefore, it is essential not only to frame a request in the most appropriate context for the source in question, but also to develop the details of the request with strict attention to the criteria, goals, and jurisdiction of that source. For example, a particular device being sought for a child may have considerable educational value, but Medicaid will not provide it on this basis. Medicaid is a program designed to meet the health care needs of poor and disabled persons. As such, its capacity to provide equipment or any services hinges on the existence of a medical justification. The purposes for which an item or service will be used play a major role in determining whether it is of a medical nature. Confusion often arises because Medicaid funds are utilized in many states to pay for "related services" provided to students with disabilities receiving special education services under IDEA. But the goods and services that qualify for payment on this basis are of a medical nature. Many devices have multiple or overlapping applications, making it plausible to seek it from more than one program-specific source; in such cases, however, the elements of the documented need or proposed use that must be emphasized in the request are those that relate to the particular service system.

Justification is a matter of form as well as substance. Each source has its own formal and documentary requirements, which must be scrupulously observed in order that requested services not be denied or delayed for reasons unrelated to their merit. In many cases, full documentation of a request requires the joint efforts of a number of practitioners and experts who reflect various disciplines. In the vocational setting, for instance, there are no formal documentation requirements prescribed by federal statute, and states have considerable latitude in conducting evaluations and assessments; the documentation task may be principally one of persuasion. Thus, a person who is seeking vocational rehabilitation support or training for a particular line of work may need to submit evidence from people in that field or documentation concerning the existence of technology that will facilitate performance of the job.

The requirement of an at least annual IEP meeting makes the educational setting slightly more formal and structured than the vocational rehabilitation setting. The documentation typically required to justify assistive technology provision includes assessments by appropriate professionals concerning the educational barriers and service needs of the student; information about ways that technology can meet these needs, either by itself or in conjunction with designated services; and data on the availability and costs of relevant devices. Where possible, it is wise to take school system assessments of need as the point of departure for recommending technology-based solutions.

Finally, Medicaid has the most formal process of all, in that the requirements for documentation (including that from physicians) of diagnosis, outcome, and medical necessity can be quite rigorous. Ideally, physicians' prescriptions, as well as justifications and recommendations prepared by ancillary health care professionals, should be consistent with the state's Medicaid plan and regulations. Diagnostic categories or clinical features for which assistive technology is most likely to be approved can be highlighted to the maximum extent possible in the supporting documents. Clinical or functional outcome or comparative data are also required in some cases.

## MAKING SUCCESSFUL APPEALS

All too often, despite the most persuasive advocacy and the most precise documentation, a bona fide request for assistive technology is denied. As service systems provide for the appeal or other reconsideration of such adverse decisions, it is critical to understand how the appeals process works.

After any denial of a request for assistive technology, the first step is to try to find out the reasons behind the denial. In the case of vocational rehabilitation, for example, the agency may have denied the request on the ground that (1) the career goal is not appropriate for its support (even though the applicant has been found eligible for services); (2) the career goal is acceptable, but there is no need for technology to achieve it; (3) the specific request is inappropriate in light of other technology that would be superior; or (4) the request is entirely appropriate, but providing the assistive technology is someone else's responsibility. Similarly, the refusal to include requested technology in the IEP may be predicated on disagreement with the applicant's assessment of his or her special educational needs; on rejection of the contention that technology can meet those needs; on acceptance that technology can meet the need, but disbelief that an appropriate device actually exists; on the conclusion that, although technology can meet the need, providing the technology goes beyond the school system's responsibility or obligations; or on the view that, while technology can meet an acknowledged need, so can nontechnological approaches that are less costly. Medicaid's denial of a request may derive from disbelief of key facts; from technical defects in the submitted documentation, ranging from the absence of a particular form to the fact that technology of the kind requested (e.g., a powered wheelchair) can be prescribed only by certain specialists; or from the reviewer's use of a standard different from the applicant's in determining medical necessity.

Of course, it is not always possible to find out why a request was denied. To whatever extent it is feasible to make the necessary inquiries or draw the needed inferences, however, it is vital to do so. In essence, the applicant wants to know, though rarely can directly ask, What difference in fact, law, or presentation would have resulted in a different determination on this request? Depending on what such inquiries, plus reasonable inferences, reveal, it may be prudent to resubmit the request rather than to appeal the original denial.

Resubmission is preferable when some defect in the request makes it likely that an appeal will not succeed. Resubmission is appropriate, too, when a denial proves to be based on a mistake of fact or law. As to the factual dimension, those who decide on requests may not read and assimilate them as carefully as necessary. On the legal side, characteristic mistakes can also occur. For example, there are anecdotal reports that some state vocational rehabilitation agencies have denied technology assistance to certain job-seeking recipients on the ground that, since the Americans with Disabilities Act (ADA, P.L. 101-336) requires employers to make reasonable accommodations, employers should bear the cost of the needed devices. An applicant who has reason to believe that the request was denied on this basis can remind the agency that such an interpretation of the law is completely erroneous.

Sometimes, inquiry into the causes for a denial may lead to creative problem solving. Those not familiar with the range of options in a particular setting often overestimate the real costs of assistive technology. If a denial was based on such a mistake, submission of additional information on costs can help to bring about a reversal of the decision.

Despite all such efforts, a formal appeal is sometimes necessary. Each of the service systems has established procedures for appeals, both in relation to overall decisions on eligibility or ineligibility for services and in relation to the specific decisions on the scope of services to be provided. As such, denial of assistive technology requests is always appealable, subject to the same attention to procedure and context discussed earlier. Typical grounds for appeal in connection with adverse decisions by various service systems include the following:

- The decision misinterprets some key fact or evidence.
- The decision is against the weight of the evidence.
- The procedures used by the agency in reaching the decision violates its own rules or some controlling provision of state or federal law.
- Though technically justifiable, the decision is irrationally at variance with other decisions made in indistinguishable cases.
- The decision, while representing a permissible exercise of discretion, is irrational in light of the fact that it negates the value of expenditures already made in the individual's education, vocational development, or medical care by the service system.
- The decision works a terrible hardship on a nice and deserving person or family.

In most public programs, the initial formal appeal is administrative, meaning that it does not go to a court, but to a hearing officer or tribunal, and that the applicable rules of evidence are somewhat less formal than those in a full-blown court case. People are entitled to assistance and representation, whether by a skilled lay advocate or by an attorney, in the presentation of their appeals. Depending on the context, people may or may not have the opportunity to submit direct, in-person testimony or to supplement the written record on appeal. Normally, any individual or tribunal called upon to review someone else's previous decision uses primarily the record of that initial determination, that is, the facts, documents, and other information that the original decision maker used in reaching the conclusion.

Whether the appellant submits new evidence or simply challenges the interpretation or use of the information already in the record, the purpose of an appeal is to convince the hearing officer or tribunal that the original adverse decision was wrong. The appellant may ask either that the prior decision be reversed outright or, in some cases, that the question be sent back to the original decision maker for redetermination in light of some guidance given by the appellate tribunal. Obviously, every effort should be made to formulate the grounds of appeal along the most favorable lines possible.

As already indicated, the process of formulating the appeal begins with a careful review of any written decision or other documents bearing on the rejection. Without some sense of the reason for rejection, simply rearguing the claim is unlikely to result in a different outcome. The appropriate appeal strategy will vary, according to the basis for the original determination. If the reason for the initial denial was a misinterpretation of the governing law, for example, then argument on appeal should focus on that error. Submission of additional factual information—more vocational evaluations, educational assessments, or medical reports—may only confuse the issue.

Although the rules of evidence are less stringent in administrative than in judicial settings, the requirements that apply to timing and deadlines are rarely waived. If allowed 15 days to appeal from the original decision, for example, the appellant should make sure that the appeal is filed within this allotted time. Giving notice of the intention to appeal or other methods of exercising the right to appeal are important procedural steps. It is arguable that more appeals are lost for procedural reasons (e.g., failure to file the required notice of appeal form within the designated amount of time) than for reasons relating to their merits. So, in studying the service system for the initial application, it is wise to prepare for the possibility of a subsequent appeal by noting the provisions bearing on the exercise of that right as well.

## USING OTHER PROGRAM SOURCES

The vocational rehabilitation system, special education system, and Medicaid have a central role in the provision of assistive technology for many people with disabilities, but these programs are not the only sources of assistive technology funding support available. A recent survey reviewed no fewer than 62 federal programs that can provide assistive technology in appropriate cases or are authorized to do so (CCD, 1994).

These programs can be divided into two broad groups: (1) programs that relate specifically to persons with disabilities and (2) programs of general applicability that can cover assistive technology within the framework of their mandate. Programs in the latter group, ranging from the Older Americans Act of 1965 (P.L. 100-175) as amended to the Jobs Training Partnership Act of 1982 (P.L. 97-300) to Head Start (P.L. 97-35) are designed to meet the needs of variously defined, disadvantaged, and underserved portions of the population rather than to address the unique concerns of people with disabilities. Although the exact terminology used will vary, the statutory provisions governing such programs, as well as an increasing number of others, authorize the use of funds to accommodate the needs of persons with disabilities. There is little or nothing to prevent the accomplishment of this goal in whole or in part through the provision of assistive technology, where appropriate.

Even where the statute and regulations governing a program contain no explicit provisions to this effect, all federal programs contain antidiscrimination provisions, and virtually all are required to comply with the provisions of Title II of the Americans with Disabilities Act (P.L. 101-336) regarding access to public services for persons with disabilities. In addition to the specific provisions contained in various federal laws, certain overarching provisions of law apply to all activities engaged in or funded by the federal government, and indeed, to many of the activities of state and local government and of private entities and commercial facilities. Moreover, organizations that receive federal funds by grant, contract, or otherwise are subject to the nondiscrimination provisions, including reasonable accommodations requirements, of P.L. 93-112, Section 503 (29 U.S.C. Sec. 793) and, more particularly, Section 504 (29 U.S.C. Sec. 794) of the Federal Rehabilitation Act.

## APPLYING CIVIL RIGHTS LEGISLATION

Federal and state-based civil rights statutes are an important potential source of assistive technology funding in many contexts. To the degree that civil rights statutes impose obligations upon government and private organizations, it has become fashionable to refer to them as "unfunded mandates." These important civil rights provisions authorize, and in many cases require, a variety of government, nonprofit, and business sector organizations to remove barriers, make reasonable accommodations, or provide auxiliary aids and services to persons with disabilities in order that they may participate on terms of equality in the opportunities available to other citizens.

Foremost among these civil rights protections is the Americans with Disabilities Act: As dramatic and as expansive as are the opportunities and protections that this act offers, it does not contain the words *assistive technology*. Therefore, as with the various service systems, terminology and context are critical to making and sustaining a credible assistive technology request under this law.

Along with access to public services, the Americans with Disabilities Act confers important rights in employment and in the use of public accommodations. Assistive technology comes into play when a barrier removal, accommodation, or auxiliary aid or service is requested or offered. In some cases, technology is the best strategy for bringing about the desired access or functional capability. Although technology is never required as such, its provision may become obligatory when it is the best or the only strategy for meeting the need, for example, because it is the lowest cost solution or entails the least modification in the existing environment.

Other civil rights protections, such as those embodied under Section 504 of the Federal Rehabilitation Act, can be applied similarly. Technology provision is not mandated in its own right, but may be required under the circumstances of a particular case. Accordingly, the would-be technology user must again understand that requesting technology out of context typically evokes a negative or an uncomprehending response, but requesting it in the context of some reciprocal understanding of the law and of its nondiscrimination and reasonable accommodation requirements makes practical and legal sense.

## OBTAINING GRANTS

For many people, the ideal source of funding for assistive technology would be a grant from a foundation or similar source. Grants to individuals are relatively rare, except in the form of scholarships for educational purposes, but they are sometimes available from various sources in health-related or other contexts. Once again, assistive technology becomes meaningful only in the context of the broader purpose for which it is sought. For example, if a student is pursuing educational assistance based on need, assistive technology becomes relevant, not typically as an object of funder interest in its own right, but rather as an expense item that must be taken into account in projecting the student's level of need.

A considerable number of philanthropic organizations include disability-related causes among their areas of concern. Although such organizations most commonly provide traditional forms of care to the sick or fund medical research, they can also support the availability of assistive technology. Charitable opportunities within a community may include not only well established programs with a relevant and clearly defined focus, but also ad hoc efforts, often resulting from knowledge of a particular individual or situation or reflecting a short-term priority of an organization that periodically adopts different causes.

Subsidies are partial grants, insofar as they reduce the net cost of needed equipment. In this connection, consumers should always be aware of the existence of product-specific or disability-specific funding subsidies. State-based telecommunications equipment distribution programs operate in about half the states, for example. Using funds collected by surcharges, typically of a few cents a month on each telephone line in the state, these programs finance all or part of the cost of telephone devices for the deaf (TDDs) or other devices that people with hearing or other impairments need in order to access basic telephone service. Similarly, a number of automobile manufacturers have offered at various times to help finance the costs of hand controls, van lifts, and other vehicle modifications needed to make their products more accessible to people with disabilities.

Finally, a wide range of manufacturer- or even retail vendor–based programs are emerging around the United States, either to make low-cost financing of specific assistive technology devices more readily available or to remove barriers to their acquisition in other ways. Such programs underscore the indispensability of careful networking not only to unearth any such programs, but also the increase in likelihood that such networking efforts will yield something of value.

## CONCLUSION

In the end, the real solution to the problem of assistive technology funding is its inclusion in the funding streams that pay for technology as a whole. Changes in laws and attitudes are helping to bring about this solution. As important, advances in design are making it more and more possible to design the physical and communications environment in ways that make them accessible to all people, thus reducing the need for and the costs of assistive technology in the future. For the time being, however, so long as the technology needs of persons with disabilities are treated separately from our overall infrastructure, individuals and families, businesses, schools, and a host of other institutions must address the funding problem with ingenuity and patience. The lack of a system for meeting these needs makes their analysis and solution in individual cases complex, but also offers tremendous scope for creativity and initiative.

---

### REFERENCES

Consortium for Citizens with Disabilities. (March, 1994). *The impact of the President's FY 1995 budget on programs for people with disabilities.* Washington, DC: Author.Economic Opportunity Act of 1965; Headstart, P.L. 97-35 (42) 9835 et seq.

P.L. 93-112. The Rehabilitation Act of 1973; USC 701–731, (29) Sec. 794, (29) Sec. 793.

P.L. 97-300. Job Training Partnership Act of 1982; (29) 1501 et seq.

P.L. 100-175. The Older Americans Act of 1965; (42) 3021 et seq.

P.L. 100-407. Technology-Related Assistance for Individuals with Disabilities Act of 1988; 2201-2217.

P.L. 101-336. The Americans with Disabilities Act of 1990; Sec. 12101 et seq.

P.L. 101-476. Individuals with Disabilities Education Act; (20) Sec. 1401 et seq.

Medicaid, Title XIX of the Social Security Act of 1965 as amended P.L. 101-508.

*The Last Word*

# Enhancing Selection through Improved Design

*Lawrence A. Scadden*

Selection of the appropriate assistive technology can lead to increased independence, greater productivity, and better quality of life for people with disabilities. In contrast, selection of inappropriate technology commonly results in frustration, disappointment, and abandonment of the technology. Both the individual with the disability for whom an assistive technology is intended and the designers of that technology have important roles to play in ensuring maximum benefits through technology.

Because personal needs change throughout life, technology that is appropriate at one point in a person's life may not remain appropriate forever. Moreover, a specific technology may be appropriate for one individual, but not others. For example, many specialized assistive devices have been designed to be used in educational and employment settings, but a large proportion of people acquire their disabilities at a later age. Many other people with disabilities in time reach the age at which they are no longer regular members of educational or employment rolls. Thus, their activities and, consequently, their technology needs will probably change. Technology selection is a lifelong process, but it always requires attention to the specific needs, desires, and activities of the individual with the disability.

People with disabilities should be involved directly in the process of selecting assistive technology for their personal use. No one else knows their personal needs and desires better than they do. Professionals and family members have important roles in the selection process, but their attitudes and opinions cannot substitute for those of the intended user.

A knowledge of the available options is also essential. Health care and rehabilitation professionals can help the individual with a disability obtain information concerning the available assistive technology options, but product vendors also play an important role in information dissemination and product demonstration. Information collection illustrates the essential partnership paradigm that must exist between product consumer and designer and should permeate the assistive technology design, selection, and training process.

Most authors who address issues surrounding the use of assistive technology emphasize the role of the consumer and the consumer's representatives in ensuring the selection of the most appropriate technology, but designers, manufacturers, and distributors of the technology also have important roles in this process. They can simplify the selection process and improve the odds that the product will be useful and used. Although information dissemination is one of their responsibilities, these companies should seek the regular participation of people with disabilities and their representatives in the design, production, distribution, user training, and maintenance of the assistive technology.

From the outset of the product development process, researchers, developers, and manufacturers of assistive technology should adopt and adhere to three tenets of good design:

1. Assess existing consumer needs and address them.
2. Involve potential users at each step in the design and evaluation process.
3. Adopt and practice principles of universal design.

These tenets are important not only for assistive technology products, but also for mass market products. The design and distribution of mass market products that can be used by people with disabilities will reduce the need for specialized assistive technology, thus reducing the cost of the tools that these individuals use in their daily lives.

The term *universal design* was first used in the 1970s by architect Ronald Mace to refer to structures designed to eliminate common barriers to people in wheelchairs (Barrier-Free Environments, 1988). For example, it focused on replacing or supplementing them with ramps of appropriate gradient, making doorways wide enough to permit wheelchairs to pass through, equipping restrooms with grab bars, and making restrooms large enough to permit a wheelchair to rotate.

Subsequently, the term was applied to the design of electronic products such as computers and consumer electronics (Scadden, 1993; Vanderheiden, 1990). In this case, the term referred to product features that would enhance the operation of the device by people with disabilities. Consideration of such features during the design phase of a product increases its marketability to a larger population and avoids the often prohibitively costly effort of adapting the product so that people with disabilities can use it. The appropriate product controls and informational displays are the features that most often can make a device usable by many people with disabilities.

The term *universal design* is now broadly used to refer to the design of any product or facility in a manner that enhances the immediate and independent use by people with disabilities (Mueller, 1993). Today, the term is often used in efforts to ensure that telecommunication systems of the future, including the national and global information infrastructures, will be designed to be usable by people with disabilities.

An underlying premise of universal design is that consideration of the needs of people with disabilities during the design phase of an architectural structure or a consumer product will facilitate its use by everyone, not just those with disabilities. Design features that are essential for people with disabilities are commonly considered to provide increased convenience for others. Curb cuts are commonly cited examples of this principle. Ramps placed at intersections to permit wheelchairs to move freely from sidewalks into streets and back onto the next sidewalk are now used more frequently for bicycles, delivery carts, and baby strollers. Adherence to the principles of universal design does not usually increase production costs significantly when appropriate design features are included at the outset of the design process.

Product designers' consideration of optimal human factors and ergonomics is a good beginning in the universal design process. It will facilitate the process of selecting appropriate assistive technology for personal use as the number of usable off-the-shelf products increase. Before the dream of widespread use of the principles of universal design can be realized, however, there must be a regular and continuous partnership between the designers of assistive technology and mass market products and people with disabilities. When that occurs, the true power and benefits of technology will be evident.

---

## REFERENCES

Barrier-Free Environments, Inc. (1988). *Universal design: Housing for the lifespan of all people*. Washington, DC: U.S. Department of Housing and Urban Development.

Mueller, J. (1993). Applying universal design: Rules of thumb for designers. Conference Proceedings, *NeoCon* 93, Chicago, Il:71–81.

Scadden, L. (1993). *Design for everyone*. Washington, DC: Consumer Electronics Group of the Electronic Industries Association.

Vanderheiden, G. (1990). Thirty-million: Should they be exceptions? *Human Factors, 32*(4), 383–396.

# Index

## B

## E

G



H

## I

## O



## P

## U



## V

W

# CD-ROM Documentation on the Cooperative Electronic Library on Disability

People with disabilities have a lot of questions.

So do their families and those who work with them. Finding the answers can make a big difference to a person's quality of life and level of independence.

The Cooperative Electronic Library on Disability brings together some of the best sources of information on disability from around the country. The library is in electronic form, to take advantage of the computer's ability to store a large amount of information and access it quickly and easily.

Not everyone is familiar with computers, so the library is designed to be very easy to use. The user does not need to have any training in computers or database searching.

The Library lets you locate—

- Products
- Services
- Information Resources
- Full Text Documents

## QUESTIONS AND ANSWERS

**Q.** I plan to go to college. Is there a machine that will let me take notes in Braille?

**A.** **ABLEDATA** lists over 20,000 products, including portable Braille notetakers.

**Q.** I found out my mother has Parkinson's. Is there an information center I can call?
**A.** Information centers around the country are listed in one of the **Cooperative Service Directories**.

**Q.** I'm paraplegic and plan to get an adapted van. Who in my area can teach me how to drive it?
**A.** **Cooperative Service Directories** list disability services such as adaptive driving evaluation.

**Q.** I'd like to get a computer so I can write and be employed. How can I pay for it?
**A.** **Publications, Media and Materials** (PMM) databases list books and pamphlets on funding.

**Q.** I heard that the ADA says my employer has to provide me with a sign language interpreter. Is that true?
**A.** The **Text Document Library** contains the full text of the ADA, plus the technical assistance manuals.

**Q.** Someone just told me about functional electrical stimulation, and I think it might help me. How can I learn more about it?[6]
**A.** The **PMM** databases let you look up publications by key words and phrases, such as "functional electrical stimulation."

**Q.** Is it possible to see some pictures of different kinds of switches and find out who makes them?[7]
**A.** **TraceBase** and **ABLEDATA** let you look at lots of different switches - many entries include pictures.

## PRODUCTS

Sometimes the difference between dependence and independence is an adaptive aid:

- A hair brush with a curved handle for a person with arthritis.
- A tactile measuring tape for a person with low vision who sews.
- An amplifying stethoscope for a doctor with a hearing impairment.

### Tools for Independent/Easier Living

Hyper-ABLEDATA and DOS-ABLEDATA provide the most complete listing of assistive devices available. More than 20,000 products are at your fingertips. Hyper-TraceBase and DOS-TraceBase provide information on products related to three specific areas of assistive technology: communication, control and computer access.

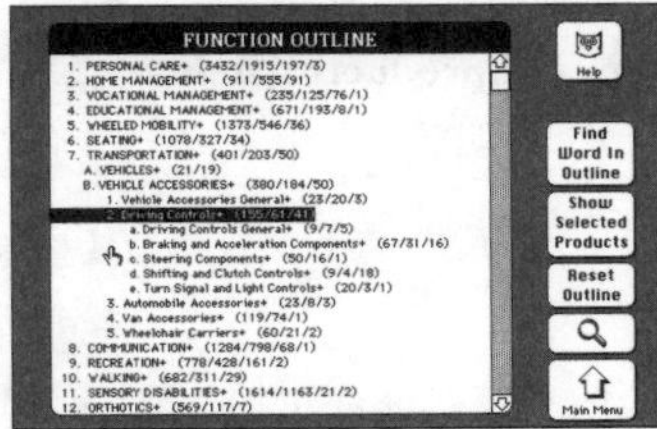


It's easy to look for products according to their functions. The "expanding outline" format lets you zoom in on any one of the 3000+ identifying terms you are interested in.

---

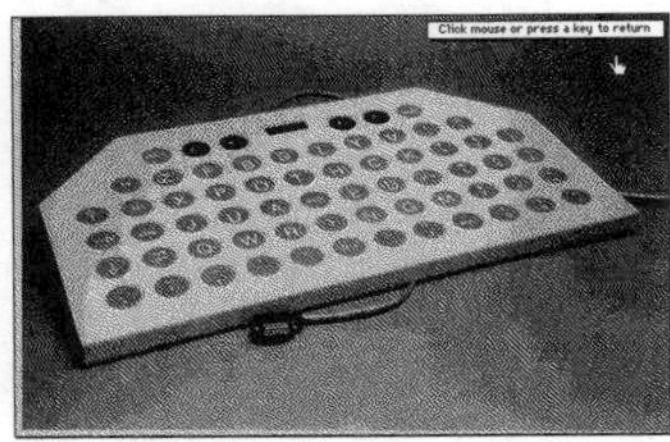


Pictures are provided for many of the products in both ABLEDATA and TraceBase.

---

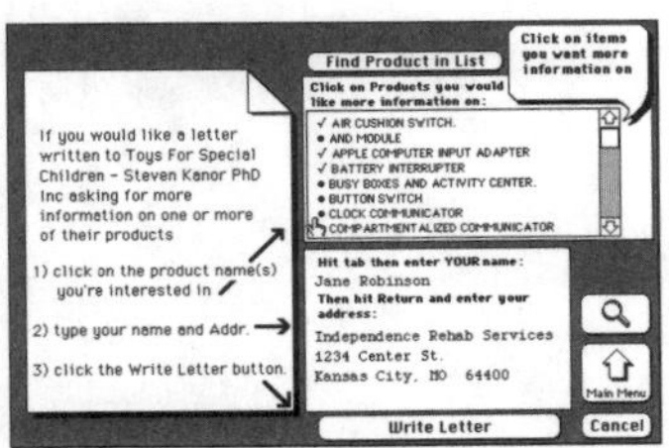


An automatic letter-writing feature lets you generate an inquiry to any company asking about specific products.

---

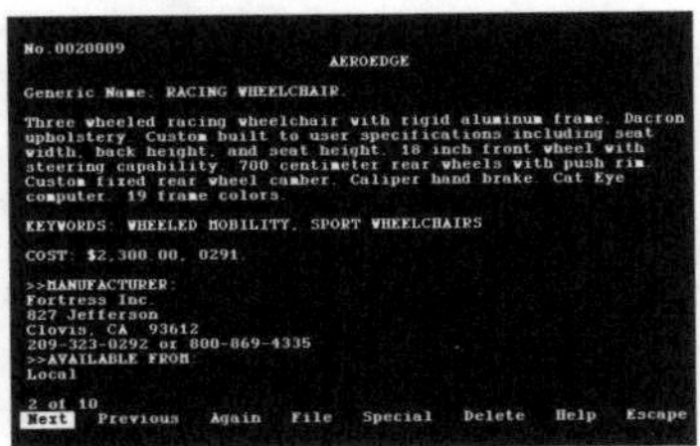


DOS-ABLEDATA and DOS-TraceBase run on IBM and compatible computers. They run on smaller and older machines (640K) and are designed to be screen reader friendly.

---

The information in Hyper-ABLEDATA and DOS-ABLEDATA comes from the ABLEDATA database, maintained by Macro International of Silver Spring, MD and funded by the National Institute on Disability and Rehabilitation Research, U.S. Dept. of Education. For more information on ABLEDATA, call (800) 227-0216.

**Here are just a few of the thousands of different types of products listed:**

- Powered stand up wheelchair
- Hair brush with extended handle
- Hand propelled tricycle
- Left foot accelerator pedal
- Auditory carpenter's level
- Sewing manual for adapted clothing
- Beach wheelchair
- Amplified stethoscope
- Braille printer for computer
- Voice output calculator
- Wheelchair picnic table
- Amplification system for television
- Talking glucose monitor
- Door handle lever
- Battery powered shopping cart
- Motorized adjustable bed
- Tactile postage scale
- Crutch tip with ice gripper
- Software for IEPs
- Prosthetic foot
- Adapted child car seat
- Automatic page turner
- One handed typewriter
- Camera mount for prosthesis
- Grab bar for bathtub
- Adjustable wheeled walker
- Telecommunication device for the deaf (TDD)
- —And many more

## SERVICES

To help people find the disability-related services they need, many organizations have developed statewide, regional, or national directories of service providers.

But how can you find them?

And is there an easier way to locate services than looking through thousands of pages in dozens of directories?

### Finding Key People and Programs

As part of a cooperative project between the Trace Center and information and referral programs around the country, Cooperative Service Directories have been collected in the Library. You can even locate services by how close they are to a certain point on the map or to a certain zip code.

---

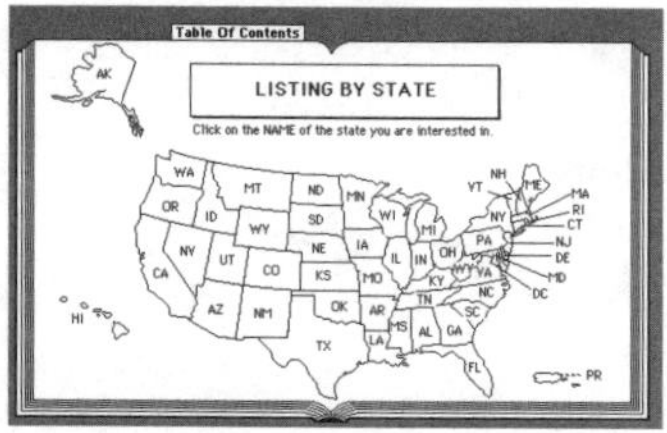


Statewide, regional, and national directories are included. Thousands of services are listed.

---

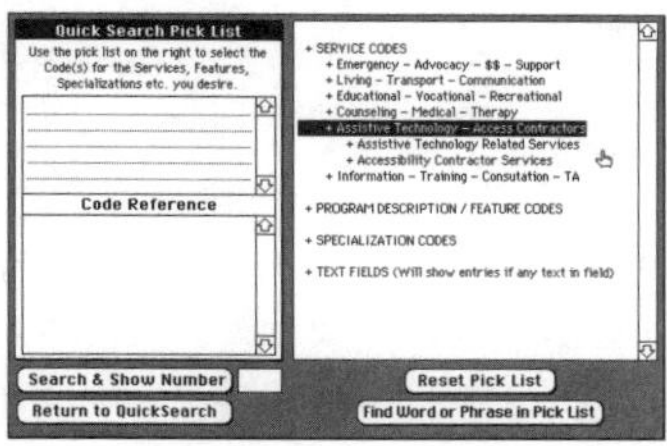


It's easy to narrow down your search for services by particular categories, such as type of service or ages served.

---

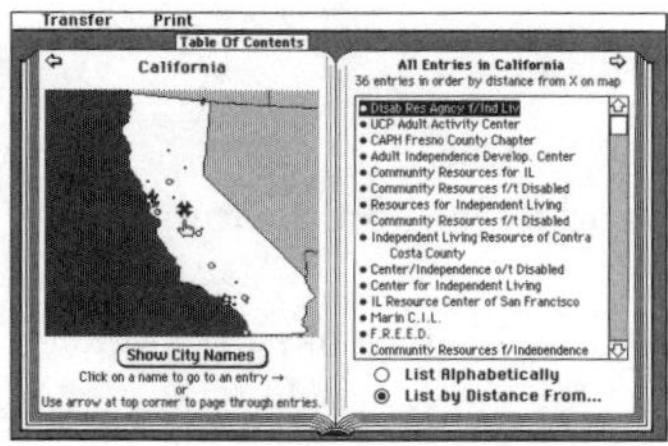


You can list service programs by their distance from a particular point on the map or a particular zip code. The program will automatically show you which services are closest to you or the person you want to help.

---

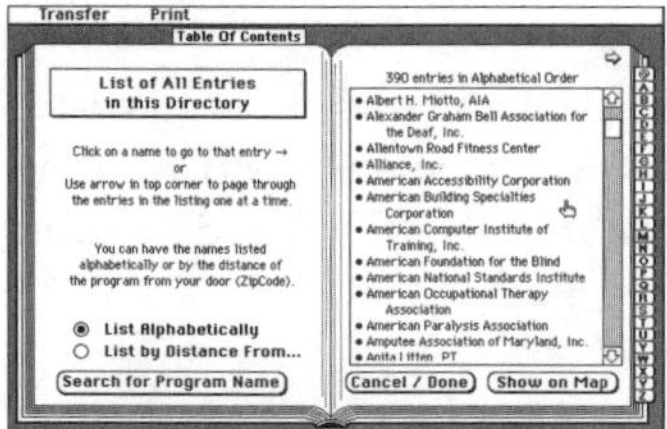


Each entry for a service provider shows the key information about that organization.

**Directories Currently in the Library:**

- Directory of Protection & Advocacy Agencies
- Directory of Resources for Older People
- National Disability-Related I&R Services Directory
- Directory of Independent Living Programs (from ILRU)
- Northeast DBTAC Directory of ADA Information
- Service Directories from Tech Act Projects:
  - — Alaska
  - — Arkansas
  - — Idaho
  - — Kentucky
  - — Maine
  - — Maryland
  - — Montana
  - — Nevada
  - — New Hampshire
  - — Utah
  - — Virginia

## INFORMATION RESOURCES

There's no shortage of good books, pamphlets, and videos on disability topics. But how do you find them?

Suppose you want something very specific: a book on how to use tax policies to help you in paying for assistive technology.

How would you locate it?

### Finding Key Documents, Videotapes, Etc.

The Cooperative Electronic Library on Disability lets you find those hard-to-find information resources—including that book on tax policies and funding assistive technology. Publications, Media, and Materials (PMM) databases make it easy, letting you search by key words, titles, authors, etc.

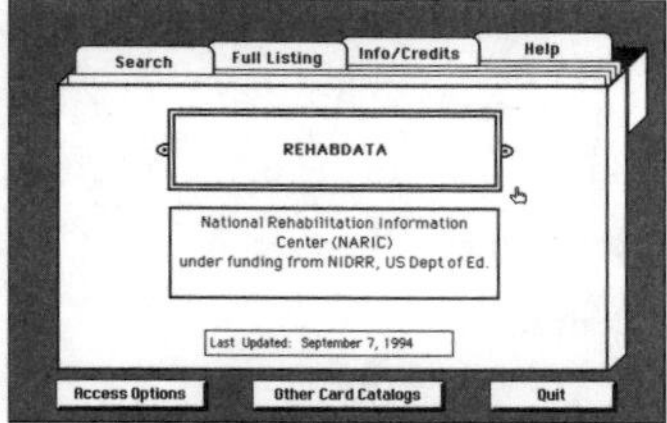


One of the PMM databases is REHABDATA, a listing of over 44,000 information resources on disability. REHABDATA is maintained by the National Rehabilitation Information Center (NARIC) in Silver Spring, Md.

---

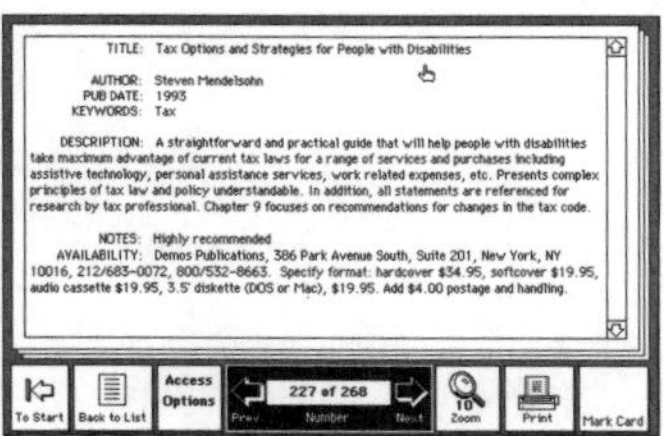


The PMM databases let you search for items by title, author, etc. You can even search for a particular word anywhere in an entry, anywhere in the database.

---

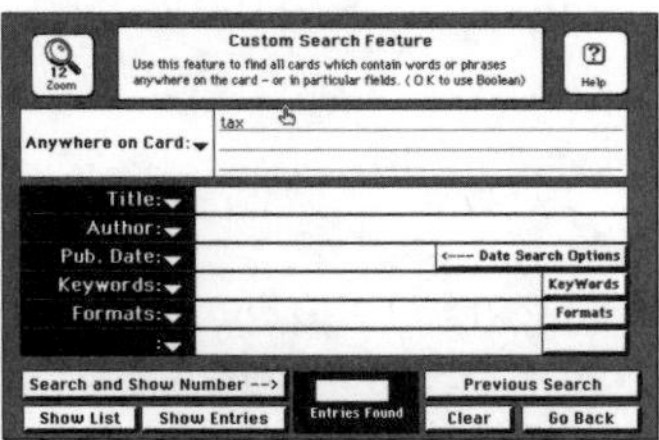


One of the PMMs is a database of resources on funding for assistive technology. Searching for the word "tax" produced ten entries—including the book shown at the left.

---

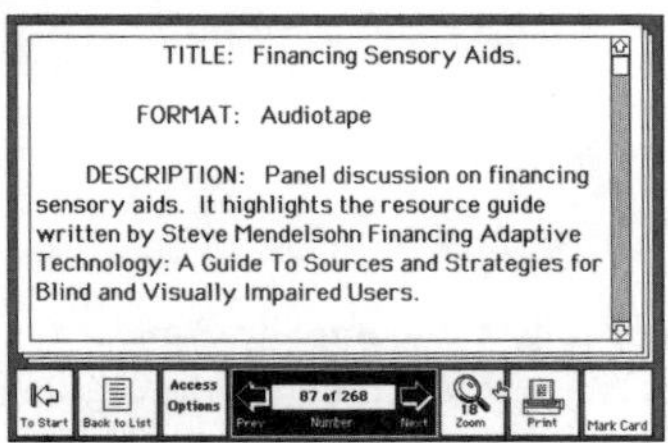


PMM databases have a "seamless interface": users with disabilities can operate the software with the same ease-of-use as nondisabled users. Features such as large print, speech output and mouse-free control are all built into the software. They can be invoked when needed, and allow access to all features of the software.

**On the Co-Net CD:**

- Full REHABDATA database—over 44,000 publications and reports
- Annotated Bibliography of Assistive Technology Funding Resources
- Functional Electrical Stimulation Information Center
- *Journal of Visual Impairment & Blindness* Listings—1990 - 1993
- Information and Referral Resources
- National Clearinghouse of Rehabilitation Training Materials
- Bibliographic Database on Disability and Statistics

## FULL TEXT DOCUMENTS

**Have you ever wanted to find...**

- A handbook on how to fund assistive technology?
- Answers to questions about the Americans with Disabilities Act?
- Guidelines for computer accessibility?

All of these publications are available in print, if you know where to find them. But wouldn't it be nice if they were all in one place, easy to retrieve and read?

### A Library at Your Fingertips

The **Text Document Library** provides complete texts of dozens of documents, including technical assistance manuals for the ADA, the Rehabilitation Act, information on funding assistive technology, and more. A special browser program is provided, making it easy for you to locate, read, and print the documents you want.

---

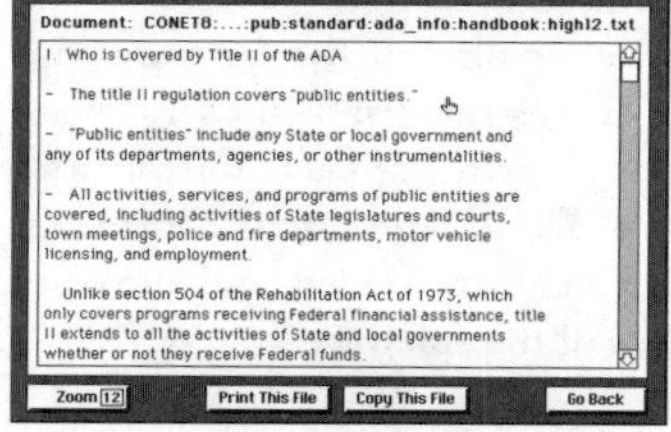


You can read not only the complete Americans with Disabilities Act (ADA), but also the regulations and technical assistance manuals which outline how the ADA is to be applied.

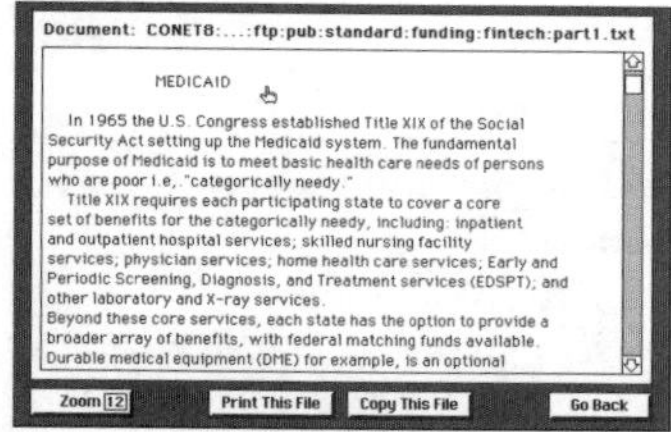


The handbook **Financing Assistive Technology**, produced by the Electronic Industries Foundation, is one of several documents in the Library that can help you learn how to obtain funding for assistive technology.

---

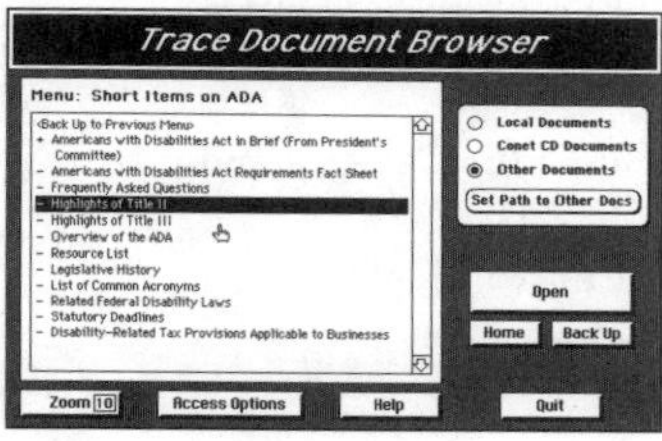


The Trace Document Browser software, provided on the CD, makes it easy for you to locate the documents you want, view them on the screen, and print them out. The Browser works with Macintosh, Microsoft Windows, or DOS. The standard ASCII files are also there, so you can format and output the documents in other forms such as Braille.

---

## Different Forms for Different Users

The Cooperative Electronic Library on Disability has been designed in two forms:

- **A graphical version**, for people who aren't familiar with computer databases. This version provides instructions, push-buttons, and other on-screen graphics to help novices use the software effectively.
- **A text-based version** for IBM PCs. This version is designed for users who want to run the databases in DOS using minimal memory or speed requirements (older, slower processors and less RAM). This version has also been optimized for use with screen reader software.

## The Library Is Not Just on CD-ROM

The Cooperative Electronic Library on Disability is provided at minimal cost on CD-ROM. But since the goal of the project is to make the information as available as possible, it is also being provided through other media:

- Parts of the Library can be purchased on floppy disks.
- Parts are available through computer bulletin board systems (BBSs).

**You can read the full text of all these documents and more:**

- Full REHABDATA database—over 44,000 publications and reports
- Bibliographic Database on Disability and Statistics
- Financing Assistive Technology: A Handbook for Rehabilitation Professionals
- Accessible Design of Consumer Products
- Checklists for Making Library Automation Accessible to Disabled Patrons
- Considerations in the Design of Computers to Increase Their Accessibility by Persons with Disabilities, Version 4.2
- Lifts and Wheelchair Securement for Buses and Paratransit Vehicles
- Making Software More Accessible for People with Disabilities: A White Paper
- Project EASI's Adaptive Computing Evaluation Kit for Colleges and Universities
- Transit Facility Design for Persons with Visual Impairments
- Visual Alarms to Alert Persons with Hearing Loss
- The Americans with Disabilities Act (ADA)
- The ADA Handbook
- ADA Requirements Fact Sheet
- ADA Questions and Answers
- ADA Technical Assistance Manuals
- Rehabilitation Act of 1973 (Revised 1992)
- Technology-Related Assistance for Individuals with Disabilities Act of 1988
- Voting Accessibility for the Elderly and Handicapped Act
- Stroke: A NARIC Resource Guide for Stroke Survivors and Their Families

. . . And dozens of other titles

- The complete Library can be downloaded from the Trace Center via Internet at no charge beyond your Internet connection.
- Any item in the Library can be copied from anyone who has a copy.

## You Can Be a Part of the Cooperative Library Effort

The Cooperative Electronic Library on Disability depends on information resources from any different organizations to be as complete and up-to-date as possible. If you are interested in contributing your information resources to the Library (as a spotter, a formatter, or a contributor), please contact the Trace Center for details.

### Many More Features

The Cooperative Electronic Library on Disability includes many more features than we could list in this booklet. Here are some key ones you might want to know about:

- **Fast Full Word Search:** Databases let you search all of the words in all of the entries, with very quick results.
- **Easy Copy to File:** Results of searches can be not only printed, but also copied to disk, for formatting in Braille or sending via e-mail.
- **Compatible with DOS Screen Readers:** All DOS versions specially designed and optimized for use with screen reader software.
- **Built-in accessibility:** Hyper-ABLEDATA, PMM, and Trace Document Browser have cross-disability accessible modes built in—including voice output for users who are blind (no screen reader required).

### What If I Don't Have a CD-ROM?

Did you know that:

- You can buy a CD-ROM drive for as little as $100 (see your local discount dealers).
- A CD holds 650 megabytes of data (more than 400 floppy disks.
- The data on the Co-Net CD would take over $200 worth of space on your hard disk.
- A CD-ROM drive is a bargain even if this is the only CD you use (and it probably won't be).

## MORE INFORMATION

Trace Research and Development Center
S-151 Waisman Center, UW-Madison
1500 Highland Avenue
Madison, WI 53705
Phone: (608) 262-6966
TDD: (608) 263-5408
Fax: (608) 262-8848
E-mail: info@trace.wisc.edu
Web site: http://trace.wisc.edu

## ACKNOWLEDGMENTS

The Cooperative Electronic Library on Disability is based on information resources compiled by many different organizations in the disability area, among them:

- ABLEDATA - Macro International, Inc.
- NARIC - KRA Corporation
- National Association of Protection and Advocacy Systems
- National Institute on Aging
- Center for Developmental Disabilities, University of South Carolina
- Independent Living Research Utilization (ILRU)
- Tech Act programs in: Alaska, Arkansas, Idaho, Kentucky, Maine, Maryland, Montana, Nevada, New Hampshire, Utah, Virginia
- Northeast Disability and Business Technical Assistance Center
- Rural Rehabilitation Research and Training Center
- FES Information Center
- Journal of Visual Impairment and Blindness
- National Clearinghouse of Rehabilitation Training Materials
- Center for Disability Statistics
- U.S. Department of Justice
- Electronic Industries Foundation
- Trace Research and Development Center
- Project EASI
- International Committee on Accessible Document Design
- UCPA Funding and Systems Change Project

### Funding Support for the Library

Support for the development of the Cooperative Electronic Library software has come from a variety of sources, including:

- National Institute on Disability and Rehabilitation Research (NIDRR), Office of Special Education and Rehabilitation Services (OSERS), U.S. Department of Education
- IBM Corporation
- Apple Computer, Inc.